The Cambridge Companion to
Modern French Culture

France entered the twentieth century as a powerful European and
colonial nation. In the course of the century, its role changed
dramatically: in the first fifty years two world wars and economic
decline removed its status as a world power, whilst the immediate
postwar era was marked by wars of independence in its colonies. Yet at
the same time, in the second half of the century, France entered a period
of unprecedented growth and social transformation. Throughout the
century and into the new millennium, France retained its former
reputation as an international centre for cultural excellence and
innovation and its culture, together with that of the Francophone
world, reflected the increased richness and diversity of the period. This
Companion explores this vibrant culture, and includes chapters on
history, language, literature, thought, theatre, architecture, visual
culture, film and music, and discusses the contributions of popular
culture, Francophone culture, minorities and women.

NICHOLAS HEWITT is Professor of French and Director of the
Institute for Modern Cultural Studies at the University of Nottingham.
His books include *Henri Troyat* (1984), *The Golden Age of Louis-Ferdinand
Céline* (1987), *'Les Maladies du siècle'* (1988), *Literature and the Right in Postwar
France* (1996) and *The Life of Céline* (1999), and his edited volumes include
The Culture of Reconstruction (1989), *France and the Mass Media* (with Brian
Rigby, 1991), *Popular Culture and Mass Communication in Twentieth Century
France* (with Rosemary Chapman, 1992), *Culture and the Liberation* (1994),
Controlling Broadcasting (with Meryl Aldridge, 1994), *European Popular
Culture, 1945–1960* (1999) and *La France et les Pays de l'Est* (2000).

Cambridge Companions to Culture

The Cambridge Companion to
Modern French Culture

edited by
NICHOLAS HEWITT

CAMBRIDGE
UNIVERSITY PRESS

CAMBRIDGE UNIVERSITY PRESS
Cambridge, New York, Melbourne, Madrid, Cape Town, Singapore, São Paulo, Delhi

Cambridge University Press
The Edinburgh Building, Cambridge CB2 8RU, UK

Published in the United States of America by Cambridge University Press, New York

www.cambridge.org
Information on this title: www.cambridge.org/9780521794657

First published 2003
Reprinted 2009

Printed in the United Kingdom at the University Press, Cambridge

A catalogue record for this publication is available from the British Library

Library of Congress Cataloguing in Publication data
The Cambridge companion to modern French culture / edited by Nicholas Hewitt.
    p. cm. (Cambridge companions to culture)
Includes bibliographical references and index.
ISBN 0 521 79123 5 (hc.)   ISBN 0 521 79465 X (pbk.)
1. France – Civilization – 20th century.   2. France – Intellectual life – 20th century.
3. Arts, French – 20th century.   I. Hewitt, Nicholas.   II. Series.
DC33.7.C27   2003
944.081 – dc21   2002045518

ISBN 978-0-521-79123-6 hardback
ISBN 978-0-521-79465-7 paperback

Contents

Illustrations

Contributors

RODNEY BALL is Senior Lecturer in French in the School of Modern Languages at the University of Southampton, where he teaches General and French Linguistics. Topics on which he has recently published include current lexical and grammatical tendencies in French, language attitudes, and the prescriptive tradition. His book, *The French-Speaking World: a Practical Introduction to Sociolinguistic Issues* appeared in 1997, followed in 2000 by *Colloquial French Grammar*.

MICHAEL BISHOP is McCulloch Professor of French and Contemporary Studies at Dalhousie University. He has published extensively in the field of modern and contemporary literature and culture, especially poetry. His most recent books include *Nineteenth-Century French Poetry* (1993), *Contemporary French Women's Poetry* (1995), *Women's Poetry in France, 1960–1995: a Bilingual Anthology* (1997), *Salah Stetie: Cold Water Shielded* (1999), *Jacques Prévert: From Film and Theatre to Poetry, Art and Song* (2002), and *Altérités d'André du Bouchet: De Hugo, Shakespeare et Poussin à Celan, Mandelstam et Giacometti* (2002). He is currently preparing books on contemporary French art and new generation French poetry.

GILLES BOUSQUET is Professor of French and Dean of International Studies and Director of the International Institute at the University of Madison-Wisconsin. His teaching and research interests range from nineteenth-century French literature and culture to contemporary social and intellectual history. In addition, he is interested in technology transfer, high-tech business and biotechnology and has long been an advocate and facilitator of international co-operation in business, science and technology as well as the arts and humanities. His publications include *Apogée et déclin de la Modernité: culture, société et révolution autour de mai 68* (1993), *Mosaïques (Cahiers d' introduction à l'analyse culturelle)* (with Andrew Irving, 1993) and *Mosaïques II (Cahiers de l'analyse culturelle)* (with Andrew Irving, 1999).

CHRISTOPHE CAMPOS was a Lecturer in French and European Studies at the University of Sussex from 1965 to 1974, and Professor of French at University College Dublin from 1974 to 1978. Since 1978 he has been Director of the British Institute in Paris. He was the founder and organiser of the Paris-Théâtre international seminar.

HUGH DAUNCEY is Senior Lecturer in French at the University of Newcastle-upon-Tyne. He has researched and published on French radio and television and new communication technologies, as well as on French sport, particularly an edited book with G. Hare: *France and the 1988 World Cup: the National Impact of a World Sporting Event* (1999). He is currently working on a variety of studies in French media, sport and popular culture, most notably edited volumes on the centenary of the Tour de France, French popular music since 1940 and French popular culture.

JILL FORBES was, until her death in 2001, Professor of French at Queen Mary, University of London, and wrote and lectured widely on French studies, cultural studies and the cinema. She was a graduate of the universities of Manchester, Paris and Oxford, and taught in Paris for several years at the Ecole Normale Supérieure and the Universities of Paris-III and-IV. Her publications include *The Cinema in France after the New Wave* (1992), *French Cultural Studies: an Introduction* (edited, with Michael Kelly, 1995), *Contemporary France: Essays and Texts on Politics, Economics, Society* (with Nick Hewlett, 1994), *Les Enfants du paradis* (1997), and *European Cinema: an Introduction* (with Sarah Street, 2000).

SUE HARRIS is Senior Lecturer in French at Queen Mary, University of London. She is the author of *Bertrand Blier* (2001) and co-editor of *France in Focus: Film and National Identity* (2000). She has published a number of journal articles and book chapters on French cinema, popular theatre and festival culture and is currently conducting research into set design in 1930s French cinema. She is Associate Editor of the journals *French Cultural Studies* and *Studies in French Cinema*.

MICHAEL KELLY is Professor of French at the University of Southampton. He has published widely on French cultural and intellectual history, including books on Catholic, Marxist and Hegelian thought, and on French cultural studies. His most recent book in this area is *French Culture and Society: the Essential Glossary* (2001). He has worked at UK and European levels on policy issues in the area of languages and is Director of the UK's Subject Network for Languages, Linguistics and Area Studies.

JEAN MAINIL is Associate Professor of French at Northwestern University. His main interests are the novel and popular, banned, and licentious literature. He is the author of an essay on the construction of gender in *ancien régime* pornographic and medical discourses, and of a book on Marie-Catherine d'Aulnoy, the first literary fairy-tale writer in French. He has also published articles on contemporary French culture, television, sitcoms, the *beur* novel, and on Belgian literature of French expression.

COLIN NETTELBECK teaches at the University of Melbourne, where he holds the A. R. Chisholm Chair of French and is Head of the School of Languages. He writes on twentieth-century and contemporary French literature, cinema and cultural history. His books include: *Patrick Modiano: pièces d'indentité* (with P. Hueston, 1988), *Forever French: Exile in the United States 1939–1945* (1991), and *A Century of Cinema: Australian and French Connections* (1996). He is presently completing a book on the impact of jazz on French culture.

ALAIN PESSIN is Professor of Sociology at the Université Pierre Mendès France, Grenoble, and is the founder and Director of the Centre de Sociologie des Représentations et des Pratiques Culturelles. He is also Director of the Réseau National de Recherche en Sociologie de l'Art (CNRS) and Co-Director of the journal *Sociologie de l'Art*. He is a specialist in the study of the imaginary in politics and the areas of arts and culture and the author of *La Rêverie anarchiste* (1982, republished 2000), *Le Mythe du peuple et la société française au XIXe siècle* (1992) and *L'Imaginaire utopique aujourd'hui* (2001).

WILLIAM R. PAULSON is Professor of Romance Languages and Literatures at the University of Michigan, Ann Arbor. His research focuses on modern French literature and on relations between science, technology and literary culture. His books include a study of Flaubert, *Sentimental Education: the Complexity of Disenchantment* (1992), and an essay on the status and prospects of literary study, *Literary Culture in a World Transformed: a Future for the Humanities* (2001).

KEITH READER is Professor of Modern French Studies at the University of Glasgow. He formally held chairs at the universities of Newcastle-on-Tyne and Kingston. He has published extensively on modern and contemporary French culture, notably in the domains of cinema, intellectual and political history and critical theory. He is co-editor (with Alex Hughes) of the Routledge *Encyclopedia of Contemporary French Culture*, for which he wrote the entries on food and gastronomy, and has also published on the history and significance of food in the journal *French Cultural Studies*.

MIREILLE ROSELLO is Professor of French and Comparative Literature at Northwestern University. Her main research and teaching interests are post-colonial literatures and theories (Caribbean and Mahgrebi areas), gender constructions and visual narratives. She has written on surrealism (*L'Humour noir chez André Breton*), on Tournier (*L'In-différence chez Michel Tournier*), on Caribbean literature (*Littérature et identité créole aux Antilles*). Her latest books are *Infiltrating Culture: Power and Identity in Contemporary Women's Writing*, *Declining the Stereotype: Representation and Ethnicity in French Cultures*, and *Postcolonial Immigration: the Immigrant as Guest*. She is currently studying the representation of moments of 'performative encounters' between France and the Mahgreb.

JEAN-CLAUDE SERGEANT is Professor of English Civilisation at Paris III-Sorbonne Nouvelle University. He is currently Director of the Maison Française in Oxford. He has published numerous books, articles and book chapters on British politics, foreign policy and media issues. His most recent publications include chapters on public broadcasting and cable television in *Television Broadcasting in Contemporary France and Britain* (1999) and a chapter on local and regional television in England and France in *Group Identities on French and British Television* (2003). He is completing *Les Médias en Grande Bretagne*, to be published by Ophrys in 2003.

ANTHONY SUTCLIFFE is Special Professor of History at the University of Nottingham. His first book, *The Autumn of Central Paris* (1970), led to further work on French urban planning and architecture. In addition to *Western Europe since 1945: an Economic and Social History* (1993), he has also published more recently on the history of the cinema and art. He is currently working on an architectural history of London since Roman times, a sister volume to his *Paris: an Architectural History* (1993).

STEVEN UNGAR is Professor of French and Chair of the Department of Cinema and Comparative Literature at The University of Iowa, where he teaches on nineteenth- and twentieth-century poetry, fiction and critical thought. His book-length publications include *Roland Barthes: the Professor of Desire* (1983), *Scandal and Aftereffect: Maurice Blanchot and France since 1930* (1995), and two co-edited volumes: *Signs in Culture: Roland Barthes Today* (1989) and *Identity Papers: Scenes of Nation in Twentieth-Century France* (1996). A study co-authored with Dudley Andrew, *Popular Front Paris*, is forthcoming. A current project, *Urban Subjects*, explores spatial practices and everyday life in fiction, essay and film.

SARAH WILSON curated *Paris, Capital of the Arts, 1900–1969* for the Royal Academy of Arts, London and the Guggenheim Museum, Bilbao in 2002, conceiving and editing the major catalogue published. She is Reader in the History of Art at the Courtault Institute of Art, University of London, and currently invited Professor at Paris-Sorbonne-IV. She has published extensively on twentieth-century European art, collaborating frequently with the Centre Georges Pompidou, Paris, and is preparing *Red Paris/Paris rouge* for Yale University Press and Editions Cercle d'Art. She has edited and introduced three volumes juxtaposing French thinkers such as Lyotard, Foucauld and Maurice Blanchot with the artists of their times, Jacques Monory, Gérard Fromanger and Pierre Klossowski, for Black Dog Publishing, London, and her developing interest in performance art has resulted in writings on Orlan, Michel Journiac and the contemporary British artist Franko.

Chronology

1900–1918: The 'Belle Epoque' and the First World War

1894   The Dreyfus Affair: Jewish Captain Dreyfus wrongly
        found guilty of espionage for Germany. High point of
        modern French anti-Semitism and beginnings of
        opposition from 'intellectuals' and a long campaign to clear
        his name

1898   Zola publishes *J'accuse*

1899   Foundation of the Royalist movement *Action Française* and the
        consolidation of the anti-republican Right

1900   Universal Exhibition held in Paris

1901   Law on the Congregations: the Catholic Church banned from
        teaching

1904   Anglo-French defence treaty, the *Entente Cordiale*

1905   Law of Separation of Church and State

1906   The Charter of Amiens: France's first trade union
        programme

1912   Establishment of French protectorate over Morocco

1914   Assassination of Socialist leader and pacifist Jaurès; outbreak
        of First World War; the Battle of the Marne

1916   The Battle of Verdun; the Battle of the Somme

1917   Mutinies in the army on the Western Front and industrial
        strikes in major cities as signs of disaffection at the conduct
        and length of the war: the first major breach in the *Union
        Sacrée* (the 'Sacred Union')

1918   Armistice

1918–39: The interwar years

1919	Signature of the Treaty of Versailles; French occupation of the Rhineland
1919	Election of the conservative *Bloc National* majority in the Assemblée Nationale: the 'Chambre bleu-horizon' (the Sky-blue Chamber), named after the colour of the French army uniform during the First World War
1920	The Socialist Party (SFIO) Congress at Tours where the majority vote to leave the Socialist Second International and join the Soviet-dominated Communist Third International to form the Parti Communiste Français (PCF)
1922	The Colonial Exhibition in Marseilles celebrates France as a major colonial power and Marseilles as both the gateway to the colonies and a major regional centre
1923	French occupation of the Ruhr in order to enforce German reparations
1924	Victory of the centre-left coalition, the Cartel des Gauches, in the parliamentary elections: Edouard Herriot is Prime Minister
1925	Defeat of rebel independence leader Abd-el-Krim in Morocco; Exposition des Arts Décoratifs in Paris
1926	Return of Poincaré as Prime Minister; stabilisation of the Franc by tough deflationary measures and the maintenance of the Gold Standard
1929	Wall Street crash and beginning of international economic crisis
1930	French evacuation of the Rhineland
1932	Further success of the Cartel des Gauches in parliamentary elections: Herriot again appointed Prime Minister
1933	Deepening economic crisis in France, with rising unemployment
1933	Stavisky Affair: a minor financial scandal perpetrated by a Russian-Jewish fraudster shows up considerable corruption within the highest ranks of Government
1934	6 February: night of rioting by right-wing *Ligues* on the Place de la Concorde over the Government's handling of the Stavisky Affair leads to resignation of Prime Minister Daladier and sets in train the formation of the Front Populaire

1934	Formation of Front populaire, uniting Socialists, Communists and Radicals
1935	Franco-Soviet non-aggression pact committing both parties to mutual self-defence
1936	Germany remilitarises the Rhineland, breaking a condition of the Versailles Treaty and exemplifying an increasingly belligerent attitude towards France
1936	April–May: victory of the Front Populaire in the parliamentary elections; Léon Blum is Prime Minister; wave of strikes and factory occupations; Matignon Agreements
1936	October: devaluation of the Franc
1936	Spanish Civil War; formation of International Brigades of volunteers to fight on the side of the Spanish Republic
1937	June: Fall of Léon Blum, effectively ending the Front Populaire; Exposition Internationale in Paris
1938	Munich Agreements: Britain and France abandon Czechoslovakia to Hitler
1939	3 September: Britain and France declare war on Germany

1939–45: The Second World War

1939–40	The 'Phoney War' (*Drôle de guerre*): France and Germany are at war but no major hostilities take place, leading many to believe that diplomacy will prevail
1940	10 May: German invasion of Belgium, Holland and France
1940	29 May–4 June: evacuation of British and French troops at Dunkirk
1940	14 June: Germans enter Paris; French government moves to Bordeaux
1940	16 June: Paul Reynaud replaced as Prime Minister by Marshall Pétain
1940	18 June: General de Gaulle broadcasts to the French from London, calling upon them to resist ('L'Appel du 18 juin'): creation of 'La France Libre'
1940	23–4 June: Armistice with Germany and Italy
1940	1 July: French government moves to Vichy; 10 July: the Assemblée Nationale votes full powers to Pétain; the beginning of the Etat Français

1940	24 October: meeting between Hitler and Pétain at Montoire: beginning of policy of Collaboration
1941–2	Admiral Darlan replaces Pierre Laval as Prime Minister
1942	16–17 July: the round-up and deportation of the Parisian Jews ('Rafle de la Vél d'Hiv')
1942	8 November: Allied landings in North Africa; 11 November: Germans occupy the Southern Zone ('Zone Libre', previously under the jurisdiction of Vichy)
1943	Establishment of the Comité National de Libération in Algiers under de Gaulle and General Giraud to plan the transition to French rule after the German retreat from France
1944	6 June: Allied landings in Normandy; 20 August: Pétain and the Vichy Government move to Germany; 26 August: Liberation of Paris; 'Guerre Franco-Française' between the Resistance and Collaborators: the 'Epuration'; de Gaulle as Head of the Provisional Government; Ho Chi Minh declares independence for the major French colony of Vietnam: beginning of the Indo-China War
1945	April: end of the war in Europe and completion of the Liberation of French territory
1945	21 October: election of Constituent Assembly; a referendum votes in favour of the abolition of the Third Republic

1945–75: The *'Trente glorieuses'*

1946	20 January: Resignation of de Gaulle
1946	Blum-Byrnes Agreements on US loans and import quotas, in particular regulating the number of US films shown in France
1946	Adoption of the Constitution of the Fourth Republic providing for an executive dependant on a parliamentary majority
1946	Sétif Massacre in Algeria: a demonstration by Algerian nationalists is brutally suppressed
1947	Vincent Auriol elected as President of the Republic
1947	Uprising in Madagascar by nationalists: 89,000 victims
1947	Foundation of Gaullist political formation, the RPF

1947	Beginning of US Marshall Aid designed to bolster the weak economies of Western democracies and forestall Communist support
1947	Communist ministers dismissed from the Ramadier Government for fomenting opposition: the PCF excluded from government until 1981
1949	Formation of NATO
1951	European Coal and Steel Agreement between France, Germany, Italy and Benelux
1953	Beginning of the right-wing anti-parliamentarian Poujadist movement; election of René Coty as President of the Republic
1954	May: Defeat of the French forces in Indo-China with the fall of Dien Bien Phu; June: Mendès-France becomes Prime Minister; July: independence granted to Indo-China; November: beginning of the Algerian War
1956	Independence granted to Tunisia and Morocco
1957	March: Treaty of Rome establishing the European Common Market
1958	Rebellion by Europeans and military in Algeria: collapse of the Fourth Republic; 28 September: acceptance of the constitution of the Fifth Republic; 21 December: de Gaulle elected President of the Republic
1962	Independence of Algeria
1965	September: Formation of the Fédération de la Gauche Démocratique et Socialiste (FGDS), under the leadership of François Mitterrand; December: de Gaulle narrowly defeats Mitterrand in the Presidential elections
1966	France withdraws from NATO as part of its independent and anti-US foreign policy
1967	The Neuwirth Law authorising contraception; the FGDS makes gains in the parliamentary elections
1968	22 March: occupation of university buildings in Nanterre; 10–11 May: student riots in the Latin Quarter, followed by wave of strikes paralysing the country; 27 May: Grenelle Agreements between employers and unions; 30 May: massive right-wing counter-demonstration on the Champs-Elysées; 30 June: right-wing victory in the parliamentary elections

1969	28 April: de Gaulle resigns; replaced as President by Georges Pompidou
1970	9 November: death of de Gaulle
1973	Death of Pompidou
1974	Election of Valery Giscard d'Estaing as President of the Republic; Yom Kippur War between Israel and the Arab states leads to an international oil crisis: end of the *'Trente glorieuses'*

After 1975: France at the end of the twentieth century

1981	May: Election of François Mitterrand as President of the Republic, followed by a Socialist majority in the parliamentary elections: a coalition government of Socialists and Communists
1982	The Loi Deferre granting limited devolution of power to the regions
1983	Demonstrations against the government's attempt to integrate Catholic schools into the state education system
1984	Founding of the anti-racist movement SOS-Racisme; the Front National gain over 10 per cent in the Dreux by-election
1986	Defeat of the Left in the parliamentary elections: Jacques Chirac becomes Prime Minister in a period of 'cohabitation'
1987	Privatisation of flagship State television channel TF1 by the Chirac Government
1988:	Mitterrand defeats Chirac in presidential elections: new Socialist government
1989:	'L'Affaire du Foulard' ('The Case of the Headscarf'): Government bans wearing of headscarves by Muslims in state schools
1989	Bicentennial celebrations of the French Revolution
1991	Edith Cresson appointed as France's first woman Prime Minister
1995	Election of Jacques Chirac as President of the Republic; death of François Mitterrand
1995	Socialist victory in the parliamentary elections: Lionel Jospin appointed Prime Minister. Second period of 'cohabitation'
2002	January: abolition of the Franc and adoption of the Euro

2002   21 April: first round of the Presidential Elections: Jean-Marie Le Pen of the Front National polls over 17 per cent of the vote, eliminating Lionel Jospin from the second ballot against Jacques Chirac

2002   5 May: second round of the Presidential Elections: Jacques Chirac re-elected President with 82 per cent, but Le Pen increases his vote to 18 per cent

2002   9 and 16 June: parliamentary elections: Chirac's conservative coalition the MSP wins outright majority

NICHOLAS HEWITT

Introduction: French culture and society in the twentieth century

In 1989 France celebrated the Bicentennial of the Revolution which overthrew the *ancien régime* and established the First Republic. Culminating in a spectacular display on the Place de la Concorde on 14 July, the celebrations were an affirmation of France's revolutionary origins and its republican tradition, a tradition which, through the first two-thirds of the nineteenth century, were eclipsed by Bonapartism but which, with the hiatus of the Occupation, had run uninterrupted from 1871. The events in Paris on 14 July 1989 were important as a statement about France's political and social identity at the end of the twentieth century, but they also adopted a cultural format of extreme theatricality in which high cultural and popular cultural traditions merged: the evening's climax consisted of the American soprano Jessye Norman singing the Marseillaise whilst circling the obelisk at the centre of the Place de la Concorde entwined in a huge *tricolore* flag. Not for the first time did France choose to celebrate its historical origins with a cultural event of high theatricality which also adopted the format of the carnival. At the same time, the Bicentennial celebrations were by no means the result of spontaneous or piecemeal enthusiasm. On the contrary, they were the culmination of years of planning at the highest levels of the State, overseen and orchestrated by the Minister of Culture, Jack Lang. As such, they were confirmation of the central role of the State in the operation of late twentieth-century, as early twentieth-century, France, and of the importance it accords to culture as a means of affirming national identity. With this role of the State, the mixture of high and popular culture, and the celebration of a republican tradition, the Bicentennial raises a number of important themes to be explored at length in the succeeding chapters of this volume.

A changing society

The nation which gathered around the Place de la Concorde on 14 July 1989 had come a long way since the centenary of the Revolution a hundred years earlier. Then, in spite of its impressive industrial achievements during the nineteenth century, France was a predominantly agricultural society and was to remain so until the outbreak of the Second World War. In the second half of the twentieth century, however, the country was transformed. Jacques Tati's film *Jour de fête*, of 1947, celebrates an apparently resilient rural society, which had remained essentially unchanged since the Revolution and was able to see off challenges to its way of life represented by America. By the time Tati made *Mon oncle* in 1958, however, the rural communities of *Jour de fête* were becoming a thing of the past and the later film casts a half-mocking, half-anxious, glance at the urbanisation and modernisation of French life.

This reflected in its turn considerable changes in the nature and output of French industry. Up until the Second World War, French industry was not merely subordinate to agriculture, it was also, by Western standards, relatively primitive, with outdated management methods and a concentration on labour-intensive luxury goods. The war destroyed an outdated infrastructure and transport network and discredited many conservative industrialists who had collaborated with the German occupiers. The Liberation and establishment of the Fourth Republic saw the beginnings of that thirty-year period of economic prosperity and industrial renewal known as the '*trente glorieuses*' (Thirty Prosperous Years), which ended only with the Oil Crisis of the mid-1970s in the wake of the Yom Kippur War. With American investment through Marshall Aid, with government ownership of the Banque de France, major clearing banks and insurance companies, and with a rational economic planning policy implemented through the Commission du Plan (Planning Commission), set up by Jean Monnet to collect data and set objectives, the French economy prospered and its population became members of an urban consumer society in full employment.

Nor did the Oil Crisis in itself seriously dent the prosperity of the nation as a whole, but it did usher in a more divided and unequal society. Just as agricultural reform in the 1960s accelerated a process of rural decline and drove country-dwellers into the cities, so the recession of the mid-1970s led to the collapse of France's traditional heavy industries: coal in the North and the Massif Central, textiles in the North and steel in the

North-East. Where France had previously known full employment, to the extent that, in the 1940s and 1950s, it had called on immigrant labour, it now had high unemployment in the former industrial areas and the suburban high-rise communities around the major cities, with consequent social unrest.

At the same time, France's position internationally in 1989 was considerably different from what it had been one hundred years earlier. When it celebrated the hundredth anniversary of the Revolution, France was a major world power with an extensive empire in Africa, South-East Asia, the Caribbean and the Pacific, a position which it held, albeit with increasing tenuousness, until the Second World War. After the war, in spite of its ambitions to resume its world role, France was obliged to recognise that it could no longer maintain its superpower status. The Indo-China War, which began as soon as France emerged from the trauma of the Occupation, ended with a disastrous military defeat at Dien Bien Phu in 1954. Although Pierre Mendès-France was able to use the experience of Indo-China to agree terms for the independence of Morocco and Tunisia, the Algerian War, which began in the same year that France pulled out of Indo-China, lasted until 1962 and brought down the Fourth Republic four years earlier. Under de Gaulle, independence was granted to France's former colonies in sub-Saharan Africa. If France needed a reminder that the glory days of empire were over, it received it as early as 1956, when its joint invasion of Suez with Britain was aborted at American insistence.

Nevertheless, even as its imperial role was receding, France had found for itself a new position in Europe. As early as 1950, Robert Schumann had proposed the creation of a European trade agreement on coal and steel, implemented the following year, and René Pleven was planning the establishment of a European army, incorporating German troops who, a mere five years earlier, had still been fighting on French soil. Although the plan was rejected in 1954, French enthusiasm for European integration continued, and in 1957 France became one of the founding members of the European Common Market, the first of many predecessors of the European Union. Under the Fifth Republic, de Gaulle found Europe an invaluable tool for the assertion of French political independence at relatively little cost, backed up by the 'force de frappe', France's independent nuclear deterrent.

In fact, even before de Gaulle, France had been trying to position herself as an important political alternative to the rivalry between the two superpowers, the US and the USSR. Under the Fifth Republic, and with the symbolic importance of the 'force de frappe', France increasingly portrayed itself as a staunchly independent power and one which was well suited to the role of honest broker between East and West. The real target of this assertion of independence, however, was the US, and in this respect French policy from the 1960s onwards was the culmination of a current of distrust present from the beginning of the century. This distrust was founded upon two distinct, but interconnected, perceptions. In the first place, France, like much of Europe, was concerned at the globalisation of American culture: even before the First World War, the French were debating American management and production techniques embodied in Taylorism and Fordism, involving time and motion studies and assembly-lines. Concerns at the global spread of features of American mass-society were prevalent throughout the interwar years and the postwar era. This concern was increasingly focussed on popular and consumer culture. At the same time, France was increasingly conscious that the United States had both the economic and military muscle to extend and impose its culture internationally. The Blum-Byrnes trade agreement of 1947, between the veteran French politician Léon Blum and the American Trade Secretary James Byrnes, was not simply about fixing levels of American imports into France, but, on a cultural level, about France's continuing identity. Hence, the aspect of the agreement which has most preoccupied cultural historians is its limiting of import quotas for US films, deemed essential both for the survival of the French film industry and, more importantly, the very notion of 'Frenchness'. In this battle against globalisation, France has been remarkably consistent: French television was severely restricted as to the number of hours of foreign programmes which could be broadcast, although these regulations were relaxed after privatisation in the 1980s, and, as late as the GATT Treaty in 1993, France was still holding out for preferential clauses which would guarantee an independent film and media industry.

The key to this continuing fight for independence, which has been fought, incidentally, predominantly on the cultural terrain, is the French language. The days are long gone when French was the international court and diplomatic language, and it has far less importance world-wide than English or Spanish. It is for this reason that, in the wake of decolonisation, the *Organisation Internationale de la Francophonie* was established, on the lines of the British Commonwealth, with the aim, not merely of perpetuating France's neo-colonial influence over the countries of her former empire, but also of preserving and fostering the language internationally. Language was also, of course, the central issue in the battle against perceived American cultural imperialism, with fierce resistance in the last half of the twentieth century against English linguistic imports.

If the nature of French industry had changed and France's colonial empire been abandoned, a profound change had come about in the nature of society itself, which was more culturally and ethnically diverse than at any time in French history. After the Revolution of 1789, the French State struggled to impose its authority over a large country whose population all too often felt more allegiance to their local region than to an imprecise concept of 'France'. The Third Republic attempted to unify the country through the dual procedures of conscription, which deliberately mixed conscripts from different localities, and education. The reforms of Education Minister Jules Ferry between 1879 and 1882, which introduced a secular, compulsory and free education system, were not merely the product of a benign and rational philosophy going back to the Enlightenment, but also the expression of a will to forge a homogenous state through a common education and language. Throughout the twentieth century, however, the regions fought back, particularly in Brittany and the South, sometimes allying themselves with the extreme Right and policies of collaboration during the Second World War in their efforts to win a modest degree of autonomy. Under the Presidency of François Mitterrand, however, the *Loi Deferre* of 1982, named after the Interior Minister and Socialist Mayor of Marseilles Gaston Deferre, gave a very real measure of independence to the regions through administrative and economic devolution, whilst education reforms in the same period permitted the teaching of regional languages within the school curriculum, albeit on a minor scale. Moreover, since the end of the Second World War, the relationship between Paris and the provinces has undergone a profound change. In spite of the reforms to regional government, the French State remains highly centralised with massive power located at the centre. However, changes in the pattern of French industry since the Oil Crisis have seriously diminished the capital's monopoly of talent and job-opportunities. The location of high-tech industry in the Rhône-Alpes region, for example, or on the Côte-d'Azur, has led to the creation of powerful regional counter-weights to Paris, no longer perceived as the most desirable place to live and work. This, in its turn, has seen the rise of real provincial capitals: not merely the historical rivals Lyons and Marseilles, but also Toulouse, with its aeronautics industry, Montpellier, Nice, Grenoble, Strasbourg, seat of the European Parliament, and a reborn

Lille. This 'désenclavement' (opening-up) of the regions and their capitals was massively facilitated by the construction of autoroutes and, particularly, of the TGV (high-speed train service).

At the same time, the composition of French society changed over the course of the twentieth century through immigration. In the 1920s, France sought a short-term remedy to losses amongst its industrial work-force due to the First World War by employing immigrant labour, essen-tially from poorer European countries: Polish coal-miners in the North and the Massif Central, or Italian industrial workers in the South. It was these workers who were the first victims of the Depression of the 1930s, and, as French industry contracted, they simply returned home. More problematic were the Eastern European Jews who fled to France in increasing numbers in the late 1930s to escape persecution in Nazi Germany. In so doing, they inadvertently helped to trigger an upsurge of anti-Semitism, which had, in fact, been a feature of right-wing, and sometimes left-wing, politics since the 1880s. The Vichy laws obliging all Jews to wear the Yellow Star and banning them from state or profes-sional employment, culminating in the round-up of the Parisian Jews on the night of 16–17 July 1942, the 'Rafle de la Vél' d'Hiv'' (from the Winter cycle-stadium, the 'Vélodrome d'Hiver', where the Jews were held) and subsequent deportation to the camps, demonstrated that the French Enlightenment values of tolerance and internationalism had their lim-its and were, in some circumstances, actively contested.

With the beginning of the *'trente glorieuses'*, France found itself in the same position as it had been at the end of the First World War: a press-ing need for industrial reconstruction and renewal together with an in-adequate work-force, due to a low birth-rate during the interwar years; and, as in the 1920s, the French opted for the expedient of immigra-tion. In the mid-1940s, however, France, devastated by the war and liv-ing in extreme austerity, could not possibly exert the same attraction on its European neighbours as it had done after World War I. Instead, it was obliged to have recourse to the colonies in North Africa: Morocco, Tunisia and especially Algeria, which received particular immigration quotas af-ter independence in 1962. To this North African immigration, was added immigration from Black Africa following on decolonisation and Vietnam in the wake of the Fall of Saigon.

Unlike the nation which celebrated the first centenary of the Rev-olution, France in 1989 was undoubtedly a multi-cultural and multi-ethnic society. The positive effects of this social change are to be seen in the areas of cuisine, music, literature and film, and were spectacularly demonstrated by France's World Cup team in 1998. At the same time, poor housing conditions, unemployment and a sense of social exclusion have given rise to tension. This is evidenced, for example, by Mathieu Kassovitz's film of 1995 *La Haine*, and the success of Jean-Marie Le Pen and the Front National which indicate that the French hostility to those perceived as outsiders visible under Vichy is still active. The shock-waves caused by Le Pen's success in the 2002 Presidential elections, in which he beat the Socialist candidate Lionel Jospin for a place in the play-off, will reverberate for many years to come.

Nevertheless, French society in 1989 was immeasurably more inclusive than its predecessor one hundred years earlier. In spite of the presence of three women ministers in Léon Blum's cabinet in 1936, women were denied the vote until 1944 and were subject to harsh legal constraints under the Code Civil, which, for example, punished a wife's adultery, but not the husband's, by imprisonment. By 1989, France had had its first woman Prime Minister, Edith Cresson.

At the same time, as the issue of multi-ethnicity and immigration indicates, France remains subject to political and social tensions which have a long history. On the one hand, much of its politics and its education system maintains that rationalist, humanist Enlightenment tradition which was the backbone of the Third Republic. On the other, resistance to that tradition has remained constant, surfacing dramatically at key moments, such as the Dreyfus Case, the Popular Front or the Occupation. If there is an uninterrupted republican tradition based upon the values of the Enlightenment, there is a no less persistent tradition stretching from the Royalist and anti-Semitic movement Action Française in the 1900s to the Front National in the 1980s, via the Vichy regime's Etat Français of the Occupation period: indeed, Jean-Marie Le Pen began his political career as an Action Française student activist in Paris in the 1940s. In other words, if France's history in the twentieth century is dominated by varying shades of republicanism, there remains a powerful right-wing anti-republican undercurrent, bolstered on occasions by the ambiguous position of the Catholic Church, the Third Republic's old enemy.

A changing culture

It is hardly surprising that French culture throughout the twentieth century should reflect the continuities, diversity and tensions visible in its political, economic and social history. French high-cultural activity enjoyed unusual and considerable prestige throughout the twentieth century and continues to do so. At the same time, it has benefited from a high level of state and local government financial support and sponsorship, whether through aid to small booksellers through resale price maintenance or through more obvious subsidies to film production, theatre and concert performances. From the era of the Popular Front, culture has been at the centre of government policy-making, with remarkable continuity: under Vichy, which paradoxically adopted and furthered many of the Front Populaire's cultural policies, but also during the Fifth Republic, with its two great Ministers of Culture, André Malraux, under de Gaulle, and, under Mitterrand, Jack Lang, the organiser of the Bicentennial.

The reasons for this unusually high profile accorded to culture in twentieth-century France are essentially to be found in its education system, which not only established a rigorous national secondary curriculum which tended to privilege arts and the humanities as well as science and engineering, but also trained the future leadership of the nation. Accordingly, this 'republican elite', whether they were engineers, technocrats, politicians, civil servants or writers, had often known each other in the same institutions and had benefited from an education which did not create an overly rigorous divide between the humanities and the sciences. Indeed, not only is it increasingly frequent for future high-flyers to study at more than one 'grande école' – the academic Ecole Normale Supérieure, for example, which trains high-level teachers, followed by the Royal Road to the top civil service, the Ecole Nationale d'Administration – it is also much easier for cultural figures to either switch careers or maintain two careers at the same time. Léon Blum, before becoming leader of the Socialist SFIO and Prime Minister of the Front Populaire government, had been a writer and a friend of Proust; Georges Pompidou studied literature at the Ecole Normale Supérieure and taught in the secondary school system before moving to the Rothschild Bank and becoming, first de Gaulle's Prime Minister in the 1960s, and then his successor as Head of State in 1969. The Nobel-Prize winning poet Saint-John Perse was also, as Alexis Léger, Head of the Quai d'Orsay, whilst André Malraux, one of France's foremost novelists of the interwar years, became a leading Gaullist politician and, as we have seen, Minister of Culture in 1959. At the same time, throughout the twentieth century there was an easy symbiosis between politics, education and culture which reinforced the prestige of the artist. Under the Third and Fourth

Republics, culture was managed at state level through the Ministère de l'Education Nationale et des Beaux-Arts (Ministry of Education and Fine Arts), which produced, as we have seen, not merely a republican leadership which included literary and artistic figures, but an essentially self-reinforcing elite in which the major actors became eventually part of the curriculum.

In other words, in France, and thanks to its education system, cultural figures, especially writers, are members of the governing elite in a way in which, in other societies, they are often excluded or, at least, more removed. In this context, it is important to emphasise the prestige and real political power of the intellectual: a figure who, whatever his or her specialist discipline, is listened to with respect on issues of general concern and who consequently wields very concrete power: from Charles Péguy at the time of the Dreyfus Case to Régis Debray, who fought with Che Guevarra in Bolivia and who became a senior foreign policy advisor to François Mitterrand.

At the same time, there was an increasingly important association between culture and national, and local, prestige, which assumed greater significance as the nation's industrial, imperial and political might diminished. Throughout the nineteenth century, France, and especially Paris, had played an important role as host to artists, writers and musicians from overseas, either refugees from less liberal regimes or simple visitors. Throughout the twentieth century, France revelled in its role as an international artistic centre. From 1900 to 1929, the Ecole de Paris attracted painters and sculptors from all over Europe, Russia and as far away as Japan. Montmartre and Montparnasse became the focus of a vibrant artistic activity, incorporating painters like Picasso, Juan Gris, Modigliani, Chagall and Max Ernst, sculptors like Brancusi and Alexander Calder, writers, especially from America, like Hemingway, Scott Fitzgerald and Ford Maddox Ford, together with rich patrons like the author Gertrude Stein. This reputation of Paris and, to a lesser extent, the Côte d'Azur, as centres of world culture, was enhanced after the Second World War by the immigration of Black American novelists, like James Baldwin and Chester Himes, and jazz musicians like Sidney Bechet, and, during the Cold War, by immigrants from Eastern Europe, like Milan Kundera. In return, France, through institutions like the Ecole des Beaux-Arts, established an international architectural tradition which exported French design theory to the rest of the world.

This role of France as an impresario of international culture was associated with its long-term view of itself as a repository of the world's cultural wealth. Napoleon's pillaging of artistic treasures from Europe and the Middle East filled the great museums of the capital and established Paris as an indispensable world-cultural site. In this context, it was no coincidence whatsoever that one of the most significant acts of Malraux when Minister of Culture was the loan of the *Mona Lisa* to the United States. The message could not have been clearer: France may well have been inferior to the United States both militarily and economically, but it had a definite and unassailable cultural edge. In other words, cultural policy reaffirmed itself as foreign policy.

It is hardly surprising, therefore, that throughout the twentieth century, but particularly since the Second World War, the State has intervened as a major sponsor and initiator of cultural activity. This was already visible in the policy of the early Third Republic to subsidise the press through preferential postage-rates and it was at the heart of the Front Populaire's cultural policy, although the government was too short-lived to see most of its proposals enacted. After the war, the Fourth and Fifth Republics poured state subsidies into a whole range of cultural activities, especially the cinema, the theatre and music. Under de Gaulle, Malraux had embarked on an ambitious project of restoring major Parisian buildings, and de Gaulle's successors lost no time in planning grandiose schemes which would stand as monuments to their own reign. Even if these 'projets présidentiels' were not themselves specifically cultural in nature, like the commercial Grande Arche de la Défense built under Mitterrand, they were intended to be significant cultural statements through the choice of major international architects. Thus, Pompidou planned the arts centre in the Rue Beaubourg which now bears his name, and launched the project for the Musée d'Orsay, put into effect by his successor Valéry Giscard d'Estaing and inaugurated by Mitterrand. It was Mitterrand himself, however, who showed most enthusiasm for the presidential projects, which brought international architects to transform the Parisian cityscape. The Louvre Pyramid, the Grande Arche, the Science Museum at La Villette, the Opéra de la Bastille and, finally, the Bibliothèque de France François Mitterrand all testify to a will to assert the prestige of France, as well as that of its President, through culture. What is significant is that, in the regions, individual mayors embarked on similar projects, designed to reinforce their own electability and to enhance the status of their city, as in the cases of Georges Frèche in Montpellier, Dominique Baudis in Toulouse, or Pierre Mauroy in Lille.

If culture in twentieth-century France had become intimately bound up with politics, individual writers, artists and musicians benefited from the same prestige. Nowhere is this more apparent than from the paradoxical success of the 1980s television literary series *Apostrophes*, in which the presenter Bernard Pivot held a weekly round-table discussion with a number of writers on the major books of the week. Not only was the programme long and the content often recondite, it was also directed at a nation whose book-purchasing statistics had long been one of the lowest in Europe – a fact which did not diminish at all the audience-ratings, which rose to some 11 million viewers. In fact, *Apostrophes*, and its successor, *Bouillon de culture*, are proof that literary culture in France has a prestige and exerts an attraction which far outstrip its mere figures of consumption. The reasons, of course, are similar to those which explain the prestige of the intellectual and the importance of culture to the State. Book-readership in France may be relatively confined to a particular class throughout the nation and, especially, to a Parisian elite, but that is precisely the reason for its prestige, produced and reinforced through the education system which has created that elite in the first place and which perpetuates it.

Yet Pivot's *Apostrophes* also strayed into the area of popular fiction, and in so doing entered a more ambiguous area. On one level, the highly successful evolution of high culture in France may be viewed as being logically accompanied by an expansion and evolution of popular, or mass culture, which benefited from the impact and development of new technologies. This popular culture may be seen as consisting initially of indigenous, local or regional traditions, often rural, and comprising folklore, artisanal production and local art-forms, and playing an important part in the maintenance of the identity of regional communities, as does the regional language. It was for this reason that this popular culture was celebrated by the creation by the Front Populaire government, in 1936, of the Musée des Arts et Traditions Populaires which continues its work to the present day. Essentially, however, by definition mass-culture is urban, the product of the shift of France from a nation of peasants to a nation of city-dwellers, and its manifestations are different. Café-culture, for example, which developed in the nineteenth century and remained a powerful vector for both popular and high culture in the first half of the twentieth, also gave rise to popular entertainment in the form of café-concert. This, in its turn, evolved into music-hall and played an important role in the evolution of popular music: from the street-singers and sheet-music sellers of the late nineteenth and early twentieth centuries to the stars made famous through recorded music. At the same time as the gramophone was transforming the popular, and classical, music industry, film became a powerful rival to both traditional theatre and the music-hall, to the extent that many music-halls were turned into cinemas before the First World War. Until the end of silent cinema in 1929, France dominated world film-production and, even in the sound era, when leadership had passed to Hollywood, still played an important role, not least because it was able to operate on two levels: a flourishing popular film industry, essentially aimed at the domestic market, and the production of serious films which, sometimes inadvertently, came to occupy the high-cultural domain and win an international audience.

These 'mechanical means of reproduction' – the phonograph and the film camera – were accompanied by other technical innovations which enhanced, and in most cases created, the modern mass media. The French daily press, which, as in all Western countries, had become a major force through the invention of the linotype machine and the rotary press, had its heyday in the years leading up to the First World War, when *Le Petit Parisien* was the best-selling international daily. Even though the sales figures of the daily press declined after the end of the First World War, they remained significant, especially in crucial periods such as the Liberation in 1944, and still exert an influence beyond that of their mere sales figures – a further example of the status of the elites to which the best-known Parisian dailies, like *Le Monde*, *Libération* or *Le Figaro*, are directed. During the interwar years, further technological advances, in particular the invention of the light-weight 35-millimetre camera, saw the birth of photographic news magazines, such as *Paris-Match*, which also paved the way for the serious weekly news press of the postwar period, still represented by *L'Express*, *Le Point*, *Le Nouvel Observateur* and *L'Evénement du jeudi*. At the same time, technological advances in the area of broadcasting ushered in the era of radio and television, which rapidly came to dominate audio-visual entertainment and, crucially, to work alongside and enhance existing forms: the relationship between popular and classical music, theatre and the radio, for example, and the importance of television in screening and funding feature films.

Finally, advances in book-production saw the extension of a popular literature which had been extant since the eighteenth century, if not earlier, but which responded to increased literacy and affluence from the late nineteenth century onwards. As in the relationship between television and film, or radio and music, popular, and more serious, literature was fostered through the commercial press, which serialised fiction before it appeared in volume-form. France was relatively late in coming to 'paperback' fiction – perhaps because its books traditionally had paper covers anyway – but after the Second World War there was an upsurge of cheap popular novels, often, as in the case of Gallimard's *Série Noire*, derived mainly from American crime fiction. At the other end of the market, the *Livre de poche* series, launched in the 1950s, brought to a mass public, swelled by a growing student and lycée population, a collection of classics in attractive format and at a low price. By the end of the 1960s, publishers had also seen the interest in producing *bande dessinée* in volume form: originally strip-cartoon serials aimed at children and adolescents and published in magazines and newspapers, but which, in the 1960s and, especially, the 1970s, acquired a following amongst students and adults. To traditional favourites like *Bécassine* or *Tintin*, there were added new heroes like Goscinny and Uderzo's *Astérix* and *Lucky Luke*, and, coinciding with May '68, more radical and sexually explicit volumes. At the same time, through artists like Claire Brétecher, *bande dessinée* became an important vehicle for social observation and comment, particularly as regards the affluent liberal middle-classes.

Significant as this vast volume of popular cultural activity was, however, its reputation, particularly amongst intellectual critics, remained highly ambiguous. It is true that some forms of popular culture, such as jazz music, film, or, to a certain extent, and belatedly, *bande dessinée*, became assimilated, at least through certain practitioners, into high culture: there is, after all, a *Musée de la Bande Dessinée*, funded by the State, in Angoulême, and there are various prestigious film festivals and numerous 'festivals du jazz'. Historically, however, cultural policy-makers and theorists of both Left and Right have tended to view popular culture with some considerable distrust, with the exception of the traditional rural regional cultures. It is for this reason that, in terms of cultural policy, the transition from the Front Populaire to Vichy was far less dramatic than might have been supposed. The Front Populaire and, in particular, its *Secrétaire d'Etat aux Loisirs*, Léo Lagrange, rightly perceived the importance of culture and leisure in a mass-society, but tended to interpret culture in a particular way. Lagrange's Ministry was attached, as we shall see, not to Jean Zay's Education Ministry, but to the Ministry of Health, and it was as a branch of public health that culture was essentially viewed. The Front Populaire and its theorists rejected passive commercial culture, the life of the café and spectator-sport favoured by most urban Frenchmen, and sponsored instead participatory activity which would take the urban working-class out of the city and out of their unfulfilled lives. Playing football and cycling, rather than watching, became all-important, as did hiking in the French countryside, an activity which would extend knowledge of France's geographical identity as well as physical fitness.

At the same time, popular culture was also regarded as intellectually and morally corrupting, as an opiate for the masses designed to keep them happy, subservient and politically undemanding. The Front Populaire government began a scheme for the Théâtre National Populaire, with prices and times which would accommodate working audiences, and opened the Louvre until late in the evening. Nowhere are its ambitions clearer than in its manifesto for a renewed state radio network, in which, instead of popular music and variety shows, listeners would have access to orchestral concerts, classical theatre, university lectures and parliamentary debates. This proposal for the reform of radio was never enacted, due to the short duration of the government, but its influence remained strong. Vichy, for different reasons, shared the Front Populaire's dislike of popular urban culture, preferring the 'arts et traditions populaires' of the provinces and a cultural network which would diffuse high cultural products designed to uplift and educate.

The post-Liberation period was highly receptive to the same cultural policies: many Resistants shared Vichy's perception of the defeat of France in 1940 as being caused by a nation weakened by urban living and demoralised by a low-level popular culture. In the 1940s, this was compounded on the Left by resistance to commercial culture, seen as the cultural wing of capitalism, and epitomised by the United States. The beginnings of the Cold War in France were accompanied, not merely by resistance to the globalisation of American culture, embodied particularly in the film-industry, but also by the perception of America as the arch-purveyor of popular commercial culture. The French Communist Party's fulminations against bookshop windows full of the works of Henry Miller and the American authors of the *Série Noire*, which, with their black jackets, were likened to 'SS troops on parade', expressed an outrage at the political threat represented by the US, but also at the perceived intellectual and moral damage being inflicted by popular culture.

To be sure, the barriers between high and popular culture have never been as high, or as rigid, as some theoreticians or policy-makers have suggested. In the first place, high culture, especially in its avant-garde phases, has always been keen to annex elements of popular culture. The Cubist painters, for example, make extensive use of popular artefacts, such as newspaper clippings, Métro tickets, advertisements and posters; Sartre, in *La Nausée*, incorporates jazz as a major element of the novel and the composers of 'Les Six' in the 1920s make use of both jazz and popular music in their work; and the *Nouvelle Vague* film-makers draw constantly on American B-Movies. Nor is it always easy to establish a precise dividing-line between high and popular culture, particularly when a high-cultural work meets with commercial success. An airing on Pivot's *Apostrophes*, like the winning of a major literary prize, was enough to boost the most inaccessible book into the best-seller lists. At the same time, and particularly since the Second World War, popular culture has become increasingly viewed as a legitimate and important object of research and enquiry by cultural theorists, such as Barthes in *Mythologies*, sociologists like Edgar Morin and social and cultural historians.

During the process by which popular culture has gradually become recognised as an important element of cultural activity, no longer automatically subordinate to high culture, it has inevitably questioned the canonical nature of that culture. It is no longer possible to view French culture as the preserve of a small number of white, Parisian, heterosexual males and as encompassing a relatively small output of works of literature, music, theatre and painting, accepted as distinguished by a particular cultural elite. The cinema, already, contrived to irremediably blur the line between high and popular culture, even if it subsequently attempted to recuperate itself as an art-house form. At the same time, the French cultural canon has been fragmented and expanded through new players and through the increased importance accorded to their work. This is particularly true in the areas of women's cultural production, regional culture and *Francophonie*. Women's writing, theatre and film, in particular, have progressed exponentially since 1945 and, particularly, 1968, and have moved to the centre of the critical stage. Similarly, in the same time-span, 'French' culture has also become a Francophone culture, encompassing the output of the Mahgreb, Sub-Saharan Africa, the Caribbean and Quebec, together with the work of practitioners originally from those areas now living in Metropolitan France.

This expansion of the traditional cultural canon, to the extent that in some respect it cannot be considered to exist, does, however, pose a methodological problem. When critics and cultural historians began to explore the importance of popular culture, the cultural production of women and Francophone culture, it was logical and legitimate to study them in isolation, and, indeed, as in all forms of cultural activity, it will continue to be so in many circumstances. In any attempt at a synthetic view of French culture throughout the twentieth century, however, it is arguable that it is now appropriate to reunite the disparate strands of that culture and to explore, for example, 'narrative fiction in French', rather than 'the French novel', followed by its inevitably subordinate categories 'the regional novel', 'women's fiction' and 'Francophone fiction'. Similarly, by looking at French classical music since 1900 alongside regional and popular music, a greater understanding may be gained of the diverse and interacting elements of a complex cultural activity. It is for this reason that this volume proceeds to examine French culture and history throughout the twentieth century, before discussing the relationship between culture and society, through themes such as architecture, consumerism, language, intellectuals, political and religious involvement and the media, before looking at areas of specific cultural production in the forms of literature, drama, music, the visual arts and film. In each of these areas, however, care has been taken to include, where appropriate, all types of cultural practitioner and all areas of Francophone cultural production.

The society which celebrated two hundred years since the Revolution of 1789 was, and is, a complex one, proud both of its international prestige and its social diversity. France's culture, throughout the twentieth century, and now into the twenty-first, has contributed more than a little to that prestige, and has been fuelled by and reflects that diversity.

1

Modern France: history, culture and identity, 1900–1945

The first half of the twentieth century was crucial in creating the identity of modern France, yet that process appears on the surface to be highly paradoxical. On the one hand, it was one of the most dramatic periods in modern French history, encompassing the four years of blood-letting of the First World War, political and economic volatility in the interwar years, culminating in the Depression of the mid-1930s, the catastrophic defeat in June 1940, followed by four years of German Occupation, and, finally, the Liberation of France, which also took the form of a near-civil war and vicious purges.

These dramatic events were accompanied by, and in some cases the product of, deep divisions in French society inherited from the nineteenth century: the fierce antagonism between republicans and anti-republicans, although mitigated after 1900, which would lie dormant for years, only to reappear at moments of crisis, like the Depression or the defeat of 1940; the battle of the Republic against the Catholic Church in the early years of the century which rumbled on right into the period of the Occupation; important social divisions between the urban working class, the peasantry and the bourgeoisie; inequalities between men and women, not least in the areas of electoral suffrage and legal status; and, finally, conflicts real or potential which were the product of ethnic divisions. Throughout the first half of the century, France was a major colonial power, second only to the United Kingdom, and its relationship to its colonised peoples, in North and West Africa, in South-East Asia and in the Pacific, was crucial in the forging of a national identity based upon a stereotype of the white Frenchman. That stereotype was often rigorously defended within France itself through periodic assertions of 'Frenchness' against those who were regarded as intruders: the period begins, after all, with the Dreyfus Case, in which a Jewish officer was wrongly convicted of treason, and throughout the first half of the twentieth century anti-Semitism, bolstered by the arrival of poor Jewish refugees from Eastern Europe, went alongside a more generalised antagonism towards non-French immigrants which reached its climax during the Occupation.

At the same time, the apparent volatility of the French political and economic system, the dramatic events which France was to experience and the very real divisions within its society belie an underlying stability and robustness which cannot be discounted. The defeat of June 1940 was due far more to particular tactical military failures than to an inherent weakness in the regime itself, which in fact had shown a remarkable capacity to survive. One of the most useful ways in which to explore these apparent paradoxes is through an important feature of the life of the period which it shared with both the previous half-century and other Western nations: the phenomena of great exhibitions, or world's fairs. These exhibitions, beginning with the London Great Exhibition in 1851, were designed to promote both individual cities and the nations which they represented, in addition to celebrating Western technological and industrial achievements in general, and were important tools in the forging of notions of national identity. As such, they were major cultural phenomena, bringing together strands of high and popular culture, and they provide an important insight into the periods in which they took place, together with the aspirations and fears of their hosts. In France, amongst a number of national and municipal events held during the period 1900–1940, three are particularly significant: the Universal Exhibition of 1900, held in Paris, the Marseilles Colonial Exhibition of 1922, and the International Exhibition of 1937, once more in Paris. Nowhere is the search for French identity in the first half of the century better demonstrated, and nowhere are the fault-lines in French politics and society, which came dramatically into play in 1940, so apparent.

Paris 1900

The 1900 Exhibition was the culmination of a series of French national exhibitions held in Paris which began under the Second Empire in 1855 and 1867, and continued under the Third Republic in 1878 and, most significantly, 1889, which celebrated the centenary of the French Revolution and left the Eiffel Tower as an indelible icon on the skyline of the capital. Its aim was to build on the recent achievements of the Republic, whilst looking forward to a new century. As the decree of 1892 setting up the 1900 Exhibition stated: 'It will be the end of a century of prodigious scientific and economic efforts; it will also be the threshold of an era whose greatness is prophesised by scientists and philosophers, the reality of which will probably exceed our wildest dreams'.[1] Accordingly, much of the Exhibition of 1900 was devoted to technological developments, displayed in the 'Galerie des machines' (Machine House), amongst which the new power-source of electricity was prominent, 'La Fée Electricité' (Fairy Electricity). At the same time, the organisers of the 1900 Exhibition were at pains to use the event as a celebration of specifically French achievements: its industrial, colonial and agricultural might, laid out in a number of halls and displays, together with its artistic prowess, particularly in the visual arts. The aim, even more than in 1889, was to reassert the prestige of France after the humiliating defeat at the hands of Prussia in 1870, and, more particularly, to celebrate the consolidation of the Third Republic as the unchallenged regime of France, a regime which had been obliged in its short career to see off a number of powerful threats: the attempt of the first President, Marshal MacMahon, to dissolve parliament in 1876, the challenge of the Monarchists and Bonapartists, nationalist groupings such as Paul Déroulède's Ligue des Patriotes, General Boulanger's bid for power, and, finally, the Dreyfus Case. At the same time, the Exhibition, by drawing on resources from all over France and its colonies, constituted a powerful assertion of nationhood, of French, as opposed to regional, identity.

The Exhibition, after a slow start, became immensely popular, attracting many visitors from the provinces and from abroad. It was also symbolic of the state of France as a whole in the period of the Belle Epoque before the First World War. On one level, France was undoubtedly justified in asserting her achievements in the field of industrial development. As James McMillan shows, although her coal and steel production was far below that of Britain or Germany, French industrial growth in the period before the war was impressive, achieving a rate of 2.6 per cent per annum between 1896 and 1906 and doubling that figure in the next seven years.[2] The deficiencies in heavy industry were offset by considerable advances in the new industries of chemicals, electricity and cars. Indeed, France became the foremost European car-manufacturing nation in the years before the war, through firms like Citroën, Peugeot and Renault, many of whom were interested in American innovations of assembly-line techniques. At the same time, the expansion of industrial development was accompanied by a similar consolidation of France's agriculture. Not only was nearly half of the labour force engaged in agriculture, but France was still predominantly an agricultural nation. In spite of some stagnancy in the agricultural sector in the last years of the nineteenth century, the rural economy remained buoyant throughout the Belle Epoque, particularly as a result of protectionist tariffs introduced by the minister Jules Méline in 1892. Finally, this economic strength was reinforced through the French colonies and diplomatic initiatives which had secured a firm working relationship with Britain through the Entente Cordiale (Cordial Agreement) of 1903 and a treaty, and economic agreement, with Russia. Both the Entente Cordiale and the Russian treaty provided for military security for France in the light of the growing power and belligerence of Germany, although they were also to prove crucial in making war inevitable in 1914.

The regime which inaugurated the Exhibition of 1900, therefore, could congratulate itself on a booming economy and impressive empire, but also upon the achievement of a constitutional stability unknown in the previous quarter-century and which seemed, with some justification, to be unassailable: by the declaration of war in 1914, the Third Republic was France's longest-serving regime since the revolution of 1789, outliving the July Monarchy and the Second Empire. This success was reflected in the recognition of Paris as the undisputed capital of the world's tourism and entertainment industry: the 'Ville Lumière', with its monuments, pleasure-quarters like Montmartre, and new transport systems, like the Métro, one line of which was introduced in time for the 1900 Exhibition, became a beacon for both provincial and international tourists. Montmartre, especially, with its music-halls like Le Moulin Rouge and Les Folies-Bergère, became internationally known and its prominence as a tourist site was fixed in the early years of the century through the near-completion of the Sacré-Coeur.

At the same time, during the Belle Epoque Paris became a magnet for the arts, particularly in painting and sculpture. The international reputation of Impressionism in the late nineteenth century had already attracted provincial artists like Toulouse-Lautrec or European painters like Van Gogh. At the beginning of the twentieth century, Paris played automatic host to the international avant-garde: Fauvism, established by Matisse, Detrain and Vlaminck, also attracted Dufy and Braque from Le Havre, in addition to Kees Van Dongen from the Netherlands, and achieved an international reputation, especially in Germany;

other avant-garde painters, like Chagall, settled in the artistic colony La Ruche (the Bee-Hive) in Montparnasse, whilst Picasso, who had visited Paris as early as 1900 and had gravitated naturally to Montmartre, founded Cubism in 1907, together with Braque, Derain, Delaunay and Léger. From 1904 onwards, when Picasso settled into the Bateau-Lavoir (literally: 'laundry-boat'), a ramshackle collection of artists' studios in Montmartre, it is possible to date the Ecole de Paris, which brought together in a loose avant-garde coalition artists from all parts of Europe, Japan and the United States. This dazzling avant-garde production during the Belle Epoque, and which continued into the postwar period, was reinforced by considerable innovative success in music, through the work of Satie, Debussy, Ravel and Fauré, and in literature. Naturalism, through the work of Zola and his successors, and Symbolism, through Mallarmé, Valéry and Claudel, continued to exert considerable prestige, but, in addition, a literary avant-garde, often closely allied to the musical and plastic arts, began to achieve a world-wide reputation, through iconoclastic dramatists such as Alfred Jarry or Modernist novelists like Gide and Proust. Journals like La Nouvelle Revue Française began to exert such an influence that, by the time of the German Occupation in 1940, it was considered one of the major French strategic assets, on a par with banks and radio stations. From 1900 onwards, Paris, with little exaggeration, could merit its reputation as 'capital of the arts'.

Nevertheless, if the France of the Belle Epoque had much to, legitimately, celebrate and congratulate itself for, there were serious underlying problems, many of which were connected to the obvious successes. One major difficulty concerned the population. Whilst other, rival, powers had increased their populations throughout the second half of the nineteenth century, France had entered a demographic slump: between 1871 and 1911, it increased its population by a mere 3.5 million, or 9.7 per cent, whilst Germany had seen an increase of 23.8 million, or 57.8 per cent.[3] This demographic crisis, which was to dog France throughout at least the first half of the twentieth century, had many causes – inheritance laws which divided property equally between all surviving children, thus rendering farms rapidly unviable; fear of political or international instability; urban poverty; or desire amongst the bourgeoisie to maximise income by limiting offspring – but the effect was clear enough. The percentage of young people in the population declined and, at some points during the Belle Epoque, the birth-rate was exceeded by the mortality-rate, with a resultant net decline in the population. The implications were stark: for a rapidly industrialising economy, the labour force was often inadequate, and, in the face of a threatening Germany, France found it increasingly difficult to put in the field a comparable army. None of these problems would go away after the carnage of the First World War.

Similarly, although French industry throughout the prewar era presented encouraging signs of growth and expansion, there were worrying trends: in addition to the relative weakness of the coal and steel industries, and set against the strengths of the new technologies represented by the electricity, chemical and automobile sectors, was the fact that French industry remained globally small-scale. Moreover, the examples of large modern plants with numerous employees and modern production techniques remained few in number, whilst the norm (1 million out of 1.1 million) was small artisanal workshops employing less than five workers.[4] Finally, the traditional pattern of French manufacturing remained unchanged during the period, in spite of the recent advances: labour intensive, cost intensive, high-quality luxury goods, designed predominantly for the domestic market. In other words, like the 1900 Exhibition itself, the French economy of the Belle Epoque looked in two directions: towards a bright and innovative future, but also back to a system of production, financing and distribution which had changed little since the mid-nineteenth century.

The same was also true of the balance between the capital and the provinces, between the urban and the rural – in fact, of the very nature of French identity in the period 1900–1914. In 1911, France was still a predominantly rural society, with the urban population accounting for only 44 per cent of the population, a factor which had considerable conservative electoral implications. However, that urban population itself was concentrated mainly in very small towns, with only 15.4 per cent living in towns of over 100,000 inhabitants in 1900, and only two centres, Lyons and Marseilles, having more than half a million citizens.[5] Paris, at 3 million, dominated the country, often draining it of its human and economic resources, and looking forward to the 'French desert' identified by Jean-François Gravier after the Second World War,[6] by which, whilst Paris continued to prosper, the rest of the nation was reduced to insignificance.

Similarly, the 1900 Exhibition and its celebration of Frenchness disguised severe social inequalities. The peasantry, although numerous and protected by the Méline tariffs, were often drastically poor. The urban working class, a relatively new minority, squeezed between the electoral power of the peasantry and the economic might of the bourgeoisie, had few rights, worked in appalling conditions and often lived in poor accommodation in the industrial suburbs. Women, who would not gain the vote until 1944, were subject to the highly discriminatory civil code, which, for example, provided for imprisonment for adultery, and in the vast majority were denied access to higher education or the professions. France's colonial population, although in some territories granted French citizenship, remained subservient.

These social inequalities were accompanied by serious ideological divisions. The Dreyfus Case split the country and opened wounds which never entirely healed: on the extreme Right, in 1898 Charles Maurras founded his royalist anti-Semitic movement Action Française, which was to become the most important anti-republican organisation of the first half-century. Action Française gained considerable support from Catholics, appalled at the policies of Emile Combes, determined to separate Church and State and to drive the Catholic Church from all positions of influence. On the Left, the Socialists, particularly the faction led by Jules Guesde, were committed to the abolition of capitalism and its bourgeois republic. In other words, although by 1900 France had achieved a republican consensus, ruled effectively from the centre, there remained powerful currents of anti-republicanism, increasingly, but by no means exclusively, on the extreme Right, which became apparent at moments of crisis and would become powerful after 1940.

Nevertheless, the republican consensus was certainly strong enough to both declare and wage war in 1914, and the 'Union Sacrée' (Sacred Union), which suspended party-political antagonisms in the higher interests of the Nation, held solid until at least 1917. Even so, there were cracks in the edifice. French industry and industrialists were not always equal to the task of a nation committed to total war, particularly with the loss or destruction of major industrial centres in the North and East. At the same time, the widening gaps between the experience of the soldiers at the Front and the civilian population at home, particularly in Paris, some of whom were blatantly profiteering from the war, led to resentments which would last throughout the interwar years. In fact, by the third year of the war, the Republic was beginning to experience what amounted to the most serious challenge to its legitimacy and power, with the wave of mutinies on the Western Front in 1917, the industrial strikes of the same year and the increasingly vociferous demands on the Left

for a negotiated peace. Victory certainly re-established the Republic's uncontested authority, but the divisions nevertheless remained beneath the
surface.

Marseilles 1922: the empire, provinces and stability

In 1922 Marseilles hosted a Colonial Exhibition, the third in a series
which began in 1906 and continued in 1916, and which culminated in
the Paris Colonial Exhibition in the Parc de Vincennes in 1931. The primary aim of the exhibition was to celebrate the achievements of French
colonial rule, but it was also an opportunity for Marseilles itself to celebrate its role as France's major imperial port, with two-thirds of all the
nation's trade with the colonies passing through it, and, incidentally, to
score points over its arch-rival Lyons.

France's empire began in the seventeenth century: in Canada, subsequently lost to the British in 1763, leaving a significant Francophone community in the province of Québec; the Caribbean, particularly
Martinique and Guadaloupe; and Africa and the Indian Ocean, initially
colonised to provide slaves for the Caribbean plantations. In the nineteenth century came the second wave of French colonialism, with the
settlement of Algeria in 1830, followed by the later North African protectorates of Tunisia and Morocco, and the occupation of the various territories making up French West Africa and French Equatorial Africa. The
empire was reinforced by the colonisation of Madagascar and Djibouti, in
East Africa, and by the acquisition of territories in the Pacific and, most
importantly, Indo-China. The process was completed by the Treaty of
Versailles, which gave to France former German colonies in West Africa
and territories in the Middle East, notably Syria and Lebanon, formerly
under the control of the Ottoman Empire.

The economic impact of the empire on France is not easy to assess.
On the one hand, the colonies were a valuable source of raw materials unavailable in France itself, ranging from minerals to timber and
food products, and an important market for French manufactured goods.
As Robert Aldrich shows, from 1928 to 1960, the empire was France's
leading trading partner, a role which assumed considerable importance
during the Depression of the 1930s, when trade with other nations often dried up. Nevertheless, overall, the empire's economic importance
can be exaggerated: in 1913, for example, it accounted for only 9.4 per
cent of total French imports and 13 per cent of exports, though these

figures were to increase during the Depression and the years following the Second World War.[7] Nor did the colonies play a determining role in the modernisation of French industry, since newer innovative sectors often preferred to trade with non-colonial markets such as Europe and America. Germany, with few colonial possessions up to 1918, nevertheless achieved a more impressive record of industrial output and modernisation than France. The same is broadly true of the empire's strategic significance: it certainly contributed troops to the war effort between 1914 and 1918, but nevertheless also absorbed French military, and economic, resources. Nor was the empire universally popular within France. The 1931 Colonial Exhibition in Paris, for example, was denounced by the French Communist Party, the Socialists and the Surrealists, who organised a counter-event and produced a pamphlet 'Don't Visit the Colonial Exhibition'. Four years earlier, the respected writer André Gide had denounced European colonial rule in Africa in his *Voyage au Congo*.

Nevertheless, it can be argued that the empire was an important aspect of the French image of themselves as they emerged from the First World War and struggled to maintain a role as a world power. In spite of the victory of November 1918, the war had inflicted huge damage on the nation. Nearly 1.3 million French troops had been killed – 16.6 per cent of all troops mobilised – and 3 million had been wounded.[8] Not only did these figures imply a huge financial burden on the State, through invalids', widows' and orphans' pensions and long-term medical costs, they also had a disastrous impact on an already acute demographic crisis. The loss of so many young men was serious in itself and led to severe shortages in the labour market. The loss of those men as potential fathers resulted in a shortfall in the birth-rate between 1915 and 1919 of some 1.75 million babies.[9] The result was that by 1938 the number of Frenchmen of military age was only half what it should have been – and that on top of the alarming demographic trends of the late nineteenth and early twentieth centuries. The labour shortage could be remedied by immigration, and France called on workers from Poland and the Mediterranean countries, but the halving of France's potential military resources was to have severe implications for her ability to wage war, both actually and psychologically, in 1939 and 1940. Finally, the war had devastated some of France's richest industrial and agricultural areas, in the North and North-East, and France emerged from the conflict heavily in debt, with a deficit of 110,000 million francs.

In the light of this, it appears surprising that the French economy should have performed so well in the years following the war, yet perform well it did. In fact, France entered a period of unparalleled economic growth which ended only with the drying-up of the export-markets during the Depression of the 1930s. In spite of France's failure to reduce the agricultural sector and her continuing heavy reliance on the artisanal production of luxury consumer goods, the economy was stimulated by the return of the steel-making capacity of Lorraine and by the further development of a modern chemical industry. Through companies like Renault, Citroën, Panhard and Peugeot, the French automobile industry was the largest in Europe, producing nearly a quarter of a million models in 1929. The underlying inherent weaknesses in the economy would only become apparent in the 1930s, when France found it difficult to emerge from the Depression as rapidly as Germany, Britain or America.

Postwar prosperity, however, was accompanied by political volatility. The elections of 1919 reflected a triumphal patriotism by returning a solid right-wing majority, the 'Bloc National'. This *Chambre bleu horizon* ('Sky-blue Chamber', named after the colour of the French army uniform) was primarily concerned with the implementation of the Versailles Treaty, particularly regarding the enforcement of German war reparations, and which led to the occupation of the Ruhr, and the search for security – from both Germany and the Soviet Union. Its financial management, however, was less successful and in 1924 it was ousted by a centre-left coalition, the 'Cartel des Gauches', dominated by the Radicals, but with Socialist parliamentary support. Under this majority, the country rapidly entered a serious inflationary crisis which was only solved by the return in 1926 of the veteran conservative politician and former President, Poincaré.

The election of the Cartel des Gauches provoked entirely baseless fears on the Right of social revolution, and this anxiety took the form of accentuated extra-parliamentary opposition. Already, under the *Chambre bleu horizon*, Action Française had reached what was to prove its peak in terms of power and popularity, although it would continue as the most important right-wing anti-republican organisation until Vichy. One of its leaders, the journalist Léon Daudet, had been elected as deputy for Paris and was urged by supporters to emulate Mussolini in Italy and overthrow the Republic. Nor was the example of Mussolini lost on other extreme right-wing activists. Georges Valois, another Action Française member, founded the openly Fascist movement Le Faisceau in 1926, and the mid-1920s saw the birth of a number of 'Leagues' which adopted the paramilitary uniforms, parades and street-fighting techniques of their Italian and German models: in particular, Pierre Taittinger's Jeunesses Patriotes, François Coty's Solidarité Française, Marcel Bucard's Francisme and Colonel de la Rocque's Croix de Feu. These Leagues, often swollen by dissatisfied former soldiers, and reinforced by the Depression of the 1930s, maintained a vociferous opposition to the Republic which came to greatest prominence in the riots of 6 February 1934 against the government's handling of the Stavisky scandal.

On the Left, the SFIO had split at its congress in Tours in 1920 (at which, incidentally, the young Vietnamese militant Ho Chi Minh had accused France of being 'a great liberal country which does not export its liberalism'), between the majority of delegates who voted in favour of joining the new Soviet-dominated Third International and the rump of the party who refused to accept Lenin's conditions. In fact, it was this rump, led by Léon Blum, who modestly adopted the role of caretaker of what had once been the grand edifice of the SFIO, styling himself 'gardien de la vieille maison' (caretaker of the old house), which was to remain electorally powerful, whilst the new French Communist Party (PCF) committed itself to class struggle and revolution. Until the Front Populaire election of 1936, the SFIO was the major left-wing political party, both in terms of membership and representation, whilst the PCF concentrated on a semi-clandestine organisation through its cell-structure and, as a party which prided itself on being 'pur et dur' (pure and hard), resisted all alliances with 'class traitors'.

Finally, unlike Britain, France refused to grant suffrage to its women citizens after the First World War, fundamentally due to the prejudices of exclusively male legislators, but also, from the point of view of the Radicals, because of spurious but politically attractive fears that women, under the influence of the priests, would be natural right-wing voters. The war itself had, if anything, reinforced gender discrimination in the workplace, and the ensuing demographic crisis rendered the emancipation of women even more difficult: not only was their role seen increasingly as being limited to the home, as bearers of much-needed children, but also legislation enacted in the early years of the *Chambre bleu-horizon* penalised birth-control information and contraception. Women, like those other vital French resources during the war, the colonial troops, entered the interwar period as disadvantaged as they had entered the war itself.

In spite of the underlying political and economic problems, the social divisions and opposition to the Republic from both the extreme Right and extreme Left, the period until the advent of the Depression was one of relative ease and prosperity. The French might look back nostalgically to what became known as the 'Belle Epoque' as a period of financial stability, and they would well know that, having lived through one 'interwar period', in the words of Léon Daudet (that between the Franco-Prussian War and the First World War), the process might well repeat itself, but the 1920s was characterised by considerable confidence, both economically and culturally. In terms of high culture, France still maintained a pre-eminent position through the Ecole de Paris, and in the avant-garde in general, particularly through Surrealism, which harnessed writers like Breton, Eluard and Aragon, and painters from France and abroad, such as Picasso, Max Ernst and Salvador Dali. France's supremacy in architecture, design and the manufacture of luxury goods was consecrated by the Exposition des Arts Décoratifs, held in Paris in 1925, which featured, amongst others, the work of Le Corbusier. In music, the progressive composers known as 'Les Six', including Honegger, Milhaud and Poulenc, became internationally known, whilst France's achievements in literature were represented, not merely by the older generation of Colette, Proust, Gide, Claudel and Valéry, but by a number of younger, often politically committed, writers such as Malraux, Drieu la Rochelle and Mauriac, and by internationally recognised journals, like the *Nouvelle Revue Française*. Even France's colonial citizens were represented in this literary Pantheon: in 1921, the Guyanese novelist René Maran won France's most prestigious literary award, the Prix Goncourt, for his novel *Batouala*.

It was in popular culture, however, that the greatest revolution occurred. In music, the phonograph replaced the street-singer and sheet music and launched the careers of modern popular singers. These singers, like Mistinguett, Maurice Chevalier or Josephine Baker, often came from the music-halls which, after the First World War, used technological innovations like modern stage-lighting and sound amplification to play to increasingly large audiences. Before the war, France had been the world capital of film production, a role which it gradually relinquished to Hollywood in the course of the 1920s. Nevertheless, France remained an important film-producing nation until the advent of sound in 1929, which revolutionised the industry and gave primacy to English-language films. Even then, France was to continue to play a major role in world cinema, both in terms of quality production, and through export to Hollywood of stars like Chevalier and Mistinguett, whilst still maintaining a strong domestic popular base. The 1920s also saw the launch of radio and the nationwide organisation of sport: the founding of the Fédération Française de Football Association (the French Association Football Federation) in 1919 was followed by that of the Fédération Française de Rugby the following year; cycling resumed its prewar popularity, through the Tour de France and the Parisian Vélodrome d'Hiver, the 'Vél d'Hiv', whilst France's international sporting reputation was enhanced by the Paris Olympics of 1924, the victory of the French Davis Cup team in 1926 and Georges Carpentier's World Light-Heavyweight crown in 1919.

The significance of the colonial exhibitions being held in Marseilles, before Paris took over in 1931, should not be lost, since it demonstrates an assertion of regional, as opposed to central, power. As we have seen, all too often Paris, with its administrative monopoly and its economic and political power, drained the rest of the country of its financial and human resources. The Colonial Exhibition of 1922 was intended as a reminder that Marseilles, like its hated rival Lyons, was an important urban centre in its own right, the major port for the empire and, some eight hours by train from Paris, an important focus of regional cultural and economic activity which owed little to the capital. In fact, Marseilles was closer to Italy than to Paris, and its frames of reference more often included its neighbours on both sides of the Mediterranean than the territories to the North. Marseilles, like the other Mediterranean cities of Nice and Montpellier, benefited from the immigration policies of the early 1920s by supplementing its work-force from workers from Italy, Spain and Portugal, just as, in the 1960s, it was to recruit labour from the Mahgreb. At the same time, it was a major centre of Provençal culture, particularly associated with the poet Mistral, and increasingly constituted a credible cultural counterweight to Paris itself: the journal *Les Cahiers du Sud*, founded by Jean Ballard in 1925, became a serious rival to *La Nouvelle Revue Française*. Similarly, building on the success of the early days of the silent French film industry, centred in studios in Nice, that dedicated Marseilles author and film-director, Marcel Pagnol, established his studios in the city throughout the interwar years.

In other words, the Marseilles Exhibition of 1922 is a potent reminder of France's role as a major colonial power and of the problems and prosperity which the nation encountered in the first decade of the interwar years. It also emphasises the fact that, in spite of its extreme political and economic centralisation, France was also a country of regions, each with their own cultural activity. The problem in the interwar years, however, was that the initial prosperity could not withstand the international economic climate and that the *Chambre bleu-horizon*'s preoccupation with security proved to be extremely well founded.

Paris 1937: the Front Populaire and the threat of war

The International Exhibition held in Paris in 1937 was to be the last of the great French world fairs. Although planned much earlier, it became the responsibility of the Popular Front government, which was blamed for the poor organisation which led to its opening late. The novelist Louis-Ferdinand Céline was not alone on the Right in disparagingly comparing the 1937 Exhibition with its predecessor in 1900. In fact, its existence at all, in the midst of a continuing serious depression and considerable political unrest, was a testimony to the resilience of the regime.

The impact of the Wall Street Crash did not come to be felt in France until 1931, when the economy went into sharp decline. Production dropped by 17.5 per cent in 1931, falling to 20 per cent of the 1929 level by 1935, and share prices declined by 33 per cent in the same period.[10] At the same time, the agricultural sector and small businesses were severely affected. The problem was that, particularly after the devaluation of sterling in 1931, resulting in an over-priced Franc, France's export trade declined massively, with a consequent balance of payments crisis. Nevertheless, seen from a certain perspective, the impact of the Depression on France was less dramatic than in other industrial countries. As we have seen, the demographic crisis, compounded by the First World War, gave France a small pool of potential industrial labour which needed to be supplemented by immigrant workers. When the Depression began to bite, the immigrant workers were the first to suffer and return home, leaving France with a relatively low number of unemployed which never rose above half a million. Similarly, women workers could simply be removed from the labour market and forced to resume their role as housewives and mothers. Nor, paradoxically, did the Depression lead to hardship amongst urban workers who remained in employment: whilst industrial wages fell sharply, prices fell more, so workers were better off. The peasantry, however, suffered more, seeing their domestic and overseas markets drying up and their income plummeting.

The Depression exposed both the underlying weaknesses of the French economy and the inability of governments of all persuasions to tackle the problem. France was still excessively reliant on both its agricultural sector and the small businesses producing luxury goods. Its heavy industry was impeded either by poor management, as in the case of the automobile sector, or by poor quality of raw materials, as in the case of coal. It was this relatively primitive nature of her industry which meant that France, unlike Britain, Germany and the United States, took far longer to climb out of the Depression, and, indeed, did not fully succeed in doing so until after the Second World War. An additional, and perhaps crucial, factor was the refusal of French governments, unlike their British counterparts, to consider devaluation as a solution: indeed, rather than countenance devaluation, French politicians placed their hopes in an increasingly rigorous policy of deflation, through public spending cuts, which made the crisis worse.

This inability to find a solution to the economic crisis was compounded by what appeared to be the inefficiency and corruption of parliament, with successive governments composed overwhelmingly of the same politicians, and culminating in the Stavisky scandal of 1933. In this case, a Jewish East European swindler, with excellent high-level political contacts, had mounted a fraud based upon the *Crédit Municipal*, or municipal bank, of the Basque town of Bayonne. When the fraud was discovered, he fled to Chamonix, on the Swiss border, where he apparently committed suicide. In the ensuing furore, the extreme Right alleged, correctly, that Stavisky could not have operated for so long and so successfully without powerful official cover and, more debatably, that he had been murdered in order to prevent embarrassing disclosures. In February 1934, the new Prime Minister, Edouard Daladier, further aroused the Right by sacking one of their own, the Paris police chief Chiappe. Incensed, the right-wing Leagues decided to demonstrate on 6 February and, in the ensuing violence which went on well into the night, fourteen rioters were killed, with many injured. It was the high point of the Leagues' activity and it brought down Daladier's government, but it also demonstrated their weakness: there was no co-ordination between the different groupings, their aims were very imprecise and the regime itself proved to be in little immediate danger. On the Left, however, the night of 6 February confirmed its worst fears of a repetition of events in Italy and, especially, Germany, and it moved to counter the threat. By July 1934 a joint agreement was signed by the two warring parties of the Left, the SFIO and the PCF, who were joined a year later by the Radical Party in the Front Populaire. This electoral alliance, which even saw the Communists holding out the hand of friendship to the Catholics, won the parliamentary elections of April–May 1936 with a massive majority of 143 over the Right.

Even before it came to power, however, in June 1936, the Popular Front government under Léon Blum encountered a major crisis which exploded dramatically as soon as the election results were known. A spontaneous wave of strikes and occupations spread across the country, involving 1,800,000 workers and 8441 factories.[11] The importance of these strikes, which were by no means restricted to industrial workers but also involved both male and female white-collar workers, such as those in departmental stores, lay in their very spontaneity: they were at one and the same time an expression of euphoria at the victory of the Left and the result of long pent-up resentment at poor wages and authoritarian management. Above all, they indicated the primitive nature of French working-class culture, with no long tradition of unionisation and discipline. This, in its turn, set the workers at odds with the leaders of the Popular Front, who seemed remote from their needs and aspirations. In spite of the exhortation of the Communist leader Maurice Thorez that 'il faut savoir terminer une grève' (you have to know how to end a strike), the strikes persisted independent of government control until the summer holidays of 1936, and they resumed in the autumn, with considerable consequences for French industrial output.

In fact, the Blum government, made up of Socialists and Radicals, with Communist parliamentary support, and with three women junior ministers, proved no better at managing the economy than its predecessors, mainly due to the same obstinate refusal to devalue the Franc, compounded by a massive flight of capital from French investors. The significance of the Popular Front governments, however, lies less in their economic record than in their pioneering legislation in terms of employment, leisure and culture. Negotiations between the government and employers at the prime minister's official residence in the Hôtel Matignon on 7 June 1936 resulted in the most radical agreement ever reached on French labour relations, with provisions for pay-increases of between 7 and 15 per cent, the recognition of union activity within the work-place, a forty-hour week and paid holidays. Although the practical effects of this legislation was blunted in the short term by the inflation of autumn 1936 and the failure of the employers to fulfil consistently the terms of the agreement, the 'Accords Matignon' became a landmark in French industrial relations.

The most visible evidence for this came in the summer of 1936, with the mass departure of the urban workers for the countryside and the coast. Under the energetic direction of Blum's Secretary of State for Leisure, Léo Lagrange, cheap railway tickets were issued and cheap accommodation organised to allow working-class families to spend the first holiday of their lives outside of the cities. Although the French bourgeois deeply resented the invasion of 'their' beaches by the urban proletariat, the newsreel films and newspaper photographs of the exodus from the cities to the countryside and the sea were emblematic of the generous nature of French labour policy. Nor was that policy restricted to paid holidays: the forty-hour week provided, for the first time, for the two-day 'English weekend', and Lagrange was determined that the urban populations would use it to benefit from healthy activities like hiking, cycling or sport. Lagrange's Secretariat was initially attached to the Health Ministry, and behind his initiatives was the perennial French concern with the health and vigour of its population, particularly those of military age, in comparison with their German rivals. For this reason, much Front Populaire leisure policy showed, as we have seen, a deep distrust of spectator sports and the life of the urban café.

This concern with the implications of increased leisure for the nation's physical health was paralleled by a similar concern for access to culture. In spite of its short life, the Front Populaire, under the Education Minister Jean Zay, embarked upon an ambitious programme of cultural reform which was to become the model both for the cultural policy of Vichy and of the Fifth Republic. In the same way that Lagrange distrusted spectator sports, Zay's advisors saw most aspects of mass popular culture as demeaning and concentrated instead on policies which would open up high culture to the masses, including theatre reform, free evening access to the Louvre and the encouragement of workers' choral societies. There were few areas of cultural activity which the Front Populaire did not begin to explore: book policy, including libraries, the uses of radio to inform and elevate and, crucially, the cinema. Jean Renoir, who had anticipated the Front Populaire in *Le Crime de Monsieur Lange*, of early 1936, and who had made *La Vie est à nous* as an election film for the Communists, presided over a co-operative film-project, *La Marseillaise*, released in 1937.

In fact, the Front Populaire was the culmination of intense cultural activity on the Left, which provoked a commensurate response from the

Right. The 1930s was a period of intense involvement of writers and artists in politics. On the Left, the growing coalition against Fascism was essentially the work of writers and intellectuals: the older generation of Gide, Romain Rolland and Henri Barbusse, and younger novelists like André Malraux, Paul Nizan and Louis Guilloux. This political commitment on the Left was reflected on the opposite side of the spectrum by Henri Massis and the directors of Action Française, Charles Maurras and Léon Daudet, accompanied by their increasingly radical disciples, Drieu la Rochelle, Robert Brasillach and Thierry Maulnier. Both sides used, not merely their fictional or dramatic work to convey their views, but also, increasingly, political or intellectual journals, such as *Marianne* on the Left and the right-wing *Je suis partout*. These cultural battles of the 1930s were to climax during the Occupation.

The International Exhibition opened in Paris after the fall of the first Front Populaire government and in an atmosphere of increasing international tension, symbolised by the massive German and Soviet pavilions placed defiantly face to face. The reality of that tension was readily apparent in the Spanish pavilion, containing Picasso's *Guernica*, and a disturbing reminder of the failure of the Front Populaire, under intense international pressure, to aid effectively the democratically elected popular front government of Spain. From the failure of the French government to resist the German reoccupation of the Rhineland and her blatant intervention in the Spanish Civil War, the road ran smoothly downhill to appeasement and the Munich Agreement of 1938, abandoning Czechoslovakia to Germany.

Defeat, occupation and liberation

France's defeat in the summer of 1940 was by no means as inevitable as subsequent commentators, often politically partisan, suggested. In spite of the short-lived nature of most governments and their inability to deal with the prevailing economic crisis, there is little to suggest that the regime was in any way mortally fragile when France declared war on Germany in 1939. Since the formation of the Front Populaire, the Communists had supported the Republic, even going so far, as we have seen, as to seek a rapprochement with the Catholic Church. Whilst the non-aggression pact between Germany and the Soviet Union of 1939, the Molotov–Ribbentropp Pact, led to the defection of a small number of PCF leaders and unjustifiably draconian repression of the Party by the

Daladier government, most of its members went to war in defence of
the Republic. The same was true on the far Right: the Leagues had accepted their dissolution by the Front Populaire in 1936, with the Croix
de Feu reconstituting itself into a legal political party, the Parti Social
Français (PSF), but, with some exceptions in the *Je suis partout* camp,
for the extreme Right, like the extreme Left, the national interest took
precedence over domestic political concerns. Nor is there evidence of defeatism amongst the population as a whole, or the army. The French went
to war in 1940 with the same dogged sense of purpose as in 1914, and,
contrary to some partisan contemporary comments, fought as coura-
geously. In fact, the French army, which was well equipped, particularly
with the B2 battle-tank, was simply, like the British Expeditionary Force,
out-manoeuvred by the German panzers under Guderian which crashed
through the Ardennes forest, broke the French line at Sedan, and, by
making for the coast, split the allied forces. The defeat of 1940 was due
to poor communications and poor generalship, but not to any more fundamental disorder, and if the Third Republic collapsed, it was through a
conjuncture of forces, including an irredeemable military defeat and the
intransigence of the French High Command, which few regimes could
have withstood.

The terms of the Armistice were severe: partition of the country into
a northern and coastal Zone under the direct occupation of the German
military, and a 'Free' Zone, south of the Loire, governed by a regime led by
Marshal Pétain based in the spa town of Vichy. In addition, the Germans
enforced crippling reparations on the French for the cost of the war,
expropriated raw materials and industrial production, and imposed a
heavy charge for the expenses of the occupying forces. Furthermore, the
Germans imposed a system of rationing which kept the French at a per-
ilously low level of consumption of food and heating.

Equally as serious as the physical deprivations to which the country was subjected were the political divisions which the Occupation
brought to light and exploited. Not that these divisions automatically
followed traditional fault-lines of Left and Right. Charles Maurras may
have felt that the emergence, and apparent capability, of Pétain was
a 'divine suprise', but Maurras himself was strongly anti-German and
many supporters of Action Française and other anti-parliamentary right-
wing groupings went on to become distinguished Resistance heroes.
The divisions were in fact more subtle, and often obscured by the
fact that, until the German occupation of the 'Free' Zone in 1942,

the majority of Frenchmen remained relatively neutral, convinced that the Marshal, perhaps clandestinely, was acting in the best interests of France.

Initially, the French Right gravitated to Vichy, enthused by the 'Etat Français', with its 'Révolution Nationale' which replaced the hated republican virtues of 'Liberté, Egalité, Fraternité' with the new trinity of 'Travail, Famille, Patrie'. The 'Etat Français' attracted a motley group of dedicated conservatives, anti-Communists and traditionalists, but also technocrats who represented an important strand of thought in French politics in the interwar years which saw an authoritarian state as an ideal vehicle for government on rational engineering principles. This led to a regime which seemed to point in at least two directions: a revival of the ethos of provincial France, together with its rural virtues, and, at the same time, centred on figures like Admiral Darlan and the Interior Minister Pierre Pucheu, the ambition for modernisation and planning which looked forward to the Fourth Republic.

Splits rapidly occurred on the Right, however, on the nature of collaboration with the Germans. The French extreme Right was always split throughout the interwar years between the 'Europeanists' who favoured the integration of France into a broader European, and anti-Communist, mission, led by Nazi Germany, and a hard, royalist and patriotic Right, which remained highly antagonistic to Germany for historical as well as ideological reasons and which wished to keep the Occupier at arm's length. This division served not only to constitute different factions at Vichy itself – represented, for example, by Pétain, Darlan and the pro-German and anti-Communist Pierre Laval – but also to alienate the more extreme pro-German collaborationists, like the *Je suis partout* team, who were rapidly exasperated by what they regarded as Pétain's weakness and moved to Paris as soon as possible. Here, in the entourage of the German Ambassador Otto Abetz, they formed part of a powerful collaborationist coterie, which included industrialists, politicians, journalists and writers. At the same time, the Occupation saw an upsurge of that French anti-Semitism which had been a powerful force in French politics since the end of the nineteenth century. The Vichy government introduced anti-Semitic legislation based upon a genealogical definition of 'Jewishness' which was even more extreme than that which applied in Nazi Germany, and its politicians and civil servants embarked on a policy which not merely excluded French Jews from the professions, but also deported them, along with Eastern European Jewish immigrants, through transit camps like Drancy in the Parisian suburbs, to death camps in the East. The Roundup of the 'Vél'd'Hiv'' in 1942 was organised by French officials and carried out by French police.

If Collaboration was a multi-faceted political phenomenon, so was Resistance. Some of the first Resistants were, as we have seen, figures from the far Right, like Lieutenant d'Estienne d'Orves, or, like the Communist Colonel Fabien, from the Left. The Communist Resistance effort was blunted by the German–Soviet Pact, but re-emerged as a powerful resistance force after Operation Barbarossa in the summer of 1941. In addition, General de Gaulle's Free French forces, established in London in July 1940, lobbied for allied support and sought to promote resistance in both metropolitan France and the colonies. Here de Gaulle and the Free French had to walk a very narrow line indeed and adopted a position both intransigent and flexible which was to fuel the massive problems of decolonisation in the postwar years. The conference of colonial administrators held in Brazzaville in early 1944, and opened by de Gaulle himself, insisted on continued French imperial rule, but nevertheless offered the possibility of decentralisation and consultation with the native populations. It is a measure of De Gaulle's political skills that, despite increasing hostility from both Churchill and Roosevelt, he was able to establish the Free French as the natural government of France following the Liberation. As the Occupation deepened, particularly after the winter of 1942–3, Resistance activity increased, with more sophisticated organisation and with a bridge-head established for De Gaulle's movement in Algeria.

It is, however, important to recognise that, in spite of the undoubted courage of the Resistance and their contribution to the Allied war-effort in terms of intelligence and sabotage, the main battle in Occupied France took place through the form of language. Until 1944, neither Vichy France nor the Resistance disposed of the logistical resources to mount a convincing military confrontation. Instead, they waged a war of words, conducted through the radio, with the collaborationist Radio-Paris fighting it out with Radio-Londres and their *Les Français parlent aux Français*, and, inevitably, through journalism and literature. It is no coincidence that some of the most prominent victims of the subsequent purges should be collaborationist journalists and writers, because that is where the battle was being waged. In support of collaboration, the prestigious *Nouvelle Revue Française* was commandeered by the Germans and given to Drieu la Rochelle to edit. It lasted only until 1942. More durable were the violently pro-German *La Gerbe*, edited by Alphonse de Châteaubriant, and that survivor from the interwar years, *Je suis partout*. Counterblasts were constituted by apparently exclusively literary journals, like Pierre Seghers's *Poésie*, and the clandestine journal of the literary Resistance, *Les Lettres Françaises*. Whilst the Académie Goncourt tended to move towards collaboration, the previously conservative Académie Française, under the guidance of the liberal novelist Georges Duhamel, proved sympathetic to Resistance ideals. At the same time, whilst most commercial publishers were pressured to sign up to the 'Liste Otto', which notably proscribed Jewish authors, clandestine presses, like Les Editions de Minuit, established by Vercors, maintained a literary production free of any taint of compromise. Other authors, like Jean Guéhenno, refused to publish at all under German Occupation.

By 1944, French opinion had polarised so much and the international situation had deteriorated so dramatically in terms of Germany's war-effort, that the country entered its most extreme period of mutual antagonism: what is known as the 'Guerre Franco-Française', a civil war between collaborationists and Resistants which, even so, only mobilised 5 per cent of the population. This war, fought on the Right by Joseph Darnand's Milice and on the Left by the military wings of the various Resistance organisations, led to set-piece battles, notably in Eastern France, in the Vercors and Glières, in which Resistance forces, heavily outnumbered by Miliciens and their German allies, were effectively massacred. The D-Day landings in Normandy in June 1944 exacerbated the situation, and the vengeful Das Reich Division of the SS, frustrated in its attempted journey to the Normandy beachheads, massacred the population of the south-western village of Oradour-sur-Glane and hanged hostages in the town of Tulle. Simultaneously, the military Resistance attacked both the Germans and the Milice, inflicting both considerable casualties and summary executions. In the early period of the Liberation, some 10,000 collaborationists were summarily executed, in addition to the more formal legal trials which followed. In other words, by the time General de Gaulle marched down the Champs-Elysées on 24 August 1944, Paris and much of France had been liberated, but there remained the process of the 'Epuration', through which the newly restored Republic sought to establish its legitimacy by a purge of its collaborationist opponents. The purges themselves did little to heal the wounds inflicted by the Occupation and, in spite of the scenes of celebration at the Liberation, many of the divisions present in French social and political life at the beginning of the century were still acutely felt. In spite of a relative eclipse of the parliamentary Right until the early 1950s, the old antagonisms remained. Women may have been finally given the vote by de Gaulle's provisional government, but one of the abiding images of the Liberation is the shaving of the heads of women suspected of having had relations with the Occupying troops. Nor, as we have seen, did the Brazzaville Conference provide a reliable base for France's postwar relations with her colonies. Nevertheless, both the Third Republic, especially under the Front Populaire, and, more paradoxically, Vichy had fostered both an extraordinary cultural output and elaborated cultural policies which were to serve the nation well in the latter half of the twentieth century and beyond.

NOTES

1. Quoted in Pascal Ory, *Les Expositions Universelles de Paris*, Paris: Ramsay, 1982, p. 30.
2. See James F. McMillan, *Twentieth-Century France: Politics and Society 1898–1991*, London: Arnold, 1992, p. 48.
3. See *ibid.*, p. 47.
4. See Alfred Cobban, *A History of Modern France*, 3, *1871–1962*, Harmondsworth: Penguin, 1965, p. 71.
5. See McMillan, *Twentieth-Century France*, p. 50.
6. See Jean-François Gravier, *Paris et le désert français*, Paris: Le Portulan, 1947.
7. See Robert Aldrich, *Greater France: a History of French Overseas Expansion*, Basingstoke: Macmillan, 1996, pp. 196–7.
8. See McMillan, *Twentieth-Century France*, p. 79.
9. See *ibid.*, p. 79.
10. See Richard Vinen, *France 1934–1970*, Basingstoke: Macmillan, 1996, pp. 10–11.
11. See *ibid.*, p. 17.

FURTHER READING

Aldrich, Robert, *Greater France: a History of French Overseas Expansion*, Basingstoke: Macmillan, 1996.
Hughes, H. Stuart, *The Obstructed Path: French Social Thought in the Years of Desperation*, New York: Harper and Rowe, 1966.
    Consciousness and Society: the Reorientation of European Social Thought 1890–1930, London: MacGibbon and Kee, 1959.
Johnson, Douglas and Madeleine, *The Age of Illusion: Art and Politics in France, 1918–1940*, London and New York: Thames and Hudson, 1987.
Looseley, David, *The Politics of Fun: Contemporary Policy and Debate in Contemporary France*, Oxford and Washington, DC: Berg, 1995.
McMillan, James F., *Twentieth Century France: Politics and Society 1898–1991*, London: Arnold, 1992.
Reynolds, Siân, *France Between the Wars: Gender and Politics*, London: Routledge, 1996.
Smith, Paul A., *Feminism and the Third Republic: Women's Political and Civil Rights in France, 1918–1945*, Oxford: Clarendon Press, 1996.

Sowerine, Charles, *France since 1870: Culture, Politics and Society*, Basingstoke: Palgrave, 2001.

Vinen, Richard, *France, 1934–1970*, Basingstoke: Macmillan, 1996.

Wilson, Sarah (ed.), *Paris Capital of the Arts 1900–1968*, London: Royal Academy of Arts, 2002.

Young, Robert J., *France and the Origins of the Second World War*, Basingstoke: Macmillan, 1996.

Zeldin, Theodore, *France 1848–1945*, I, *Ambition, Love and Politics*, Oxford: Oxford University Press, 1973.

  France 1848–1945, II, *Intellect, Taste and Anxiety*, Oxford: Oxford University Press, 1977.

2

Culture and identity in postwar France

Historical overview

If one understands the term *mutation sociale* (social transformation) in the sense in which it was established in French sociology around the work of Georges Balandier at the beginning of the 1970s, it is with just this kind of phenomenon that French society in the second half of the twentieth century was confronted: values and principles of social organisation no longer held, broke down and disappeared even while surviving as a reflex of thought and in the form of superficial ritualism. Meanwhile, new problems and new collective concerns developed under the effects of imported cultural behaviours, the impact of innovation, and the discovery of social forms unforeseeable from the vantage point of what France had been since the nineteenth century. In examining such a shift, the word 'culture' is to be taken in its widest sense. Thus, it refers not only to cultural objects produced and distributed by practitioners, but also and more generally to all of the styles of doing, thinking and feeling that distinguish a particular group, its conscious or semi-conscious shared beliefs. This is because a shift always affects, at differing rates, all levels of experience. It is also because culture, as a collective concern, has become broader in its contemporary definition, and its globalisation has become an important issue today. Finally, it is because many social and political problems can be, and are, treated as cultural issues.

The second half of the twentieth century in France was marked by significant disappearances: the disappearance of colonial France was followed by that of rural France. Likewise, there was the disappearance of the major political confrontation between anti-Communism and anti-Fascism that characterised the middle years of the century. In its place, new elements unceasingly emerged, those of a society that was becoming a mass society: the transformation of the industrial world, the reorganisation of work that no longer defined the individual in the same fashion as before; the erasure of the great divide, in politics and labour relations, between clearly recognised classes, which gave rise to the spread of new, multi-form social movements; feminist demands and modifications in sexual and marital practice; new relationships to the body, to nature, to health; the environmentalist wave; the slow progression of European unification; the many levels of regionalist aspirations; the problems of multi-culturalism. Such were some of the principal issues to gain prominence during this fifty-year period without war.

The right demanded by both groups and individuals to maintain their cultural differences still collided, at the end of the century, with the old instincts upon which the Republic was built and which charged France with being one and indivisible. For the past fifty years, all the sources of French cultural inventiveness, with their varied forms and diverse intentions, have chipped away the power of the centralised political regime. This chapter is concerned with these new elements and the uncertainty they provoked.

It is interesting here to begin with the fable that opens *Les Trente glorieuses* (Thirty Years of Prosperity) by Jean Fourastié (1979), a title that symbolises the postwar period of accelerated and profound economic and social change in France. As a prelude to his numerical analysis, the author juxtaposes two very different villages. He writes that the first, Madère, remained in a traditional or pre-industrial stage of development. Its way of living and quality of life still closely resembled those of the nineteenth century. In contrast, in the second village, known as Cessac, the principal traits of economic development characteristic of the post-industrial age shone brightly: demographic vitality, increased life expectancy, population mobility, omnipresent machines, and an enviable level of comfort and convenience. This was exemplified in the domestic triad of automobile, refrigerator and television set that embodied technological progress and the renewal of attitudes. In short, these two villages belonged to two different worlds, two civilisations.

And yet, as the author soon reveals, the two villages were one and the same, the Quercy village of Douelle, at two moments in postwar France, 1946 and 1976. Today, *Les Trente glorieuses* can be read on two levels: on one hand, it is a perceptive study of economic metamorphosis, lifestyles and the attitudes that, on the threshold of the 1960s, created a new social and cultural order; on the other, it is testimony to a particular vision of French modernity, nourished by technocratic ideology and political ambition, shaped by Gaullist rhetoric, and whose brutal impact is masked by upward progress towards better living as revealed by statistics, studies and polls.

Between 1946 and 1975, and more intensely still since 1960, France has lived through a transformation whose depth, rhythm and amplitude have been exceptional. The abrupt demographic shifts in themselves constituted a revolution. The French population rose from 40 to 52 million between 1946 and 1975 (an increase equal to that of the period from 1800 to 1946). This spectacular growth was simultaneously due to a natural boom (the 12 million beautiful babies de Gaulle wished for at the Liberation had arrived!) and to high immigration during the 1950s and 1960s that the war-shrunken working population required for reconstruction and industrialisation. This was a break with regard to the first half of the century, when population declined. Although a break, it was also a new social order: with the swelling population, a generational logic developed, and, with the beginning of the 1960s, youth culture stamped its new imprint on French society. New perspectives unfolded as well on the length of life. Infant mortality plummeted (eighty-five deaths per thousand in 1946, fourteen per thousand in 1975!). Over the same span, men gained close to eight years in life expectancy and women almost ten years. Longer life-spans led to new behaviours, in particular to the desire to retire earlier in order to enjoy new leisure pursuits. The birth of this *troisième âge* (the post-retirement years) also contributed to this generational logic, a new direction for analysis of the way the French live.

The profound changes affecting the make-up of the working population were decisive. The primary sector – mainly agriculture[1] – shrank at an unheard of rate. In 1946, 36 per cent of the working population was still employed in the primary sector, versus 9.5 per cent in 1975. These numbers tell in short and brutal fashion one of the characteristic and highly symbolic facts of the *'trente glorieuses'*: the disappearance of many agricultural workers who were often marginalised from the perspective of the new values of the consumer society. This represented a clear reversal of national values from the central importance placed on rural life and agricultural workers throughout the nineteenth century and the first half of the twentieth. S. Berstein correctly reminds us that up until the Second World War the system of societal values and attitudes was imbued with the notion that the 'reality of France was one of a country made up of small land-holders working the plots that secured their independence and freedom'.[2] In the new economy, open to international competition, a few farmer-businessmen managed huge agricultural holdings in accordance with the dictates of the market and competitiveness, cultivating vast acreages through the extensive use of machines, chemical fertilizers and laboratory-developed seed. Moreover, this transformation was sought by many farmers themselves and accelerated by government policy, in the hope that French agriculture would become more competitive in European and world markets. A less symbolic, but equally important, change for society during this same period was the rapid growth of the tertiary[3] sector from 34 per cent to 51 per cent. Three-quarters of the new jobs created during the 1960s were in the service sector, particularly in financial institutions, distribution and public administration.

In addition to demographic upheaval, there was economic revolution. In the same way as agricultural production changed in nature, rhythm and outlook, so too did the production of manufactured goods. Government policy was committed to free trade among the countries of Europe. The French economy would have to face up to international competition and prove its robustness and innovation in unprotected and highly competitive markets. The State elected to open the economy to the outside world, beginning with its European partners. A decisive turning-point was reached during the '*trente glorieuses*' in the sense of an irreversible internationalisation of the economy. By 1970, half of French exports were destined for Common Market countries, compared with 10 per cent in 1960. Europe thus replaced France's colonies as her largest trading partner. Extrapolating from this result, government policy favoured the creation of large conglomerates of international scope. Mergers and acquisitions followed one after another to the detriment of small and medium-sized firms ill-adapted to compete in this environment. Cottage industry in the manufacture of clothing and textiles, and in woodworking disappeared, as did small businesses that lacked expertise in distribution. The economic centre of gravity shifted and so did the discourse of those responsible. The new buzzwords were 'profitability', 'growth', 'competitiveness' and 'investment'. Small, independent owner-operators in manufacturing, trade or the crafts, the individual producers who were so recently the cornerstone of the French economy, vanished or found themselves marginalised, albeit in a less spectacular fashion than agricultural workers. Henceforth *le cadre* (the business executive) was to be the victor par excellence of the social competition.

The context of life, the standard of living, behaviours and values were transformed in time with the beat of this accelerated modernisation. The disruption was evident in the ways people lived and the environments where they lived. The France of 1946 had been largely rural; that of 1975 was already highly urbanised. This was a phenomenon of major proportion in its own time and one with numerous long-term consequences. Urbanisation developed in a state of quasi-permanent crisis because of long delays in making new housing available even as more people were pouring into the cities. The hasty construction of suburbs seemed to be a solution until they gave way to housing projects and 'new cities'. At issue, however, was the same failure to provide the new urban dwellers with any local context for their lives beyond that of soulless bedroom communities with no social or cultural life, leaving them vulnerable to a breakdown of the social order.

Rapid technological progress, a revolution in productivity, industrialisation that was willingly embraced and planned, and phenomenal urbanisation all joined to change forever the settings for living and working. A considerable increase in purchasing power during the period entailed, for the 1960s and beyond, 'the greatest and fastest improvement in material progress that history has ever known'.[4] The French were part of a revolution in consumption that was transforming the conditions of existence. Thus, in inventorying the indicators of change, Fourastié concludes in *Les Trente glorieuses*, 'This great adventure of development is truly, for better or worse, the advent of a new humanity'.[5]

During the period with which we are concerned the changes in behaviour, tastes and values were revealing. The newness was concentrated around two poles that deserve particular attention: youth on the one hand, and the consumer society, the civilisation of objects, on the other. The large contingent of young people was clearly the direct result of the demographic renewal. Moreover, the generation born during the postwar years would form a distinct and autonomous group within society. The young had their own music, their own magazines, their own style. New forms of expression adapted to youth appeared. This group was non-conformist and more sensitised than others to cultural phenomena coming from abroad (music in particular). Young people pulled the whole society along in their wake, speeding up its openness to novelty and, in so doing, disputing the traditional values that still shaped it. These youths also represented a tremendous clientele for whole sectors of manufacturing and services. Mass communication channels (radio and magazines in particular) were responsible for promoting and disseminating their distinctive tastes and behaviours (consider *Salut les Copains*,[6] *yéyé*[7] concerts, pop music, etc.). The dawning of massive urbanisation amplified distinct generational and cultural behaviour styles. City life became a vector of what was modern, while the young and the not-as-young were susceptible to fear of the outdated, the backward, not only in the city, but also in the countryside, as E. Morin notes in his study (1967) of a Breton village.

Commenting on small landowners, shopkeepers, the bourgeoisie and part of the *classe dirigeante* (the governing class), an analyst of postwar France noted: 'The curmudgeonly old France, attached to its small annuity and keeper of old-fashioned values, is still there when economic expansion tears the social fabric'.[8] The postwar years of the *'trente glorieuses'* brought the most dramatic socio-economic, cultural and geopolitical change France had experienced since the Revolution. As others have pointed out, this period was remarkable for the scope of change as much as for the fast pace with which change affected the fabric of everyday life. In retrospect, one may ask, 'Why?' What made such sweeping change possible in so short a time? Why, at that particular moment, in a society for so long suspicious of industrial and economic modernisation? Why, in a society that clung to traditional values and whose centre of gravity lay in the permanence manifested by the rural world, that cornerstone of French identity?

At least three elements came together to make such transformation possible. First was the postwar international context which broke France's isolation, until then limited to the confines of its own world of colonial empire, and brought it into new economic, political and geostrategic movements of global magnitude. Next, the will of many and the vision of a few: a collective desire to bring about change to regain moral standing, to overhaul the political system, to modernise production methods, to bring social justice and refresh the promises of the Revolution. Many, who witnessed the suffering, humiliation and powerlessness of the defeat and Occupation wanted to draw a line through the past and were ready to usher in a new beginning. A new social discourse emerged: France would henceforth ride upon the shoulders of her workers. Productivity would be the key to recovery of France's status as a world power. Lastly, such tremendous change was possible because a new generation, the millions born during the *'trente glorieuses'*, would shatter the traditional framework of life and its moral and cultural tenets. Millions who grew up in a new world formed a generation that felt itself free of the past, that looked to the future and to the 'modern'. New values and attitudes took a firm hold as the social groups who embodied traditional values – as well as the values themselves – had been tainted by the moral and political failure of Occupation, Vichy and collaboration. Many in this group were willing and eager to attain new horizons. A tremendous energy, directed towards change, was palpable at the end of the war. 'La modernisation ou la mort!' (Modernisation or death!) proclaimed a leading politician of the time.

It is one of the cultural markers of the postwar years that we are witnesses to the waning influence of the purveyors of written culture. The great men of letters (novelists and playwrights) who represented the spiritual power of the 1930s, were followed by philosophers during the period of existentialism, when Sartre and Camus could still insist on a way of being in the world, of feeling, and of appreciating life that links the adventure of individual experience to the historical nature of collective life. They would be followed, for a time, by the leaders of the 'structural revolution' (M. Foucault, J. Lacan, R. Barthes, C. Lévi-Strauss) who illustrated the breakthroughs of the social sciences in their own new fashion, one that heralded the disappearance of the subject/agent and the end of humanism.

The result of these changes and the consequence that followed from them was the loss of key thinkers. The next generation of young men and women would discover little that was new, except occasionally (Marcuse, perhaps, represented such an instance). Their culture would soon be made more of images than ideas, of images conveyed through artistic media – music and film in particular – and readily diffused more and more by television. Their way of thinking would have to be structured according to a new grammar required by new technologies. To whatever extent one could still speak of key thinkers, it would be in terms of the creators of images, those engaged in the exploration of new technical languages and their unique characteristics (Jean-Luc Godard is an exemplary figure in this regard).

But images and myths continuously invaded communal life and accompanied the beginnings of mass consumption. Jean Baudrillard and Georges Perec, in their works devoted to consumer society, as well as Edgar Morin, in his investigation of the first transformations of mass culture, identified the complexes of the imagination that shaped the experience one could have of 'things' and the happiness they promised.

Wonderment before an unbelievable burgeoning thicket of objects – a virgin forest, unfamiliar and full of promise, but which had also grown up around the French without their noticing – was offset by the sense of a trap. The arrangement of these objects, their amassing in an array or a collection, where each object called for another which completed it and would soon replace it, removed them from any concern of use or functionality. They became a system of socially conventional and ephemeral signs; they were sources of an artificial prestige. Advertising, magazines, film and television created a new mythological category, that of 'Olympians', the inhabitants of the world where movie stars, royalty, sports heroes, famous artists, adventurers and the occasional CEO mingled. With one foot in the profane and the other in the sacred, they were tracked through the twists and turns of their most intimate dramas as they accomplished great heroic and erotic feats. As with objects, they figured in the life of the average person, where they played the same role: in a society with a strong work ethic, where pleasure was always somewhat suspect, they erased the stigma of uselessness and made the case that happiness no longer needed to be earned. They made up a world of consumable images that were the images of life itself: life was thus a consumable good.

May '68 and its aftermath

The May '68 student movement constituted a landmark moment in the French postwar period when the triumphant spirit of modernisation struck a sour note and was undermined by those very youths who, it was thought, were to be the immediate beneficiaries of the tremendous economic leap forward. The millions who would come of age in the 1960s were to assure the future of France as a powerful, modern and confident nation. The student rebellion and the workers' strikes lasted barely more than a month, from 3 May to mid-June, yet they ushered in a period of social and cultural questioning and displayed a new style and new fronts of political action that would last well into the 1970s. May '68 was truly an *entre-deux* (interval) in the sense of Capdevielle and Mouriaux: at the same time archaic in its revolutionary pretence and already postmodern with its unique brand of protest, a mix of media-savvy, individualism and cultural eclecticism.

The arrest of about 500 student protesters at the Sorbonne triggered student demonstrations of solidarity, which grew not only in number, but also in scope when workers – and eventually their unions – joined the students for marches, the like of which France had never seen before. Paving stones were torn up and barricades erected in the nineteenth-century tradition of insurrection. A general strike brought France to a standstill. In the short term, the fear of social unrest, the lack of political alternatives, and an inculcated 'fear of the unknown' prevailed. In the legislative elections of 17 and 30 June, Gaullist supporters won a stupefying majority. 'L'imagination au pouvoir' (Government by imagination) and 'Rien ne sera plus comme avant' (Nothing will be as it was before) were among the slogans of that May. In April 1969, a dispirited de Gaulle stepped down. Less than a year had past since demonstrators throughout Paris were chanting, 'This is only the beginning!' Thirty-five years later, testimony still continues to emphasise the originality of May '68 and how it attacked the foundations of the socio-political and cultural order.

May '68 offered a critical vision of French society as it was being re-shaped during the '*trente glorieuses*', the society of the refrigerator, the automobile and the television set. The Movement brought to the surface widespread and unvoiced anxieties about the scope of change and the speed at which France was losing the compass of its traditions and way of life. Familiar surroundings were being shaken in unfamiliar ways by labour migrations, the disappearance of rural communities, the dominance of consumerist and materialistic values, and a loss of meaning. The targets of the Movement were political: de Gaulle and his particular authoritarian style of government, censorship and other forms of control. The extraordinary liberation of speech manifested during May '68 is still considered today as one of the key distinctive features of the Movement. Creative and critical effervescence in student-occupied Paris led to the invention of a number of slogans and expressions that captured in words the anxieties of a society ambivalent about its new identity and hesitant about its future. 'Empoignons cette société et retournons-la comme un gant' (Grab hold of this society and turn it inside out like a glove), 'dessous les pavés, c'est la plage' (Beneath the cobblestones is the beach), 'l'imagination au pouvoir' (Government by imagination), 'nous sommes tous des juifs allemands' (We are all German Jews,[9] this in reference to the expulsion of Cohn-Bendit from France), 'cours, camarade, le vieux monde est derrière toi' (Run comrade; the old world is right behind you) and 'objet, cache-toi' (End materialism) were examples from a political, social and cultural protest movement, new in its style and bold in its tactics.

May '68 as a movement was also about youth, the university system, and the socio-economic order in flux as a result of the *'trente glorieuses'*. The student movement began on the Nanterre campus before spreading to the Sorbonne. Hurriedly built to house the overflow of students from the Sorbonne, Nanterre, like many French cities of the time, was in a permanent state of construction. Students lived there in isolation from a real urban centre and from each other, as no social and cultural space had been included in the plans. Nanterre was a concrete shell; the result of demographic explosion and the ever rising demand for education, it carried the hope for renewal in the university system even as it embodied the blatant failure to fulfil that hope. Between 1959 and 1969, the number of high school and university students tripled. The French system of secondary and post-secondary education, designed by tradition to train a small and elite body of students, strained under the high enrolment figures. For decades afterwards, the educational system would register, with the sensitivity of a photographic plate, the hopes, anguish and dysfunction of an entire society and the permanent, sometimes bitter, struggle between the old and the new in France.

The politics of the generation preceding May '68, Left as well as Right, was shaped by the many burning questions that were the legacy of the Second World War. The political avant-garde, which fuelled the student/ workers' protest, turned to the revolutions of Latin America and Asia and to the anti-colonial struggles of the late 1950s. This lent the May '68 student movement a distinctive dimension: its internationalism. For the politicised youth of the 1960s, the struggles for liberation in South America, Asia and Africa served as an immense reservoir of revolutionary images, episodes and faces from which the theory and practice of revolution emerged renewed. The 22 March Movement,[10] formed at Nanterre when local Vietnam Committee[11] militants were arrested, named itself in deliberate reference to the Movement of 26 July,[12] the name Castro's closest companions gave themselves. A universal and heroic actor, the Chinese, Cuban, South American or African partisan offered proof to the militant youth in the cities of the West that hope for a free and happy humanity, for work that was not alienating, for a classless society, was not lost. The tales that reached the young European activists created a 're-enchantment of history'; it mattered little whether they were true for they were believed and widely retold. (Régis Dubray's writings of the time, particularly in *Les Temps modernes*, are indicative of this vision.) The return of revolutionary discourse, the overload of references to insurrections of the past century, led to the staging of revolution, which as a means of bringing down of the State, was already outdated in 1968. Protest targeted language, the given cultural order, and its representations; May '68, as a cultural revolution, challenged the forms of meaning a culture had adopted to think of itself and to communicate. May '68 illustrated a vast movement of cultural liberation. The *Situationnistes*[13] (Debord, Vaneigm) and the return of anarchist thinking contributed to bringing forth for open reflection issues which, until then, had remained unarticulated. In many areas, May '68 anticipated social and political struggles that would emerge more fully in the 1970s, and that exemplified a changed political sensibility and represented new forms of action. In particular, sexual behaviour, the relationship between the sexes and representations of the body became objects of the new questioning. The concerns of feminist and homosexual constituencies opened up new fronts of political struggle. Critiques of the educational system, of the judicial system, and of institutions housing prisoners and the mentally ill would all have found fertile ground in the protests and spirit of May '68.

There would be yet another twist to the cultural and political agitation of May '68. Fifteen years later in his description of the postmodern individual unfixed in his references and beliefs, engaged in living free and unconstrained, demanding the right of personal fulfilment, and the right to be absolutely oneself, Lipovetsky[14] saw in May '68 a movement that was relaxed and without rigor, a revolution without an agenda, but 'cool', the germ of the postmodern world in search of identity and communication, which has dismissed the grand projects of transforming man and society. Will May '68 have been simultaneously the harbinger of new fronts of political and social struggle throughout the 1970s and of the cultural eclecticism of the age of hedonistic individualism?

Cultural openings

During the period we are examining, the spread of American models is more or less rapid and spectacular depending on the plane in which it occurs. From the beginning of the 1960s, apart from a certain influence from the beat culture that had a marginal effect, it was the arrival of rock with all of its accompanying practices and attitudes that signalled a considerable transformation in the status of youth. First came French-style rock with its *yéyé*[15] wave that eclipsed the traditional French *chanson* (song), and which, in 1965, was drowned in the tidal wave of the Beatles and pop music. A youth culture emerged, a 'young' category for the generations born after the war who adopted blue jeans as their distinguishing feature, who enjoyed the minor independence of their own pocket money, and who first found their rallying ground in musical expression, before music was wed to politics in 1968.

Proceeding more slowly, but more deeply, the penetration of television into French households would be the engine of familiarisation with American lifestyles, values and ways of thinking. This was a drawn-out penetration since one must wait until the mid-1980s before the quasi-totality of French homes would be equipped with television sets and for French broadcasting to become an important purveyor of American shows and films. Moreover, these media played a large part in turning politics into spectacle; the progressive disengagement of the French with regard to political parties and grassroots activism was accompanied by an episodic passion for large televised electoral contests.

In even slower and more regular fashion, the transformation, at least in appearance, of the social structure followed the model observed several decades earlier in the United States: despite the persistence of fundamental inequalities and even of ruptures between social classifications, a certain homogenisation of life styles unfolded along with an apparently limitless expansion of the middle class.

While the definition of culture continued to expand in the second half of the century, it was more than ever becoming a social issue. The role of culture holds a unique place in France, as it is a sphere in which political prerogative is vigilantly exerted and where the need for a certain authority is constantly reaffirmed. This view, long-held in France, dates from the sixteenth century, when the monarchy styled itself as the protector of arts and letters. New life was breathed into this old tradition during the period with which we are concerned. Cultural policy is a peculiarly French invention that has no counterpart elsewhere. It recognises that the State has a political responsibility for the arts and creativity, which implies that these are not solely the province of a cultivated elite, but that they must be made available, through appropriate measures, to each and every individual. Revitalised by the Popular Front in 1936 and then confronted by real problems of creation and dissemination in the field by Jean Vilar and several others when the Festival of Avignon was organised in 1946, cultural policy was the object of regular revivals – and of as many passionate debates. Most notably, in 1959 the first Ministry of Culture was created and entrusted by General de Gaulle to André Malraux;

in 1981, under the first Socialist government and the policies of Jack Lang, the budget for cultural spending exceeded the threshold of 1 per cent of state spending for the first time.

The State and public institutions were thus charged with a cultural mission that actively accompanied the cultural explosion that France has known over the past thirty years: the spread, in very decentralised fashion, of festivals dealing with all aspects of artistic expression, the intense valorisation of national heritage, the developing manifestations of scientific and technical culture, etc. For instance, when Malraux created the 'Maisons de la Culture' it was so that each *département* (an administrative unit, roughly the equivalent of a county) might have a space available that would permit access to the great works of humanity for the widest possible public. In the same way, it is generally a question of political policies that support cultural offerings: aid to creators, or even to the industries of production and distribution, up to and including the imposition of entry barriers to economic competition (as, for example, with the 1981 single-price book law which required that a book be sold everywhere in France at the same set retail price). All this was done in the belief that the public's desire for culture would be stimulated by having a maximum of high-quality cultural objects at its disposal.

Vectors of cultural change

In the 1960s, when Pierre Bourdieu and Jean-Claude Passeron analysed the functioning of the educational system, it was to bring to light the social conditions that made for unequal schooling. The results from all levels of schools and universities were proof of social inequality in access to degrees. These sociologists thought that French schools played a conservative role in that they sanctioned, reinforced and renewed the social hierarchy by treating equally those who were, in fact, unequal. It remained to be seen what contributes to social inequality in academic success. Success owes little to innate abilities, which have been shown to be an unreliable indicator of one's aptitude for learning; a secondary factor is the economic disparity between families. Without ignoring the latter, success stems primarily from the cultural capital that accumulates in families over generations without their needing to make a conscious effort. Familiarity with educational institutions, the knowledge that one is expected to have in certain career paths, the extent of the vocabulary used in the home, and contact from an early age with cultural works all combine with other factors, such as residence in an urban or rural setting, to determine early-on the odds for success in school and society. The conditions for success are thus largely cultural.

Have forty years of active cultural policy by public institutions – of their methodical attempt to make all works, past and present, available to everyone, to make culture egalitarian and democratic – really reduced cultural disparity? Since 1973, the Ministry of Culture has been measuring the evolution of French cultural practices; the results of these investigations have been regularly published. Their latest results (1998) show the following: strong tendencies, already present during the 1970s and 1980s, have been accentuated: the French continue to acquire more audio and video equipment, and to devote more time to its use. Most French homes already had television sets by 1973, following which one observes the success of the VCR (72 per cent) and the rising numbers of personal computers (23 per cent). The French spend an average of forty-three hours per week watching television, using the VCR, and listening to the radio, CDs or cassettes – which exceeds the amount of time they spend at work. The use of electronic media has not come at the expense of reading. A decline in the readership of the daily press has been offset by an increase in the readership of magazines and journals. Even as the base of serious readers remains stable, the number of books read has generally fallen. Half the population of France had actually read five books in the twelve months prior to the survey. Amateur artistic pursuits are slowly gaining popularity in the population as a whole, and more rapidly among young people.

Even if one observes a certain global infatuation with culture – having opened wide the notion of culture to those pursuits that may be simply hobbies – it cannot obscure the maintenance or reinforcement of discriminatory cultural practices and massive non-attendance at cultural venues. Widespread accession to 'classical' forms of cultural expression in the theatre, concerts, museums, *maisons de la culture* and even books, as it was conceived and put forth after the Second World War, has not happened and will not happen. Increases in attendance at cultural venues between 1989 and 1998 were extremely modest. Aside from multi-media libraries whose subscriber numbers rose sharply from 23 to 31 per cent, patron attendance at amateur shows rose in the range 4 to 6 per cent, at museums by 3 per cent and at theatrical and dance performances by only 2 per cent.

What is most important about this trend is that it in no way represents a change in the make-up of the population concerned. Attendance rates for university graduates, Parisians, senior executives and professionals, and, to a lesser degree, mid-level professionals remain distinctly higher than they do for other categories of the population. To better appreciate this reality, one must take into account that for some people cultural practices are cumulative in nature. Thus, one can classify the French by cohorts to discern overall patronage at libraries, cinemas, performance halls, exhibition spaces and heritage sites: 24 per cent never go; 27 per cent rarely go, 28 per cent go from time-to-time; 12 per cent go often; and only 10 per cent attend regularly. A great deal of cultural life depends on this 10 per cent from whose ranks are drawn over half the attendees at concerts and museums and 60 per cent of theatre patrons.

During the last decades of the twentieth century, the cultural landscape of France found itself radically altered. A great many observers think a genuine revolution has taken place, whose effects are at least as important, if not more so, than those of the Revolution of 1789. It is, at any rate, a profound social and cultural shift that is displacing most of the fundamental problems familiar to French society.

Here we can touch only briefly and in passing on some of its aspects. First, we note that French centralism, the old multi-secular effort to unify France, is under attack from all sides by claims for local differences and the diversity of individual interests. The forms of individual participation in public life bear witness to this. At the same time as political organisations and unions have stagnated or regressed, one observes a spectacular proliferation of associations. Forty thousand were created in 1992, yet only a few thousand were established during the postwar years. This is but one indicator, among so many others, of the waning identification with large groups and the ideologies they represent, and of the new culture of individuals and the multiplicity of possible ways in which they can come together.

New groups, new cohorts present society with issues that cannot be evaluated using the old political rhetoric, particularly not that of the historical clash between social classes. These are transversal issues that implicate individuals from all levels of the social hierarchy in the same quest for identity. The women's movement provides the most visible and best-known example. It seems to have infiltrated political discourse and practices, and with good reason: women's access to educational programmes, including higher education, is growing enormously, and the number of women in careers that were once closed to them, continues to rise. Nonetheless, this in no way resolves the question of the balance of power between the sexes, but rather it complicates the experience of inequality. The assessment recently offered by sociologist François Dubet supports this: while girls are more successful in school, they are drawn towards the least well-paying careers; the wage gap between men and women has been maintained and, in fact, is widening; autonomy for working women often means hardship at home since the domestic division of labour was unaffected by the rights they gained in the workplace. But if the present state of affairs bears the marks of its profoundly difficult history, it is nonetheless the case that women's issues have become a central cultural concern, and that no important social question can be addressed without including them.

Politics and culture are tightly interwoven through many seemingly disquieting aspects of end-of-the-century French society. Certain nationalist and populist pressures, the demands of ethnic groups, new manifestations of racism, urban violence, the reappearance of deep social schisms in the society of plenty, acute poverty, the evidence that large numbers of men and women bear all these social handicaps at once and are neglected in the sense that they can no longer live with a even minimal degree of autonomy – these, as Michel Wieviorka elaborates, present a good many challenges for democracy. One can measure the full complexity of today's political and legal issues against the contradiction between secular equalisation that is one of the fundamental building blocks of the Republic and that rests on a notion of individuated citizenship, and the recent proliferation of ethnic groups or reconstituted communities that claim a collective identity. In a recent work, Jean-Loup Amselle maintains that the republican position finds itself torn between the defence of the rights of peoples and that of the rights of individuals.

In this landscape, the concern of culture is again to effect transformation and broadening. A large portion of contemporary artistic undertakings, especially in music, can be labelled 'cross-cultural'. In France, perhaps more than elsewhere, urban cultures, spawned by hip-hop, blend ethnic and artistic pretensions, and, according to Jean-Pierre Saez, demand admittance into the common culture.

This same dialectic between the whole and the parts, between the rights of individuals guaranteed by the State and the autonomy of the subject/agent, has become a source of renewal for French society today. This is illustrated in the most recent research on non-traditional alternative environments. After the first alternative wave in the years following 1968 that gave rise to rural communal ventures, a new movement has been developing over the past few years in urban neighbourhoods: the search for new paths to living differently here and now. It borrows freely from utopian concepts and effectively bears utopian aspirations. Nonetheless, it is characterised by a fairly clean break with the primary conceptual orientation of important socio-political utopian schemes from the Renaissance through to the nineteenth century. What is in the making today is a collection of experiments, validated day-to-day, that we know and wish to be incomplete and ephemeral. These experiments take many shapes and concern themselves with all spheres of communal activity, work, health, food and nutrition, and culture. They are based on mutual assistance and individual self-realisation. In this they are unlike classic Utopias which never relented in hunting down the individual, that is, the unpredictable.

When asked what is the main advantage to European integration, the French respond that it is peace on the Continent. This sentiment shored up the support of the generation that lived through the last world war. Those who grew up in the 1950s and 1960s witnessed the birth of the European Community with a closer bond between nations fuelled by the spectacular reconciliation of France and Germany, an increasingly open economic space, and a growing number of concerted policies that have changed the relationship between regions and nations, the individual and the law, often enabling forward-looking measures in areas where national governments or specific interests had failed to act. But after thirty-some years of major policy initiatives, over the past decade a widespread sentiment has surfaced, particularly in France, that European integration has been led by political elites with the appearance of consent on the part of the people whose daily lives and futures are increasingly shaped by the European Union.

With the September 1992 referendum for the ratification of the Maastricht Treaty, the situation changed dramatically. Since then, the nature, organisation and finality of the Union as a political entity have become a subject of public debate. Voices have bemoaned the lack of a communal, democratic political space. Will the Euro serve as the instrument through which economic achievement and political, citizen-based integration coincide? Many in Europe today talk about *chantiers européens* (Europe-building projects), to underscore that rather than being an end, the Common Currency is merely the beginning in the construction of citizenship, of culture, of shared history and common defence. François Mitterrand often said that Europe was the great adventure of his generation.

In spite of the divisions around Maastricht, opinion surveys show that the concept of Europe has infiltrated even the lowest, most out-of-touch tiers of society. Will it open new horizons for the dawning century? Will it awaken the French political imaginary[16] and a belief in shared values?

Conclusion: an uncertain France

SOFRES, a polling institute, has regularly asked the following question of a representative sample of the French population: 'Do you feel that people like yourself live less well today than before?' In 1966, 26 per cent replied 'yes'. In 1998, it was 37 per cent; in 1985, 51 per cent; and in 1993, 60 per cent. This type of response seems to rely less on data related to the quality of life than on a hard-to-define anxiety that colours much of the current outlook. Without doubt, along with Georges Balandier, we can classify the present-day experience of France and of all super-modern societies by this indication of uncertainty.

It is in the realm of culture, the latter term being used in its broadest meaning, that the greatest changes of our age are occurring. We have only just begun to speak hesitatingly of the investigation of 'new New Worlds', those scenarios and problems handed to us by science and technology, the globalisation of exchanges, the creation of world-wide networks, the displacement and scarcity of jobs, the dream and the effort to uncover the secrets of life, the invasive profusion of images.

Clearly, a cultural problem is being raised today: the anthropologist asks, how shall we civilise these 'new New Worlds', when each after its own fashion is virtually a vehicle of non-civilisation?

NOTES

The authors would like to thank Peter Vantine and Carol Witzeling for their assistance in preparing this chapter.
1. The primary economic sector also includes fisheries, mining, lumbering and other extractive industries.
2. Serge Berstein, *La France de l'expansion*, vol. I, *La République gaullienne 1958–1969*, Paris: Editions du Seuil, 1989, p. 186.
3. This is the service sector.
4. Berstein, *La République gaullienne*, p. 210.
5. Jean Fourastié, *Les Trente glorieuses*, Paris: Fayard, 1979, p. 12.
6. This monthly magazine, published from 1962 to 1976, chronicled the French pop/rock music scene.
7. 1960s French bubblegum rock.

8. Dominique Borne, *Histoire de la Société Française depuis 1945*, Paris: Armand Colin, 1988, p. 20.

9. An expression of solidarity with Nanterre student leader and anarchist theorist Daniel Cohn-Bendit. A German citizen of Jewish origin, Cohn-Bendit was deported for his role in the events of May '68.

10. On 22 March 1968, students at Nanterre, Cohn-Bendit among them, occupied the administration building. The anarchist student organisation took its name from these events.

11. Student members of the National Vietnam Committee had been arrested in February '68 during violent anti-Vietnam War protests.

12. On 26 July 1953, Fidel Castro was arrested when he led a small group against the Moncada Army Barracks in Santiago de Cuba.

13. The *Situationnistes* were a revolutionary group that advocated the complete destruction of existing society in favour of a more humane, non-materialistic, non-hierarchic, individualistic and creative world. This was to be achieved through the 'construction of situations', subversions which would confront modern society with its own irrelevance.

14. Professor of Philosophy at the University of Grenoble, Gilles Lipovetsky is a social philosopher and author of several critically acclaimed books on modern life. His works include: *L'ère du vide* (1983) and *L'Empire de l'éphémère – La mode et son destin dans les sociétés modernes* (1987).

15. See note 7.

16. The symbolic and representational frame of reference that includes images, symbols and symbolic discourse.

FURTHER READING

Balandier, G., *Sens et puissance*, Paris: PUF, 1971.

Baudrillard, J., *The System of Objects*, trans. James Benedict, London: Verso, 1996.

 The Consumer Society: Myths and Structures, London: Sage, 1998.

Berstein, S., *The Republic of De Gaulle, 1958–1969*, trans. Peter Morris, New York: Cambridge University Press, 1993.

Berstein, S., and J. P. Rioux, *The Pompidou Years, 1969–1974*, trans. Christopher Woodall, Cambridge: Cambridge University Press, 2000.

Bourdieu, P., and J. C. Passeron, *The Inheritors: French Students and Their Relations to Culture*, trans. Richard Nice, Chicago: University of Chicago Press, 1979.

Bousquet, G., *Apogée et déclin de la modernité*, Paris: L'Harmattan, 1993.

Capdevielle, J., and R. Mouriaux, *L'entre-deux de la modernité*, Paris: FNSP, 1988.

Crozier, M., *The Bureaucratic Phenomenon*, Chicago: University of Chicago Press, 1964.

Donnat, O., *Les pratiques culturelles des Français*, Paris: Presses de Sciences Po, 2000.

Fourastié, J., *Les Trente glorieuses*, Paris: Fayard, 1979.

Gildea, R., *France Since 1945*, Oxford: Oxford University Press, 1996.

Hoffmann, S., *Decline or Renewal? France Since the 1930s*, New York: Viking Press, 1974.

Hoffmann, S., and W. Andrews, *The Impact of the Fifth Republic on France*, Albany: SUNY Press, 1981.

Hoffmann, S., G. Ross and S. Malzacher (eds.), *The Mitterand Experiment: Continuity and Change in Modern France*, New York: Oxford University Press, 1987.

Johnson, R. W., *The Long March of the French Left*, New York: Macmillan, 1981.

Lipovetsky, G., *L'ère du vide: essai sur l'individualisme contemporain*, Paris: Gallimard, 1983.

Maffesoli, M., *The Time of the Tribes: the Decline of Individualism in Mass Society*, trans. Don Smith, London: Sage, 1996.

Monnet, J., *Memoirs*, trans. by Richard Mayne, London: Collins, 1978.

Morin, E., *Penser l'Europe*, Paris: Gallimard, 1990.

    Commune en France, la métamorphose de Plodémet, Paris: Fayard, 1967.

Perec, G., *Things: a Story of the Sixties*, trans. David Bellos, Boston: D. Godine, 1990.

Pessin, A., *L'imaginaire utopique aujourd'hui*, Paris: PUF, 2001.

Touraine, A., *Critique of Modernity*, trans. David Macey, Cambridge, MD: Blackwell, 1995.

    May Movement; Revolt and Reform: May 1968 – the Student Rebellion and Worker's Strikes – the Birth of a Social Movement, trans. Leonard F. X. Mayhew, New York: Random House, 1971.

    The Post-Industrial Society: Tomorrow's Social History: Classes, Conflicts, and Culture in the Programmed Society, trans. Leonard F. X. Mayhew, New York: Random House, 1971.

Wihtol de Wenden, C., *La citoyenneté européenne*, Paris: Presses de Sciences Po, 1997.

Winock, M., *Chronique des années soixante*, Paris: Seuil, 1983.

3

Architecture, planning and design

The historical foundations of French design

France entered the twentieth century with one of its greatest assets, a
rich national culture, in full vigour. More than any other European country, French society set cultural standards which most creative people observed and the population respected. Since its origins under Henri IV
(1589–1610) and Louis XIV (1643–1715), this comprehensive culture had
been associated with national unity and power, formal training, and the
dominance of Paris within French society.

Most French design was inspired from the late sixteenth century by
an aesthetic derived from the Italian Renaissance, and given a clear national form from the seventeenth century by architects such as Mansart,
Lemercier and Blondel. In this chapter the term 'classical' will be used to
describe this aesthetic. It was a system of harmonious proportions, enhanced by details associated with the ancient world. It often made use of
the classical orders but many features, such as turrets and steep roofs covered in slate, finials, filigree work, and massive fire surrounds, were medieval French. These traditional features had faded, however, by the late
seventeenth century except in small towns and the countryside where tradition still dictated design. In the eighteenth century, symmetry, repetition, archaeological study of ancient remains, the classical orders, and
precisely shaped masonry blocks, marked most new public buildings and
the homes of the royalty and aristocracy.

In the nineteenth century French architecture was further regularised
by the Ecole des Beaux-Arts, set up by the government in 1819 as the national centre for design training. Work followed training and half the architects in France practised in Paris by 1914. Haussmann's reconstruction

of Paris (1853–70) generated a Second Empire version of the classical style which spread all over France.

After 1871 the example of Charles Garnier's grandiose, ornate opera house (at last completed in 1875) was the biggest single influence until the First World War on French architects, and Garnier was recognised as the doyen of French architecture until his death in 1898. Only industrial design pursued the goal of pure efficiency, but most French people were oblivious to its implicit modernism. Church design, for its part, drew on mainly regional traditions expressive of faith and morality, leaning towards a Romanesque eclecticism. Exhibition architecture, on the other hand, made little impression. The biggest international exhibition, at Paris in 1900, was eclectic, fantastic and international to a degree that cut it off from most French architecture, apart from the great technical contributions of the city officials, Louis Bonnier and Eugène Hénard.

The twentieth century

French architecture thus entered the twentieth century with its classical tradition intact. The curvaceous version of Art Nouveau architecture, imported from Belgium from around 1895 and promoted in Paris notably by an enthusiastic Hector Guimard, flourished for only a few years after its triumph at the 1900 Exhibition and Guimard's unique Metro entrances. The turning-point was the new Samaritaine department store building of 1905 which the modernising owner, Ernest Cognacq, had commissioned from Frantz Jourdain. Its two huge cupolas, rich colours and undulating façade treatments, were intended to challenge Paris classicism by what amounted to a central European vision. On the removal of the canvas sheeting which had protected the decorators, the press and part of the city council declared the design to be an insult to the historic Seine frontage on which it stood. Almost overnight, Art Nouveau was rejected by Paris, even for interior and commercial design. More strongly seated in the German-occupied provinces in the east, notably in Nancy and Metz, where it was linked to the more elegant German Jugendstil, the geometric version of Art Nouveau, it faded there also after French rule resumed in 1918. This fate was really no surprise, for the expressionistic and ugly features of French Art Nouveau, which clung to its Belgian origins above all, were as crude a challenge to French tradition as could be imagined. The same was true of Art Nouveau interior decor and furniture, with their heavy polished wood treatments and

Figure 1. Théâtre des Champs-Elysées (Perret), 1912.

dark monochrome. Only the specious link with modernism had briefly justified it.

The other challenge to classicism came from the architecture developed to make use of concrete. French engineers were pioneers in the development of this material and from the 1880s urban and church architects had started to use it. Although it could be moulded into the classical style, it offered great structural potential which justified simplicity. In the cities, however, it was used mainly for concrete frames and, when used in the façades, it tended to reproduce traditional forms. François Hennébique, for instance, the Parisian specialist in reinforced concrete from as early as the 1870s, used the potential of the material for moulding complex forms to emulate designs which elsewhere were being carried out in masonry. Auguste Perret's Théâtre des Champs-Elysées of 1910–13, with its striking, rectangular openings and bas-relief frieze, looked forward to his neo-classical work in the 1930s despite its very assured use of concrete. Between 1900 and 1914, however, urban France saw a spate of new apartment blocks. Most of those with architectural pretensions were in the rich, eclectic style which followed Art Nouveau – best described as the 'Paris luxury style' or modern academicism, and related to the Louis XV style of ornate facades, caryatids, small glazing bars and shallow arches. They followed rich Parisians and foreign tourists to their favourite resorts including Nice, Deauville and Vichy. Hotels and railway stations were built in the same style, as at the Gare d'Orsay (1900) and the Gare de Lyon (1902) in Paris. A generation of hotels for the rich grew up. With French stone-carving skills now reaching their peak, carving was often incorporated sinuously into the design of façades rather than being simply applied. Natural forms, only remotely connected with the defunct Art Nouveau, acquired even a structural function.

This taste for the ornate detracted from the simple symmetry applied to cities in Haussmann's time, but the aesthetic of the rectilinear street survived in the newer districts, and also in the new urban planning of the French empire. Rather as in London at the turn of the century, architecture and town planning represented imperial aspirations. This French version was, however, exclusively French and the Viennese urban design theorist, Camillo Sitte, with his intimate, asymmetrical spaces promoted in his book of 1889, had virtually no influence in France, partly because his complex German style barred his work to most French architects. The coming French ideal of 'urban art' owed little to foreign example other than Belgium, while the British 'garden city' approach was adopted only, and in a limited form, for a few rich suburban enclaves and, after 1918, for part of Henri Sellier's programme of public housing around Paris.

The French tradition of practical, industrial architecture had been greatly reinforced during the nineteenth century, without securing critical recognition beyond the engineers. After 1900, however, it was increasingly combined with a new modernism in which innovative French architects were prepared to look to the rest of Europe and America. Viollet-le-Duc's efforts to promote practical design during the Second Empire had assembled a number of followers, especially those specialising in industrial and commercial buildings. The launch of a programme of primary school building from 1879 had been linked to state encouragement for simple structures which recalled the concepts and methods of Viollet-le-Duc, and which extended to secondary schools.

The First World War weakened the classical tradition in French architecture. After 1918, more building was done in the public sector, while demand for luxurious apartment blocks and villas was reduced. A variety of new styles emerged from the early 1920s, including Art Déco, neoclassicism, and (streamline) modern. Modernism (sometimes referred to as the International Style), led by the concrete specialist, Auguste Perret, was especially influential in its reduced form using large, rectangular concrete panels. The Parisian modernist, Robert Mallet-Stevens, designed sets for Marcel l'Herbier's avant-garde film, *L'Inhumaine*, in 1923,

Figure 2. Maisons La Roche-Jeanneret, 16ᵉ Arrondissement, Paris, 1923.

while completing a street of comparable houses in Paris itself. Most interwar building, however, did not make a complete break with the nineteenth century, especially in its proportions and the quality of its execution. Even the radical, Swiss-born modernist Le Corbusier, leader of
the world-wide Modern Movement in architecture which had achieved
consciousness since the war, honoured the French cultural tradition and
took up French citizenship in 1930.

After 1918 Le Corbusier took up a single-handed struggle against the
traditional elements in the French architectural profession. His coherent architectural system, fully articulated by the end of the 1920s, led
him to devote much of his effort to advocacy, presenting ideal schemes
at exhibitions and entering for competitions which he was unlikely to
win. Most of the buildings which he built between the wars were for
rich clients of artistic aspirations, and their love of abstract art was reflected in the designs, as at his big suburban commission, the Villa Savoie
(1929–31). Le Corbusier's ideal city plans could not be financed by individuals and he used many means to publicise his concept of high-rise cities,
criss-crossed by rapid motor roads, and almost completely devoted to
open space. *A Contemporary City of Three Million Inhabitants*, an alternative Paris, was exhibited in 1922, and was followed by another Parisian
scheme, the *Plan Voisin*, in 1925. The sweeping *Radiant City*, developed
and adapted from about 1930, played a big part in the CIAM (Congrès

Figure 3. 'La Construction Moderne', contents page, 22 April 1928, showing a typical Roux-Spitz apartment house.

Internationaux d'Architecture Moderne) discussions of modern architects from 1929 and in the influential *Athens Charter* statement of 1933. These ideas had little impact until the Second World War but Le Corbusier developed a number of practical schemes for tall apartment blocks designed to house the masses without class distinction. He also developed plans for high-speed urban roads.

Although Le Corbusier is now seen to look forward to postwar modernism, his sense of frustration before 1939 reflected a reality in which French architecture retained its national tradition. From the very end of the First World War a debate sprang up about the design treatment of the *Voie triomphale*, the extension of the Champs-Elysées to the northwest, which was intended to commemorate the French victory in 1918. Very little emerged from a number of projects, competitions and pious hopes, but the numerous proposed layouts and buildings reflected the best that French architects could offer. The schemes were dominated by the concept of the monumental tower. Unlike Le Corbusier's *Plan Voisin* towers, those on the *Voie triomphale* were taken seriously. Lying outside the city boundary, they did not infringe the Parisian official ceiling of around 25 metres which had been confirmed at the end of the nineteenth century. Perret suggested a great avenue of towers, while Henri Sauvage put forward his ziggurat idea in grandiose form. Others suggested pairs of towers at some of the great crossroads. Concrete would have played a large part in the construction of most of these towers, and some resembled the tall, narrow church towers which were built in the period. Nothing, however, came of these schemes before the war.

The 1930s saw a strong tendency towards neo-classical design, mainly in its stripped-classical variant, in public buildings. This reflected the political conservatism of the decade, in which the rise of Hitler was producing a neo-classical revival in Germany. The Palais de Chaillot and some other French-designed public buildings at the Paris international exhibition of 1937 were in this style, and were influenced by political considerations. The official competitions so common at this time prompted architectural debates which tended to direct the designs into a single path. Even Auguste Perret joined the trend, for instance with his Musée des Travaux Publics (1937), and his example influenced many French modernists. Neo-classicism made little impact on domestic and commercial building in the 1930s, however, owing to the deep depression of the building industry. A combination of modernism and neo-classicism developed in commercial architecture, often using concrete, with simple columns holding up massive lintels, with rectangular openings and powerful glazing. Churches and cinemas, whose construction proved less vulnerable, had something in common with their big interior spaces and simple exteriors. The cinemas veered towards modernism in the 1930s, at least on the outside, but the church architects ranged widely between blatant historicism, with Romanesque much favoured, and modernism like that of Perret's church of Notre-Dame at Le Raincy-Villemomble, a Paris suburb, built in 1922–3. Perret's airy, well-lit nave, with the altar and pulpit in full view, contrasted with the heavy, gloomy interiors of the predominant tradition in church design between the wars.

Much less public housing was built in France after 1918 than in Britain and Germany, but what was built mainly took the form of blocks of flats on the fringes of Paris and the industrial cities. Economy was essential and brick was the main material used in the early 1920s. Where the architects sought character, they did so by rustic features for which brick was suitable. There was no equivalent of the modernistic architecture developed in the Netherlands, as in De Stijl, and Germany, for example Ernst May's work at Frankfurt. However, the Quartier des Gratte-Ciel at Villeurbanne and some of the estates of flats built around Paris in the 1920s and early 1930s with the aid of state funds, and under the direction of Henri Sellier, mayor of Suresnes and a minister, created a modernistic impression thanks to their size and their use of concrete. Marcel Lods, determined modernist and architect, with Eugène Beaudoin, of the Drancy estate, added towers to a carefully designed layout of medium-rise blocks of flats in a simplified style. Lods made some progress here in the industrialised techniques of which he was a leading advocate in France.

The design of private housing was very varied in the 1920s. Le Corbusier, Adolf Loos and others carried out commissions for small houses in the Paris area in the 1920s but most of the new villas – apart from Le Corbusier's – were variants of traditional styles, albeit using some fashionable geometrical features and smooth surfaces. Gradually a modernistic style for apartment houses emerged. Robert Mallet-Stevens developed an entire street at Auteuil in 1925–7 with modernistic white houses and flats. The specialist apartment house architect and developer, Michel Roux-Spitz, did most to disseminate a new Parisian style with the dozens of apartment houses which he built in Paris from 1925. Broad, cavernous windows and vertical bays with angled lights, combined with a cladding in polished Hauteville stone, were almost always to be found in his work. His formula was much emulated, in Paris and elsewhere, although Roux-Spitz himself turned towards neo-classicism from the later 1930s. This style suggested clients and architects seeking a secure modernism at a time of uncertain economic circumstances. Modern design could flourish in the southern resorts, however, as at Saint-Tropez where Georges-Henri Pingusson built the streamlined Hôtel Latitude, with its sweeping, shaded balconies, in 1932.

Industrial building pursued a separate evolution between the wars. Some industrial sectors, such as aircraft, railways and motors, were technically very advanced. Their architecture made widespread use of reinforced concrete on a scale not seen elsewhere in Europe. Steel and glass, including transparent bricks, though by no means unique in Europe, were also used freely. Bernard Lafaille, Eugène Freyssinet and André Coyne were the leading designers of dams, bridges, factories and hangars. In 1939 a combined theatre and civic market built at Clichy, near Paris, by a partnership led by Beaudouin and Lods, made extensive use of prefabricated metal components and its rolling partitions allowed for flexible use of the floor space. In the later 1930s Bernard Lafaille built a number of huge roundhouses for the railways in concrete and glass. As the work of engineers for the most part, it had limited links with the rest of French architecture. However, commercial buildings in Paris generally made use of concrete frames and extensive glazing, though the building regulations of 1902 restricted the freedom of architects in terms of height and frontage treatment. In Paris the Rue Beaubourg, a street widening completed in the 1920s, accumulated two ranks of mainly commercial buildings which sought efficiency and the maximising of space to an extent that almost broke away from Parisian traditions but which in proportions and overall treatment belonged to the Parisian cityscape.

Church architecture largely pursued its own course after 1914. The Church did its best to ensure that the new suburbs were equipped with new churches, especially around Paris, and a number of peripheral churches, started before 1914, were completed. Most of the designs were a combination of neo-Byzantine and modernistic, combining the influence of the Parisian basilica of the Sacré-Coeur, at last completed in 1919, and the potential of reinforced concrete. The church of Sainte-Odile at the Porte Champerret, Paris, begun in 1935, with its three domes and towering 'minaret', and massive, lowering interior vaults, was echoed by dozens of new churches all over the country. Most church architects, though conventionally trained, specialised in church design from early on, and a big church could occupy their entire careers. They absorbed the aesthetic and philosophy of the Church insofar as it related to religious design. The result was a unique architecture of geometrical, natural and historicist forms, often using industrial materials, which remains sadly neglected by architectural historians. In Québec, where church design has been more respected, a similar transition took place.

The advance of modernism

The years from 1939 to 1945, dominated by the Vichy regime of 1940–44, saw very little building in France. Architects, particularly student and junior architects, played a full part in government reconstruction competitions, as did many architects who languished in prisoner-of-war camps in Germany. However, the results veered well away from prewar trends in most cases. Cottage or village styles were seen as representing the best national traditions, and Nazi neo-classicism influenced schemes for slum clearance and inner areas. Le Corbusier directed a study group of young architects, known as Ascoral, to express the openness of its views, which allowed him to develop his *unités d'habitation* in slab rather than zig-zag form. He also incorporated more open space and smaller buildings, including the single-family houses favoured by some members of his team.

Figure 4. Calais postwar reconstruction on neo-traditional lines.

After 1945 Le Corbusier was acknowledged, along with the older Auguste Perret, as the leading French modernist architect and urban planner. In the design of housing areas and reconstruction sectors he saw no essential distinction between architecture and planning and the new generation of French architects took a similar view which affected their work on reconstruction areas and housing estates from the later 1940s, helping to generate the controversial *grands ensembles* (giant estates of public apartments) at Sarcelles and elsewhere. However, the Saint-Dié and La Rochelle postwar reconstruction schemes allotted to Le Corbusier failed, mainly because of local opposition to widespread expropriation. His sweeping *unité* landscapes never emerged. He was reduced to building a small number of single blocks, the most influential being at Marseilles (1947–52). This block, with its striking row of dolmen-like *pilotis* (heavy concrete supports), persuasive horizontal lines, and sculpted playground on the roof, applied the modernist aesthetic of the Villa Savoie and other houses for rich people to public housing. This most admired of Le Corbusier's postwar buildings influenced the design of tower and slab blocks all over France from 1950, not so much in terms of design features but in the basic decision to build on a large scale, using reinforced concrete. Le Corbusier built only three more *unités* in France, and one in Berlin, but by now his world reputation won him

Figure 5. Neo-modern housing at La Villette, 1991.

contracts for buildings and city plans which, far from being derided, were carried out down to the last detail. His new city of Chandigarh, capital of the Punjab, planned in 1951, incorporated much of his Radiant City concept and several unique government buildings. He built for the Brazilian government in Rio de Janeiro. In France he built a suite of revolutionary churches, at Ronchamp (1950–55), the monastery of La Tourette (1956–59), and Firminy (1973–74).

Although concrete was often associated with great architectural quality, the flats, schools, factories and other utilitarian structures which multiplied in the 1950s and 1960s, as France caught up two decades of building deficit, were grimly repetitive. Little of Le Corbusier could be detected and the main influence came from the concrete flats of Marcel Lods in the 1930s. Industrialised building, originating in the later 1950s for public housing construction and using a multitude of identical panels, made matters worse. As these gloomy, boring buildings nevertheless represented modernisation and improving facilities to the bulk of the French people, their aesthetic was not questioned, and in design terms the country slipped back overall. Then, after the early 1970s, the world depression allowed a breathing space, and a florid emergence of new architectural styles took place in France. Normally known as postmodernism, they drew on historicism, colour, asymmetrical forms and outright fantasy. Brick came into favour, even on very large buildings. At the same time, the demolition of older buildings slowed down and owners started to value the refurbishment of the urban past. In the 1990s there was a return to more modernistic styles which nevertheless tended to conform in detail or general character to French tradition. Concrete and steel rods allowed exteriors and interiors to be merged, as often at new airport terminals and railway stations, with sweeping glass roofs and atria. The predominant grey colour of the visible metal recalled a naval dockyard on a rainy day but this did not disturb the French. Even the stranger designs of the 1980s generally added to the urban environment, and the new architecture of the 1990s was original and elegant for the most part. Meanwhile, the unique French expertise in concrete continued to produce the world's most elegant water towers.

Like the cathedrals of medieval France, the *grands projets* of the Presidents of the Fifth Republic amazed, frightened and inspired. Charles de Gaulle, in office from 1958 to 1969, was more concerned with economic success, but his successors (with the partial exception of Giscard d'Estaing) felt the need to emulate Louis XIV by building great monuments in Paris. All were practical, most were very large and visually striking, and their architecture was modernistic. In most cases the designs were chosen through international competitions, and many of the winners came from abroad. Most of these huge projects challenged the existing, traditional aesthetic of Paris and a great deal of acrimonious controversy took place, some of it related more to party politics than to aesthetics or history. The lofty Tour Montparnasse, topped out in 1973, was a commercial project, but government involvement and response to the resulting outcry foreshadowed the *grands projets*. The first *grand projet* to be completed, in 1977, was the Pompidou Centre, designed by Renzo Piano and Richard Rogers. Later projects took care to show more respect for Parisian architectural traditions and many were a welcome stimulus to design in the capital. O. von Spreckelsen's Grande Arche de la Défense, completed in 1991, prolonged the three-century Parisian tradition of the triumphal arch, while I. M. Pei's Louvre pyramid, finished in 1989, transformed the palace both inside and out. A new Paris of space, light and grandeur emerged from these schemes, thanks partly to foreign architects. However, the French designers of smaller buildings were ready to learn and a spate of 'neo-modern' buildings went up in the 1990s, using bays, strong glazing bars, colour, glass and varied shapes, with interior greenery, flowing water, and music. Echoes of Art Déco and Moderne were deliberate and other historical allusions were accepted.

Street façades were softened by the use of voids. Architects were more aware of their sites and designed for space much more than in the past. Similar buildings went up in the provinces in cities such as Lyons, Montpellier and Toulouse, though the *grands projets* were limited to Paris and its region.

French architecture in 2000 faced the new century and the new millennium in a creative, convincing condition. The repetitive classicism which Haussmann had confirmed had been partially replaced by a more individualistic, varied design method. At the same time, the great rectilinear thoroughfares and the moderating building regulations which had spread from Paris to the provinces after 1860 generated a townscape of harmony and equilibrium, notwithstanding the new architecture. Here, French architects were the prime movers. They showed that they could learn and they could create. As a rich, modern country, France had acquired an elegant, exciting environment without parallel in Europe, while retaining its great historical and aesthetic traditions.

Town planning: achievement and delay

Town planning, in its modern form, originated around the turn of the nineteenth century, but France lagged in the development of planning theory and the necessary powers. This delay was partly due to the success of Baron Haussmann's urban renewal techniques in mid-century. As Prefect of the Seine from 1853 to 1870 he achieved the spectacular reconstruction of some of the inner districts of Paris and inspired similar works in Lyons, Marseilles and other cities. His work was based on sweeping clearance and the creation of large streets, squares, public gardens and parks. New building, most of it financed by private capital, was guided by the new streets and by revised building regulations which produced a healthy habitat and a model aesthetic. This reproduced the classical forms of the Renaissance and the later Absolutism of the eighteenth century, though on a much bigger scale. In doing so, it reinforced French national culture and combined classicism with modernity. Meanwhile, the outer districts of Paris and the other cities were left largely under the control of private interests.

Although Haussmann's methods were very expensive, they were generally admired and after 1870 most French cities tried, with reduced resources, to carry through his plans. The result was a network of canyon-like streets with tall apartment houses, and uncoordinated peripheral districts with varied structures and little green space. Some towns, ruled by strong and perceptive mayors, such as Jules Siegfried's Le Havre at the end of the century, broke free from this standard, and were well known among the reformers, but the idea of comprehensive planning was slow to emerge. Around 1900, Robert de Souza and other urban reformers began to point to the emergence of new concepts of town planning, especially in Germany and Austria, whereby the entire city could be brought under control at little cost. The public health law of 1902 laid the basis for a general improvement of urban conditions. Planning and related innovations figured in the 1900 and 1911 universal exhibitions. In Paris, the new building code of 1902 allowed greater heights while requiring coherent roof lines. The impending removal of the Paris fortifications led to a growing interest in open space in the form of a 'green belt' around Paris, with the suburbs spreading outside. Charles Beauquier's parliamentary campaign for powers to protect beautiful countryside and historic sites had a similar effect.

However, efforts to create powers to plan new districts of towns (*plans d'extension*) on German lines by putting a private member's bill through parliament had achieved little by 1914. Charles Beauquier's committee on local government was the main channel but even when the Chamber voted the bill in 1915 it met delay in the Senate. No government department wanted to be involved until 1915, when the war gave a new urgency. The Senate 'lost' the file for most of the war. However the war prompted a general conviction that planning powers were needed in the damaged areas. In 1919 the Cornudet Law, named after Beauquier's successor, extended them to the whole country. However, the law was very little applied outside the damaged areas, mainly because it did not confront the problems of expropriation and compensation. Towns of 10,000 or more people were encouraged to draw up, within three years, 'a development, embellishment and extension project', but few did so. By 1940 the law was largely a dead letter. Meanwhile, there was little slum clearance anywhere in France and the only planned layouts were prepared for public housing schemes.

Paradoxically, the best French planning was done overseas. The Ecole des Beaux-Arts taught urban design, and its students often specialised in a brilliant combination of architecture and urban design. From the 1880s a growing number of architects entered for urban planning competitions abroad. Their successes are too many to be listed here; Henri Prost, for instance, won first prize in the Antwerp extension plan competition of 1910. Others prepared plans for the French colonies in North Africa, under military direction, which were far more ambitious than legislation and practice would have allowed in France. South America was another area which welcomed French architects and planners. This tradition continued after 1918, for instance in the work of Henri Rotival in Venezuela and the USA, and especially in Henri Prost's planning in French North Africa. French architects continued to build abroad into the 1960s, and some even continued after 1968, when most French colonies became independent. This architecture responded well to the climate, using concrete but creating shade by close grouping. Public buildings used white surfaces and arcades to create shade. Apartments for the rich were modernistic and stressed air and light, with a white, luxurious appearance, like the Liberté building in Casablanca, built in 1951.

Town planning under the Vichy regime produced little apart from emergency reconstruction using mainly traditional layouts and elevations. However, in 1943 the government decreed a general town planning law. Similar to a law passed by the Fascist government in Italy, it provided stronger acquisition powers and accelerated procedures which were suitable for war damage reconstruction. Despite its provenance it remained in force until 1955 when a more overtly modernising planning law was passed. The 1955 law made it easier to create new housing areas and transport links without prompting speculation. As urbanisation speeded up from the later 1950s, new legislation was passed to control land values in areas designated for rapid development under public control. Where estates of public or co-operative housing were to be designated on the urban periphery, 'zones set aside for priority urbanisation' (ZUP) had their land values frozen from the moment of their designation. Areas of cities planned for redevelopment (ZAD) (this meant slum clearance or urban renewal) benefited from similar controls.

French town planning turned towards growth and modernisation from the mid-1950s as urban populations, especially those of Paris, began to increase. De Gaulle's modernisation programme after 1958 increased the need for urban space, and for rapid movement within that space. Henri Prost's Paris regional plan, which had remained in force since 1939, was replaced in 1960 by the PADOG (Plan d'Organisation Général). This was intended to revitalise the suburbs by creating a number of 'urban nodes', including La Défense, some miles outside the city boundaries. There would be a regional motorway network and a regional express Metro system. Paul Delouvrier, de Gaulle's appointment as the 'new Haussmann', adopted conventional solutions which drew more on American than on French traditions. However, his regional approach to Paris spread the congestion more than it concentrated it. Tall blocks of offices were linked by express roads and public transport to high-rise residential areas but in his 'new towns', announced in 1963, lower dwellings could be built. The RER (express metro) was made an urgent target. Similar results were sought in the main provincial cities but they had less impact there, mainly because people and employment, under de Gaulle, could flow into the Paris area almost unchecked, while the decen-tralisation strategy of the 1950s was pursued with less vigour. However, Delouvrier and the prime minister, Georges Pompidou, both wanted ur-ban France to adapt readily to the motor car. The resulting aesthetic could be regarded as a debased version of Le Corbusier's urban landscape, or as a French Chicago. Where carefully planned, as at an expanding, mod-ernising Toulouse, main home of the French aircraft industry, it could secure national admiration by the 1980s. Moreover, the spreading urban area of the 1960s and thereafter provided more space in the inner districts for modern architecture. New towns like Marne-la-Vallée provided a spa-cious environment, generous public transport and striking, youthful ar-chitecture of the neo-modern type. The huge Part-Dieu development at Lyons, dominated by A. Cossuta's pencil-like Tour du Crédit Lyonnais (1974), its crowded TGV station, and its labyrinthine shopping centre, would have troubled Godard's hero from *Alphaville*, Lemmy Caution.

Meanwhile, the past made a growing contribution to French plan-ning. The link between French culture and French national identity was confirmed in 1959 when de Gaulle made André Malraux the first Min-ister of Culture. Malraux quickly acted to secure the conservation of historic districts of towns, securing the so-called Malraux Law in 1962. This counterbalanced the depressing rise of concrete which had occurred since around 1950. The repair and preservation of historic buildings was more extensively funded and respect for pre-industrial styles, never ex-tinct in France, increased. These twin trends were partly combined from the later 1970s when a colourful, asymmetrical 'neo-modern' style trans-formed the appearance of new blocks of flats and schools. Fantasy and the grotesque were often used to liven up blocks of flats on public and co-tenancy housing estates. The most striking feature was large areas of contrasting primary colours, challenging the monochrome of the tradi-tional French cityscape. These innovations did not, however, do much to resolve the social problems of these newer housing areas.

Design: the French gift to the world

The French enjoyed a very high standard of design throughout the period. It was seen as essentially *French* design, with any imports from the Renaissance onwards absorbed into 'French' culture. Behind it, as in architecture, lay a national education system stressing a common, and superior, knowledge, and formal training for design skills. Paris couturiers, for instance, led the world and their fashion shows figured in magazines and newspapers every year. Men's clothes, at least in the middle and upper classes, were of a high standard. The jewellery worn by rich women was the best in the world. French cuisine was universally recognised as the world's leader. House furniture was drawn heavily from antiques, mainly of the eighteenth century, but the French were prepared to buy reproductions in the same styles, and their impressive but often uncomfortable interiors were thus available to all but the working class. Most stylish salons sported a parquet floor and a large Turkish carpet. The moquette and the plywood furniture of the lower-middle and working classes did not emerge until after 1945. The design of magazine layouts, many of which dealt with artistic and quality consumption matters, was always very good. These high design standards were self-supporting and self-sustaining. They sometimes led to superiority and snobbery, and originality could suffer, for instance in the choice of furniture and of pictures for the walls, which were often faded or darkened paintings of ancestors, but in the modest provincial towns where many of the middle and upper classes lived, this conservative taste was appropriate. The French were aware of these high standards, and proud of them. They looked down on the cultural and behavioural features of almost all foreign countries, even when countries like the USA enjoyed higher living standards and advanced technical equipment.

This was an ambivalent climate for the development of modern design. However, it was promoted from 1903 by the Salon d'Automne, an annual exhibition launched by the modernising architect, Frantz Jourdain. From 1922 the Exposition Internationale des Arts Décoratifs further promoted Paris as a world centre of design, with Art Déco emerging from the exhibition as a new luxury style combining decoration and modernity. French exports generally conformed to high design standards. The huge French Line passenger liner, the *Normandie*, conceived in 1928 and making its first transatlantic crossing in 1936, outshone its British contemporary, the *Queen Mary*, with its hull design, engineering and above all its modernistic interior design scheme on Art Déco lines – prepared by some of the leading French architects of the day – which unified the whole ship, in contrast to the more fragmented design of the British boat. Almost forgotten since she caught fire and capsized in New York in 1942, the *Normandie* was arguably the greatest French design achievement of the century.

Many other areas of French design excellence could be cited here but the connection between advanced technology, unique design concepts and exports – so productive in the *Normandie* case – merits special attention. We shall concentrate on two areas, motor cars and aircraft. Both of these originated at the turn of the century and France became a leader in both. At first their designs were practical rather than elegant, but in the 1920s and 1930s many manufacturers sought to produce an original aesthetic based on integrated fuselages and body shells, moving towards sculptural forms.

In motors the design leader was André Citroën. The front-wheel drive saloon car (Citroën Traction Avant) which he launched in 1934 was as revolutionary in its external design as in its engineering. As the first mass-produced monocoque (single body shell) car its exterior conformed to a single design concept. Details were as important as the whole: the door-handles, for instance, were an Art Déco concept.

After the war the producers of smaller French cars also sought a coherent body design. Renault's 4CV, launched in 1946, 'the first peasant's car', used a single, rounded shell. It was surpassed in 1949 by Citroën's 2CV, also designed for the rural market, which used curved lines though with flat doors and body panels which the owners could remove from the car for repairs or awkward loads. Both cars did well in the cities, as they were easy to park and gave good visibility. Curved body shells reached their zenith in the late 1950s with the comfortable Panhard three-cylinder saloon with its nearly identical, semi-circular, front and rear treatments.

In 1955 Citroën pursued its goal with the luxury DS19, its completely original body shell looking like a marine form or spacecraft, with wheels partially hidden. Headlights, indicators and external mirrors were completely integrated within the lines of the body shell. This futuristic design was accompanied by appropriate advertising suggestive of space travel. In *Mythologies*, Roland Barthes compared the technical prowess of the DS to the architecture of French medieval cathedrals. The DS quickly became the flagship of the French cultural world. Politicians, businessmen and civil servants all rode in them. When nearly all the French colonies gained independence in 1958 and after, their new rulers invariably acquired them.

Renault launched an elegant four-seater, the Dauphine, in 1956. Though derived mechanically from the 4CV, its clean, monocoque exterior gave it considerable appeal to young people. Its big sales elsewhere in Europe boosted France's image as a source of modern design.

A distinctively French design was not always required. however. Simca, previously producing cars for other companies, launched in 1957 the first popular French car to have transatlantic lines. This, the Simca Aronde, made liberal use of chrome and recalled the 1957 Chevrolet. Simca went on to produce an open-top luxury car similar to the Ford Thunderbird.

Car owners preferred French models, just as they preferred French wine, and into the 1980s they outnumbered foreign vehicles on French roads. The result was a small number of types which were recognised as typically French, not only in France but all over the world. The French valued car ownership; in 1991 76.8 per cent of households owned one car or more, compared to 68 per cent in Germany and 66 per cent in the UK. The story of French car design was a cultural triumph for the conservative, classical country with which we began.

The scope for conservatism in aeronautical design was less than for cars, but French makers sought clean lines and coherent forms from the start. The Bréguet 14, the first aircraft to be used on passenger flights after the First World War, was already a handsome biplane. In the 1920s French Farman airliners, such as the F180 Oiseau bleu, were an elegant presence on the popular Paris–London route. Its competitor on this route, the Loiré et Olivier 213, looked powerful on the outside and its interior, designed like a railway dining car for the lunchtime service to London, was the lap of luxury with its strip windows and studded leather seats, not to speak of its well-stocked bars.

The French did not get heavily involved in passenger airships and a series of powerful passenger airliners emerged in the 1930s. These were metal monoplanes and they were more attractive than the giant biplanes used by Imperial Airways until the end of the 1930s. Dewoitine, Potez and Bloch produced some very attractive twin and tri-motor airliners which outshone most of their German equivalents in visual terms. The Bloch 220, an all-metal bi-motor which Air France brought into service in 1937, would still be in regular use after the war. The Dewoitine D338, a long-range tri-motor, was introduced in 1936, allowing Air France to provide the fastest service (one and a half hours) between Paris and London, as well as flying a multi-stop route to Hong Kong. These planes looked attractive in service and also in the inventive posters used by Air France all over the world.

The development of the jet engine gave France a chance to make a new start in aircraft design after the barren Vichy and early postwar years. The two British Comet disasters in 1954 set back the British plane by four years and the smaller French Caravelle, designed and built by Sud-Aviation at the modernising city of Toulouse, was able to meet medium-range demand throughout the late 1950s and the 1960s, selling 280 examples. It went into service, with Air France, in 1959. This was the first commercial jet to be built in France, and the first anywhere to have its engines mounted on the tail. In terms of its aesthetics, the Caravelle was the aerial equivalent of the DS. By moving the two engines back, the thickness of the wing could be reduced and the design of the fuselage was unified. The curved silhouettes of the wings and tail were completely in harmony with the fuselage. The interior design was made simple and elegant, helping the passengers to relax. The Caravelle generated record-breaking exports throughout the world and became a universal symbol of French design prowess.

It was followed by the supersonic BAC/Aérospatiale Concorde, whose wings and fuselage were fully integrated. The product of Anglo-French co-operation, agreed in 1962, Concorde flew for the first time in 1969. The unique range of problems generated by Concorde meant that only sixteen were ever built, but the design input, which came mainly from the French side, made it a work of great beauty.

Prompted by these elegant planes, Air France made sure that stewardess outfits, hair and makeup, and steward uniforms were of the highest standards. The airline had close links with the best Paris couturiers, and the introduction of new uniforms was normally accompanied by a fashion show in Paris. Using its dominant sky blue, Air France made sure – following a prewar tradition – that leaflets, instruction cards, baggage tags, souvenirs and ashtrays used designs and motifs which were at one at the same time restful and memorable. Many were taken away by passengers as decorations for their homes, or presents for their children. Airline cuisine usually offered a little more quality than the rest. As the front line of French design, Air France was probably the country's best salesman.

Design was one of the greatest strengths of twentieth-century France. Sustaining that design was the French tradition of quality, together with French taste. France has shown that high standards, and belief in high standards, can bring economic success just as readily as strength, effort and long hours of toil. Where those standards, as in France, are based on tradition, a nation can never fail and even the newest of its products will inspire confidence. This eternal French secret is fully reflected in the work discussed in this chapter.

FURTHER READING

Cook, Malcolm, *French Culture Since 1945*, London: Longman, 1993.

Gans, Deborah, *The Le Corbusier Guide*, New York: Princeton Architectural Press, 2000.

Lesnikowski, W., *The New French Architecture*, New York: Rizzoli, 1990.

Le Wita, Beatrix, *French Bourgeois Culture*, Cambridge: Cambridge University Press, 1994.

Middleton, Robin, and David Watkin, *Neoclassical and Nineteenth Century Architecture*, 2 vols., London: Faber and Faber, 1987.

Perry, Sheila (ed.), *Aspects of Contemporary France*, London: Routledge, 1997.

Reynolds, John, *André Citroën: the Man and the Motor Car*, London: Wrens Park, 1996.

Sutcliffe, Anthony, 'Cities, Modernization and Architecture: Before and After the Paris Building Code of 1902', in Colin Holmes and Alan Booth (eds.), *Economy and Society: European Industrialisation and its Social Consequences*, Leicester: Leicester University Press, 1991, pp. 175–97.

Paris: an Architectural History, New Haven and London: Yale University Press, 1993.

Towards the Planned City: Germany, Britain, the United States, and France, Oxford: Basil Blackwell, 1981.

Wakeman, Rosemary, *Modernizing the Provincial City: Toulouse, 1945–1975*, Cambridge, Mass: Harvard University Press, 1997.

Wall, Robert, *A History of Airliners*, London: Quarto, 1980.

4

The mass media

The role of the State

The most original feature of French media is perhaps to be found in the role of the State which to a large extent has shaped the current situation of the broadcasting media and plays a supporting role in the survival of national papers with strong political commitments but devoid of sufficient advertising resources.

Media broadcasting emerged in France as the result of the initiative of wireless set manufacturers (Radiola) or of publishing groups (Le Petit Parisien). The government lost no time in asserting the State's monopoly over 'the sending and the receiving of radio-electrical signals of all kinds' (1923 Finance Bill) on the basis of the scarcity of national radio frequencies considered as a national asset. This restrictive approach to a new medium, enshrined in an article of the Finance Bill of 1923, was in fact the logical continuation of the traditional official position defined as early as 1837 which restricted the use of telegraphic signals to the suppliers licensed by the government.

In 1923, however, the law allowed the government to grant licences to private radio broadcasters under the control of the Ministry for Post, Telegraph and Telephone (PTT). Radio-Paris was in fact the only private radio station licensed by the administration, later to be relaunched by the State under the title of Poste National. By 1929, broadcasting was taken away from the supervision of the PTT Ministry to be put under the sole control of an Information Commissar directly responsible to the Cabinet (Council of Ministers).

The link between broadcasting and the government was strengthened under the Vichy regime which set up an Information Ministry. Postwar governments did not wind up the Ministry and even requisitioned all the private radio stations which had sprouted in France by the end of the war. The RTF (Radiodiffusion Télévision Française), set up in 1952, was a corporation under the control of the Ministry of Information which supervised both radio and television suppliers, all of them state supported with the exception of peripheral radio stations – Radio-Luxembourg and, later, Europe N°1 – which broadcast from outside the national territory but reached millions of listeners in the northern part of France. However, the state monopoly over the production and broadcasting of radio or TV programmes was reaffirmed in the 1953 Finance Bill for broadcasting services which stated that no one could be granted a licence to produce or broadcast radio or television programmes without the approval of Parliament.

Six years later, the RTF was recognised as a full-fledged corporation with a budget of its own, while the ultimate responsibility to the Information Ministry remained. It was not until 1964 that the RTF was granted the status of a semi-autonomous *Office*, which meant that its performance was supervised rather than controlled by the Ministry of Information. At the same time, the law defined the mission of the ORTF as a public service broadcaster whose remit included the provision of news, cultural and educational programmes as well as programmes of a more entertaining nature. The ORTF was run by a Board whose members were half appointed by the government and half made up of representatives of the staff, the viewers and listeners and personalities chosen by the government. The financial resources of the *Office* were to be provided by the proceeds of the licence fee, the amount of which was approved every year by Parliament.

Seen as the stronghold of government influence, the ORTF could not but be affected by the 1968 'events' which rejected the sort of paternalistic society supported by the *Office*, caricatured on the posters of the rebelling students as a member of the police force in full riot gear addressing the country on an ORTF microphone. Yet, far from being the stooges of the government, the staff of the ORTF had taken an active part in the general protest against the authoritarian control of broadcasting which had hitherto prevailed. The endless marches of strikers around the new headquarters of the ORTF, 'La Maison de la Radio', sitting on the right bank of the Seine, are part of the history of the May '68 saga. Once the revolution had dispersed in the hot air of the summer months, the government retaliated by laying off a substantial number of staff known to have been involved in the strike movement. At the same time, the government decided to introduce a number of reforms meant to reconcile the ORTF with modernity: advertising was allowed, although to a limited extent and two separate news units, one for each of the two TV channels, were set up in order to increase diversity. Additionally, the opposition parties were officially allowed some modest air time.

This liberalisation of national broadcasting policies was, however, precarious. The resignation in 1972 of Premier Jacques Chaban-Delmas, who had tried to steer French politics towards a 'New Society' based on more liberal values, put paid to his efforts to give the ORTF more leeway. Soon after his Prime Minister's resignation, President Pompidou said at one of his press conferences that French television was the voice of France.

At the time, there were about 11 million TV owners who welcomed the launch in 1973 of the third national TV channel called FR3, France Régions, which was dedicated to the cinema and the reporting of regional news. The election of Valéry Giscard d'Estaing as President in 1974, following the death of Georges Pompidou, triggered off a complete break-up of the ORTF, carved out into seven autonomous companies, which stopped short of a more radical solution, including the privatisation of parts of it, that his advisers supported. In fact, the role of the government was in no way reduced by the fragmentation of the ORTF and the state monopoly over broadcasting remained undiluted in spite of the apparently more liberal approach to television articulated by the President.

This monopoly was not to remain unchallenged long. Various political and cultural groups decided to make their voices heard, aided by the relatively simple FM technology which provided them with access, albeit illegally, to the airwaves. The sprouting of 'free' radios, officially labelled 'pirate' radios, constituted the thin end of the wedge which was to bring about the abolition of the state monopoly of the making of audiovisual programmes under the Socialist government of Pierre Mauroy in 1982. Even by the end of the 1970s, Socialist leader François Mitterrand had been prosecuted for running an illegal radio station called Radio-Riposte which broadcast from the headquarters of the Party in the Rue de Solferino. This radio station was only one among the eighty 'free' stations which had been set up in the Paris area alone, prior to the victory of the Left in both the Presidential and General elections of 1981.

The liberalisation of broadcasting had been part of Mitterrand's manifesto and the law of July 1982 constituted a landmark in the history of French broadcasting. For the first time, it stated that 'audiovisual communication' was free, echoing the 1881 law which proclaimed the freedom of the press, and consequently declared the end of the state monopoly over broadcasting. The use of frequencies, however, was to be regulated through a system of authorisations for local radio and TV services or licences for national TV channels. Moreover, the monopoly was retained regarding the transmission of TV channels, both local and national, which TDF (Télédiffusion de France, one of the seven state-owned companies set up in 1974) was to operate.

But the major innovation was the creation of a broadcasting regulator, the Haute Autorité de la Communication Audiovisuelle, to which the government delegated a number of the responsibilities hitherto exercised by the former Ministry of Information or by the government as a whole. In particular, the law provided that this High Authority was to appoint the chairpersons of the state-controlled broadcasting companies, including the three public TV channels and Radio France. This was seen as an irrevocable decision to sever the umbilical cord which had for so long linked French public broadcasting to its political masters, although broadcasting regulation could not be totally immune from political influence. If the 1982 law removed the broadcasting system from the government's strict political control and allowed the emergence of hundreds of independent radios, it nevertheless reaffirmed the key role of public service broadcasting in the field of audiovisual communication.

In fact, French broadcasting was not so much affected by the law as by political decisions and concessions to commercial pressures. In 1984, the government agreed that the new independent radios, originally meant to allow cultural and interest groups to make their voices heard, be funded by advertising. By the end of the year, the government gave up imposing sanctions on the Paris-based music station NRJ, along with a number of other independent radio stations. Obviously, the tens of thousands of young demonstrators who marched in Paris against the possible suspension of NRJ impressed the government who felt it would be politically unwise to silence a radio station which proved so popular with young people so close to the General Election year of 1986. Furthermore, the government acquiesced to NRJ's request that independent local radios be allowed to link into networks, which in fact amounted to agreeing to the setting up of national commercial radio networks and was in direct contradiction to the spirit of the 1982 broadcasting law.

The law had not anticipated the creation of national commercial TV channels either, and yet three of them were authorised by the government between 1984 and 1985. The creation of Canal Plus in 1984 was the conjunction of a technical opportunity and a political project. The frequency network used by TF1 had been vacated by the channel, whose colour programmes were transmitted on different frequencies from the old black-and-white network. Turning down a project based on cultural programmes and films, President Mitterrand announced that a new fourth network would be allocated to an independent channel, devoted to the encrypted transmission of films. The status of Canal Plus was defined in a convention passed between the State and Havas, one of France's major media companies, which awarded a twelve-year licence to the operator with very few constraints in return, except that of investing 20 per cent of its turnover in the cinema. The High Authority was not even consulted. However, few observers would have predicted that Canal Plus was to become so successful, even though its existence was soon threatened by the ease with which its encryption system could be broken, and, more importantly, by the launch in 1985 and 1986 of two more national terrestrial channels. Mitterrand felt that by creating private TV channels he would deter the right-wing opposition from privatising one of the existing public TV channels.

As it was, the National Assembly was hastily convinced to adapt the 1982 broadcasting law to provide for the operation of these two new channels, one of which, La Cinq, was aimed at the general public, while the other, called TV6, would supply the under-thirty audience with music programmes. As in the case of Canal Plus, La Cinq in particular benefited from substantial exemptions from the traditional constraints that the older channels were saddled with, in terms of quotas of French fiction programmes to be shown and the size of investments to be made in the national film production industry.

Not everybody was pleased with the launch of these channels which departed so much from the traditional Socialist concept of what good-quality television should be. Opponents to La Cinq were even to be found at the heart of the government while the High Authority issued critical advice which was ignored. What dismayed people most was the fact that Mitterrand had agreed to entrust the operation of La Cinq to a consortium of French industrialists who had joined sides with Silvio Berlusconi, whose company Fininvest had set up a very popular independent TV network in Italy. In fact, La Cinq was to be the French version of Canale Cinque which broadcast a daily diet of films, games and variety shows. The dumbing-down of television had begun and was soon justified by the 20 per cent of the viewing audience La Cinq managed to reach by the end of 1986. Yet the success of the channel was thwarted by the slow progress of its coverage of the country. By 1987, only 56 per cent of French homes with TV could receive the programmes of La Cinq.

By the time Jacques Chirac's government, set up in 1986, decided to introduce its own broadcasting reform, France numbered six terrestrial channels, three of which, all commercial, had been launched in the previous two years, which put the three, so-called 'historical', public service channels in a difficult situation. Chirac's intention to cut state-owned companies down to size was well known. Antenne 2, the least viable of the three state TV channels, seemed earmarked for the axe. In fact, it was TF1, the oldest and most popular channel, which was put on the market. The sale of the channel was organised under the terms of the 1986 law concerning the 'Freedom of communication', an important signpost in the history of postwar French broadcasting which was to remain the foundation of all subsequent legislative developments introduced by successive governments.

The importance of the new law also lay in the fact that it no longer referred to public service broadcasting which, as a concept, all but disappeared. It was to be understood that 'public service' amounted to the 'general interest' which all TV channels, both public and independent, were supposed to serve. In practice, public and commercial channels had to provide a diversified range of programmes, including cultural, educational and arts programmes, while reflecting the plurality of opinions and 'currents of thought' in news programmes in particular. However, public TV channels – and Radio France – had to carry a certain amount of religious programmes and to broadcast, whenever necessary, government messages and statements. The traditional triptych which defined public service broadcasting in France – to inform, to educate, to entertain – had by then been consigned to oblivion.

Moreover, the law reinforced the powers of the regulator, whose composition was drastically altered. The control of all broadcasting operators – including cable and satellite TV – was to be exercised by a new thirteen-strong body called the Commission Nationale de la Communication et des Libertés (CNCL), which replaced the former High Authority. The CNCL's field of competence included the authorisation of the setting up and operation of all terrestrial and satellite communication systems, as well as the licensing of cable systems. However, the CNCL suffered from the wish of the governing team to erase the legacy of the previous Socialist governments. And, indeed, the decisions of the CNCL justified the concerns of those who were suspicious of its capacity to act independently. The appointment of new heads to run the three TV channels, Radio France and the two external radio services, RFO and RFI, showed an unsurprising political subservience also perceptible in the awarding of the licence for the newly privatised TF1 or the renegotiation of the conventions allowing the operation of La Cinq and M6. Competing against the Hachette group with a less attractive bid, the Bouygues group, one of the world's leading construction companies, was awarded TF1 in spite of the insistence of the government that the CNCL should give a premium to quality and choose the more culturally ambitious bid. Media mogul Robert Hersant, who had been persuaded not to bid for TF1, was eventually rewarded with the permission to team up with Berlusconi in the running of La Cinq which was already facing financial difficulties. The last round of beauty contests resulted in the jury deciding in favour of CLT, the Luxembourg-based media company, to take over from the original operators of M6.

This whiff of political subordination did not help the CNCL to regain its credibility, already dented by its inability or reluctance to make the commercial TV channels and independent radio stations respect their programme commitments or their requirements regarding quotas or transmission standards. It was clear that the Socialists would seize the earliest opportunity to replace the controversial commission by a new regulator, set up in effect by the law of 1989, barely seven months after the Socialists had regained control of the government.

The new body, called Conseil Supérieur de l'Audiovisuel (CSA), looked like the reincarnation of the previous Haute Autorité. Its nine members were appointed by the same procedure, although for a shorter term (six years instead of nine), three of them being renewed every two years. Its missions were identical in essence, even if its field of competence had been enlarged by the development of satellite and cable television. In practice, the CSA acts as a consultant to the government and Parliament and as an appointment board when the Chairs of France Télévision (the two channels were brought under a common chairmanship in August 1989), Radio France, RFO and RFI come up for renewal. It also runs the spectrum of frequencies which are attributed to independent radio and TV operators to whom it awards a licence. The CSA also licences cable networks for thirty years once their setting up has been agreed by local authorities.

The CSA has been a more formidable regulator than its predecessors but it still cannot intervene to block the acquisition of a broadcasting station or channel by a larger media group when it feels that the projected takeover is likely to lead to an unhealthy level of concentration in radio or television. The CSA can only refer the matter to the competent administrative or judiciary authority. There is always the risk that a decision made by the CSA may be nullified by the Conseil d'Etat, the supreme administrative court.

Broadcasting's legislative framework was to be completed by a law passed in February 1994 which increased to 49 per cent of the capital of a commercial national terrestrial channel the limit of the stake controlled by an investor (originally set at 25 per cent by the 1986 law in order to reduce the risks of concentration). The law also provided for the creation of a new channel dedicated to culture, training and employment called La Cinquième, which was to share with the Franco-German Arte (founded in 1990 by a bilateral treaty) the frequency left vacant by the bankrupt La Cinq which had gone off the air in April 1992.

Five years later, the Socialist government led by Lionel Jospin felt compelled, once more, to adapt the contours of the broadcasting scene by reinforcing the capacity of public broadcasting to fulfil its mission in an increasingly competitive environment, both structurally and financially, and by charting the course towards terrestrial digital television. This law brings together the various components of public TV broadcasting – France 2, France 3, La Cinquième – within a single holding company called France Télévision, led by a Chairman appointed for five years by the CSA (rather than three as in the previous system). The law also provides for the reduction of advertising time on France 2 and France 3, the loss of revenue for the two TV channels being compensated for by the State's payment of F2.4bn (€366 million), corresponding to the unpaid licence fees of the 3.4 million people exempted on social grounds. The new law was well received to the extent that it included elements likely to satisfy all categories of broadcasters. The public sector was pleased that its long-standing demand to get the full proceeds of the licence fee that they were entitled to had been finally heeded. For their part, commercial broadcasters could only benefit from the limitation of commercial air time on the public television channels. More generally, everyone recognised the importance of preparing the digital revolution that French leaders had been slow to take on board.

The role of the State is not limited to that of a rule-setter for broadcasters or protector of public radio and TV service providers. It also contributes to the survival of the press through various direct or indirect subsidies. The most symbolic, if not the most costly, of these actions concerns the contribution of F26.6m (about €4 million) made in 2000 to national newspapers with limited advertising revenues. Five titles benefited from this subsidy, the major recipients being *La Croix* and *L'Humanité*, both struggling to keep afloat but contributing to the balance of the political spectrum covered by the press. Regional dailies and weeklies also benefit from state funds, which are also used to encourage the home delivery of dailies, the launch of multi-media operations by publishers and to compensate the national rail company (SNCF) for reduced tariffs applied on the transport of newspapers across the country (F101m – €15.5 million – in the 2000 Budget). In all, direct subsidies amounted to F260.8m (€40 million) in 2000, to which can be added the much more substantial cost of indirect subsidies – F6.6bn (€1 bn) – covering revenue losses due to exemption of certain local taxes, the reduced VAT rate applied to newspapers and magazines (2.1 per cent against the current standard rate of 19.6 per cent) and the F1.9bn – €290 million – losses incurred by the national mail company La Poste through discounts on the distribution of press products.

Media supply and consumption

Media consumption takes up a substantial amount of the leisure time of the average French individual, who spends about 25 minutes every day reading a national daily, 20 minutes reading a regional daily, 193 minutes listening to the radio and 183 minutes watching television. Regarding television, it does not seem that the growth of cable and satellite TV has substantially increased the amount of time the average viewer spends watching the screen. Obviously the use of the Internet services to which about 7 million of people in France have access provides a credible alternative to the consumption of traditional media. At the turn of the twentieth century, the daily number of web pages visited was greater than the number of copies of both national and regional daily papers sold. Adapting to this new competition has become a stark necessity not only for the press but for the broadcasting media as well.

The Press

Broadly speaking, the French press is made up of three elements of unequal importance: the national press, the regional press and the magazine sector. The national press is by far the most prestigious segment, not in terms of its readership which is declining, but because of its involvement in the current affairs of the country. Yet the French national press is underdeveloped. Only one French person in five reads a national daily. By international standards, France is far from being in the forefront in terms of newspaper readership. In 2000, she ranked only in 38th position in international table leagues for daily newspaper readership.

The relative commercial weakness of the French press, particularly its national component, is partly compensated for by its status as a major contributor to the political and social debate of the day. It was not always commercially vulnerable, however: in the latter half of the nineteenth century the press was to transform itself into an industry with the emergence of new technical devices – the rotary press, the linotype machine – and the growth of a reading public willing to buy cheaper newspapers catering for a wider range of interests. The success of *Le Petit Journal* launched by Moïse Millaud in 1863 testified to the capacity of entrepreneurs prepared to invest in cutting-edge technology to bring newspapers to the general public. By 1869, this daily selling at five centimes had reached a record circulation of 350,000, a success story later to be repeated by *Le Petit Parisien* started in 1889 which, under the energetic stewardship of its owner *cum* editor Jean Dupuy, established itself as the world's best-selling daily in 1904 with a circulation of 1.3 million.

Not only did the press attract investors but it also benefited from a liberal legal status defined by the law of 1881 which was retained throughout the twentieth century. Freed at last of political control and tax regulations (the stamp duty for example), the press thrived until the First World War and became a major component of the political and social life of the country. The role of the press during the Dreyfus Case (1894–99) has often been underlined, as has the importance of newspapers in the ideological debate which preceded the outbreak of the war, best illustrated by the role of Jean Jaurès, the leader of the Socialist party, as editor of *L'Humanité*. By 1914, the press had reached its climax with a total of 309 dailies published in the country while four national dailies – *Le Petit Journal*, *Le Petit Parisien*, *Le Journal* and *Le Matin* – sold over one million copies each.

The strict censorship imposed on the press during the First World War altered its image in the eyes of the public. Its tarnished status was compounded by the consequences of the heavy slump of the early 1930s which affected the survival of many titles. Only the few belonging to large industrial conglomerates, such as the Prouvost group which published *Paris Soir*, could weather these difficult times. Concern for maintaining the political diversity of the press was voiced as early as 1928 by Léon Blum, the leader of the SFIO – the French Socialist party of the time – who suggested a system of state support for the political press. Once in office in 1936, the Socialists and their allies in the *Front populaire* stopped short of implementing the nationalisation scheme that Blum, by then *Président du Conseil*, had developed eight years earlier.

The defeat of 1940 and the ensuing four years of Occupation were to prove traumatic for the press. Two-thirds of the dailies in the northern zone, including a number of national dailies like *Le Figaro*, *Le Populaire*, *L'Aube*, ceased publication; others, like *Le Petit Parisien*, were requisitioned and put under German control, while the rest chose to collaborate. The most notorious case was *Le Temps*, which, the war over, made way for *Le Monde* run by a new management team headed by Hubert Beuve-Méry. Like the Revolution of 1789 or the Commune of 1870–71, the period of the Liberation produced a large crop of new titles. There were no fewer than twenty-six national dailies in 1946 reflecting fine shades of ideological persuasion.

The current situation of the national Press at the turn of the twenty-first century stands in stark contrast to what it was in the heady days of the Liberation. Then, some 6 million copies were sold every day compared with 2.6 million in 1999, and that figure includes two sports dailies, *L'Equipe* and *Paris Turf*, which have little to do with general interest newspapers like *Libération* or *Le Figaro*. By the early 1980s, seven national dailies born before or just after the war had folded, among them the highly respected *Combat*, initially edited by Albert Camus and which often included contributions from leading intellectuals of the time. The only lasting addition to the range of titles is *Libération* which in its current format is a far cry from the extreme leftist journal it was when it was launched in 1973 by a group of militants who attempted to keep the 1968 spirit alive. Other creations inspired by the belief that there was a market for dailies with a political message failed: *Le Matin* and *Le Quotidien de Paris* are notorious examples. More original experiments based on the unadorned presentation of hard news proved even less successful. *Info Matin*, for instance, launched in 1994, never sold more than 75,000 copies a day and had to fold the following year.

As Table 4.1 shows, the national daily press, more appropriately called the Paris-based press, is struggling to keep afloat with a few exceptions. Although the circulation figures given in the table are conservative in that they only represent actual sales in France, they do, however, reflect a

Table 4.1 *Circulation figures of national dailies (000s)*

	1999	1981
La Croix	85	118
Le Figaro	353	336
France-Soir	139	428
L'Humanité	54	140
Libération	160	70
Le Monde	346	439
*Le Parisien/Aujourd'hui**	478	342
Les Echos	119	60
La Tribune	84	N/A
*L'Equipe***	374	223
Paris Turf	97	119

(Source: Office de Justification de la Diffusion OJD)
* *Le Parisien*, formerly known as *Le Parisien Libéré*, has now become a regional daily with a number of different editions in the Ile-de-France area. The national edition of the daily is called *Aujourd'hui* and sells 129,000 copies daily.
** *L'Equipe* has higher circulation figures for its Monday and Saturday editions.

general decline or, at best, a stagnant situation. The figures for *Libération* which seem to contradict the general trend ought to be put in perspective. In 1985 Serge July's daily had a circulation of 200,000 corresponding to its break-even point. The fact that *Libération* had to accept the temporary intervention of Pathé and, later, of the British investment group 3i suggests that it needs financial support to keep afloat. But the most pressing concern is over the fate of *France-Soir* and *L'Humanité*. The former is the heir of *Paris Soir*, the successful prewar popular daily whose tradition was continued by Pierre Lazareff, a key figure of broadcasting journalism as well of the press. At the peak of its career in the early 1960s, *France-Soir* was selling over a million copies a day. But whatever market there was for national popular dailies in France seems to have shrunk rapidly with the development of television. At the turn of the last century, an ailing *France-Soir* was sold for a token franc to the Italian publisher, Poligrafic Editoriale. After trying several recipes to win back readers, it would seem that *France-Soir* has been put on a life-support system which can merely delay the terminal phase of its life.

L'Humanité might well be another casualty to be added to the list of defunct dailies despite the recent injection of cash by a number of groups including TF1 and Lagardère-Média (May 2001). This unusual move, if one considers that the official organ of the Communist Party has always denounced the rule of capitalism, may not be enough to save the daily founded in 1904 which has lost three-quarters of its circulation in the last twenty-five years. In fact, the decline of *L'Humanité* reflects the drop in the support of the Communist Party in the country, itself a consequence of the collapse of the Communist regimes in Eastern Europe.

But *L'Humanité* and *France-Soir* are not the only titles facing difficulties even if they are the most vulnerable of the national dailies. As we have seen, *Libération* had to agree to the intervention of a British investor in its capital to compensate for the withdrawal of Pathé. Similarly, in 1999, the Hersant family which owns *Le Figaro* and its associated supplements, brought in Carlyle, an American risk-venture fund, which for some time held nearly 5 per cent of the group's capital prior to the involvement in 2002 of Serge Dassault, head of a leading French electronics company. It is perhaps encouraging that British and American investors should see the French national press as financially attractive at a time when the sales are at best stagnant and advertising revenues less buoyant than at the end of the 1990s.

Obviously the situation of each title differs on the basis of the financial support it can command. In that respect, *France-Soir* as a foreign offshoot of an Italian group could legitimately worry more about its future than *Le Monde*, secure at the heart of a large media group with a turnover of F2bn – €305 million – (in 2000). Socpresse, one of the two pillars of the press empire run by the Hersant family, controls, besides *Le Figaro* and *Paris Turf*, some of the best-selling regional dailies – *Le Progrès* and *Le Dauphiné Libéré*. The other pillar of the group includes a cluster of titles in the French West Indies and in the eastern regions of France. The other substantial press group is the one made up of *Le Parisien* and *L'Equipe*, the highly successful national sports daily.

Concentration of press ownership, which once had been seen as threatening the balanced expression of opinion, particularly at the time when Robert Hersant controlled three national titles (*Le Figaro*, *L'Aurore* and *France-Soir*), is no longer considered a key issue. The real problem is to retain enough readers, particularly among the young who have yet to be persuaded to buy a daily, to keep the current titles going. The growing lack of interest in politics does not augur well for the survival of a

Table 4.2 *Circulation figures of leading regional dailies (000s)*

	2000	1990
Ouest France (Rennes)	767	795
Le Parisien (Paris)	355	–
Sud Ouest (Bordeaux)	336	370
La Voix du Nord (Lille)	320	372
Le Progrès (Lyons)	262	250
Le Dauphiné Libéré (Grenoble)	255	296
La Nouvelle République du Centre Ouest (Tours)	247	267

(Source: Office de Justification de la Diffusion OJD)

number of dailies which have broadened their coverage of non-political events and increased their specialised sections and supplements to appeal to new categories of potential readers. A key obstacle to the expansion of the national daily press is, however, the cover price of newspapers. *Le Monde*, for instance, put up its price to F7.90 (€1.20) in September 2000. At the beginning of the twentieth century, the price of a daily paper was the same as that of an inland postage stamp. A hundred years later, a first-class postage stamp cost F3 (€0.46) while, with the exception of *France-Soir* and *Le Parisien*, no national daily could be bought for less than F7 (€1).

The regional daily press, whether confined to a *département* or spreading over more than one region, like *Ouest France* with its forty-two local editions, is financially stronger than the national press. In 1998 it accounted for 25 per cent of the total turnover of the press (F63bn – €9.6 bn) and received more advertising revenue than any other sector of the press. Moreover, readership surveys suggest that four out of ten French people over fifteen years of age actually read a regional or local daily, half of these readers being in the 15–49 age group. Although the regional press is traditionally associated with rural France, one-third of its readers are to be found in towns with a population over 100,000.

With a daily circulation of slightly over 6 million – three times the size of that of the national dailies – the regional press is a vital segment of the country's press. The best-selling French daily is *Ouest France* with a circulation of three-quarters of a million, while seven regional titles are to be found in the league table of the ten most popular French dailies (see Table 4.2).

Yet, with few exceptions, the regional press has shown a steady decline. While in 1960 there were about 120 regional dailies with a combined circulation of 7 million, the number of dailies had been halved by the end of the century with a total circulation slightly under 2 million. Local press groups are also confronted with competition from national publishers trying to establish monopolies in specific areas. Thus the Hersant family finds itself in a dominant position in the Rhône-Alpes region (*Le Progrès*, *Le Dauphiné Libéré*) or in the northern and eastern areas where it indirectly controls or has a substantial stake in the leading local titles (*La Voix du Nord*, *Le Courrier Picard*, *L'Est Républicain*).

There is, however, a limit to the expansionist drive of local publishers or national press groups, which is the market itself. Far from expanding, it is constrained by the competition with local radio and the limited amount of advertising resources available. An additional source of development lies in the Sunday editions of daily titles which most publishers have launched, and, perhaps more promisingly, in the setting up of local TV channels, licensed by the CSA. The first of these, based in Lyons (TLM) and in Toulouse (Télé Toulouse), were started in the mid-1990s and are by now getting weekly audiences of half a million viewers each. In September 2000, Clermont Première, a local TV channel owned by the local daily *La Montagne*, went on air with two and a half hours of new locally produced programmes every day. In early 2001, Sud Ouest, the Bordeaux publishing group, was selected by the CSA to provide local TV programmes through its TV subsidiary TV7. Seven other regional dailies have applied for a licence to launch local TV programmes and services.

On-line versions of printed products constitute another way of stemming the decline of the sales. Most dailies have by now set up a website increasingly offering a substantially different content from that available on paper. Based on the constant updating of the information provided as well as on the interactive use of databases, these sites are fast gaining in popularity. In May 1999, 20 per cent of them registered over 1.5 million visits per month while, by comparison, the site of *Les Echos*, part of the UK-based Financial Times group, notched a monthly average of 1.5 million hits in the same period.

In contrast to the regional dailies, the magazine sector is more unpredictable and constantly adapting to new interests and tastes developing in a fast-changing society. More dependent on advertising revenues than the daily press and to that extent more vulnerable, the magazine sector accounts for half the turnover of the press industry and about 50 per cent of the total circulation figure.

With one of the widest ranges of titles available in any country – over 2,000 if technical and professional magazines are included – the magazine market is dominated by large publishing groups, some of which, like Bayard, specialise in particular segments of the market such as senior citizens and younger readers. Among the largest French magazine publishers are Hachette Filipacchi Médias, part of the Lagardère group (*Télé 7 Jours*, *TV Hebdo*, *Paris Match*, *Parents*, *Elle*), Bayard (*Notre Temps*, *Le Chasseur Français*, *Pélerin Magazine*) and Excelsior Publications (*Auto Moto*, *Science et Vie*, *Biba*, *20 ans*). But competition has increased with the arrival on the French market of German and British rivals. Prisma Presse, in particular, the French subsidiary of Grüner & Jahr, itself part of the Bertelsmann empire, has made its presence felt in little more than ten years to the extent that in 2000 three of their titles were included among the top ten best-selling magazines. The British group EMAP has also done well on the French market. They started by buying a number of periodicals from the Hersant group (*L'Auto-Journal*, for example) and have also introduced French editions of their successful British titles (*FHM*). With three of their titles over the one million mark, EMAP is now one of the dominant magazine publishers alongside Hachette Médias and Prisma Presse. Yet not all best-selling magazines are published by large groups as Table 4.3 shows. *Télé Z*, a TV listings magazine with no frills sold at €0.30 and published by Médias et Régies Europe, a little-known publisher with a limited portfolio of titles, is number two in the league table. Similarly, *Famille et Education*, number ten in the table, is published by a parents' association.

The fact that half of the titles listed above are TV listings magazines suggests that in spite of the fears which the emergence of television might have spawned, TV has been on the whole an objective ally of the press. In 2000, there were ten TV listings weeklies with a combined circulation of nearly 18 million, to which could be added *Télérama* published by the group La Vie Catholique which has become the cultural bible of the liberal bourgeoisie.

However, more interesting developments have taken place in less intellectual areas, namely celebrity magazines, which the French call '*la presse people*' and men's magazines. At least half a dozen titles are trying to tap the prurient interest of readers in the doings of famous people. This field, which until recently had been the preserve of *Paris Match* and the defunct *Jours de France*, has now been encroached upon by *Voici*, *Gala*

Table 4.3 *The ten best-selling consumer magazines (000s)*

Title	Publisher	Circulation
Télé 7 Jours	HFM	2,606
Télé Z	Médias et Régies	2,246
Télé Star	EMAP	1,788
Télé Loisirs	Prisma	1,710
Femme Actuelle	Prisma	1,634
Télé Poche	EMAP	1,666
Notre Temps	Bayard	1,040
Prima	Prisma	1,030
Pleine Vie	EMAP	823
Famille et Education	Association	762

(Source: Office de Justification de la Diffusion OJD, 1999)

and *VSD*, all stable mates of the Prisma Group, and *Oh Là* published by the Spanish group Hola and which is falling short of its sales targets. Trying to outdo its rivals, in 2000, Hachette Médias launched *Entrevue*, a semi-erotic magazine which falls in the category euphemistically labelled '*presse de charme*'. Although the five most popular magazines read by men are TV listings magazines, the last ten years have seen the launching of a number of titles aimed at the under thirty-five age group with the traditional recipe of physical fitness, sex and consumer goods, although not all of them are flourishing.

Perhaps one of the most significant areas of magazine publishing concerns the weekly news magazines – *Le Nouvel Observateur, L'Express*, and *Le Point* – none of which sells more than half a million copies. Yet they often set the political agenda or contribute to keeping the national debate alive by their extensive reports or investigations. Mostly read by the urban middle classes, French news magazines remain unsure of their future. *L'Express*' fate, in particular, remains doubtful. Started by Jean-Jacques Servan-Schreiber, a journalist with political ambitions, in the 1950s *L'Express* was revamped in 1964. A carbon copy of the American *Time Magazine*, it articulated left-of-centre political views which made it one of the mouthpieces of the opposition to General de Gaulle. Those views were felt to be too radical for the taste of a dissenting group of *Express* journalists who decided in 1972 to start a rival magazine called *Le Point*. Although French news magazines constitute a very small niche in the magazine market, the difficulties they have been facing for many years reflect the growing disaffection of the public for periodicals with strong political coverage.

Broadcasting

In spite of its long history, radio has managed to retain its attraction for the French people, 28 per cent of whom listen to one of the thousand stations available. A declining medium until the late 1970s, radio was boosted by the 1982 Broadcasting law. Until then, radio amounted to the four stations of Radio France, supplemented by the programmes of its local stations, and by the mainstream peripheral stations, Radio-Luxembourg, Europe 1 and Radio-Monte Carlo. But the real impetus occurred when the government, as we have seen, authorised the new local stations to get advertising funding (1984) and to organise into networks. These new radio stations provided the sort of musical programmes which proved instantly popular with the younger section of the population. As early as 1985, 62 per cent of the 15–34 age group in the Paris area listened to one of the music stations.

Over the last twenty years, the situation of the radio market has been polarised by the competition between the mainstream, generalist stations and the new commercial radios, themselves split between the truly independent stations and the networks (NRJ in particular which broadcasts on 200 frequencies over the country). The more traditional stations have tried to meet the challenge by creating their own music-orientated stations on the FM band (RTL2, Europe 2) or by launching new stations based on original concepts, such as France Info, started by Radio France in 1987, which provides a non-stop programme of news and features. A more recent addition to the range of stations offered by Radio France is Le Mouv', a station based in Toulouse aimed at 16–30-year-olds which went on air in 1998.

The past two decades have also been characterised by a process of concentration which has led to the domination of large radio groups, themselves part of larger empires, such as Ediradio (RTL, RTL2, Fun Radio) or Europe 1 Communications (Europe1, Europe2, RFM) respectively included in RTL Group and Lagardère. Beside these dominant operators, NRJ has managed to increase its own share of the market through its four networked brands, NRJ, Nostagie, Chérie FM and Rire et Chansons.

Table 4.4, which gives the list of the most popular radio stations in terms of audience reach, also includes the group of seventy-eight

Table 4.4 *Radio weekly audience share (Monday to Friday) (%)*

	Nov.–Dec. 2000	Nov.–Dec. 1999
General interest radio stations		
Europe 1	11.5	11.3
France Bleu*	6.5	NA
France Inter	11.7	10.7
RTL	13.2	17.2
Music radio stations		
Chérie FM	6.6	6.1
Europe 2	4.9	5.2
Fun Radio	6.7	7.1
Nostalgie	8.7	7.9
NRJ	11.5	12.0
RFM	4.4	4.9
Rire et Chansons	3.6	3.2
RTL2	4.7	4.8
Skyrock	6.7	5.9
Other radio stations		
France Info	12.2	10.1
Independent radios	10.8	10.0

Source: Médiamétrie (1% = 475 800 listeners over fifteen)
* *France Bleu* is the general name for the thirty-eight local stations of Radio France.

independent radio stations, which are commercial stations but not linked to any of the three commercial networks.

What Table 4.4 shows is the gap between the leading stations, in which RTL is the dominant player, and the rest of the league. A more unexpected development was the continued success of France Info which for the very first time ranked second after RTL in terms of audience reach at the end of 2000, a development which reflects a steady demand for news. With 7 per cent of total media advertising spend, radio in France has reached the age of maturity. Yet, the market can only grow through the awarding by the CSA of franchises for the surplus frequencies relinquished by Radio France.

Paradoxically, television is no more popular than radio, since on average, radio or television consumption amounts to three hours per day. In spite of the development of cable and satellite television, the traditional

Table 4.5 *Audience share of the terrestrial channels (%)*

TF1	32.7	M6	13.5
France 2	21.1	*Arte/La 5e**	3.5
France 3	17.1		
Canal Plus	3.6	Non terrestrial	8.5

Source: Médiamétrie (2001)
* *Arte* and *La 5e* share the same channel, *Arte* taking over from the cultural channel at 7 p.m.

terrestrial channels have retained their leadership in terms of audience share. In homes with cable and satellite TV, the share of terrestrial channels was still as high as 71 per cent in 1999 and even reached 78 per cent in the early evening prime time slot (6–8 p.m.). Among the 23 million TV households, three-quarters of which still do not have access to either cable or satellite channels, the audience share of the terrestrial channels was 92 per cent, the 'historical' channels – TF1, France 2 and 3 – towering above the more recent channels as is shown in Table 4.5.

In spite of its privatisation in 1987, TF1 remains the preferred channel of the French while France 2, which used to be its respected rival, is now struggling to keep its lead over France 3, the increasingly successful other channel of French television. The other success story of French Télévision is M6 which has managed to attract new viewers among the younger age groups with a clever mixture of US imported soaps, music programmes and reality shows such as *Loft Story*. Although it broadcasts on a national terrestrial frequency, Canal Plus is essentially providing encrypted programmes to its 4 million subscribers.

After a sluggish start, cable television has by now established itself as a credible complement to traditional television. The number of subscribers stood at about 3 million in 2000 and had more than doubled in the previous six years. The main attraction of cable is not so much cheaper telephone services, but rather the wider range of channels to suit all tastes and interests. By the end of 1999, there was a total of 137 channels available on either cable or satellite, 86 of them in French. The main providers of themed channels were France Télévision, Lagardère, Pathé and Canal Plus/Vivendi. Only seven of them however had an audience share of more than 1 per cent. These were: RTL 9, Eurosport, LCI (the news channel of TF1), Ciné-Cinéma, Cinéstar, Disney Channel and TMC (a film channel).

As in any other country, sports, films and children's programmes were the main reasons for getting cable television although the prospect of superior interactive services, available to only 600,000 digital cable homes in 2001, was also a strong motivation.

Among those who chose satellite television rather than cable, one of the main reasons was the quality of pictures and sound provided by digital technology. The marketing efforts made by the main satellite TV operators – TPS and CanalSatellite – also played a part in the ultimate decision to buy an aerial, the cost of subscribing to a satellite package being marginally lower than a monthly subscription to a cable company for a similar mix of channels. CanalSatellite, started in the mid-1990s by Canal Plus, had a total number of subscribers of 1.5 million by the end of 2000, while the other main operator, TPS, in which TF1 is a key partner, claimed a number of subscribers just over one million. It seems that the rate of signing up new subscribers for both companies is slackening while cable television is still making steady progress.

The launching of digital terrestrial television in 2003 at the earliest is likely to have a marked impact on French television. In June 2002 the broadcasting regulator – CSA – began assessing the sixty-nine files sent in by the applicants to one of the thirty-three frequencies to be awarded on the six multiplexes announced in the 2000 broadcasting law. If France Télévision, the public service broadcaster, has already been promised three frequencies, the other current terrestrial broadcasters TF1 and M6 who have also reserved frequencies on one the multiplexes have shown a strong opposition to DTT which they fear will undermine the growth of cable and satellite TV in which they hold a substantial stake.

If successful, which remains to be seen if the recent failure of DTT in Britain and Spain is anything to go by, digital terrestrial television will raise the visibility of regional and local communities which have hitherto been sidelined on existing traditional channels. The decisions to be made by the CSA may also strengthen some media groups which are not yet present on the television scene (NRJ and EMAP in particular) or which are seeking to expand their limited presence on cable and satellite (Lagardère group).

DTT in France will succeed only if it is seen as a reasonably priced complement to cable and satellite television, the only other growth segments in an otherwise stagnant or saturated sector. If radio maintains its position because of its virtually endless capacity to cater for changing tastes and aspirations, the press, particularly the Paris-based newspapers, is struggling and can only survive by investing in local radio and/or television. In this respect, France is no exception. As in other Western countries, multi-media groups combining interests in broadcasting and the press will be better equipped to take on foreign competitors and to adapt to the unpredictable cycle of the advertising market.

FURTHER READING

Bourdieu, P., *Sur la télévision*, Paris: Liber, 1996.

Campet, J., *L'Avenir de la television publique*, rapport au ministre de la Communication, Paris: La Documentation française, 1993.

Charon, J.-M., *La Presse en France de 1945 à aujourd'hui*, Paris: Le Seuil, 1991.

Dibie, J.-N., *La 5ième étoile – L'Europe de l'Audiovisuel*, Paris: Femis, 1992.

Farchy, J., *La Fin de l'exception culturelle?* Paris: CNRS Editions, 1999.

Kieffer, P., and M.-E. Chamand, *La Télévision, dix ans d'histoires secrètes*, Paris: Flammarion, 1992.

Schneidermann, D., *Du Journalisme après Bourdieu*, Paris: Fayard, 1999.

Scriven, M. (ed.), *Group Identities on French and British Television*, London: Berghahn Books, 2002.

Sergeant, J.-C., 'The Future of Public Broadcasting' and 'Cable Television' in Scriven M. and M. Lecomte (eds.), *Television Broadcasting in Contemporary France and Britain*, London: Berghahn Books, 1999, pp. 46–56 and pp. 107–19.

Wolton, D., *Internet et après?* Paris: Flammarion, 1999.

5

Consumer culture: food, drink and fashion

Consumption is a heading so all-embracing as to be potentially infinite in its scope. We have chosen to concentrate on the fields of cuisine and fashion for a number of reasons. They are, as this chapter will show, to a large extent related ('show what me what you eat and drink and I will tell you what you wear' is perhaps an exaggeration, but not much of one); they have perhaps unsuspected political and ideological resonances; they are probably the two areas of French popular culture most significantly ignored by Anglophone academics, as the dearth of articles on them in major journals suggests; and yet their presence not only 'on the ground' in mainland France but in French literary and cinematic texts is an often vitally important one. Much more important work remains to be done in exploring the resonance and significance of these two most inescapable of areas. The French all eat, drink and dress themselves, but until now little has been done, in English at any rate, to investigate how and why.

Food and drink

France's cuisine is among her major cultural and economic assets. Indeed, it could be argued that it is the area more than any other in which she clearly leads the world. German philosophy, Italian art and architecture, the American cinema, the British theatre are worthy rivals and sometimes more to their French counterparts, but nobody would question France's position as the cradle of gastronomy and the world's leading producer of top-quality wine.

This is not to say that that position has not in recent years come under attack. The growing popularity within France of, on the one hand, ethnic cuisines and, on the other, American fast-food means that the young in particular are likely to opt for a couscous or a 'MacDo' rather than the *boeuf bourguignon* (beef stewed in Burgundy wine) or *sole meunière* (cooked with butter and lemon juice) earlier generations might have preferred. Eminently drinkable table wine at reasonable prices is more likely, outside France at least, to come from Australia or Eastern Europe than from the less prestigious French provinces such as Languedoc, and within France the young in any event – judging by recent films and television programmes – tend to prefer marijuana or beer. One possible narrative of gastronomy in France in the past hundred years is that of its obsolescence, if not decline – a view reinforced by the contrary example of Britain, where the restricted and dreary range of foodstuffs available half a century ago is even in remote or peripheral areas now largely a thing of the past.

This, however, is but one strand among many in an evolution of which we shall have the time to give only a summary account. Attitudes towards and discourses about food and drink are of course shaped by tendencies within the wider society, most important of which have been the greater concern with health and the shift from a primarily agricultural to a largely industrial economy characteristic of post-Second War France. Those attitudes and discourses are relayed in a host of forms – through journalistic writing on gastronomy, whose leading practitioners have included Curnonsky and La Reynière, but also through fiction and cinema. The importance of meals in the novels of Balzac or the films of Chabrol is plain to see, and it is no accident that those two bodies of work count among French culture's leading chronicles of bourgeois life and mores. The restaurant, which came into its own after 1789, is perhaps the bourgeois social institution par excellence, so that the history of representations of gastronomy in twentieth-century France will be inextricably bound up with the vicissitudes of the bourgeoisie. Two texts chosen for close attention here – Marcel Rouff's 1924 short novel *La Vie et la passion de Dodin-Bouffant, gourmet* (The Life and Passion of Dodin-Bouffant, Gourmet) and Marco Ferreri's 1973 film *La Grande Bouffe* (Blow-Out) – both tell us as much about a particular stratum of the French bourgeoisie as they do about the drinks and dishes its members, in frequently daunting quantities, consumed.

The early years of the century

1900 and the years immediately following marked a number of important events in French gastronomic history. A vast official banquet was held in 1900 to which the mayor of every commune in France was invited, and the same year saw the Exposition Universelle in Paris, which featured temporary restaurants showcasing a range of world cuisines, including those of Hungary, Bosnia and even China. For Alberto Capatti this exhibition marked a dietary watershed, preparing as it did 'a new gastronomic language accessible to the masses'.[1] Across the range of restaurants, classic dishes revived from bygone days coexisted with exotic innovations – a spectacular early example of the interplay of nostalgia and progress that was to be so characteristic of the later development of gastronomy in France.

1903 saw the publication of Escoffier's *Guide culinaire*, which rapidly became the bible of the professional cook. Escoffier's career was spent in luxury hotels – briefly in Monte Carlo, Paris and Rome, but for the most part in London, where he presided over the kitchens first of the Savoy, then of the Carlton. The internationalisation of French cuisine thus owes much to him, as does the standardisation of the restaurant menu familiar to this day, from hors d'oeuvres through to dessert. He also helped to popularise the *prix fixe* menu, though a present-day diner confronted with an Escoffier meal might have difficulty in believing the simplificatory impact often credited to him. Luxury ingredients such as truffles, *foie gras*, crayfish tails abounded, and most of his sauces were based on a *roux* (an amalgam of flour and butter) – one of the staples of *haute cuisine* to be called into question much later in the century by the apostles of *nouvelle cuisine*, Henri Gault and Christian Millau.

Such richness was of course simply not available to the bulk of the population, who continued to make do with the local dishes later to be canonised by the label *cuisine du terroir*. Serious interest in gastronomy among the bourgeoisie was fostered by two major factors: rising motorcar ownership, which led to a growth in tourism, and the proliferation of articles and columns about food in the press. Burgundy has always been among the premier gastronomic and wine-producing regions of France, but its dominance was favoured by the fact that the main road routes to Provence and the Côte d'Azur run through it, making it an ideal staging-post for enthusiastic gastronomes en route to the sun. 1900 also marked the first appearance of the *Guide Michelin*, whose combination of maps of the principal towns and cities and brief notes on their best hotels and restaurants was clearly aimed at the burgeoning car-owning population. The restaurant-guide industry was born, and has continued to thrive ever since.

The shift from Parisian *haute cuisine* to an appreciation of the wealth of different regional dishes, favoured by the growth of tourism, was also in large part the doing of writers on gastronomy – first among them by common consent (he was elected 'prince of gastronomes' in a 1926 press ballot) was Maurice-Edmond Sailland, who wrote under the pseudonym of Curnonsky. Curnonsky always retained a soft spot for the cuisine of his native province Anjou, characterised by light wines and sauces and the use of poultry and freshwater fish. His proverbial maxim that 'things should taste of what they are' predates the move towards greater naturalness and simplicity that became dominant from the 1970s onwards – though advocates of *nouvelle cuisine* might bridle at his injunction that 'nothing can replace butter'. His *La France gastronomique* – all twenty-eight volumes of it – divides French cooking into four species: *haute cuisine* (as practised by Escoffier), *cuisine bourgeoise* (more modest and less extravagant – that of the celebrated woman cooks, the *mères de Lyon*, who gave their names to such restaurants as La Mère Brazier and Chez Léa, also known as La Voûte, fits into this category), *cuisine régionale* and *cuisine paysanne* – the last two much more widely consumed than the others, yet paradoxically, and doubtless for that very reason, in his day far less well known.

The comparative scarcity brought about by the First World War led to restrictions (restaurants were briefly banned from serving both cheese and dessert, though protests swiftly led to a change of policy), and to a significantly increased consumption of vegetables, hitherto very much the poor relation of the table. Vegetarianism is to put it mildly less widespread in France than in Britain or the USA, but the International Vegetarian Congress of Paris had held its first dinner in 1900 (inevitably upstaged by the more sumptuous repasts mentioned earlier) and the first French vegetarian restaurant was to open in Paris in 1908, serving vegetable soup, braised endives and croquettes – dishes that would not blush to appear on far grander menus in later years.

Austin de Croze, author of *Les Plats régionaux de France* (1928), organised in 1923 and 1924 week-long sessions promoting regional gastronomy at the Paris autumn trade fair – an idea taken up by Curnonsky in 1939 and one that was to become an annual event between 1949 and 1959. Another important showcase for hitherto little-known or neglected types of cuisine was the Colonial Exhibition of 1931, at which a variety of exotic foodstuffs were served. Red mullet soup and roast warthog were tasted by many diners for the first time, establishing a place for non-European delicacies whose commonest manifestations, after the war in particular, were to be couscous (from North Africa) and Vietnamese food.

For the rest, the history of gastronomy in France until the Second World War is a fairly tranquil one, in which technological innovations – the motor car, the expansion of journalism, the spread of radio in the 1920s which sparked off a vogue for recipe competitions – brought about a wider diffusion of information and discussion rather than revolutionising the bases of culinary practice. *La Vie et la passion de Dodin-Bouffant, gourmet* – whose author was a friend and collaborator of Curnonsky – proclaims that 'the table is still waiting for its great classic century',[2] and celebrates the joys of gastronomy among a small provincial circle of male friends. The central character Dodin-Bouffant, like Curnonsky or his illustrious eighteenth-century predecessor Brillat-Savarin, is a bachelor, albeit far from a celibate one – at least until half-way through the novel when he marries his cook in order to prevent her leaving him for a richer master – and the overwhelming maleness of gastronomic discourse is perhaps one of its least appealing attributes. Thus, Raymond Olivier, France's first television chef, refused to take part in a television programme with his British equivalent Fanny Craddock, alleging that women were not capable of great cooking.

Dodin-Bouffant is, however, not the reactionary hymn to copiousness and over-indulgence we might imagine. Its hero is invited to dinner by a 'Eurasian prince' who serves a string of at once banal and over-elaborate dishes. For the 'revenge match', Dodin contents himself with a *pot-au-feu* – a dish at the time regarded as fit only for the lower orders, *cuisine paysanne* at its most subaltern – whose combined simplicity and succulence delight the guests. His favourite wines include many local ones (notably from his province, the Jura in Eastern France), now firmly ensconced on menus throughout the country but in those days likely to be dismissed by many a 'serious' gastronome. Dodin/Rouff's diatribe against the stifling uniformity of *haute cuisine* sauces strikingly prefigures those of Gault and Millau half a century later, while his brief period on a diet at his doctor's insistence, including an unhappy sojourn in a German spa, suggests the privations to which the gouty gourmet was likely to be subject before Michel Guérard opened his *cuisine minceur* restaurant in the spa-town of Eugénie-les-Bains in 1974. Rouff's novel is at once a glowing evocation of the gastronomic mores of a bygone age and a straw in the wind of the revolution French cuisine was to experience in the later part of the century.

The Second World War and its aftermath

For most of the population at least, the war years were a time of alimentary scarcity. Imports were (at best) difficult to come by and meat and dairy produce subject to severe rationing. Marshal Pétain's speeches contained a number of part melancholy, part hortatory summonses to gastronomic ingenuity and inventiveness. Gaston Derys, coauthor with Curnonsky of *Anthologie de la gastronomie française*, provided a series of suggestions for how to deal with the besetting shortages that were calling the very existence of gastronomy into question for many. Salads could be dressed with home-made lichen oil, and béchamel sauce be made without milk (which was reserved for children), with a mixture of artichoke-water, flour, lemon juice and – for the lucky ones – egg-yolks. Some of his other suggestions appear strikingly modern – the extolling of *tête de veau* (calf's head), a *plat du terroir* par excellence and a notorious passion of Jacques Chirac; the advocacy of stews such as *ragot de mouton aux haricots* (mutton casseroled with beans); and even a recipe for making one's own pasta. These *pis-aller*, as they would have been perceived at the time, would be a great deal more to most modern tastes than the richer and more elaborate cooking they were designed to replace.

Vegetables, an accessory in *haute cuisine*, perforce acquired greater importance when meat and fish were in short supply. Much of the discourse of *nouvelle cuisine*, lauding simplicity and (comparative) abstemiousness, can be traced back to the diverse ways in which writers about food made a virtue of necessity under the Occupation. The writer and Vichy partisan Paul Morand – himself most unlikely to have been severely affected by rationing – has his two imaginary gastronomes M Lefauché and M de Quatresous (= M Broke and M Sixpence), in *Chroniques de l'homme maigre* (1940), console themselves for the meagreness of the times with allusions to how food had helped to cement French national unity and how some of the pompous and turgid classics of *haute cuisine* had never been a particularly good idea in the first place.

The great cooks of the prewar years resumed 'normal service' at the Liberation. *La mère* Brazier, foremost among the *mères de Lyon*, began once more serving in the restaurant that bears her name a menu still unchanged after over sixty years – artichoke hearts filled with *foie gras*, *quenelles* (sausage-shaped dumplings made of pike), and pullet in a truffle-based sauce. Yet this most conservative of establishments was to be the training-ground for France's most celebrated and innovative cook of the modern epoch, Paul Bocuse, who began his apprenticeship there in 1946.

Bocuse went from *la mère* Brazier to work under an even more venerated chef, Fernand Point, whose restaurant La Pyramide in Vienne, between Lyons and Grenoble, had enjoyed immense status since the early 1930s. Point is often cited as a forerunner of *nouvelle cuisine*, not least because many of its leading figures trained under him, and his insistence on using only the freshest of ingredients certainly prefigures later developments. Convenience foods seem to have enjoyed a certain bizarre cachet at the time of their introduction, judging from a 1920s advertisement for Liebig stock-cubes which proudly proclaimed: 'What use is fresh flesh to me now that I've got meat extract?' – a question Point would doubtless have treated with the contempt it deserved. However, other aspects of his practice are in sharp contrast to *nouvelle* and what might be called post-*nouvelle cuisine*. Point's cooking was heavily reliant on sauces – not absent from *nouvelle cuisine*, but certainly not its linchpin – and his watchword 'Butter, always butter' was to be outpaced by later generations' creative use of herbs, lemon juice, olive oil and vinegar. His imposing bulk bore witness to his adherence to his own precept, as alas doubtless did his death in 1955 in his late fifties.

The other key pre-*nouvelle cuisine* figure was France's first television chef, Raymond Oliver, whose restaurant Le Grand Véfour is situated in the Palais-Royal, at the heart of Paris. Televised cooking in 1953, when Oliver started, was far from an easy activity, since programmes went out live and scope for making mistakes was consequently limited. It was Oliver who first imported into French cuisine ideas and ingredients from the Far East – the result of his being in charge of cooking for the French contingent at the 1964 Tokyo Olympics. *Nouvelle cuisine*'s fondness for steaming, its horror of overcooking, the imaginative 'non-classic' use it made of often unusual flavourings all owe much to the Oriental influence which Oliver did a great deal to spread.

The names most closely associated with what can fairly be described as the culinary revolution of the 1960s and 1970s did not, however, belong to cooks at all, but to two journalists – Henri Gault and Christian Millau, journalists for *Paris-Presse* whose first guide to Paris restaurants sold 100,000 copies. Their often sectarian zeal now appears dated, but this is in large part because so much of what they were campaigning for has become part of the mainstream of French cookery. The 'ten commandments' they originally published in 1973 are reproduced below, with annotations illustrating how widely each has been adopted:

- Thou shalt not overcook. (Readers may find it difficult to credit that the French ever did such a thing, but the serving of for example salmon either raw, tartare-fashion, or cooked on one side only is a distinctively *nouvelle* phenomenon.)
- Thou shalt use fresh, high-quality produce. (Any self-respecting chef, of course, always has; but modern refrigeration technology has made it much harder to get away with serving food in less than pristine condition. Paul Bocuse published *La Cuisine du marché* in 1976, stressing the importance of getting the freshest possible ingredients each day.)
- Thou shalt lighten thy menu. (The catalogues of starchy *haute cuisine* dishes that clogged many a menu and many an artery are now virtually a thing of the past. The *Larousse gastronomique* gives a range of recipes for these, worth perusing if only for curiosity value.)
- Thou shalt not be systematically modernist. (This was frequently honoured more in the breach than in the observance in the early days of *nouvelle cuisine*, when bizarre combinations of ingredients ran rampant. Nowadays, above all with the revival of *cuisine du terroir*, over-modernity is scarcely an issue.)
- Thou shalt seek out what new techniques can bring you. (The growing use of woks and steamers is a good example of this. Even convenience food has benefited from improved techniques of preservation; the vacuum-packed dishes sold under the names of such top chefs as Joël Robuchon can often be difficult to distinguish from their freshly prepared counterparts.)
- Thou shalt eschew marinades, fermentations and their like. (Food that can be prepared rapidly is not nowadays thought to be by definition inferior to more elaborate and time-consuming recipes.)
- Thou shalt eliminate white and brown sauces. (The heavy *roux*-based sauces characteristic of *haute cuisine* have now become largely a thing of the past.)
- Thou shalt not ignore dietetics. (Concern for the well-being of diners' digestions, and indeed of their health in general, was a leitmotif of *nouvelle cuisine*.)
- Thou shalt not tart up thy presentations. (The ceremonial presentation of courses, complete with the raising of the silver dome from the serving-dish, now appears distinctly antiquated. Aesthetic presentation, however, did become something of an obsession in the early days of *nouvelle cuisine*; one favourite trick was to place the fish or meat on top

of its vegetable accompaniment, sometimes unkindly thought to be a way of trying to mask the sometimes minuscule size of portions.)

• Thou shalt be inventive. (So used are we now to finding for example salmon served with a sorrel sauce that it is easy to forget that this was an invention of the Troisgros brothers, whose restaurant is situated in the Rhône valley town of Roanne. Inventiveness often, as here, consisted in raising to 'classic' status ingredients hitherto thought of as workaday or down-market; Pierre Bourdieu's exploration of the phenomenon of 'distinction' is as valid in the gastronomic world as anywhere else.)

Michel Guérard claims in the introduction to his *La Grande Cuisine minceur* (1976) that it was at his wife's instigation that he set about devising gastronomic recipes that might actually help to lose weight – a consideration, as Point's girth of itself suggests, that would not have counted for much with earlier generations of chefs. One of the main reproaches levelled at *nouvelle cuisine* – that it offered minute portions and poor value for money – is more likely to have been true of the bastardised or inferior versions of it that were for a while popular in the Anglophone world.[3] Guérard's book and its successor, *La Cuisine gourmande* (1978), were both translated into twelve languages – at least in part a reflection of the new, more health-conscious attitudes towards the body that at the same time were leading to a decline in smoking and the booming of the exercise industry.

This in turn can not implausibly be traced back to the cultural upheaval of May '68 and the radical re-evaluations of the self that sprang from it. French cultural history is even more than that of most other nations far from ideologically innocent, and in a matter so central to national identity as cuisine that is especially true. Commentators such as Régis Debray and Gilles Lipovetsky in their different ways have suggested that May '68 had a greater impact in the spheres of culture and individual (re)definition of identity than in the political world it so ardently sought to change. Jean-Robert Pitte's linking of the unpretentiousness of *nouvelle cuisine* with the 'post-'68 aspiration to absolute sincerity'[4] is thus less implausible than it may at first appear. The new bourgeoisie that emerged from the melting-pot of 1968 turned its back on the hierarchical formality of its predecessors, and this was as true in the domain of cooking as anywhere else.

It is surely no coincidence that *La Grande Bouffe* was made at about the time *nouvelle cuisine* was carrying all before it. Its four central characters – a chef (Ugo Tognazzi), a judge (Philippe Noiret), a television producer

(Michel Piccoli) and an airline pilot (Marcello Mastroianni) – lock themselves away in a country house and literally eat themselves to death on the finest and most elaborately prepared produce. Even the less *recherché* dishes are on the heavy side (pasta comes in a cream and mushroom sauce), and the orgy culminates in a vast dome of pâté. The humour, unsurprisingly, tends to the scatological, notably in one scene where the lavatory explodes and in the memorable episode where Piccoli literally farts himself to death while playing the piano. This of course is in the line of descent from Rabelais, but the tone here is much darker. *La Grande Bouffe* functions as a requiem for a style of life and eating, intimately associated with the bourgeoisie of which its four central characters are such sterling representatives. That bourgeoisie, of course, was to survive the aftermath of 1968 in far better shape than might have been predicted at the time – a survival in which *cuisine minceur* may conceivably have had its part to play.

The current situation

Nouvelle cuisine is no longer an operational concept, so swiftly have its innovations become generally accepted. The chef as superstar is a fact of contemporary life, so that Bocuse is as often to be found on a jumbo jet or endorsing this or that product as slaving over a hot stove. Along with this promotion to celebrity status, however, has come, as we suggested earlier, a growing indifference to gastronomic refinement, especially among the young. As against this, it is probably harder to find a truly inedible meal, or an actively repellent bottle of wine, in the France of 2001 than in earlier years, technology abetting the increasingly educated palate. Regional dishes are widely available outside their provinces of origin; there can scarcely be a French province whose specialities are not available in one or more Parisian restaurants. Thirty or so years ago the average medium-sized provincial town would have had one or two North African, Chinese/Vietnamese and Italian restaurants (as well of course as a scattering of burger bars). Nowadays Indian, Spanish and Japanese cuisines are much more likely also to be represented, and the burger bars have multiplied apace. Non-French – even non-European – wines and exotic or luxury beers are also readily available more or less anywhere. French wines themselves have altered significantly over the years, becoming stronger in alcohol (12 per cent is now the norm rather than the erstwhile 10 per cent for vin de table) as well as broader in range. New *appellations contrôlées* and the wider availability of palatable wine from areas such as the Aude, which until twenty or so years back produced almost exclusively the roughest red wine, generally sold in plastic bottles, evidence this latter change. French cuisine is obviously being squeezed, but this is not to say that it is not at the same time prospering. It will be a very long time, if ever, before France's reputation as the world's leading gastronomic nation is overturned.

Fashion

Food and drink keep body and soul together, but apart from these things that people put in their mouths and the cultural discourses and narratives that arise about them, the story of consumption in post-1900 France needs to consider other commodities. If cuisine, wine and the practice of gastronomy are something in which France excels and which contribute in no small way to the image of France, what then are the equivalent goods, products, services and practices which characterise the non-alimentary aspects of French consumption? The stereotypes of national expertise in the production of commodities and services appear to suggest that Italy and Germany produce the finest cars and motorcycles, that Britain is good at finance, pop music and maybe latterly cinema, and that French consumers are spoiled for choice in cinema, food and drink and...fashion. Arguably since the *ancien régime* and the splendour of pre-Revolution courts such as that of the Sun King Louis XIV, European and American fashion has been dominated by French styles, and France's production of luxury clothing, perfume, accessories toiletries and other 'designer goods' forms an important component of the contemporary image of *la Maison France* – or France's identity in the globalised marketplace. Apart from films and gastronomy, France is known for Chanel No. 5, Hermès, and Louis Vuitton.

Fashion and luxury goods do indeed seem to be the nearest counterpart to food and drink in this perspective on consumption: the body fed or pleasured by a *menu gastronomique* (or by a *MacDo*) is adorned by costume and apparel to become the body dressed. Just as *haute cuisine, grands crus* and gastronomy constitute a major economic and cultural asset, so have *haute couture* and *la mode* both bolstered France's balance of payments and symbolised the pre-eminence of French style over the decades. The parallels between the consumption of fashion (understood in the widest sense) and the attitudes towards and discourses about food and drink are many and varied: fashion has suffered in periods of scarcity and habitu-ally negotiates a pathway between extravagance and minimalism; fash-ion is made up of a multitude of socio-economically and socio-culturally differentiated reflexes ranging from *haute couture* through *prêt-à-porter* to US-inspired youth street garb; fashion problematises issues of masculin-ity and femininity and of the representation of the body and the self; fashion is driven creatively by an artistic tension between traditionalism and innovation.

Just as French cooking can be divided into different 'species' such as *haute cuisine, cuisine bourgeoise, cuisine régionale* and *cuisine paysanne,* the consumption of fashion is multiple and differentiated. Firstly, fashion is consumed as *haute couture*; secondly, what people tend to wear in 'everyday life' is consumed as *prêt-à-porter,* and thirdly, fashion is infor-mal leisurewear, or, more markedly, streetwear – clothing often worn as a kind of 'inverted' *distinction sociale* in which individuals distinguish them-selves from others not by the choice of formal clothing, but rather by a marked adoption of styles apparently at variance with their social posi-tion.

French consumer culture since 1900 has been continuously irrigated by the trickle-down glitter of such fashion-houses as Patou (founded 1919), Coco Chanel (founded 1924), Nina Ricci (1932), Balenciaga (1937), Balmain (1945), Dior (1947), Lapidus (1949), Cardin (1950), Givenchy (1951), Yves Saint-Laurent (1962), Lacroix (1987) and others, who in pro-viding products for the rich, have influenced fashion in society in general. Fashion and its consumption, particularly what might well be consid-ered, in the sense defined by Veblen[5] as the 'conspicuous consumption' of *haute couture,* has periodically become the subject of controversy. As Bourdieu has demonstrated, in the 'field' of fashion tensions between the stylistically traditional and the stylistically innovative overlap and coalesce with generational conflicts between the old and the young to produce fluctuating patterns of production and consumption.[6] For Bourdieu, taste is, sociologically, that which brings together people and things that go together and divisions within the sphere of production match divisions within the sphere of consumption. As these divisions and tensions are articulated as discourses and attitudes towards 'style and its consumption', fashion becomes polemical.

In the postwar austerity of reconstruction, general rationing and culi-nary austerity, Christian Dior's exuberant use of material in his 1947 styles was considered by some as immoral and an affront to decency;

more recently, in the 1990s, in an interesting reversal of preoccupations Colonna's 'deconstructed' clothes attracted considerable criticism for evoking the poverty of utility clothing. Above and beyond the traditional issues of oppression of women through unrealistic expectations of beauty, and male voyeurism – although such concerns enjoy arguably much less currency in France than they do in the US or in Britain – the fashion industry and the meaning of clothing in France seems to be becoming increasingly politicised. One of the early instances of this politicisation came from Yves Saint-Laurent in 1971 when his 'Mourning for Vietnam' collection shocked the consciences of usually tranquil and politically untroubled consumers of *haute couture*, and in the 1980s and 1990s new sensibilities about inequality, race and ethnicity, and revisionism came to undermine (or inform in different directions) the unbridled freedom of expression of designers by making people increasingly aware of the semiotics of their clothing choices. Thus Jean-Paul Gaultier's use of nuns, Eskimos and Hasidic Jews as inspirations for his designs provoked controversy, and in 1994 a public discussion-debate with Karl Lagerfeld at the Sorbonne turned sour as students challenged his constant use of status logos and the elitist influence of his *haute couture* on the development of French culture. In 1995, approaching the fiftieth anniversary of the liberation of Auschwitz, the *Comme des Garçons* collection of pyjama-striped apparel shown by shaven-headed and painfully thin models provoked a furore over the apparently insensitive commercial exploitation of memories of deportation and images of the suffering of the Nazi death camps. In France's multi-ethnic 'rainbow society' the sorority of mainly white supermodels employed in the fashion industry came in the 1990s to be seen as something of an affront to multi-culturalism. Although the French-born black Muslim model Adia was a star fashion model in the mid-1990s, Jean-Paul Gaultier's pointed use of only black models for his 1997 show in protest at apparently rising xenophobia amongst many French people was a striking example of how the consumption of fashion could be exploited to make political points.

In the 1980s and 1990s, often iconoclastic newcomers such as Jean-Paul Gaultier arguably started to blur distinctions between the *haute couture* fashion of *la grande société* and that of ordinary French citizens, and the rise of *prêt-à-porter* clothing evolved from high-society fashion exemplifies one way in which the consumption of fashion has been at least partly democratised in postwar France. Fashion houses and designers such as Azzedine Alaïa, Balenciaga, Cerruti, Gaultier, Kenzo, Lagerfeld, Rykiel and Mugler all produce lines carrying their own labels (known as *griffé* or 'designer label') for the general public beyond the financially elite and numerically highly restricted world of those who purchase true *haute couture*. *Prêt-à-porter* fashion has been spread by famous high-readership women's magazines such as *Elle* and *Marie-Claire*, and by a variety of well-known mail-order clothing catalogues such as *Les Trois Suisses* and *La Redoute*, which have helped promote a certain 'decentralisation' of fashion from its source in the *Place Vendôme* in Paris, overseen by the industry's governing body – the *Chambre syndicale de la couture parisienne* – to the six corners of *L'Hexagone*. Since the 1980s *Les Trois Suisses* has popularised styles by Rykiel, Gaultier and Alaïa for the mass market, and in 1996, in a neat demonstration of the trickle-down not of glamour alone but also of emancipation and democratisation, *La Redoute* celebrated its thirtieth anniversary by bringing Yves Saint-Laurent's celebrated women's dinner jacket ('le smoking' – which had itself been launched in 1966) to the mass consumer market for the first time.

The social consumer phenomenon of mail order and its spreading of fashion styles has found a significant counterpart in France's celebrated *grands magasins*. As Miller (1981) has demonstrated for the early years of French mass consumption, an important feature of the everyday experience of buying clothes is represented by department stores such as *Prisunic*, *Printemps* and *Galeries Lafayette*, which have popularised styles and designs launched by the fashion houses, at prices accessible to the mass of consumers. Diametrically opposed to the designer boutiques of the *Place des Victoires* and the *Place Vendôme* of central Paris in the socio-cultural and socio-economic hierarchies of fashion consumption, the famous *Tati* shops have provided inexpensively costed – and some would argue – unfashionable clothing for the masses. Representing the antithesis of *haute couture*, both in siting and pricing, arguably the best-known branch of *Tati* is to be found in the working-class and immigrant quarter of Paris of Barbès-Rochechouart. However, in the 1990s *Tati* stores did offer ranges of styles designed specially by Azzedine Alaïa, which in symbolic defiance of the dominance of high fashion in establishing the agendas of social and sartorial acceptability, were democratically entitled 'La rue c'est à nous' (The streets are ours). A similar quantitatively important and socially significant aspect of the consumption of everyday fashion is the role played by hypermarkets such as *Leclerc* and *Mammouth* in providing value-for-money apparel for the man and woman in the street. As France modernised during the postwar years, the decline of *le petit commerce* (small retail) in the face of competition from supermarkets and other forms of *grande distribution* (large-scale retailing) contributed to the demise of local clothes production and retail and favoured the homogenisation of clothing style through the consumption of standardised ranges of mass-produced ranges of clothes.

Indeed, the trickle-down dissemination of 'Parisian' *haute couture* style through *prêt-à-porter griffé* and the influence of *haute couture* on the clothes industry in general (known as *la confection*), combined with generally increasing prosperity and social and geographical mobility have significantly attenuated some traditional disparities of clothing style. Although regional idiosyncrasies of dress have all but disappeared save self-conscious displays of 'folklore' for tourists, fashion and style nevertheless remain reasonable indicators of some aspects of social status in France, ranging from the famous workmans' blue overalls (*le bleu de travail*) through the designer suits, raincoats and briefcases of civil servants in the ministries of the prosperous and socially exclusive area of the 7e *arrondissement* of Paris to the pearl necklaces, Hermès handbags, scarves, hairbands and American-style penny-loafers of bourgeois young women from the expensive 16e or the Neuilly-Auteuil-Passy suburbs of Paris. The initials NAP have indeed become an acronym describing this last particular style, as a sub-class of the general category of *bon-chic bon-genre*. BCBG – or chic, conservative, conventional upper middle-class – attire is demonstrated notably in some fields of higher education, where students in the more prestigious law faculties, institutes of political studies and some *grandes écoles* use more formal dress codes to differentiate themselves from the majority of other students.

More than simply categorising a social class and its sartorial characteristics, descriptions of dress-style such as 'rocker', 'hippie' and 'punk' refer to French incarnations of American and British music-related youth culture and their associated vestimentary clichés. The consumption of such styles, often with the elements of personal 'reappropriation' through individuals' modification of clothes and accoutrements reflects many elements of 'Anglo-Saxon' influences on French popular culture, particularly since the 1950s and 1960s. More specifically French is the *baba-cool* ('hippy') style. Originating in the questioning of authority and dominant modes of behaviour prevalent in the 1960s, *baba-cool* fashion is environmentally friendly, politically correct and informal, continuing the *gauchisme* of May '68 throughout the 1970s and beyond and is therefore an example of the ways in which an 'alternative' fashion style can, to some degree, demonstrate at least some measure of autonomous control of consumption. In the 1980s and 1990s, street style influenced by American rap and hip-hop music has been adopted by youth culture and French bands such as IAM and their fans. Large numbers of alienated young French people, often of immigrant origin, express their anomie in their choice of music and what appears an aggressively informal style of dress (baseball caps, trainers, leather sports jackets). Such trends amongst young people demonstrate the general trend towards an increasing acceptance of informality. Distinctions between formal and informal dress have been lessening progressively, as French society has become less rigid since the 1960s and as demarcations between the public and private spheres have blurred: it has been claimed that one of the major effects of May '68 was that some people stopped feeling obliged to present themselves at work in suit and tie, and more recently, some French companies – copying American customs – have even encouraged 'dress-down' days at the workplace.

The proportion of households' disposable income spent on clothing is in constant decline (1970: 9.6 per cent; 1995: 5.4 per cent), despite the financial emancipation of adolescents and the consequent rise in specially marketed lines of fashion clothing such as Naf-Naf (founded 1973) and Chevignon (1979). The fashion industry in the 1990s has reflected French society's new desire for a blend of individualism and conformism. The cyclical, intertextual nature of fashion (interweaving old styles with new modes) engages it in constant dialogue with the past; French fashion is in many ways the product of recurrent French preoccupations with eroticism, exoticism, spectacle, the mixing of genres and deconstruction. Arguably since the Dior 'New Look' of 1947 which luxuriously 're-feminised' women's dress after the privations and scarcities of the war, much of French fashion exploits the tension between seduction and the socially or politically correct with a postmodern playfulness perhaps best encapsulated by Dim's advertising slogan for their colourful clothes: 'La vie est trop courte pour s'habiller triste' (Life is too short to dress sadly).

The importance of fashion in French intellectual life is suggested by its inspiration of literary critics and philosophers such as Roland Barthes and Gilles Lipovetsky: Barthes formulated a semiotic analysis of a corpus of articles from the women's fashion magazines *Jardin des Modes* and *Elle*, elaborated in 1967 in *Système de la Mode* and Gilles Lipovetsky (1994) has interpreted modern democracy in the light of fashion and trends. Most importantly though, perhaps, consumption in general has itself been the focus of much investigation by Jean Baudrillard (1996, 1998).

French sociologists first began fully to focus their attentions on consumption in the 1960s and then, after the questioning of social, material and personal values of May '68, in the 1970s. The economic policies of governments of the late 1940s had targeted reconstruction and infrastructure development, and macroeconomic priorities in the 1950s and 1960s had likewise focused on growth and the encouragement of industrialisation, generally at the expense of the production of consumer goods. Sociological interest in the evolution of the French version of the US mass consumer society grew in the 1960s as it became evident that pent-up demand for consumer goods combined with the feeling that workers were not sharing fully in the distribution of the fruits of growth was creating a situation of explosive possibilities. The cultural importance of a number of consumer practices in the decolonising 1950s has been dazzlingly analysed by Ross (1996), whose analysis focuses on the symbolic or signifying value of cars – mostly *belles américaines* or ('beautiful Americans'), housekeeping – most germanely *électroménager* (household electrical goods), couples and masculinity.

French fashion is linked closely to the visual arts, continuing the cross-fertilisation established by Cartier-Bresson in photography, by Chanel in 1939 in providing costumes for Renoir's *La Règle du jeu* (1939) and Cocteau's postwar *La Belle et la bête*, and in 1997 with Gaultier's futuristic frocks for Luc Besson's *Le Cinquième elément*. Each of the reflexes of fashion has produced companion corpuses of clothing in cinema and photography especially, and also in literature. The discourses and narratives that arose around consumption, materialism and the 'Americanisation' of French daily life through the adoption of US products and practices were given artistic form and reflection in a number of films and novels of the 1960s in particular, including Perec's novel *Les Choses* (1965), Tati's film *Mon oncle* (1958) and Godard's *Weekend* (1967). Christiane Rochefort's *Les Petits enfants du siècle* (1961) similarly depicted the effects on couples' consumption patterns of the system of state *allocations familiales* in which, most famously, social security payments for successive babies born to families came to represent less the children themselves than the consumer goods of which they allowed the purchase.

In *Les Choses*, subtitled 'une histoire des années soixante' (a story of the sixties), Georges Perec traces the consumption (of commodities, accommodation, food, leisure and transport) and materialistic dreams of the twenty-something couple Sylvie and Jérôme. As an almost sociological description of the acquisitive materialism of a pair of pyschosociologists whose work is concerned with determining the effectiveness of advertising, *Les Choses* lays bare the preoccupations of many French babyboomers caught up in the seemingly soul-less stalemate society of the 1960s. Where the material *bien-être* called for after the austerity (culinary and material) of the 1940s had been assured through the rising prosperity of the Fourth and early Fifth Republics, French society increasingly became concerned with finding the improved well-being (*mieux-être*) which would reconcile consumerism and moral comfort. Roudiez suggests that Perec's following novel *Un Homme qui dort* (1967) forms a counterpart to the focus on material acquisitiveness examined in *Les Choses* by focusing on a nameless protagonist whose ambition is to withdraw and detach himself from the world of material things.[7] Taken together, the two works unarguably present some of the uneasiness experienced by many over the consumerist tendencies of French society which found varied expression in May '68, and which, recuperated in the early 1970s by normal politics and by Gaullism, allowed Chaban-Delmas to suggest that the *nouvelle société* he was calling for was 'la société de consommation avec un supplément d'âme' (a consumer society with a soul).

May '68 is an obvious watershed in French attitudes towards consumption and the discourses and narratives that arise about it. Adapting Touraine's interpretation of the 'epochal originality' of the time of Balzac's novels – the take-off of French industrialisation – and the significance of 1848 as a prism which brought the rising issues of industrial work and the proletariat to visibility, Ross has suggested that May '68 is a similar socio-cultural epiphany. In this perspective 'May '68 would be the new 1848, the confirming afterthought, the event that certified the massive social upheaval and the land grab of the decade that preceded it . . . It was the event that marked the political end of that accelerated transition into Fordism: a protest against the Fordist hierarchies of the factories and the exaggerated statism that had controlled French modernization.'[8]

The academic and everyday critiques of consumerism and materialism that fuelled May '68 and which evolved from it combined with trends in the macroeconomics of the French economy during the 1970s, 1980s and 1990s to produce a complex set of postmodern, post-Fordist attitudes towards consumption. The end to the '*trente glorieuses*' (Thirty Glorious Years) brought by the oil crisis of the mid-1970s heralded a new period of what might be termed 'self-conscious' consumption, where those in

society who could afford to continue the patterns of ostentatious acquis-
itivism redolent of the previous era did so in the knowledge that growth
and its claimed trickle-down of prosperity were not guaranteed for all,
and where others increasingly came to realise that for the first time since
1945, their generation was not necessarily to live better than that of their
parents. Although France has continued to enjoy rising levels of prosperity, current concerns over the fracturing of French society into haves and
have-nots – most noticeably debated during the presidential campaign
of 1995 – concentrate on the division of France into those who manage to
maintain their socio-economic status and those who, increasingly, find
themselves 'excluded' from consumption by virtue of unemployment,
lowly-paid jobs or skills that have become unsaleable in the increasingly
globalised economy.

To return for a moment to food and drink, it could be argued that the
nouvelle cuisine born in the 1970s was a typical manifestation of the trend
towards self-conscious consumption. Self-conscious consumption can be
either 'knowing' – in which case it is a form of conspicuous consumption – or 'naive', when the style of commodity or service consumed becomes – by virtue of its essence – 'modest'. *Nouvelle cuisine* appeared as
a form of 'knowing' self-conscious consumption, since it was a form of
food and drink enjoyed by the minority of eaters able to afford its prices
and whose purchase occurred in settings of fashionable high-visibility.
Doubtless as with all gastronomy, but perhaps to a higher degree, *nouvelle cuisine* divorced the use-value, exchange-value and symbolic value of
food as a commodity in a particularly flagrant way, as its own high-priest
Paul Bocuse suggests when he opines that 'meals are always too large' and
that diners should 'always leave the table feeling slightly hungry'.[9]

The (apparent) 'self-denial' of the small portions and large white
plates of *nouvelle cuisine* and even more so the almost equally expensive
and socially distinctive *cuisine minceur* reflects one of the trends of consumption in the post-May '68 and post Oil Crisis context of the *'vingt
rugueuses'* (the Twenty Rough Years which followed the *'trente glorieuses'*
of growth from 1945–75), namely minimalism. The sociologically traditional hedonism of consumption characteristic of industrialisation in the
earlier periods of the twentieth century was replaced by a modern (or perhaps more accurately, 'postmodern') hedonism represented by the success of minimalist design and by the trends away from the consumption
of the 'classic' products of consumerism towards that of leisure, information and communications. An illustration of the postmodern hedonism

of minimalism is afforded by the career of France's foremost contemporary designer, Philippe Starck. Starck's creations are to be found everywhere in the pages of design and life-style magazines and are seemingly possessed by everyone who can afford them. They are a clear example of products whose signifying value in the creation of social distinction is patently of greater importance than their use value (as a citrus fruit juicer, for example). Interestingly, however, Starck products of the 1980s and 1990s are conceived and consumed as commodities of their time to the extent that in the paradoxically work- and leisure-obsessed turn-of-the-century the conspicuous consumption of expensive designer goods is rationalised by an appeal to their claimed *functionality*.

Despite the continuing celebrity of supermodels and designers, the *haute couture* industry is now, however, increasingly questioning its future viability in the face of public scepticism about its ethics and role. Perhaps somewhat paradoxically, given the continuing postmodern vogue for production and consumption of celebrity, Balenciaga reputedly lost faith in fashion because 'there was no one left to dress', and the managing director of YSL has predicted that *haute couture* will disappear at the death of Yves Saint-Laurent (born 1936) himself. Ironically, French *haute couture* has long been dependent on the signal success of foreign designers such as Gianfranco Ferré at Dior, Karl Lagerfeld and, most recently, the Britons Galliano (Givenchy, then Dior), McQueen (Givenchy), and McCartney (Lagerfeld), and since the 1970s a Japanese influence has derived from Kenzo and Issey Miyaké. As with the globalisation of the agroalimentary industry and the challenges to French gastronomy posed by regional, ethnic and convenience foods, the consumption of fashion in France is being forced to evolve, but is doing so from a position of considerable strength.

NOTES

1. A. Capatti, *Le Goût du nouveau: origines de la modernité alimentaire*, Paris: Albin Michel, 1989, p. 69.
2. M. Rouff, *La Vie et passion de Dodin-Bouffant, gourmet*, Paris: Le Serpent à Plumes, 1994, p. 70.
3. See S. Mennell, 'Food and Wine', in M. Cook (ed.), *French Culture since 1945*, London and New York: Longman, 1993, p. 182.
4. J.-R. Pitte, *Gastronomie française: histoire et géographie d'une passion*, Paris: Fayard, 1991, p. 200.
5. See T. Veblen, *The Theory of the Leisure Class: an Economic Study of Institutions*, London: Allen and Unwin, 1925.

6. See P. Bourdieu, *La Distinction: Critique sociale du jugement*, Paris: Minuit, 1979.

7. See L. S Roudiez, *French Fiction Revisited*, Elmley Park: Dalkey Archive Press, 1972, p. 292.

8. K. Ross, *Fast Cars, Clean Bodies: Decolonisation and the Reordering of French Culture*, Cambridge, Mass.: MIT Press, 1996, p. 3.

9. P. Bocuse, *The Cuisine of Paul Bocuse*, London: Grafton Books, 1988, p. xvi.

FURTHER READING

Baudrillard, J., *The System of Objects*, London: Verso, 1996.

    The Consumer Society: Myths and Structures, London: Sage, 1998.

Bocuse, P., *The Cuisine of Paul Bocuse*, London: Grafton Books, 1998.

Bourdieu, P., *Distinction: a Social Critique of the Judgement of Taste*, Cambridge, Mass.: Harvard University Press, 1984.

Lipovetsky, G., *The Empire of Fashion: Dressing Modern Democracy*, trans. C. Porter, Princeton: Princeton University Press, 1994.

Mennell, S., 'Food and Wine', in M. Cook (ed.), *French Culture since 1945*, London and New York: Longman, 1993.

Perec, G., *Les choses*, Paris: René Julliard, 1965.

    Un homme qui dort, Paris: René Julliard, 1967.

Rochefort, C., *Les petits enfants du siècle*, Paris: Grasset, 1961.

Rouff, M., *La Vie et la passion de Dodin-Bouffant, gourmet*, Paris: Le Serpent à Plumes, 1994. Originally published 1924.

Ross, K., *Fast Cars, Clean Bodies: Decolonization and the Reordering of French Culture*, Cambridge, Mass.: MIT Press, 1996.

Roudiez, L. S., *French Fiction Revisited*, Elmley Park: Dalkey Archive Press, 1972.

Veblen, T., *The Theory of the Leisure Class: an Economic Study of Institutions*, London: Allen & Unwin, 1925.

6

Language: divisions and debates

A crumbling monolith?

Issues relating to language have been debated in Francophone culture ever since French replaced Latin in the sixteenth century as the dominant medium for writing. But the nature of the debates, and the assumptions underlying them, have evolved markedly over the centuries, reflecting the fortunes of the language itself. This chapter will mainly be devoted to presenting a picture of twentieth-century tendencies and the controversies accompanying them. Particularly relevant is the most recent change to affect French speakers' linguistic beliefs and attitudes: since the Second World War especially, confidence and optimism about the state of the language and its prospects have tended to give way to uncertainty and even pessimism. Partly as a consequence, traditional norms and practices are nowadays increasingly liable to be challenged and even disregarded.

The erstwhile mood of confidence set in three-and-a-half centuries ago, when the speech of the royal Court was gradually established as the cultivated standard – essentially the formal written French of today. Seventeenth-century grammarians prided themselves on creating a new and perfected language: 'worthy of the greatest monarch on earth', as one of them put it (in a reference to Louis XIV). Far from adopting a conservative, backward-looking perspective, theirs was an innovative approach, and they made a particular point of distancing themselves from the chaotic usage of the sixteenth century, dismissing it contemptuously, though quite inappropriately, as *le gaulois* ('ancient Gaulish').

By the time of the Revolution, standardised French had come to be viewed – not least by the revolutionaries – as clearer and more logical than other languages: even as the language of thought itself. 'What is not clear is not French; what is not clear may well be English, Italian, Greek or Latin.'[1] This belief was not unconnected with the fact that the cultural and political importance of France had made French the international medium of Europe's educated classes – a role previously filled by Latin, and later to be taken over by English. The following opinion, expressed in the early nineteenth century, must have seemed entirely plausible at the time: 'The French language is spreading so rapidly that we can soon expect to see it adopted throughout Europe'.[2]

Paradoxically, the 'language of liberty' was largely unknown to the mass of the population, who, even in and around Paris, spoke a very different, 'popular' variety of French, and elsewhere used either one of a variety of local dialects (Burgundian, Norman, Picard...) or a distinct regional language (Alsatian, Breton, Provençal...). During the nineteenth century, successive national governments pursued a vigorous policy of imposing standard French throughout the land – the single most effective measure being the introduction in 1881–83 of free, compulsory primary education (exclusively in French, of course). By the First World War, regional languages and dialects had embarked on a steep decline.

The domestic expansion of French was paralleled overseas. Symbolically, Jules Ferry, the reforming Education Minister of the early 1880s, was, as Prime Minister, an enthusiastic colonialist. By 1914, the French empire was second in extent only to the British: the new French colonies and protectorates in North and West Africa, Oceania (Tahiti, New Caledonia) and Asia (Indo-China and the trading stations in India) combined with earlier possessions in the Americas to give the language a presence on five continents.

With a standardised and 'perfected' French at last available for use throughout the national territory and beyond, the first half of the twentieth century was – linguistically – a period of consolidation rather than one of change. But since mid-century, central control has gradually been replaced by fragmentation, and assertion by questioning. Modern linguistics has had its part to play, providing, for example, abundant evidence that despite the still-current belief in the special 'genius of the French language', no language is, in itself, clearer or more logical than any other: clarity is a matter of language *use*. But no less significant are the linguistic practices and attitudes that have come to characterise contemporary Francophone society more generally. These are closely related to a range of recent social, cultural and political developments: the post-1968 challenge to established authority, the move to greater social informality, the emergence of a distinctive 'youth culture', the recognition of women's rights, the independence of former colonies, France's changing world role. All these factors have had a number of consequences for the language which will be explored in the rest of this chapter:

- Linguistics specialists, unlike traditional grammarians, have come to accept non-standard varieties of the language as valid systems in their own right: indeed, they dispute the very notion of 'bad', or 'substandard' French.
- 'Ungrammatical' colloquial usage is encountered more and more widely today, even in writing. And since the early 1980s, unconventional styles of speech – particularly those of adolescents – have become fashionable, finding their way into newspapers, novels, advertisements, specialist and standard dictionaries. But some people find such developments disturbing, even threatening.
- During the last two decades also, the comfortable traditional assumption that, in French grammar, the masculine gender has precedence over the feminine has been called into question and linked to wider issues of gender bias.
- In a parallel development, the traditional, Academy-approved spelling system was challenged in 1989–90 by a highly controversial reform project, although in this case tradition eventually won the day.
- As the twentieth century progressed, French, from being a net exporter of terminology to other languages, became a net importer from English – a state of affairs which has caused so much concern about its integrity and 'purity' that, since the 1970s, various official attempts have been made to reverse the trend.
- In the 1950s, a more positive view of regional languages started to replace earlier 'Jacobin' hostility, and, however hesitantly, central government began enacting measures in support of them.
- On the world stage, French – a century ago the principal international language – has yielded an enormous amount of territory to English. Moreover, in the post-colonial era (c. 1960 onwards), it is questionable to what extent there really remain valid links among the world's various 'Francophone' countries.

'Good' and 'bad' French

By the early twentieth century grammarians had come to see their task as one of maintaining the standardised language in its allegedly pristine state and protecting it from misuse and decadence. The 'prescriptivist' or 'normative' defence of the language essentially involves imposing (prescribing) and, as far as possible, justifying the established norm, while warning against deviations from it. If taken to extremes, the result is the 'purist' view that language change is synonymous with deterioration and must always be resisted. Such an approach has been taken in many books intended for the general public, often with alarmist titles like *Le Péril de la langue française* (The French Language in Peril) (C. Vincent, 1910); *Les Incorrections du langage, la décadence de la langue française, le sans-gêne moderne* (Bad Grammar, Decadent French, Shocking Modern Behaviour) (A. Dejean, 1936); *Hé, la France! Ton français fout le camp!* (Watch Out, France! Your French is Going to the Dogs!) (J. Thévenot, 1974).

As the proliferation of such publications implies, 'mistakes' are widespread in everyday speech and even in writing. Here are just four examples (the 'correct' use is given first, and the usual justification for it indicated).

> 1. Indicative not subjunctive with *après que* ('after'). So 'after she left' ought to be *après qu'elle est partie* (not *soit partie*). A mood expressing uncertainty and doubt should not be used in connection with events that have already occurred.
> 2. *En revanche* not *par contre* ('on the other hand'). No less prestigious a figure than Voltaire took exception to this juxtaposing of two prepositions.
> 3. *A bicyclette* not *en bicyclette*. One travels 'on' the bicycle, not 'in' it.
> 4. *Pallier un défaut* ('make good a defect') not *pallier à un défaut*. The Latin verb *palliare* meant 'to cover something with a cloak (*pallium*)', and *pallier* should therefore also take a direct object, not an indirect one.

Given such divergences between 'correct' and 'actual' usage, many Francophones have developed an inferiority complex about what they take to be the poor quality of their French. Typical comments: 'We make mistakes all the time ... My mother's a very snobbish woman, and careful about how she speaks. But her French is bad all the same.'[3] One of the twentieth century's leading French linguists, André Martinet, a follower of the Swiss scholar Ferdinand de Saussure, commented as follows on this state of affairs:

> French people dare not speak their own language any more. It has been turned into a minefield by generations of professional and amateur grammarians.[4]

Linguistics specialists like Martinet cannot accept that forms used most or all of the time by 90 per cent of speakers should simply be dismissed out of hand. And they are sceptical about the shifting criteria advanced by normative grammarians. Thus in the examples above, logic, etymology (word history), tradition, the opinions of famous writers, are all pressed into service. Linguists point out that the appropriateness of a form often depends on the circumstances in which it is used – a conversation in a café is a different matter from a formal speech. And pursuing the implications of Saussure's view that each language is a system composed of interdependent and interlocking units, their scientifically orientated 'descriptivist' approach seeks to account for 'incorrect' forms in terms of the language system as a whole, taking into account its natural development – not as deviations from an arbitrarily fixed and/or outdated norm.

So a descriptivist analysis of the four 'mistakes' just listed might be as follows:[5]

1. If the subjunctive is used after *après que*, this is because of the parallelism with the 'correct' subjunctive that follows *avant que* ('before'). The tendency in modern French is for the subjunctive to be less and less 'meaningful': the purists themselves insist on its use in *quoiqu'il fasse beau* ('although the weather's fine'), even though the verb here expresses a fact, just like the verb with *après que*.

2. *Par contre* and *en revanche* are not interchangeable: *par contre* introduces a drawback, whereas *en revanche* introduces a compensatory factor: *Il a réussi à son examen; par contre sa femme l'a quitté* ('He's passed his exam; on the other hand, his wife's left him'), but *Sa femme l'a quitté; en revanche il a réussi à son examen* ('His wife's left him; on the other hand, he's passed his exam'). And not the other way round. Everyday language in such a case is more subtle than the norm – as another prestigious writer, André Gide, once pointed out approvingly.

3. The pattern is for *en* to be used if an 'artefact' of some kind is involved: *en voiture* ('by car') of course, but also *en tandem, en planche à voile* ('on a windsurfing board'). Not even a purist would recommend *à* in these two cases. *À* is used for 'natural' means of locomotion: *à pied* ('on foot'), *à cheval* ('on horseback'), *à genoux* ('on one's knees'). As bicycles are artefacts, the use of *en* is quite consistent: being 'inside' or 'outside' is not the point.

4. The model for *pallier à* is the perfectly standard *remédier à* which has the same meaning ('to make good', 'to remedy'). The ancestry of *pallier* is irrelevant, since French usage, not Latin, is at issue. One might as well recommend *je et Marcel* instead of *Marcel et moi* ('Marcel and I'), on the grounds that the Romans said *ego et Marcellus*.

Successors of Martinet like Françoise Gadet, Claude Hagège, Danielle Leeman-Bouix or Henriette Walter have, since the late 1980s, been presenting their descriptivist views quite forcefully on television or in successful books – one sign among others of a tendency to call into question the rulings of normative grammarians.

The spread of colloquial usage

The gulf that has emerged since the seventeenth century between the aristocratic standard language and the everyday speech of ordinary people (even in the Paris region) is almost large enough for colloquial French to be considered a separate, parallel language. One relatively minor grammatical difference has just been mentioned (the use of the subjunctive after *après que*). But others affect wider areas – the structure of questions, negative sentences or relative clauses, for example. And colloquial vocabulary offers a whole range of alternatives to standard terms: *flotte* for *eau* ('water'), *bagnole* for *voiture* ('car'), *cramer* for *brûler* ('burn') – and thousands more.

Despite the efforts of the normative grammarians, it has proved impossible to suppress non-standard forms. The omission of *ne* from *ne... pas* negatives, for example, or the use of questions without inversion (*Tu veux du café?* for *Veux-tu...?*) are well on the way to becoming universal in conversation. Sometimes the conventions of standard French are disregarded deliberately – for example in the conspicuously colloquial remark made not long ago in an official statement by Jean-Pierre Chevènement, when he was a member of the French Cabinet: *Un ministre ça ferme sa gueule ou ça démissionne* ('Ministers should shut up or resign'). *Ça* is here used of a person, *un ministre* is 'detached' from its verb; *fermer sa gueule*, 'shut up', is not the most polite of expressions.

Colloquialisms are also an increasingly prominent feature of written French. They have long been used by avant-garde novelists like Céline (1930s) or Queneau (1950s), and it is traditional for detective stories to make use of criminal *argot* (the first dictionaries of slang appeared in the nineteenth century). But today familiar and popular French have really 'come in from the cold', and are to be found in novels of all kinds – in the narrative as well as in the dialogue – and are a stock-in-trade of many journalists and broadcasters. Advertisers (even staid government agencies) have also taken advantage of the possibilities offered by colloquial language. Thus *Soyez pas nuls, filez vos globules* ('Don't get stuck in the mud, let's have some of your blood') was a linguistically controversial slogan invented in the mid-1990s to encourage blood doning. (No *ne* with *soyez* here, and two informal vocabulary items: *nuls* = *sans valeur*, 'worthless', and *filez* = *donnez*, 'give'.)

The influence of the media and the entertainment industry in this kind of development is of course a powerful one – they have done far more than descriptive linguists ever could to make traditional colloquial French more respectable, and they have also been important vehicles for new developments. In particular, during the last two decades, much media attention has been paid to the speech of adolescents – especially those who are of immigrant origin and live in dilapidated high-rise estates. Further publicity was given to this in the 1980s by pop singers – Renaud Séchan in particular – and later by the work of film-makers like Matthieu Kassowitz, whose *La Haine* ('Hate') (1995) attained almost cult status.

'Youth language' (*le langage des jeunes* – alternatively *le langage des cités* or *des banlieues*, 'suburban high-rise estate language'), closely follows traditional colloquial patterns as far as grammar and pronunciation are concerned (apart from some distinctive features of rhythm and intonation). What has attracted the attention of magazine feature editors, authors of books about adolescent culture, film-makers and, inevitably, academic researchers and dictionary compilers, is its innovative vocabulary. Some of this consists of English terms, especially from the drug and popular music scenes, but for the most part youngsters draw on the resources of French (or increasingly Arabic), creating picturesque figurative expressions like *pot de yaourt* ('yoghurt pot') for a person of European origin, shortening words to just their final syllable (*blème* for *problème*, *dwich* for *sandwich*) or restructuring standard items like *métro*, *femme* or *Arabe* as *tromé*, *meuf*, *Beur* respectively, a type of formation known as *verlan* ('backslang': from *à l'envers*, 'back-to-front'). *Verlan* is actually a centuries-old phenomenon, and not unique to French. But only recently has it achieved celebrity – a good example of the effects of media publicity.

Reactions to youth language vary. Many linguists and sociologists praise its inventiveness and resourcefulness, claiming that French is being revitalised, expressing admiration for the virtuosity of young practitioners of *verlan*, and even suggesting that teachers should become French/*verlan* bilinguals. Others (and not only normative grammarians) see *la langue des cités* as an overrated ghetto jargon, lacking a written tradition, and with limited range and function – useful for insult, invective and wordplay but for little else, and least of all a means of escape from unemployment and the soul-destroying environment of the high-rise estate.

Towards gender-neutral French

A specific point of standard grammar which is currently a focus of debate is the convention that the masculine serves as a 'common' or 'default' gender when no differentiation is being made between the sexes. Thus in a reference to a mixed group, even if females are in the majority, adjectives, past participles and pronouns are required to be masculine (*Deux étudiants et mille étudiantes se sont rassemblés: ils ont protesté vivement...*), and the masculine form of nouns has to be used (*tous ces étudiants*).

Though an individual female student is *une étudiante*, in some cases (typically occupations to which women have obtained access only recently), the feminine form of the noun refers to the wife of a (male) member of the profession in question. Thus *Madame l'ambassadrice* would not herself be an ambassador, but would be married to one. Women who actually are ambassadors (teachers, government ministers, etc.) are *Madame l'ambassadeur* (*le professeur, le ministre*).

Despite the paradoxes that can result (*le directeur est enceinte*, 'the director is pregnant'), this state of affairs was long accepted unquestioningly: 'It is flattering for a woman to have a masculine title', declared a columnist writing in 1948 for the Paris newspaper *Le Figaro*. And the meaning of words as well as their gender sometimes illuminates traditional assumptions about 'woman's place'. Thus an unflattering view of women emerges from contrasts like *homme public* (respected public figure) versus *femme publique* (prostitute), or *courtisan* (courtier) versus *courtisane* (woman of easy virtue).

Such features of the language, and the attitudes underlying them, have been fiercely challenged in the last few decades – not only in French-speaking countries, of course. Some of them are too deeply rooted for remedial action to be easily undertaken: the meaning of words or expressions cannot be altered by fiat. But the restricted area of professional names has proved more amenable. Specific feminines *are* standardly used for occupations with long-established female membership (*une vendeuse, concierge, actrice*), and it is basically a matter of extending this pattern to the more prestigious, male-dominated ones. If *une secrétaire* is acceptable for an ordinary office worker, it is a small step for a female minister to become *la secrétaire d'Etat*. Many feel that the language should acknowledge the fact that more and more women have come to occupy such positions: they should not have to suffer 'linguistic invisibility'.

In 1985 the Socialist government set up a commission to draft recommendations for the feminisation of professional names. The preferred solution in most cases was simply to use a feminine article, rather than add a suffix to the noun itself: *la maire*, *une recteur*, *une ingénieur*. Except, that is, when a straightforward feminine can be formed: *une lieutenante*, *une avocate*. Inevitably it was not always clear what was 'straightforward' and what was not: *une écrivain* or *une écrivaine*? Moreover, when a mixed-sex group is involved, then, in the absence of a common gender, either the masculine still has to be resorted to (*tous les maires de France*), or else both genders have to be used in a rather cumbersome repetition (*les Français et les Françaises*).

Even these timid proposals elicited much mockery from sections of the media: flippant coinage of new pairs like *la juge/le jug* ('judge'), *la vedette/le vedet* ('film-star'), or ironic expressions of relief that the feminisation project post-dated the famous World War Two broadcasts 'Les Français parlent aux Français'. More seriously, there was determined opposition from the French Academy – led, surprisingly, by the anthropologist Claude Lévi-Strauss. The Academy's view was that the use of the masculine as the 'default' or 'unmarked' gender is a time-honoured feature of French grammar, the masculine having taken over the role played by the neuter in the three-gender Latin system. To which the rejoinder from linguists, feminists and others was, firstly, that languages like Latin which have a neuter normally reserve it for inanimate objects, and, secondly, that the default role of the masculine is precisely what is being objected to. What French lacks is a 'common' gender, and the feminisation proposals are an attempt to fill the gap.

The debate hung fire for several years, but was reopened in 1998, when a relaunched commission came up with the essentially traditionalist compromise recommendation that when general reference is made to the office of, say, Secretary of State, then *le secrétaire d'Etat* should continue to be used; but when specific reference is made to a female occupying that position, then *la secrétaire d'Etat* should be acceptable.

Many academicians and private individuals (women as well as men) remain unconvinced, and usage fluctuates considerably. But a number of new feminines are standardly used nowadays on radio and television (particularly the minimalist kind where only the article changes: *la ministre*), and they are quite often encountered elsewhere, so there does seem to have been some movement. Interestingly a tendency has emerged for the Gordian knot to be cut by the substitution of abstract nouns for masculines and feminines alike: *La direction propose que*... ('Management suggest that...') instead of *Le directeur/la directrice propose que*... ('The manager/manageress suggests that...'). An ingenious (and spontaneous) way of simulating the missing common gender!

Finally, to compound the impression of fragmentation, Francophone Belgium, Canada and Switzerland have diverged from metropolitan France. In particular, extra-Hexagonal users rely less on the feminine article and more on adventurous feminine forms like *chirurgienne* ('surgeon'), *sapeuse-pompière* ('firefighter') and even *cheffe* ('chief, head').

Spelling: the perennial debate

Further evidence that established linguistic traditions, though they may be challenged, are not easily overturned, is provided by recent attempts to reform French spelling. Unlike pronunciation, grammar or indeed vocabulary, spelling is essentially a matter of agreed convention, and on various occasions in the past, revisions have been approved by the Academy, the ultimate authority for orthography. Until the end of the eighteenth century, for example, imperfect tense endings were written *-ois/t*, not *-ais/t*, and spellings like *enfants* (replacing *enfans*) or *très digne* (replacing *très-digne*) were introduced in the 1830s. Moreover, the *tolérances* of 1901, issued by the Ministry of Education, allowed certain deviations from the norm (affecting past participle agreement for example) to be exempt from penalty in public examinations.

Nevertheless, today's system essentially represents the pronunciation of the twelfth century, not the twenty-first. It uses different sequences of letters for the same sound (*pin, peins, peint, pain*). Conversely, distinct sounds can be represented by the same letter: *g* has different values in *gris, cage* and, as a liaison or linking consonant, in the formal pronunciation of *sang* [k] *impur*: in *doigt* it is not pronounced at all. One or more 'silent letters' are to be found in many other words: the seven letters of *heaumes*, 'helmets', correspond to just two sounds in pronunciation: [om].

French is not the only language with a conservative spelling system, but it is unusual in that the proliferation of silent letters results in some fundamental grammatical differences between the written and spoken codes. For example, an orthographic *-e* is added to the masculine of many adjectives in order to form the feminine (*gris/grise*). But in pronunciation it is the masculine that ends in a vowel, not the feminine: [gri/griz]. Other differences are seen in verb endings (-*é*, -*és*, -*ées*, -*er* are identical in pronunciation) and in the plurals of adjectives and nouns (-*s* is added in writing – *auto/autos* – but not in speech – [oto/oto]). As may be imagined, the rules of *orthographe grammaticale* are a serious problem for school pupils, who in effect have to master a new grammatical system when they learn to read and write their own language.

It was particularly with the interests of pupils in mind that the latest spelling reform project was launched in 1989, with the backing of Michel Rocard's Socialist government, and guided by a panel that included several linguistics specialists. Earlier twentieth-century attempts at reform encountered so much hostility that they were abandoned, so, ironically, the Rocard reform had to be a very modest affair if it was to have any chance of succeeding. In particular (to the disappointment of progressives) there was no question of introducing a radical *ortograf fonétik*. The complexities of *orthographe grammaticale* were therefore untouched by the proposals. These focused on such relatively trivial points as the use of the circumflex and the tréma (*voute* for *voûte*, *ambigüe* for *ambiguë*), hyphenation (*contramiral* for *contre-amiral*), compound plurals (*un sèche-cheveu/des sèche-cheveux* for *un/des sèche-cheveux*) and sundry anomalies (*ognon* for *oignon*, *exéma* for *exzéma*).

Hostile critics commented that such a reform would be of little help to bad spellers, and would 'traumatise' good ones. This was just one argument in the lively and sometimes impassioned debate which set anti-reformers (including many language professionals: writers, journalists, some members of the Academy) against pro-reformers (academic linguists, schoolteachers, government ministers). By and large the general public and much of the press sided with the anti-reform group. There was a widespread conviction that the spelling system was the language itself, not just its outer garment, that 'the language' belonged to the people, and that self-proclaimed 'language experts' had no right to tamper with it.

One of the more curious anti-reform arguments was that it would become impossible to read the seventeenth-century classics 'in the original'. But pro-reformers responded that spelling has already changed considerably since Molière's day. Many other arguments were, from a linguistic point of view, equally suspect. Some anti-reformers found traditional spelling endearingly picturesque: the circumflex of *voûte* ('vault'), for example, was claimed to conjure up an image of the meaning. (Response: this is just sentimental fantasy!) Circumflexes like the one in *île* (representing the *s* of earlier *isle*) were said to preserve word history. (Response: many circumflexes have no historical justification, like the one in *extrême*.) Proposals like *un sèche-cheveu* ('hair-dryer') were predictably ridiculed – how could it be possible to dry just a single hair? (Response: the advantage is that the general rule 'add -*s* or -*x* for the plural' will apply to all such compound nouns.) Decisions about spelling should be left to usage, not to government commissions, said some anti-reformers. (Response: this is a recipe for chaos.)

And so on – with a counter-argument for each argument. The Academy was unable to reach unanimity, and by the end of 1990 the forces of reason had been defeated by those of sentiment (reinforced no doubt by a fear of 'dumbing-down'). Today the reformed spellings are 'tolerated' in public examinations, but otherwise are to be found only in a few books and pamphlets published by linguists and other reform enthusiasts. Though Francophones may find the spelling of their language daunting, they do for the most part appear to be attached to its idiosyncrasies – the popularity enjoyed by Scrabble and by the annual televised dictation contest, Les Dicos d'Or ('Golden Dictionaries'), is further evidence of this.

Is English a threat?

Spelling would appear to be a more 'sacred' aspect of the language than vocabulary, if the outcry over the 1989 Rocard proposals is contrasted with the lack of public concern about the growing number of anglicisms used in contemporary French.

A large proportion of the vocabulary of modern English is of French origin – from medieval, post-Norman Conquest imports like *joy* or *chief* via seventeenth-century acquisitions like *grotesque* to modern ones like *carnet* or *tranche*. But lately the flood has been reduced to a trickle, whereas the trickle of English words passing into French has, by contrast, become a flood (or so many would claim) – a reflection of the change in international status of the two languages.

Public attention was first alerted to this in the 1960s, when the term *franglais* was coined. R. Etiemble's classic attack, *Parlez-vous franglais?* of 1964, does not in fact distinguish very clearly between different categories of anglicism. Long-established borrowings like *comité*, *club*, *tramway* or *sport* entered French before the twentieth century. Other 'anglicisms' are in effect original French creations (*wattman*, 'tram driver', *pressing*, 'dry cleaners'). Others again changed their meaning after entering the language, adding an arguably useful nuance to its vocabulary (*shopping*, 'shopping for enjoyment' not for necessities). Some, however, do seem merely to duplicate existing French terms (*in*, 'à la mode'; *loser*, 'perdant'). Only the last category really fits the usual definition of *franglais*: 'unnecessary or superfluous English word'. But it could be argued that even these 'true' *franglais* items have different associations from their French equivalents (smartness, internationalism, up-to-dateness).

Descriptive linguists take a relaxed view, and regard the alarm over the influx of anglicisms as misplaced. Similar, and (as it turned out) unjustified controversies have occurred in the past – over an alleged influx of Italian words in the sixteenth century for example. All languages borrow vocabulary from one another, they say, and French has been a major contributor in its time. Moreover, even though lists of anglicisms look dauntingly large, the proportion occurring in running texts is small – perhaps 1 per cent in the average newspaper. If an anglicism usefully 'fills a gap', then it will be assimilated (as *week-end* and many others have been); otherwise it will be merely a passing phenomenon. Etiemble and others, it is claimed, fail to make this important distinction.

Defenders of the language, however, are unconvinced – in part because they see the 'anglicisation' of French as just one symptom of the wider advance of Anglophone culture world-wide. They point out that in some kinds of usage (technical writing, articles about popular music, advertising), the proportion of anglicisms is higher than 1 per cent, and they take the view that, when there are gaps, it is better to fill them with genuinely French words than slavishly borrow from English.

Accordingly, various government ministry terminology commissions, set up by legislation passed in 1972 and now co-ordinated by the Délégation générale à la langue française ('General Delegacy for the French Language'), have been devising appropriate 'indigenous' items, increasingly in collaboration with organisations from other Francophone communities – notably Quebec. A few of the coinages have proved very successful: *logiciel* and *matériel* have ousted *software* and *hardware* respectively – and indeed have given rise to further widely used neologisms like *didacticiel*, 'teaching software' or *ludiciel*, 'computer games'. Other new terms are having to struggle to survive, however (*baladeur*, 'walkman', *restauration rapide*, 'fast food'). Others again, for whatever reason, have not caught on at all, and exist merely as alternatives listed in dictionaries (*bouteur*, 'bulldozer').

There have even been two controversial attempts to make the use of anglicisms illegal in situations where equivalent French terminology is available: the Bas-Lauriol law of 1975 and its successor, the Toubon law of 1994. These apply to the relevant government departments of course, but, more controversially, to private sector provision of goods and services – on the grounds that Francophone consumers are legally entitled to have these supplied in their own language. From time to time, language defence associations like *Droit de comprendre* (The Right to Understand) have succeeded in prosecuting firms for illicit use of anglicisms, but the number of such prosecutions is tiny and the penalties derisory. Moreover, following an appeal by Socialist deputies to the Constitutional Council in 1994, the legislation was deemed to contravene the principles of human rights enshrined in the Constitution, and was judged invalid in its application to private firms. Today the legislation may be considered null and void (state institutions apart), with public indifference mirroring the laissez-faire attitude of the linguists.

The use of individual English words or expressions within a French text is not the only contentious issue. There is, perhaps more justifiably, concern about the growing tendency in business, industry and the academic world to abandon the use of French altogether. The managing board of Renault, for instance, holds its meetings in English nowadays; some civil service committees operate in English only, even in their Paris ministries; English is increasingly the sole language of instruction in French business schools; and the possible shape of things to come is foreshadowed by the controversial statement made in 1999 by the then Education Minister, Claude Allègre: 'English is no longer a foreign language'.

Some would claim reassuringly that, although the formal business at Renault and elsewhere may be in English, the subsequent informal drinks session will still be in French. But defenders of the language would retort that it probably will *not* be in French if colleagues from non-Francophone countries are present. More importantly, they would add, this state of affairs is disturbingly parallel to the relationship obtaining a century or so ago between French itself and regional speech forms. In that case, the 'prestige' language quite rapidly came to be used in all circumstances, whether formal or informal, even though many had been convinced that local *patois* was indestructible.

Regional languages and dialects

Before the present-day relationship between French and 'regional speech' can be examined, three different aspects of the latter need to be distinguished.

Dialects. In the French context, these are vernaculars like Burgundian, Norman, Picard, Gallo (eastern Brittany) or Walloon (south-eastern Belgium). Like standard French itself, they all derive from the Latin spoken in different localities in northern Gaul, and though not mutually comprehensible, have many common features. But, from the early Middle Ages onwards, for political, economic and social reasons connected with the dominance of Paris and the surrounding Ile-de-France, they were gradually eclipsed by an amalgam of Ile-de-France speech and elements from a number of other dialects. *Francien*, as this mixed, central, variety is sometimes called, was the ancestor of today's national language. The local dialects have by now disappeared from almost all urban areas (Picard is still used in towns in the Nord-Pas-de-Calais), but they cling on in some country districts. However, these rural *parlers* have no official status or standard form, and for the most part lost their written traditions many centuries ago. It is symptomatic of their decline that they should now be referred to as mere 'dialects of French'.

Regional languages. South of a line from Bordeaux to Geneva, the modern descendents of Latin are sufficiently different from those to the north for them to be regarded as dialects of a distinct language – *Occitan*. Unlike French, this 'language' has never been standardised: 'Occitan' is simply a collective – and sometimes disputed – name for Béarnais and Gascon (in the south-west), Languedocien (south centre), Provençal (south-east), Auvergnat and Limousin (Massif Central), etc. Members of the group show numerous 'family resemblances', the best-known being *oc*, the word for 'yes' (hence *Occitan* and *Languedoc*, 'language of *oc*'). Around the edge of the Hexagon, several other regional languages are spoken. These are less closely related to French even than the Oc dialects. True, *Catalan* (Perpignan region) and *Corsican* are also derived from Latin, but their nearest relatives are Spanish and Italian respectively, not French. *Flemish* (Dunkirk region), *Francique* (Thionville region of Lorraine) and *Alsatian* are all Germanic languages; *Breton* (western Brittany) is Celtic, having many similarities to Welsh; *Basque* is an isolate, with no relationship to any other Western European language.

Regional French refers to local varieties of the national language. Essentially this is the same colloquial French that is spoken in and around Paris, but with influence from dialect or a regional language, especially in pronunciation. There is full mutual comprehension between the various *français régionaux* and standard French, and, perhaps as a result of this closeness, younger speakers, particularly in northern France, increasingly follow Parisian patterns, though not necessarily middle-class ones. Paradoxically, it seems that speakers today value local accents more than they used to, even though they may be heard less and less often. Parisian centralism is unfashionable, but in spontaneous usage it is evidently difficult to resist its influence.

Regional languages have proved somewhat more tenacious than the 'dialects of French'. Many of them have affinities with prestigious languages spoken in neighbouring countries (Corsican with Italian, for example). Their speakers are geographically more distant from Paris and may well have a stronger ethnic and cultural identity. Indeed, following the Revolution, regional languages were seen as a threat to the integrity of the Republic. Throughout the nineteenth century and much of the twentieth, their use was actively discouraged by central government, and they were referred to dismissively (and inaccurately) as 'dialects' or, more disparagingly still, as *patois*. Consequently, though up to a third of the inhabitants of Corsica are still fluent speakers of Corsican, Flemish is rarely heard in the Dunkirk region these days, fewer and fewer young people speak Alsatian or Francique, only an estimated 9 per cent of a regional population of 12 million regularly use Occitan, and the figures for other languages also show a decrease.

Ironically, now that they are no longer perceived as a threat, regional languages have come to enjoy more government support (the first step was the Deixonne law of 1951, and further legislation was enacted notably by the 1981–86 Socialist government). There has been much talk of 'the right to be different' and local speech is actually coming to be valued as part of the national heritage. Bilingual schools are tolerated (though only a few per cent of local children attend them), many of the languages can be studied as *baccalauréat* options, they are allowed a modest amount of time on state radio and television (as well as being used on various private stations) and bilingual street signs can be seen in some town centres. 'Eleventh-hour' official projects apart, there is no lack of organisations dedicated to preserving local languages and cultures – but with many monolingual Francophones among their members, it must be said. Regionalist groups are particularly active in Brittany, Corsica and the Basque Country, where the years since 1970 have been marked periodically by violent protests. In Alsace-Lorraine, however, and even more so in French Flanders, a certain wartime collaborationist stigma still attaches to the local Germanic speech.

But none of the regional languages comes anywhere near to attaining the official status enjoyed by Welsh in Wales or by Basque and Catalan in Spain. Indeed the French Constitution was amended in 1992 to incorporate the explicit statement that 'the language of the Republic is French'. And the European Charter for Regional or Minority Languages (1992) has not been ratified by France. The Charter encourages the use of regional languages in local government for example. But, unlike harmlessly bilingual street signs intended mainly to appeal to tourists, such large-scale provision of special administrative arrangements for particular groups would infringe the fundamental constitutional principle that all French citizens are to be treated equally. At the same time, pressure from Corsican nationalism led in 2000–01 to concessions like the inclusion of Corsican in state school syllabuses on the island. Such developments could encourage similar moves elsewhere – albeit at the cost of much argument about constitutionality.

French world-wide

Though Parisian speech varieties are dominant in the Hexagon, French is no longer the international auxiliary language that it was before the First World War. And there are at least a dozen other languages in the world with more native speakers. Nevertheless, because of extensive colonial settlement in the nineteenth century particularly, French is probably the world's most widely disseminated language after English: any advantage it has in the 'league table' of languages lies in its large number of non-native users – or potential users. These are increasingly to be found outside Europe and North America: the reservoir of future Francophones is located above all in West Africa, where, in around twenty countries, French is the language of government, law, administration and, most importantly, education. But it should be borne in mind that in Third World 'Francophone' countries the proportion of those sufficiently well educated to have any worthwhile proficiency in French can be as low as 10 per cent.

The rather ambiguous situation of French world-wide has contributed in no small measure to changing attitudes about its future. The move towards a more multi-polar approach, discussed earlier in relation to non-standard usage within the Hexagon, is beginning to apply also to non-metropolitan varieties, which are increasingly regarded as alternatives to the Paris norm, not as deviations from it. This is particularly true of Canadian usage – a Quebec standard is well on the way to becoming a reality – and more and more Canadian, Belgian and Swiss vocabulary items and variants are listed in standard dictionaries published in Paris. Not long ago they would have been relegated to prescriptivist collections with titles like *Chasse aux belgicismes!* ('Eliminating Belgian turns of phrase'). The distinctive forms of expression being developed by writers from Africa and the Caribbean are further evidence of emergent alternative *Francophonies*.

The view that the future of the language lies in its international dimension is echoed in the attempts to establish links between the various 'French-speaking' countries and regions, creating a counterweight to 'Anglo-Saxon' dominance. International associations of Francophone writers and journalists have existed since the 1920s, but it was only after the French and Belgian colonies gained independence in the 1960s that steps were taken at government level to create what has been described as a 'Commonwealth à la française'. Like the Commonwealth itself, the *Organisation Internationale de la Francophonie* supports various subsidiary bodies and holds regular summit meetings for its heads of state (the first in Versailles in 1986, with subsequent summits every other year in, for example, Quebec, Senegal, Mauritius, Vietnam, Lebanon). In 1997, a permanent post of Secretary General was established.

But the organisation is by no means clear about its exact nature and role. Certainly there is much rather cloudy rhetoric about the unifying function of the French language:

> *Francophonie* is not just a word, but a thousand years of memory, dispersed over five continents. In the sands of the Sahara, the creeks of Louisiana, the jungles of Cameroon or the snows of Quebec it reproduces that ingenious interplay of vowels and consonants which expresses the soul of a people called on to add its voice to the great symphony of mankind.[6]

In actual fact, it is far from obvious what, say, Chad, Quebec and Vietnam really have in common. Even the linguistic ties between them are weak: proficiency in French in Vietnam has become limited to some 5 per cent of the population since the demise of French Indo-China in the 1950s, while in Chad the figure has never risen above 10 per cent, due to the country's underdevelopment. Moreover, despite the post-colonialist background of the organisation, the richest member states (Belgium, Canada, Luxembourg and Switzerland) are not former colonies, and what is more, are themselves multi-lingual.

All this makes the *Organisation Internationale de la Francophonie* considerably more heterogeneous even than the Commonwealth. And recently, membership has been extended to countries whose Francophone credentials are still more tenuous – Albania, Bulgaria, Israel, Poland, Slovakia. In fact the only member state which approaches monolingualism in French is France itself. As some 80 per cent of all native speakers of the language are concentrated there, the risk of 'neo-colonial' domination by Paris has always been present – something which of course runs counter to the doctrine of international diversity. Alongside this lack of coherence, the relative lack of economic power of the group should be kept in mind (many of the member states are among the world's poorest) and so should its comparative collective weakness in the domains of science and technology.

So the Francophone 'bloc' has had difficulty in establishing itself as a significant player on the international stage. Even for the general public, the activities of the organisation are remote and bureaucratic. Its reluctance to expel or suspend member states for violations of human rights (in contrast to the Commonwealth) was a major course of discord at the 1999 summit in New Brunswick, and epitomises the uncertain status of the organisation: is it a political or merely a cultural grouping?

The middle way between excessive diversity and excessive centralism is clearly hard to attain. The dilemmas of post-colonial *Francophonie* mirror the evolution of the language itself, as it oscillates between an ideology of uniformity (in the seventeenth, eighteenth and nineteenth centuries) and a tendency to fragmentation (before the seventeenth century, and again, it would seem, in our own time).

NOTES

1. Comte de Rivarol, *Discours sur l'universalité de la langue française*, Paris, 1784.
2. D'Hautel, *Dictionnaire du bas-langage ou des manières de parler usitées parmi le peuple*, Paris, 1808.
3. M. Fischer, *Sprachbewusstsein in Paris*, Vienna, Cologne, Graz: Böhlau, 1987, pp. 103, 162.
4. A. Martinet, *Le Français sans fard*, Paris: Presses Universitaires de France, 1969, p. 29.
5. See D. Leeman-Bouix, *Les Fautes de français existent-elles?* Paris: Seuil, 1994.
6. A. Maillet, quoted in *Lettre(s)*, 25:2, 1999.

FURTHER READING

Ager, D., *Francophonie in the 1990s, Problems and Opportunities*, Clevedon: Multilingual Matters, 1996.

Ball, R., *Colloquial French Grammar*, Oxford: Blackwell, 2000.

Gervais, M.-M., 'Gender and Language in French', in C. Sanders (ed.), *French Today*, Cambridge: Cambridge University Press, 1993, pp. 121–38.

Goudaillier, J.-P., *Comment tu tchatches! Dictionnaire du français contemporain des cités* (3rd edn), Paris: Maisonneuve et Larose, 2001.

Judge, A., 'France: "One State, One Nation, One Language"?' in S. Barbour and C. Carmichael (eds.), *Language and Nationalism in Europe*, Oxford: Oxford University Press, 2000, pp. 44–82.

Lodge, R. A., *French: From Dialect to Standard*, London: Routledge, 1993.

Parker, G., 'Orthographe: une affaire d'Etat', *Modern and Contemporary France* 48 (Jan. 1992), pp. 33–43. (In English.)

Thody, P., *Le Franglais: Forbidden English, Forbidden American*, London: Athlone Press, 1995.

7

Intellectuals

Dictionaries define the noun *intellectuel* as a person devoted by profession or taste to the exercise of intelligence, to the life of the mind. Yet the word – in both French and English – has a more specific meaning that, while widely recognised, almost never makes it into these definitions: that of a person of recognised intellectual attainments who speaks out in the public arena, generally in ways that call established society or dominant ideologies to account in the name of principle or on behalf of the oppressed.

This more pointed definition of the intellectual must be given pride of place in a chapter such as this one, which obviously cannot begin to cover all the French-language intellectual contributions of the twentieth century, or attempt a synthesis of philosophic, scientific, linguistic, literary, aesthetic, sociological and anthropological thought. At the same time, the porous boundaries between the different definitions of the intellectual make it impossible to remain solely within this canonical perspective. At times philosophic, literary or scholarly work by itself has sufficient impact to give its authors a role in public life. Perhaps more disconcertingly, the public intervention of the intellectual on behalf of a cause has become a stereotypic act that can seemingly be performed (or mimicked, purists would say) by individuals who lack the imprimatur of their peers as legitimate contributors to the life of the mind: entertainers, celebrities or essayists not esteemed within the intellectual community. The questions of definitions, limits and legitimacy raised by these activities loom increasingly large as the twenty-first century begins under conditions very different from those that gave birth to the intellectual at the end of the nineteenth. They point to a disturbing and as yet unanswered question: does the history of the intellectual coincide with that of the twentieth century, not only in its beginning but in its end?

'J' accuse!'

That beginning, at least, can be pinpointed in space and time. On 13 January 1898, the newspaper *L'Aurore* published Emile Zola's 'Letter to the President of the Republic' on controversies surrounding the espionage conviction of Captain Alfred Dreyfus. Given the title 'J'accuse!' by the paper's editor, Georges Clemenceau, Zola's letter denounced an elaborate web of judicial errors and of wrongdoing by high officials of the army and the government. In the days that followed, as Zola himself was accused and convicted of libel in an atmosphere of nationalistic frenzy, the press began publishing petitions of scholars, scientists and men of letters in solidarity with Zola and in favour of a review of Dreyfus's case. Among the organisers of these positions were Lucien Herr, the influential librarian of the Ecole Normale Supérieure, Charles Péguy, then a student at the same school, the (as yet) little-known author Marcel Proust, and Léon Blum, at the time a young civil servant with ties to Symbolist literary groups. Among the leading signers were Emile Duclaux, director of the Institut Pasteur, Anatole France, the novelist Octave Mirbeau, the physicist Jean Perrin, and the literary historian Gustave Lanson. On 23 February Clemenceau wrote of this movement: 'Is it not a sign, all these *intellectuals*, coming from every corner of the horizon, who are organising around an idea and holding to it unshakably?'

Clemenceau was not the first in French to describe people as *intellectuels*, but this was the first instance in which it designated followers of the life of the mind who were taking positions on public issues. The word had been used as a noun with apparently increasing frequency in the 1880s and 1890s, notably in Paul Bourget's 1889 novel *Le Disciple*, an early attack on philosophy teachers as corrupters and demoralisers of youth, but also in the writings of Guy de Maupassant, Edmond de Goncourt, Maurice Barrès and Anatole France. It often, though not always, carried a pejorative connotation of one who lives too much in thought to the neglect of action. But the Dreyfus affair made it a common usage and associated it with principled intervention in public life. Zola's letter became the prototype of an individual act of intellectual commitment to truth and justice; the petitions, a model for collective statements of intellectual solidarity.

Not only the intervention of the intellectuals but even the very concept of them drew quick criticism from those who felt that the real danger in the Dreyfus affair was not to truth or justice but to military honour and national cohesion. Barrès, the person most responsible for the development of *nationalism* as a concept and ideology, denounced the Dreyfusard intellectuals as a self-appointed pseudo-elite who erroneously believed that society should be ordered according to the dictates of abstract, universal reasons rather than according to traditions rooted in place and custom. The author of *Les Déracinés* (The Uprooted, 1897), a novel critical of the Republic's secular schools, Barrès stated flatly that Zola was not a Frenchman but an 'uprooted Venetian' whose novels violated French taste and who could not be expected to understand or sympathise with the needs of the French nation and its army. The literary critic Ferdinand Brunetière objected that 'intellectuals' did not really form a single category and that their pronouncements deserved no special respect outside of their specialties. In acting as if their views had strong claims on the attention of the public, he concluded, intellectuals showed themselves to be a symptom of the modern malady of individualism. The sociologist Emile Durkheim responded on two fronts: by defending the individualism of autonomous moral subjects from confusion with the selfishness of economic individualism, and by defining the intellectual professions not via high intelligence but via their autonomy: their use of knowledge for the production of more knowledge and not for external ends.

The criticism of Barrès and Brunetière featured what were to become recurrent themes of anti-intellectualism. The Dreyfusard protest was made in the name of truth, justice and the rights of the individual; it was opposed in the interest of tradition, national particularism and social cohesion. These were not new antitheses; indeed, they point to strong continuities between the 'new' figure of the intellectual and the Enlightenment *philosophe*, and between the intellectuals' detractors and the tradition of modern reactionary thought that first emerged clearly around the period of the French Revolution. Shortly before the Revolution, the moralist Chamfort wrote a definition of the *philosophe* that would do as well for the Dreyfusard intellectual: 'What is a philosopher? A man who sets nature against law, reason against custom, his conscience against public opinion, and his judgement against error.' The case of established law and above all of custom and particularity against abstract reason was to be argued by thinkers of the counter-Enlightenment and opponents of the Revolution and its effects, first and most famously by Edmund

Burke (*Reflections on the Revolution in France*, 1790). In France, Barrès's attack on the Dreyfusard intellectuals had already been that of the Emperor Napoléon I against the *idéologistes*, a group of late Enlightenment rationalist philosophers who hoped to develop the philosophy of Locke and Condillac into a science of ideas and who held positions of institutional power in the French educational system in the later phases of the Revolution. Napoléon felt that the ideologists and their philosophic brethren, by valuing head over heart and neglecting historical experience, bore major responsibility for the social disorder of the revolutionary era.

'La Trahison des clercs'

As the intellectual's filiation from the *philosophe* and the struggles over the legacy of the Revolution suggests, the Dreyfus affair was a crucial moment in the long process of completing and consolidating the work of the French Revolution of 1789. The chief Dreyfusard organisation took the name *Ligue des droits de l'homme* (League of Human Rights), alluding explicitly to the 1789 *Declaration of the Rights of Man and of the Citizen*. Their opponents banded together in a *Ligue de la patrie française* (League of the French Fatherland), thus emphasising the fault-lines between individualism and the prerogatives of the collectivity, between abstract principle and localised tradition, between a potentially universalist conception of France and one devoted exclusively to national interest.

A striking difference between the Dreyfus-era controversy over intellectuals and earlier oppositions of reason and tradition lay in its institutional setting. Teachers and journalists were the largest professional groups among the pro-Dreyfus petitioners, with scientists and writers also prominent, and their opponents – many of them writers, too – argued that France was endangered by the hold of unpatriotic, abstract thinking on its schools, universities and news media. The question of intellectuals was thus a key part of the increasingly tense conflict between the secular culture of the Republic's educational institutions and the still major role of the Catholic Church.

The parties of the Left benefited politically from the exoneration of Dreyfus and attendant discrediting of many conservatives, and in 1902 Dreyfusards and Socialists entered the government of the 'bloc des gauches', which undertook to secure and strengthen the secular and republican character of both the State and society through a policy of anti-clericalism. The cause of many Dreyfusard intellectuals thus became that of assuring the institutionalised cultural victory of secular knowledge over the teachings of the Church as a means of securing the stability of the Republic. The law separating Church and State was approved under the left coalition government in 1905. With the Republic decisively committed to secularism, the forces of tradition became more aggressively anti-republican. The *Ligue de la patrie française* was displaced and in effect superseded in 1906 by the more pugnacious, anti-democratic, and monarchist *Action française* founded by the combative nationalist Charles Maurras (1868–1952), who – unlike Barrès – thought that the Revolution could and should be reversed.

The causes of Dreyfusism, Socialism and nationalism converge in an individual (and arguably idiosyncratic) way in the work of the poet and essayist Charles Péguy (1873–1914). Péguy is arguably the first major writer or thinker to be thoroughly identified with the question of the intellectual, Zola and Barrès already having had significant reputations before the Dreyfus Affair. A young and ardent Dreyfusard and soon thereafter an independent Socialist editor and polemicist, Péguy's most memorable contribution to the Affair probably lay in his later interpretations of it, in which he denounced the actions and influence of what he called the 'intellectual party' in the name of an idealised, even mystical concept of the mission of the intellectual.

Protesting the injustice against Dreyfus had been, for Péguy, a holy cause, an affirmation of eternal and universal values against the temporal expediency of a *raison d'état* that saw national cohesion and the reputation of the military as more important than the life of liberty of a single man. 'We were heroes', he would write of the Dreyfusards in *Notre jeunesse* (1910). But Péguy considered what he took to be the subsequent political opportunism of the Dreyfusard forces, and especially their participation in the anti-clerical project of *bloc des gauches* governments, as a betrayal and a moral disaster. The secular philosophy of the anti-clerical Republic did not represent, for him, the removal of metaphysical teachings from education, as partisans of the Separation generally argued; instead it was itself a metaphysical philosophy, a poor and vulgar one at that, and worst of all it was being promoted and for all purposes enforced as a *métaphysique d'état* (state metaphysics), which struck him as completely incompatible with the victory of principle over state power won in the Affair. In *Notre jeunesse*, Péguy generalised his view of the fate of the Dreyfusard cause into a famous maxim: 'everything begins as mysticism and ends as politics'.

And, for Péguy, the political project of what he called the 'parti intellectuel', that coalition of journalists and professors turned politicians, was nothing less than a disaster for France. His own Socialist ideal was one of vital reorganisation and internal integration of particular societies – an organic Socialism compatible with, rather than opposed to, the development of individual nations. A raging critic of capitalist modernity and of faith in science, Péguy believed that nations and peoples only had value because they were the products of long and variegated histories; any and all attempts to remake them according to the ideas of the present were abusive and ultimately doomed to failure. In this sense, and in his designation of the misguided and even perverse *parti intellectuel*, Péguy's thought had affinities with that of Barrès and other cultural conservatives going back to Burke, but Péguy never truly made common cause with the anti-Dreyfusard nationalists. He considered the reactionary thesis that the Dreyfus affair was an intellectuals' conspiracy to be itself a characteristic error of excessive intellectualism; for him, the thinkers of the nationalistic right were no less intellectual, no less modern and shallow, than their anti-clerical adversaries.

Péguy's lament for the fall of the Dreyfusard cause from mysticism to (ordinary) politics was a strong and unusually personalised version of a very widespread characteristic idea about intellectuals: the 'otherworldliness' of their values and interventions. The underlying fidelity of the intellectual, on this view, must be to the order of ideas (or beauty or science) rather than to the necessities and compromises of governing the world as it is. To have agreed to condemn Dreyfus, he argued, might have given the French some short-term advantage of national unity or military morale, but at the cost of their soul, for the nation would be ruined in the eyes of eternity if it committed an injustice. But for an 'intellectual party' to try to govern the country and impose its philosophy on it was no less a betrayal.

A somewhat different but no less absolute stand on the purity of the intellectual's mission was made by Julien Benda in La Trahison des clercs (1927), probably the most famous of all French pronouncements on the intellectual (though by no means one of the most read today). By designating intellectuals as clerics, Benda emphasised what he regarded as their necessary unworldliness: for him, the transhistorical function of the cleric, whether a member of a religious order or a secular intellectual, is to represent universal, immutable principles and to exert a countervailing force against the passions and projects of society and its leaders when these conflict, as they almost certainly must, with the claims of justice, truth and reason.

What Péguy and Benda agreed on was that to be an intellectual one had to be faithful to something beyond the ordinary politics and interests of the temporal world. What divided them was the question of the nation and its interests. For Benda, the use of intellectual authority in the interests of a nation's advancement or defence could only be a perversion of intellectual values, since these are universal and the nation is always particular. He likewise condemned what he considered the modern tendency of intellectuals to value the practical and the realistic more than ideals or spirit. Of course, he acknowledged, those in power have always had intelligent counsellors urging that they pursue parochial and pragmatic interests; what Benda found new and deplorable was the move to see this kind of advice given and endorsed by clerics who ought to be combating it, and who were instead trying to give it moral and philosophic authority. Although he reserved special scorn for French nationalists like Maurras, his real targets included all modern thinkers, such as Nietzsche, who in his judgement were wrongly proclaiming the morality or at least inevitably of worldly and selfish passions. He was, in effect, intent on denouncing what he saw as an anti-Socratic turn in the relation between philosophy and the life of the city.

For all his insistence that intellectual values transcended those of politics, Benda was not shy about his own commitments. He justified the fierce nationalism he himself displayed during the Great War by identifying the cause of France with universal values, that of Germany with vile particularism. He was an outspoken anti-Fascist and anti-pacifist during the 1930s. In a new edition of *La Trahison* published in 1946, he described intellectual support for the Marxist doctrine of dialectical materialism as yet another betrayal of universal principles for temporal interest, but this did not prevent him from being himself a loyal fellow traveller of the French Communist Party in his last years. Whatever the potential for contradiction in these positions, Benda's 1927 essay remains a reference for a resolutely idealistic and universalist conception of the French intellectual's mission, and a rallying point for those who refuse any complacency on the part of intellectuals with nationalism or with the compromises and expediency that are inevitably part of governance.

As the Dreyfus Affair and the strikingly individual cases of Péguy and Benda suggest, the relationship of the thinker to the nation was a crucial and problematic one for intellectuals throughout much of the twentieth century. As heirs of Enlightenment universalism and opponents of injustice and intolerance, most intellectuals were well disposed to denounce the anti-Semitism, authoritarianism, and politicised Catholicism of the nationalist Right. Nonetheless, that very nationalism continued to attract significant intellectual support until 1945, often thanks to the identification of the French nation with the achievements of its people (or of Europe more generally) in the field of high culture, or because of a rejection of capitalist modernity as incompatible with morality and cultural traditions.

France and its intellectuals split along the fault-lines revealed in the Dreyfus Affair after Hitler's rise to power and the menace of a French Fascism revealed in the riots of 6 February 1934, provoked by rightist leagues such as the Croix de Feu as a protest against the parliamentary regime and its supposed corruption. An Intellectuals' Antifascist Vigilance Committee was promptly formed, presided by the anthropologist Paul Rivet, the founder of the *Musée de l'homme*, with the essayistic philosopher Alain (pseudonym of Emile Chartier) and the physicist Paul Langevin as vice-presidents. The Intellectuals' Committee, which significantly brought together radicals, Socialists and Communists while remaining itself outside the control of the parties, was able to contribute to the establishment, the following year, of the *Front populaire*, which united the hitherto divided parties of the Left in an uneasy alliance against the internal and external Fascist threat. On the Right, Maurras and the monarchists of *Action française* were joined by young writers such as Pierre Drieu La Rochelle (1893–1945) and Robert Brasillach (1909–45) who embraced Fascism on the Italian and (especially) German models as a radical alternative to capitalism, modernity and parliamentary democracy.

The divisions of the 1930s continued, of course, under the German Occupation following the defeat of 1940, with prominent writers like Drieu and Brasillach taking up key cultural posts such as editorships so as to advocate active collaboration with the German occupiers, while others served the Resistance to varying degrees. (In general, more resistance heroes came from the ranks of scholars and scientists than from those of creative writers.) Following the Liberation, non-collaborationist intellectuals divided on the question of whether and how to punish their collaborationist colleagues. Brasillach, sentenced to death for treason, was executed by firing squad after General Charles de Gaulle, then head of the provisional government, refused to grant him the clemency requested by a petition of fifty-six writers. The elderly Maurras, convicted and sentenced to life in prison, shouted 'It's the revenge of Dreyfus' when his sentence was announced.

Although most collaborationist writers were able to resume their lives under surprisingly normal circumstances, the war and Occupation broke the back of the right-wing intellectual nationalism that had flourished from Barrès to Brasillach. There was a brief flurry of mainstream media attention to the doings of right-wing intellectuals, baptised the *Nouvelle droite*, in the late 1970s, but this quickly faded. The more recent electoral resurgence of a crudely nationalist political party, Jean-Marie Le Pen's *Front National*, has not had a serious intellectual counterpart. In some ways the rise of the FN revives the critical mission of anti-nationalist, anti-xenophobic intellectuals. Yet the very marginality of the extreme Right – the fact that it is opposed by the very centrist politicians whom many intellectuals consider to be at best tepid managers and reformers – makes it difficult to consider opposition to the *Front national* to be a specifically intellectual cause. Le Pen has no intellectual supporters of the calibre of a Barrès or even a Drieu, so there is no real debate of ideas with FN sympathisers. When intellectuals take up the matter of the extreme Right, it is generally to debate the most effective means of combating it or to denounce politicians from the governing parties for complicity or complacency with FN themes. In April 2002, when Le Pen reach the final round of the presidential election, mass demonstrations by high-school students were a far more prominent form of moral protest against his candidacy than declarations from intellectuals.

Intellectuals and the Left

If intellectuals were key figures in the belated combats to secure the republican legacy of the Revolution of 1789, they were no less involved in the great revolutionary drama of the twentieth century, that of class struggle and proletarian revolution. This drama is that of the 'short twentieth century', we may say, the one that began in 1917 with the Russian Revolution and ended in 1989 with the collapse of Communism in Eastern Europe, although Socialism was already the cause of many intellectuals from the Dreyfus affair to the Great War. The cause of the proletariat and the reaction to nationalism were often intertwined, since both Socialist and Communist parties had universalist goals and belonged to international movements, but it could also be allied, as in the case of Péguy, to nationalist aspirations.

Commitment to class struggle on behalf of the proletariat was both attractive and problematic for intellectuals for two main reasons. In the first place, intellectuals do not belong, almost by definition, to the working class, and few of them come from it. So the activism of intellectuals on behalf of workers involved speaking on behalf of others – something that can seem both a responsibility on the part of those who enjoy education or high status towards those who do not, and an unstable position with risks of misrepresentation and divergence of interests.

More important, however, is that Socialism – especially in its Marxist form – seems to indicate a clear direction of history towards which intellectuals could work: the triumph of the proletariat, the only class bearing universal aspirations. This seems to reconcile the demands of objective rationality and commitment to a specific cause. If the proletariat not only has the claims of justice on its side, but embodies the rational and necessary direction of history, then the intellectual who works for its triumph is defending truth and reason, not betraying them for particular or partisan interest.

Given these possibilities and constraints, it is not surprising that the vexed relation of intellectuals to Communist parties should have been an enduring problem, or that their actions in this regard should have become the objects of intense recrimination and polemics late in the century following the massive discredit of the Soviet system and the fall of Communism in Eastern Europe. The pattern was established early, soon after the split of French Socialism at the *Congrès de Tours* (1920) established the *Parti communiste français* (PCF) and the *Section française de l'internationale ouvrière* (SFIO), the principal direct ancestor of the *Parti socialiste* (PS) of the last thirty years. In a famous speech at the Tours meeting, Léon Blum of the SFIO had refused to rally to the new Communist International based in Moscow, in part out of concern for the essentially intellectual values of openness and freedom of thought. Yet because of the SFIO's reformist tendencies, and because of the tremendous forward step for Socialism that the Soviet Union seemed to represent, many intellectuals saw support for the PCF as the only true, pure commitment to Socialism. Since the PCF and the Soviet Union were not organised to allow for much intellectual freedom, intellectuals almost immediately faced the problem of how, whether and to what extent they should subordinate their commitment to free enquiry and truth to their support for the Communist cause. This was the fundamental issue in a written exchange between the pacifist writers Romain Rolland (1866–1944) and Henri Barbusse (1873–1935).

Barbusse, author of France's most memorable Great War novel, *Le Feu* (1916), defended the need to support the positions of the PCF; in the years before his death, he became the party's most prominent writer and intellectual.

The tortuous history of relations between Surrealism and the PCF provides a striking example of the attractions and incompatibilities that the Communist cause presented to an aesthetic avant-garde movement. The Surrealists were above all revolutionaries of culture and the psyche, determined to use literary and artistic invention to break open and expand the mindset and social possibilities of a post-First World War Europe that seemed at once narrowly conventional and spiritually and morally exhausted. They were attracted to Communism for its possibilities of radical destruction and renewal, and believed they could offer it an avant-garde aesthetic that would help to undermine the bourgeois order. But their attempts to collaborate with the PCF, whether as members or as fellow-travellers, met with disapproval, warnings and often disavowal on the part of an organisation determined to promote and endorse only 'proletarian literature' and what would soon come to be known as 'socialist realism'. Especially after Stalin's consolidation of power in 1929, it became difficult for the Surrealists (or any other writers) to support the PCF on anything but the latter's own strict terms; even Barbusse was, for a time, suspect in the eyes of Moscow. By 1932, this led to a break between those Surrealists, like André Breton, who were unwilling to accept the Party's aesthetic dictates, and those, like Louis Aragon, who gave their allegiance to Stalinism.

André Gide's experience as a soon-disappointed fellow-traveller of Communism the mid-1930s was, for all his divergence from the Surrealists, similar. The brilliant writer and polemicist Paul Nizan, a self-proclaimed Communist, was never fully trusted by the PCF. Nonetheless, some intellectuals remained firmly within the Party orbit: a special issue of *Les Lettres françaises*, the Communist literary weekly, on the occasion of Stalin's death in 1953, featured front-page contributions from Aragon and the physicist Frédéric Joliot-Curie.

Commitment to Socialism occupied a crucial (though not truly central) place in the work of Jean-Paul Sartre (1905–80), the most famous French intellectual of the century. Largely apolitical in the 1930s and on the sidelines during the Occupation, Sartre became the archetype of the committed (*engagé*) writer and thinker in the postwar years. Commitment, he argued, was an inevitable consequence of existential freedom:

it is in the nature of human beings to fashion themselves and to remake their world through their choices and actions. To say that it is not one's business to try to change the world is thus to choose to reinforce the status quo. Although Sartre's existentialism is not, at its core, a philosophy of history, for much of his career he argued that a commitment to universal justice and freedom implies placing oneself on the side of the proletariat, the only class whose interests can be truly identified with universal ones, against the bourgeoisie, whose claims to universality for its values, plausibly advanced in the days of its struggle against the nobility, are false because it has become exclusionary and repressive in its struggle to retain power over the proletariat. Sartre thus agreed with the Marxist teaching that history has a direction, one that enables intellectuals to orientate their commitment to universal values towards particular causes and struggles. The extent to which this direction should correspond to that espoused by the Communist movement remained a vexed question for existentialist intellectuals: in the early postwar years, Sartre and his fellow philosopher Maurice Merleau-Ponty (1908–61) each for a time came close to supporting the positions of the PCF, only to decide that this was incompatible with intellectual freedom and integrity and to pull back. Sartre's sense of solidarity with all those whose claims represent a struggle of universal rights against the always particular forms of exclusion and oppression remains a powerful ideal of intellectual commitment; at the same time, his statement that his new postwar review, *Les Temps modernes*, would take a stand on every major issue that came along seems symptomatic of the pitfalls of superficiality and misjudgement to which such a general concept of commitment can often lead.

As events of the second half-century – the invasions of Hungary in 1956, Czechoslovakia in 1968 and Afghanistan in 1980 – inexorably discredited the progressive hopes once placed in Soviet-style Communism, support for the PCF among intellectuals all but collapsed. The decisive moment in the process was the publication of the French translation of Alexandr Solzhenytsen's *The Gulag Archipelago* in 1974: only then did denunciation of Soviet totalitarianism and rejection of the PCF become a major preoccupation of French intellectuals. (It was a central theme in the first works of Bernard-Henri Lévy and André Glucksmann, polemicists whom the media feverishly baptised the *nouveaux philosophes* in the late 1970s.) Around the same time, following the Czechoslovakia debacle and the rigid stance of the PCF during the May '68 student uprising in Paris, some intellectuals on the Left went through a period of intense admiration for the Communist China of Mao Zedong, but the influence of 'Maoism' quickly faded around 1976–7. By the time the PCF obtained four ministerial posts in the French government following the election of the Socialist François Mitterrand as President of the Republic in 1981, their presence seemed more a quirk or an aberration than a triumph to most of France's intellectuals.

May '68 and after

In recent generations, French intellectuals have increasingly been engaged by problems and issues related, in one way or another, to the economic and geopolitical changes of the postwar world. France has become both far more prosperous, and more obsessed with both the opportunities and the insecurity of a dynamic and open economy, than the intellectuals who flourished in the Third and even Fourth Republics could have imagined. At the same time, the country's position and identity have been affected by its relative decline in geopolitical importance, by decolonisation and new patterns of immigration, and by vast increases in the flow of money, information and cultural products across international borders. These conditions have given rise to situations in which it is difficult to distinguish a direction of history or to separate the application of intellectual ideals from the kind of realistic and worldly interests condemned by Péguy and Benda.

Such issues, of course, are by no means entirely new. The Algerian war of the 1950s was the most intense crisis of French decolonisation, but colonialism and its discontents were already major themes of French-language intellectual life between the wars. The colonial question divided intellectuals in ways not reducible to positions taken on nationalism or Socialism. Early in the century many partisans of the secular, anti-clerical Republic – anti-nationalists in this sense – approved France's colonial activities as part of a project of spreading the benefits of Enlightenment and modernity. As late as the Algerian War in the 1950s, it was possible to hear, in opposition to support for Algerian independence and denunciations of the French army's recourse to torture, intellectual arguments of a theoretically progressive character in favour of maintaining Algeria within the French Republic.

Of more lasting impact than the varying positions taken by the French, however, was the emergence of intellectual figures among the colonised peoples: individuals capable of articulating the demands and aspirations of their communities in ways that would be taken seriously within European culture. The *négritude* movement, founded by Martinique's Aimé Césaire (1913–) in collaboration with Sénégal's Léopold Sédar Senghor (1906–2001) in the 1930s, is in this regard exemplary. The art, music and poetry of Africa had been attracting the sympathetic attention of European avant-gardes since before the Great War, but only with Césaire, Senghor and their colleagues of the 1930s do African writers, chiefly poets, acquire the kind of cultural legitimacy and status that will enable them to bring the perspective of the colonised into the French intellectual field. As an affirmation of African identity and a challenge to the universality of European culture and thought, *négritude* was one of the first and most important of many identity-based challenges to the traditional identification of the modern alliance between the universal and the progressive. Both Césaire and Senghor had distinguished political careers, something almost inconceivable in France itself for poets and intellectuals of their stature; their trajectories emphasise that social power and symbolic capital were much less distanced from each other in Martinique and Sénégal than in France.

Another kind of intellectual intervention based in embodied identity can be found in feminism, for the long-standing cultural assumption that the masculine is the norm or universal causes the intellectual work and interventions of women to be judged in relation to their sex in a way that men's have seldom been. Women who made their mark on the intellectual life of the first part of the century included the physicist Marie Curie (1867–1934), the journalist and feminist Marguerite Durand (1864–1936), and the journalist and libertarian Socialist Séverine (Caroline Rémy, 1855–1929). But the most important woman intellectual of the century was the novelist and existentialist Simone de Beauvoir (1908–86). Companion to Sartre and his major collaborator in *Les Temps modernes*, Beauvoir became a major intellectual figure with the publication of her philosophical examination of woman's condition, *Le Deuxième Sexe* (1949). In this founding work of late twentieth-century feminism, Beauvoir emphatically refused the idea of a female or feminine essence: 'One is not born, but rather becomes, a woman'. Bringing the resources of post-Enlightenment philosophical criticism to bear on the question of woman's nature and place in society, Beauvoir argued that it is an illusion and a mystification to speak of female nature as a given, since the character and condition of women are socially constructed through a culture that excludes women from the public sphere and assigns them to roles of passivity and inaction. Arguably more existentialist and Marxist than specifically feminist, *Le Deuxième Sexe* nonetheless became a touchstone for women's movements world-wide throughout the second half of the century. Beauvoir herself was to declare herself a feminist and commit herself to women's causes only much later, beginning in the mid-1960s and especially in the wake of May '68.

The intellectual struggles of decolonisation, the *négritude* movement, and *Le Deuxième Sexe* could all be said to prefigure the emphasis on place, identity and embodiment that would take centre-stage in intellectual work and activism following May '68. The May 'events' were in many ways the emblematic moment of a new historical configuration far less defined by the issues of the French and proletarian revolutions. The student uprising was spontaneous and unexpected; in contrast to the Dreyfus affair and the creation of the Popular Front, intellectuals did not play a leading role. In its most radical aspirations, the spirit of May '68 was a condemnation of both the old rigidity and the new consumerism of French bourgeois society, a rejection by youth of the role of 'guard dog' for the established order, a position that Sartre saw as the inevitable alternative to progressive intellectual commitment for those who have received advanced education. Yet in other respects May '68 seems to have prepared the way for a more fully developed consumer society structured by a commitment to hedonistic values and differentiated market preferences, a society that blurs Durkheim's distinction between the good individualism of moral autonomy and the bad individualism of economic selfishness. The attempt to make the students' cause that of the workers, though it succeeded in briefly paralysing the country through strikes and thus creating the sense of a regime in crisis, ended with more incomprehension and mistrust than solidarity, and the government's deal with the unions to end the strikes by raising wages ultimately helped to fuel consumerism and diminish the clarity of traditional class oppositions.

One of the central features of the May '68 movements was what the historian Michel de Certeau called its insistence on 'speaking out' or 'taking the floor': a demand for liberation from the condition of being spoken for and represented, of being an object rather than a subject of knowledge. In the aftermath of May '68, the imperative for individuals and groups to speak out for themselves, in their own specificity, became part of a turn towards what has been called micropolitics, associated with what in the English-speaking world are often referred to as the

New Social Movements: the women's movement, the gay/lesbian movement, political ecology, the activism of racial minorities. These brought intellectual manifestoes and commitments of a largely new type, one that involved the body as well as the mind. This kind of activist stance had already been prefigured by *négritude* and feminism, and articulated in the writings of Jean Genet (1910–86) and Frantz Fanon (1925–61) – for example, in the latter's cry, 'O mon corps, fais de moi toujours un homme qui interroge!' (My body, always make of me a man who questions). Probably the most striking instance of an intellectual activism grounded in embodied particularity rather than abstract rationality was the 1971 'Appeal of 343 women' published in the left-leaning weekly *Le Nouvel observateur* on behalf of the right to legal abortion. Evoking the estimated 1 million women undergoing illegal and often dangerous abortions in France each year, the appeal stated, 'I declare that I am one of them. I declare that I have had an abortion.' Some of the signatories were well known as writers, scholars and artists, but many were not, and the authority of their intervention was based more on their experience of abortion than on their intellectual status.

While causes based in identity and experience, like that of abortion legalisation, often have the support and participation of intellectuals, they raised new problems for the practice of intellectual intervention. Together with the discredit of the Soviet Union and more generally of Marxism, the post-1968 changes in social movements undermined the notion of a unitary subject of history (such as the proletarian, the colonised subject, or the citizen of the Third World). What could a total intellectual on the Sartrean mould bring to the cause of women, of homosexuals, of prisoners, of second-generation immigrants? At best, expression of a general solidarity; at worst, a usurping of the specific subjectivity located in particular bodies, communities and cultures. It was no accident that the arguably most prominent intellectual of the 1970s, Michel Foucault (1926–84), was a systematic critic of the confinement and marginalisation to which those defined as deviant – the insane, prisoners, non-heterosexuals, etc – were subjected by the institutions of supposedly liberal society and the modern state. Characteristically, Foucault's most notable role in intellectuals' activism was as a co-founder of the *Groupe d'information sur les prisons* (Prison Information Group), which attempted to document and denounce conditions in the French penal system. It is consistent with Foucault's insights – and with the May '68 imperative to 'speak out' – that some of the most characteristic movements on behalf of rights and justice in recent years, such as the anti-racist *SOS-Racisme* and the gay anti-AIDS organisation *ACT UP*, have been neither founded nor directed by intellectuals, although in many respects they seek a role as national conscience not unlike that with which intellectuals were once strongly associated.

Identity- and community-based movements have even come into conflict with the tradition of intellectuals rallying to defend the secularism and universality of the French Republic. For some thinkers, any emphasis on particular communities carries the risk of corporatism or even privilege, forms of social organisation incompatible with a conception of the Republic based on the abstract equality of individuals. This concern sometimes focuses on the ideal of secularism, as in the notorious *affaire du foulard* of 1989–90, in which many intellectuals of the Left defended the State's right to prohibit Muslim women from wearing the *chador* or veil to school on the grounds that as a religious symbol it violates the principle of republican education. To many observers outside of France's particular republican traditions, such a prohibition seemed a strange cause for intellectuals, opposing as it did both individual freedom in general and the expression of an already much vilified minority culture in particular. Opposition to the politics of identity-based communities often takes the form of anti-Americanism, a rejection of putatively American multiculturalism as being inherently anti-republican and even un-French; this sort of argument is particularly common in anti-feminist polemics.

Comparison of France to the United States, often in the context of polemical reporting on the USA as the country of modernity, has been a major topic of intellectual pronouncements throughout the century. In the early part of the century, critical views of the USA often rehearsed themes of conservative nationalism such as the danger of racial mixing or the threat posed by mass society to the traditions of French and European culture. During the early years of the Cold War, opposition to American economic aid and influence via the Marshall Plan was more often than not a corollary of support for Soviet Socialism. In recent years, however, the United States are much more identified in France with the dynamism and competitiveness of the global economy and with the ubiquity of English as an international language. In this context, a somewhat defensive nationalistic reaction can be discerned, one that is neither reactionary nor pro-Communist but that is organised around a defence of republican and social-democratic values. Thus when many categories of French workers struck in November and December 1995 to protest against government plans to curtail pension and health benefits, they were supported by a petition of intellectuals led by the prominent sociologist Pierre Bourdieu (1930–2002). The intellectuals' petition stated that the strikers were defending not special interests or privileges but 'the most universal benefits of the Republic . . . equality of rights for all'.

Bourdieu was arguably France's most prominent intellectual at the century's end, in part for his specifically sociological work on the ways in which educational and cultural inequality reproduce social inequality in France, in large part for his defence of social democracy and denunciation of globalised *laissez-faire* capitalism, and to an increasing extent for his defence of the specificity and function of the intellectual. Although a critic of Sartre's philosophy and of the tendency of some intellectuals to pronounce on anything and everything, Bourdieu in the main defended a canonical conception of the intellectual as one whose authority must be conferred by peers rather than by the public or the mass media, and whose interventions defend universal values. He saw the status and rule of the intellectual as under attack above all from the workings of new media such as television, at least in their current economic configuration: the mass media confer visibility (and, by extension, authority) on those who are capable of reaching the largest audiences rather than on those who are recognised by their fellow cultural producers. Television thus fosters an intellectual demagoguery that consists of persuading the public rather than convincing one's peers.

Bourdieu therefore linked his defence of the legitimately conferred authority and the critical mission of the intellectual with his critique of the extension of market mechanisms and behaviour into ever more areas of life. It is a serious argument for maintaining a role that has a largely honourable history of over a century. As the reflexive stance of an intellectual writing about the role of the intellectual, it is well suited to the retrospective character of much recent intellectual life in France: biographies and re-evaluations of major figures like Sartre, Jacques Lacan and Michel Foucault; re-examination of collaboration and the crimes of the Vichy regime; judgement with the benefit of hindsight of the intellectual support once extended to Stalin and Mao.

In contrast to Bourdieu's defence of the canonical role of the intellectual, Régis Debray (1940–) argued in a 1998 memoir that it is a role whose best days are in the past: one that, if it survives at all in the new century and media environment, will have to do so on more modest terms. For Debray, who in his recent work has tried to define a field of *mediology*, or study of cultural transmission and mediation, the canonical figure of the intellectual was strongly linked to the organisation of mature print culture: the forms of literacy needed to enter the category of possible intellectuals, the authority acquired within a field of cultural producers sharply differentiated from its audience, the network of publication that would assure the diffusion of declarations. Of course, all networks of publication and distribution have always been partial and finite, the propagation of ideas always fragile and imperfect. But when the order of the print media was so well established as to seem almost natural, the problem of transmission could largely be set aside and intellectuals could assume that their writings were doing what writings were supposed to do. That is no longer the case in the still emerging multi-media order in which television and the Internet bid to outweigh print. The new media do not just bring different forms of communication: having arisen in different historical contexts, they are different kinds of social institutions, organised in response to different imperatives.

Under these conditions, it may be impossible to insist on the norms of intellectual autonomy and legitimacy once so crucial to defining who could be an intellectual and to establishing the public authority of those so defined. The confusion of genres and the intervention of 'television intellectuals' can be contested, but it surely cannot be stopped. Indeed, to try to do so would be to stifle one of the zones in which, for better or worse, active transmission of ideas – as opposed to their mere publication – has the best chance of taking place. There are surely many citizens capable of having their minds engaged by people skilled in audiovisual communication who would never be touched by a printed tract, and by what right should their form of reception and participation be deemed an unworthy object of intellectual life? The recent phenomenon of *cafés philosophiques* and of associated activities and publications on the Web shows the interest in an active and public intellectual life outside the traditional institutions of scholarly and writerly legitimacy and the unidirectional transmission of print publication. However uncertain the fate of the canonical role of the intellectual in the twenty-first century, it seems safe to say that as long as France continues to benefit from a fundamentally strong system of secondary education, it will continue to be a society comparatively rich in serious intellectual productions, pronouncements and exchanges of many kinds, one in which the life of the mind will follow both old and new paths to the public sphere.

FURTHER READING

Benda, Julien, *The Treason of the Intellectuals*, New York: Norton, 1969 (*La Trahison des clercs*, 1927).

Judt, Tony, *Past Imperfect: French Intellectuals, 1944–1956*, Berkeley: University of California Press, 1992.

Julliard, Jacques, and Michel Winock (eds.), *Dictionnaire des intellectuels français*, Paris: Seuil, 1996.

Lilla, Mark, *The Reckless Mind: Intellectuals in Politics*, New York: New York Review Books, 2001.

Lottman, Herbert R., *The Left Bank*, Boston: Houghton Mifflin, 1982.

8

Religion, politics and culture in France

Introduction

In 1873, the French National Assembly voted to build a church on Montmartre hill, looking over Paris, as a better way of dealing with social unrest than the alternative proposal of an army barracks. This Church of the Sacred Heart (Sacré-Coeur) is now a national symbol and tourist attraction. But it was originally designed as a gesture of national contrition, seeking divine forgiveness for a military defeat, in the Franco-Prussian War (1870–71), and for a Socialist revolution, in the Paris Commune (1871), the short-lived people's government which refused to surrender and tried to introduce a new social order in the besieged city. In many ways, this moment sets the scene for the complex and passionate relationship between religion and politics in twentieth-century France, and for the deep and long-running conflicts they have embodied. It also provides a benchmark against which to measure the changes that have taken place over the past century or more.

This episode raises three enduring issues, which continue to preoccupy French society today. The first is the relationship between religion and the State. The builders of the Sacré-Coeur were staunch advocates of an inseparable link between the Catholic Church and the French State, but that link was decisively broken thirty years later. In the ensuing century since then, France has groped towards new ways of addressing the place of religious beliefs in the life of the nation, and managing the surges of passion that the question arouses. The second issue is the relationship between religion and politics. The Catholics of the nineteenth century struggled for the soul of France in opposition to Socialists and radical republicans, and both sides defined their own identity in the process.

But in the twentieth century, many creeds and doctrines have struggled for the hearts and minds of French people. Spiritual and secular movements have elicited equally staunch levels of partisanship, with a surprising similarity of methods, and in a bewildering dance of shifting alliances with each other. The third issue is the role of culture in politics and religion. The French State built the Sacré-Coeur as a rampart against social revolution, counting on its symbolic power and architectural dominance to awe, bully or persuade the people of Paris into an acceptance of the new order that had put down their insurrection in blood. Since that time, political and religious movements, as well as the State, have attached great importance to the role of culture (broadly understood) in gaining acceptance of their ideas and objectives. This chapter will explore these three themes through the religious and political culture of France of the twentieth century, and will conclude by suggesting that recent cultural events enable us to benchmark the distance that France has travelled from an anti-modern to a postmodern state.

Religion and the State

The link between Church and State was a long and contentious one in French history, even before the French Revolution of 1789 sought to sweep away the Catholic Church with the Monarchy. Thereafter, and for most of the nineteenth century, the Church positioned itself firmly in alliance with the succession of kings and emperors who offered authoritarian political systems, and against the 'modern' movements that tried to reintroduce republican and democratic institutions. It kept its powerful position in the early years of the Third Republic, as the building of the Sacré-Coeur demonstrates, but began to lose some of its strength during the 1880s with the onset of accelerating industrial development. The growth of working populations in the larger cities and towns was largely ignored by the Church, which saw them as dangerous seedbeds of revolution. Church power was also undermined by the rapidly expanding state education system, designed to reverse the economic, technological and military backwardness that had proved so disastrous in preparing the defeat of 1871. The emergence of a large workforce of lay teachers throughout the country was seen as a threat to religious authority. Many a village was torn by conflict between the opposing figures of the priest (*curé*) and the teacher (*instituteur*), the one nurturing faith and obedience while the other taught reason and free enquiry. These developments were echoed in many areas of national life, with urban workers and educated professionals swelling the opposition to traditional Catholicism. Much of the conflict was crystallised in the Dreyfus Affair, around the eve of the twentieth century. It revolved around the case of Alfred Dreyfus, an Alsatian Jewish army officer, found guilty in 1894 of passing military secrets to the Germans. He was convicted of treason and imprisoned on Devil's Island. Evidence of his innocence was suppressed by the army general staff, but growing disquiet led to a press campaign for the case to be reviewed, sparked by a celebrated article in 1898 by the novelist Emile Zola, entitled 'J'Accuse' (I Accuse). Dreyfus was pardoned in 1899 and his conviction eventually quashed in 1906. In the meantime, supporters and opponents of Dreyfus became increasingly impassioned, driving many sections of French society to take sides in the Affair. The Church became embroiled, aligning itself with the army and the values of authority. The professions and the middle-class intelligentsia opposed them, rallying round calls for truth, justice and human rights.

The divisions provoked by the Affair increased the polarisations in French society to the point of national crisis. It was in part resolved by a constitutional change, which provided for the separation of Church and State, officially promulgated in 1905. The key provision was that priests and religious observances were formally excluded from state schools and from the state apparatus. This was expressed in the doctrine of '*laïcité*' (roughly meaning a secular state), a much-debated concept originally designed to demarcate the responsibilities of the State and the Catholic Church, especially in education. Over the years, it has been expanded to accommodate a variety of social changes, and broadly means that the State is separated from religious institutions and has a policy of neutrality towards them. Religious organisations have no official standing within the institutions of the State, which in turn plays no role in organised religious bodies. The difficulty of *laïcité* is that it highlights a difference between the State and the Nation. Whereas in many respects, the French State presents itself as the embodiment of the nation (*la patrie*), in particular respect of religious and ideological beliefs it is neutral. Standing apart from these passionately contested matters, the State can therefore not embody a significant dimension of the real life of the nation.

The movements of both Left and Right energetically exploited this difficulty. The Left, with limited success, argued that religion was a thing of the past, which had no place in a modern democratic society. These views were expressed with some virulence by anti-clerical groupings, linking with the centrist Radical republican parties. The Right, with perhaps more success, argued that the Third Republic was inherently unable to represent the 'real' nation, because it did not reflect the overwhelmingly Catholic composition of the population. These views were most forcefully articulated by the leading right-wing nationalist newspaper, *Action française*, and the movement grouped around it. Led by the writer Charles Maurras, it argued for an 'integral' nationalism, which could only be achieved by the restoration of the Monarchy and the former rights of the Catholic Church. The newspaper offered vitriolic polemics against the institutions and parties of the Republic, attributing France's ills to a combination of scheming foreigners, unpatriotic traitors, and lack of strong leadership. Jews, freemasons and Socialists were prominent among its targets. It became highly influential, especially in Catholic circles, and enjoyed the support of Pope Pius X (1903–14), who took the opportunity it offered to strengthen Vatican control over the French bishops.

The institutions of the Third Republic survived, however, and if anything were strengthened by the outbreak of war in 1914. All sections of the population were mobilised in different ways. President Poincaré formed a broad national coalition government, which he called the Sacred Union (*union sacrée*). It set aside many divisions in the interests of pursuing victory, and largely secured national unity across the political spectrum for the duration of the war. The postwar governments of the early 1920s were ultra-conservative, much like those of the 1870s, and sought to negotiate restored relations between Church and State. Though opposed by the depleted republican Left, these moves were even more strongly opposed by the Catholic bishops, who wanted no compromise with the Republic and its associated values of democracy, secularism and social reform. The bishops' intransigence delighted *Action française*, but dismayed the Vatican, which now favoured an accommodation with the French government. Rome also feared that the integrist newspaper was beginning to appear too much as the political voice of the Church, usurping the latter's authority. In 1926 it was announced that the paper was henceforth on the *Index of Prohibited Books*, which Catholics were therefore forbidden to read. This disavowal provoked tectonic movements, which eventually saw the emergence of a moderate centrist movement catering for a mainly Catholic constituency within a democratic republican context, in the form of Christian Democracy. The late 1920s also saw the emergence of a series of Catholic action movements, aimed at young people from particular social groups, including urban workers (*Jeunesse ouvrière chrétienne*), rural workers (*Jeunesse agricole chrétienne*), students (*Jeunesse étudiante chrétienne*) and the professional classes (*Jeunesse indépendante chrétienne*). Working within mainstream social and political institutions, their members were trained to provide the Catholic elite of the next generation.

The reluctant accommodation of the Church with the Republic proved surprisingly durable, but not before it had been tested in the painful circumstances of the Second World War. After the Fall of France in June 1940, and during the Nazi Occupation, Marshal Pétain's ultra-conservative Vichy regime provided an opportunity to restore the fortunes of the Catholic Church in France. Declaring a 'National Revolution' to return France to its traditional values, he replaced the Third Republic with the *Etat français* (French State), and replaced the republican motto of Liberty, Equality and Fraternity with a Catholic-inspired alternative: Work, Family, Fatherland (*travail, famille, patrie*). Amid the overwhelming popular support he initially attracted, Pétain's most loyal and fervent supporters were the French bishops, some of whom outdid him in their enthusiasm for collaboration with Nazi Germany. A remarriage of Church and State seemed the inevitable outcome, encouraged by the strong representation of *Action française* leaders in the corridors of Vichy, and the strongly Catholic orientation of the Vichy youth movements.

Inspired by Mussolini's example in Italy, Pétain planned a new Concordat redefining relations between the Church and State. However, it never came about, owing to the perhaps unexpected complexity of those relations. While the integrists, and perhaps Pétain himself, looked forward to a union that would be dominated by the State, the Catholic bishops were reluctant to submit to direct state control, even by an avowedly Catholic state. The Vatican too was reluctant to envisage state intervention in such matters as the appointment of bishops and priests, or to hand over control of important Catholic institutions such as youth movements and charitable works. In the early months of 1941, there was a concerted effort to restore the Church's role in education, led by the Catholic philosopher Jacques Chevalier. As minister for education he introduced state aid to private Catholic schools and reintroduced religious teaching and Catholic symbols into state schools. He closed teacher training schools, noted for their enthusiasm for *laïcité*, and dismissed hundreds of teachers suspected of being freemasons or otherwise anti-Catholic. The result was met with such hostility in the schools that his successor, Jérôme Carcopino, had to rescind the more aggressive pro-Catholic measures.

At the end of the Occupation, the Church found itself deeply compromised by its enthusiasm for Vichy and the timidity of its response to the oppression and atrocities carried out by the regime and by the occupying forces. At the same time, religious practices had rarely been more popular, and the potential of the Church to assist in unifying the nation was sorely needed after the Liberation. The delicate balance was demonstrated by the service held in the cathedral of Notre-Dame de Paris on 26 August 1944 at the end of the week in which the French capital was liberated. The *Magnificat* was sung, in thanksgiving for victory, in the presence of General de Gaulle, newly arrived leader of the provisional government. But the Cardinal Archbishop of Paris, Monsignor Suhard, did not greet him, and was not present at the service, at the request of de Gaulle, who considered him compromised by his previous support for Pétain and Vichy.

Although in a formal sense, the separation of Church and State was reaffirmed at the Liberation, the spirit of their relations was in reality much more co-operative than it had been. The bishops had every incentive to make amends for the blemishes (or ambiguities) of their wartime record, and accepted the demarcation of responsibilities with little demur. De Gaulle was a devout Catholic, and so were the Christian democrats who formed a major force in most of the governments of the Fourth Republic. The Church operated in a climate of general public tolerance, and was left largely alone to pursue its spiritual and pastoral purposes. The return of *laïcité* was remarkably consensual, even in the area of education, where a judicious compromise was reached protecting the secularity of state education but providing a measure of state support for private Catholic and Jewish schools. Compromise also included the continued exemption of the Alsace and Lorraine region from the separation, which it had missed in 1905, since at that time the region had been under German administration. This postwar religious settlement was never thereafter seriously threatened. The Catholic voice has certainly been heard in politics, but as the voice of reason rather than authority. It has generally found a range of allies when it has argued, for example, for measures against prostitution, for stricter censorship of publications, for restrictions on contraception or divorce, or for improvements in social welfare. An echo of former conflicts emerged in 1984, when the Socialist minister, Alain Savary, proposed changes in the conditions for state subsidy of private education, and was met by huge public protests. The predominantly Catholic protesters were almost immediately successful in persuading President Mitterrand to withdraw the changes and accept the minister's resignation. It was generally noted, however, that the concerns of the protesters were at least as much about educational opportunities as about religious rights.

The comfortable relations between the State and religion were challenged during the 1990s by the emergence of awareness that Islam had by then become a substantial religious group in France. Largely as a result of successive waves of immigrants from North and sub-Saharan Africa, there are now around 4 million Moslems in France. They remain a minority in comparison to 39 million Catholics, but they already outnumber Protestants (1 million), Jews (600,000) and Buddhists (500,000). For the most part, Moslems have readily accepted the secular nature of French society, though so far no Moslem schools have been authorised to receive state support of the kind available to Christian or Jewish denominations. A series of incidents began in 1989, when Moslem girls were sent home from school because they were wearing headscarves (*foulards islamiques*, sometimes called *hejab*), deemed to be tokens of their religion and therefore in breach of *laïcité*. These sparked off a series of public debates about the nature of *laïcité*, the compatibility of Islam with French law, and the position of women in Islamic doctrine. In purely legal terms, these episodes have been settled without much difficulty. Courts have consistently ruled against the exclusion of girls for wearing such headscarves, maintaining that religious believers have the right to express their faith in school premises and other public places, though they are prohibited from proselytising there. In other words, they may display religious tokens, but must not attempt to convert others to sharing their beliefs within state institutions. The same restriction applies to members of other religions.

The controversy over headscarves may be at root an ethnic rather than a religious issue, though it is difficult to separate issues of belief from issues of culture and identity. It is often observed that Christians and Jews have for many years worn their religious symbols without challenge from those who now object to headscarves. The strictures of *laïcité* are invoked against the latter with a passion that does not apply even-handedly to other religions. There are some contemporary advocates of *laïcité* who regard it in the same terms as the militant secularists of the republican Left in 1905, that is, as a compromise position which should be used to advance an agenda of opposition to all religions. But these are a dwindling group within an increasingly secular society, where religion is regarded as a personal lifestyle choice, and viewed with indifference by a growing proportion of the population. Paradoxically, the well-documented decline of traditional religious practice may itself be reason why some French people express a fear of Islam. They may feel disarmed in the face of religious enthusiasm which they cannot match.

More generally, though, the Islamic challenge has been debated in terms of the French Republic's long-term commitment to 'universalism'. Arguing that a democratic republic must apply universal principles, advocates of universalism have taken the principle of equality to mean that all French citizens should be treated equally, with no concessions to the specific requirements of particular groups or identities. This position has always been contested by the anti-republican and nationalist Right, who argue that France is a particular country with a specific history and personality, which should be recognised in laws giving a special preference to the majority ethnic and religious group. This is a thread common to the 'integrism' of *Action française* in the 1890s and the 'préférence française' of the *Front national* in the 1990s. However, universalism is also contested on the Left, by those who argue for a 'multi-cultural' society in which the specific identities of all cultural groups should be recognised and respected, whether the identities are based on ethnicity, language, religion, class, gender, sexuality or lifestyle. Within the centre ground of French politics, some proponents of universalism undoubtedly use it as a means to enforce a *status quo*, to which they wish everyone to conform. But others argue that universalism is an indispensable principle that enables France to remain a single and undivided country in the face of pressures which could pull it apart, especially the drive for regional autonomy. The example of former Yugoslavia is often invoked to illustrate the consequences which might so easily follow. It is unlikely that this debate will be rapidly concluded. The dialectical relationship between unity and diversity is a dynamic one, and with a covert pragmatism that belies the widespread rhetoric of absolutes, the French state apparatus still manages to negotiate working arrangements with the diverse and often conflicting identities of a complex modern society.

Religion and politics

One of the most feared recent developments in the rise of Islam in France is the growth of Islamic fundamentalist groups, referred to as 'Islamists'. Taking their religious beliefs to have direct consequences for political and social action, they tend to reject any clear-cut distinction between politics and religion. They profess an integral faith, which combines political and religious commitment in ways that recall the integral Catholics who were so prominent in France a century previously. The fear they inspire in some parts of French public opinion can to some extent be traced to those earlier struggles, in which the separation of the religious and political spheres became a condition for the emergence of a democratic and republican form of government.

With hindsight, it may be argued that the Separation of Church and State in 1905 spelled the end of integral Catholic nationalism as a viable political force. However, the success of the separation was for a long time in doubt, and it continued to be fiercely contested for a further forty years. That contest shaped public perceptions of the relationship between religion and politics, not least by providing a sense of polarity between two logically opposed positions. The integrists on one hand advocated religion as an indispensable component of their political programme, while the secularists on the other hand advocated the exclusion of all religious considerations from the political arena. In practice, a spectrum of intermediate positions was possible, and most of those positions were catered for by various political groupings. The more militant anti-religious or anti-clerical positions were focused in the centrist parties, with Emile Combes of the Radicals as their emblematic representative, though they were also well represented in the Socialist parties of the Left. However, the Left also had other significant currents, including those that looked to the Christian spirituality of the Sermon on the Mount to inform their social awareness, and those that considered religious belief to be a matter of private conscience for the individual. On the moderate Right, there were many whose political authoritarianism or social conservatism drew explicitly or implicitly on their Catholic beliefs, but who kept their politics at arms length from their religion.

The integrist advocacy of a Catholic state for a Catholic people attracted sympathy across a wide range of Catholic opinion, even among those who did not share its view that this could only be achieved through a restored monarchy. But it was ultimately dependent on at least tacit support from the Church itself. So when the Vatican announced its prohibition of *Action française* in 1926, the plausibility of the integrist position was fatally undermined. Not surprisingly, *Action française* supporters rose in revolt against the papal act of authority, but by doing so they made themselves easier to identify and isolate. Many of its supporters among the clergy were swiftly removed from positions of influence, particularly from the key areas of education, vocational training, sensitive chaplaincies and youth work.

Fellow-travellers of *Action française* among the Catholic intelligentsia began to reconsider their position. Particularly influential among them was the philosopher Jacques Maritain, who had made his reputation with a detailed reworking of the thought of the medieval philosopher St Thomas Aquinas, and with some scholarly polemics against the 'modernist' ideas of Protestantism and the Enlightenment. He opposed Maurras's view that politics should come first (*politique d'abord*), and argued that spiritual matters should have priority (*primauté du spirituel*). This echoed the bishops' concern that they were being railroaded into support for a political programme over which they had no control, and it was common knowledge that, despite his pro-Catholic politics, Maurras was himself an atheist. Maritain proposed a distinction between two types of political actions open to the faithful. Some actions were a necessary consequence of Catholic faith, and therefore required of all Catholics, *en tant que catholiques* (by virtue of being Catholic). Other actions, he argued, might be undertaken by Catholics, *en catholiques* (in a Catholic manner), carrying them out in a way that was informed by Catholic values, but concerned matters on which conscientious Catholics could hold different views from each other. Since most of the political domain fell into the second category of actions, the distinction gave Catholics a greater sense of freedom to choose between parties, rather than feel obliged to follow the 'Catholic party line' proposed by *Action française*.

Through the 1930s, political parties of the Left and Centre began to develop Catholic support. A small Christian Democratic party emerged, and became a minor current within centrist politics. Catholics began to join the Socialist Party in larger numbers, despite the fierce anti-clericalism they often encountered there. A small number joined the Communist Party, and some went so far as to form a small revolutionary Catholic movement, *Terre nouvelle* (New Earth), with a striking logo that combined the Christian cross with the Communist hammer and sickle emblem. These shifts were visible in the rapid growth of broad anti-Fascist movements in France, culminating in the Centre-Left coalition that formed the Popular Front government of 1936. On the other hand, many Catholics also gravitated towards the extreme right-wing movements that were looking for inspiration to Mussolini's Italy and Hitler's Germany. The growing diversity of Catholic political choices was also reflected in French responses to the Spanish Civil War. The insurgent Generals, led by Franco, had gained the support of the Spanish bishops, declared their actions to be a crusade, and sought international support from Catholics. Images of gutted churches and executed priests were circulated in order to stir up feeling. However, prominent figures like the writers François Mauriac and Georges Bernanos wrote openly expressing their reservations about the Franco side, and in general this discouraged French Catholics from being stampeded into a holy war.

The Popular Front elections were notable in inaugurating a key shift in the political and religious landscape. In a much-commented radio broadcast of April 1936, the leader of the French Communist Party (PCF), Maurice Thorez, announced that he was offering an outstretched hand (*main tendue*) to Catholic workers, whom he regarded as brothers to their secular fellow workers, sharing the same problems and concerns (women did not at this time have the right to vote). The short-term effect among Catholics was to sow consternation among priests who were alarmed at the prospect of their congregations turning Communist, and to encourage a small number of workers and intellectuals to consider supporting the Communists for the first time. Within the year, Pope Pius XI issued an encyclical letter, *Divini Redemptoris* (March 1937), denouncing atheistic Communism, and warning against Communist attempts in several countries to woo Catholic workers. The announcement also caused alarm among Communists who were often accustomed to identifying Catholics as ideological enemies, though it allowed others to feel more relaxed about the Catholic background which many members of the party had in common, and enabled them to cast their political alliances even more broadly. The iron discipline of the Party meant that Thorez's policy brought an abrupt end to Communist attacks on religious believers and Catholic organisations. The longer-term effects were more important, however. Rather than being a temporary gesture of electoral opportunism, the outstretched hand gradually became established as a permanent stance of Communist preparedness to co-operate with Catholics, with its first dramatic results during the Occupation.

The shift also revealed an unexpected parallelism between the Catholic Church and the Communist Party. Founded in 1920 as a result of an acrimonious schism within the French Socialist movement, the Party gradually developed as an alternative community with a close-knit organisational structure, an increasingly codified belief system, and a cadre of professional organisers. It was a member of the Moscow-based

Third International, also known as the Communist International (or Comintern), the organisation that directed the activities of Communist parties throughout the world. This affiliation mirrored the Church's allegiance to Rome, and it proved able to inspire conspicuous acts of loyalty and self-sacrifice. Like the Church, the Communist party also built up a wide array of associated movements catering for different groups (such as women, youth, students or farm workers), campaigning for different causes (such as anti-Fascism, social welfare, international friendship), and developing a range of publications and cultural activities. It also drew on a powerful source of support and dissemination in the trade union movement. Although other political parties had developed significant social and cultural networks, none could match the extent and integration of the Communist network or the discipline of this party, which prided itself on being unlike the rest (*un parti pas comme les autres*). As a result, the incipient dialogue between Catholics and Communists became a defining feature of the mid-century, from the 1940s to the 1980s, with surprising points of convergence alongside the perpetual tension between them.

The first fruits of convergence came during the Occupation. Despite the Pétainist leanings of the Church hierarchy, many lay Catholics and substantial numbers of junior clergy gradually entered the Resistance movements. There they found a diversity of non-Catholics including strong and well-organised Communist networks. The desire for national liberation was a strong incentive to set aside old ideological and political differences in the common struggle to end the Nazi Occupation. The outstretched hand policy provided a useful framework, and as a result, many firm bonds of co-operation and mutual respect were forged in action. They were famously celebrated by the Communist writer Louis Aragon, in his much recited poem 'La rose et le réséda' (The Rose and the Gillyflower), with its recurring chorus 'Celui qui croyait au ciel, celui qui n'y croyait pas' (He who believed in Heaven, he who did not). Catholics and Communists both had their share of heroic figures and martyrs in the Resistance and in deportation to concentration camps. But while both could point to a proud wartime record, neither was entirely unblemished. The collaborationism of senior Catholic clergy was a particular embarrassment, but the Communists also had some difficult questions to answer about their activities between the signing of the Hitler–Stalin non-aggression pact (August 1939) and the Nazi invasion of the Soviet Union (June 1941).

At the Liberation, there were many points of common action between Catholics and Communists, all of whom felt the overwhelming need for national unity to reconstruct their country. While a significant number of young Catholics joined the Communist Party at that time, more Catholics turned to the Popular Republican Movement (MRP), a Christian Democrat party founded in 1944, which together with the Socialists and Communists formed the coalition governments of the early Fourth Republic. Initially inspired by progressive projects of reform, the MRP was led by elites who had been formed in the Catholic Action groups of the 1930s and in the Resistance. They had no immediate competition for Catholic support, since the conservative Right and the extreme Right *Action française* movement had been thoroughly discredited by their wartime collaboration with Nazism. The MRP also reflected the social conservatism of its mainly Catholic constituency, especially in its policies on matters of health and social security. However, unlike the powerful Christian democratic movements of German or Italy, it proved unable to exercise a monopoly over its constituency. Many Catholics moved over to the conservative Gaullist movement when it was launched in 1947, or drifted back to other right-wing groupings which emerged from their enforced quiescence in later years. The MRP was a depleted force by the end of the Fourth Republic (1958) and attracted much of the blame for the latter's demise. The movement was formally disbanded in 1967, to be replaced by a series of small groupings, usually allied to the Right.

The decline and fall of the MRP marked the last attempt to institutionalise Catholicism in mainstream French politics, though several parties attract a strong base of support among Catholics. This is especially true on the Right, which regularly gains two-thirds of the Catholic electorate. However, a significant number of devout Catholics militate in left-wing and Green parties, expressing an ardent commitment to improving conditions in the Third World, ending capitalist exploitation, or protecting the global environment. And most parties are conscious of the need to accommodate Catholic opinion among their voters. For the most part, this is reckoned a normal issue of political marketing, and parties also keep an eye on the attitudes of other religious groups. Jews and Protestants have more often been attracted to the parties of the Left, and the Socialists in particular have produced prime ministers from both these traditions.

More recently, the emergence of a large Islamic community has posed challenges to all parties, and the Socialist, Communist and Green parties have responded with some energy to develop political participation in groups from immigrant backgrounds. Conversely, the Right, and especially the far Right, have been inclined to identify Moslems as essentially foreign and therefore having no role in French politics. In response, the majority of Moslem voters look to existing parties to represent their interests. But a small minority, especially among young people, have looked to Islamist movements, associating themselves with one or other of the many international politico-religious movements and operating in a quasi-clandestine fashion in areas with large immigrant communities. These have so far made only a marginal impact on political life, not least because of the variety and divisions within the Muslim population, which does not provide a large homogeneous political constituency. However, Islamic 'integrism' is felt as a potential threat among the majority population, and the emergence of a specifically French Islamism remains a widespread fear.

This fear echoes the concern of universalists that coherent and self-contained communities are factors of division in the nation. However, they are also concerned that the rapid social changes in modern globalised society may be undermining traditional forms of community affiliation, with potentially damaging consequences for national identity. The steady decline of religious practice in the Catholic, Protestant and Jewish communities is noticeably diluting these identities. And the same phenomenon appears to be affecting the main political parties, who register an increased volatility and shifting loyalties among their constituencies, accompanied very often by growing 'apathy' among voters. Increasing mobility of population and access to communications technology are factors in loosening traditional bonds, and reducing the loyalty of individuals to particular organisations. In the market of public opinion, beliefs and values appear as matters for consumer choice rather than the obligations of life-long membership in a political or religious community. New political groupings and new religious sects compete with the established ones, and both compete for attention with the attractions of sporting and leisure activities, single-issue social campaigns, self-improvement techniques and media events. French people now have a boundless variety of options from which to develop their social profile and sense of personal identity. Increasingly the evidence is that they are exercising their options in the *à la carte* mode, composing a portfolio of personal preferences for which they are answerable only to themselves, rather than accepting the *table d'hôte* approach of a set menu of life choices offered by the traditional political parties and religious organisations.

Culture, politics and religion

In a society where the media are now so pervasive, the power of shared public images is universally recognised as crucially important in binding French people into a sense of community. This recognition has grown more prominent in recent years, but the construction of the Sacré-Coeur in the mid 1870s is a reminder that the State and the Church were already aware of the potency of cultural symbols at that time. As the twentieth century developed, this awareness extended to all aspects of cultural life, and was developed with growing effectiveness by political parties, especially on the Left.

Imposing symbols of the French State are built into the architecture of the country, especially in Paris. The Eiffel Tower, built for the 1889 World Fair, and commemorating the centenary of the French Revolution, has become the universally recognised symbol of the country and its capital. As a striking but abstract geometrical construction, it has no figurative meaning, despite its often remarked phallic connotations and the feat of engineering involved in its construction. Nor does it have any specific social function, despite the restaurant, viewing platforms and broadcasting equipment now built into it – the tower is not a restaurant or radio mast as such. In this sense, the Eiffel Tower is an assertion of universal principles. It may be seen as a counter-point to the Sacré-Coeur, which has the social function of a church, and is named after the Sacred Heart of Jesus, one of the most specifically Catholic of Christian religious emblems.

Though there were further world fairs, including those of 1900 and 1937, and great exhibitions, including the Colonial Exhibition of 1931, for most of the early twentieth century the dynamism of French culture came from civil society (individual initiative, religious and political organisations) rather than the State. Publishing of books, newspapers, reviews and magazines developed into a powerful industry. Sport assumed growing importance as France built on the prewar achievements of people like the Baron Pierre de Coubertin, founder of the modern Olympic Games. Football, rugby, tennis, cycling, motor racing and winter sports all developed into large-scale activities for both spectators and participants, drawing substantial industrial sponsorship. Paris and Chamonix hosted the 1924 Olympic Games, crowning thirty years of Coubertin's presidency of the Olympic movement. The 1920s and 1930s were a golden age of cinema-going and film production. They also saw the birth of radio as a mass medium, developed partly by state action, but increasingly through private radio stations. Alongside private enterprise, an energetic voluntary sector entered the cultural domain. Religious organisations, trade unions, political parties and other affinity groups saw the opportunities and dangers in the new media, and in mass access to culture. They were important actors in organising cinema clubs, reading groups, exhibitions and musical venues. They were arbiters of taste and of moral or political acceptability, with an influential voice in the institutions of the State. No doubt the best organised groupings were those sponsored by the Communist Party and the Catholic Church. The PCF's political strategy of a broad front against Fascism led to the creation (and takeover) of several associations of left-wing intellectuals, and a plethora of associated magazines and media production enterprises. The Church's strategy of guiding the spiritual nourishment of the faithful and restoring moral standards to the modern world led to the founding of companies to produce Catholic-orientated entertainment. This was at the origin of the Tintin comic strips from 1929, for example. They were launched when their author, Hergé (Georges Remi) a scoutmaster, was commissioned by Belgian church leaders to develop cartoon material suitable for Catholic children as an alternative to the popular American products by Walt Disney and others. The Church also produced several voluntary codes of practice, and its system of film classifications exercised a pervasive influence well into the Fifth Republic.

The election of the Popular Front government in 1936 marked a turning-point in the State's role in culture. Spurred by the Socialist aim of democratising culture, or at least popularising it, the new government began to develop a programme of strategic intervention. It sought to give ideological direction to existing cultural activities, especially those concerned with young people and those associated with the movements participating in, or supporting, the government. It aimed to articulate a cultural policy, including pioneering work on popular culture by minister Léo Lagrange. And it sought to give increased order and structure to the industries and professions engaged in cultural activity. Because the Popular Front government (1936–8) was, in the event, too short-lived, many of its initiatives did not bear immediate fruit. But the ideas remained active, and their fruits were harvested in the cultural policies of Vichy, aligned to a different ideological agenda, and in the practice of successive postwar governments.

The Vichy government (and the German occupying authorities) introduced an elaborate system of control and censorship over publications, performances and broadcasts. It developed Radio-Vichy as its propaganda arm, in parallel with the German-run Radio-Paris. Despite severe material shortages, French cultural life flourished unexpectedly, to the point where many in the creative professions later looked back on it as a 'golden age'. The lack of imported cultural goods gave market opportunities for French producers of films and comics, for example. Cinemas and theatres were well attended, and sporting events were enthusiastically supported. Churches were full to overflowing and people flocked to popular festivals, pilgrimages, exhibitions and concerts. Youth movements flourished. Vichy established a number of official bodies, such as the Commission for General Education and Sport, or the Committee for the Organisation of the Cinematographic Industry, and contributed to the extension of state involvement in the cultural realm, which had been inaugurated by the Popular Front. Among the opponents to the Vichy regime, culture was mobilised in the cause of national liberation. They were active abroad, for example, in the battle of the airwaves broadcasting through the BBC, Radio-Moscow and the Voice of America. And within France an active clandestine and semi-clandestine culture developed, with a swelling underground press, the circulation '*sous le manteau*' (under cover, literally 'under the overcoat') of songs and poems calling for Resistance, and eventually an underground publishing house, Les Editions de Minuit, producing high-quality literary works by major writers (usually contributed under a pseudonym).

At the Liberation, de Gaulle and the provisional government launched a programme of reconstruction which had a strong cultural component. Radio broadcasting was nationalised, as the most strategically vital medium of communication. Radio and then television remained a state monopoly, under close control until the mid-1970s. The government also recognised that French culture had a powerful appeal internationally, and could be used in the effort to restore France's position in the postwar world. The Ministry of Foreign Affairs funded a very active schedule of foreign visits, performances and exhibitions by writers and artists of all descriptions. In response, Jean-Paul Sartre complained in late 1945 that literature was being nationalised as well, with every young novelist being treated as an ambassador for his country. His point was well founded, at least to the extent of recognising the State's strong interest in culture, and the strong current of nationalism that henceforth ran through French culture.

Religious and political groups also felt the increased importance of mobilising culture in support of their aims. Cultural associations, newspapers, magazines and book collections blossomed and then struggled in the difficult postwar years. Only the strongest survived to take advantage of the economic prosperity that took hold in the 1950s. The most successful of the groupings were again the Catholics and Communists, who increasingly made common cause, despite their divergent perspectives. Both shared a deep antipathy to the products of American culture; the Catholics for fear of its licentiousness and its defence of individualist values, and the Communists for fear of its advocacy of capitalist and imperialist objectives. The two groupings co-operated in a vocal campaign against the 'Blum-Byrnes agreement', when a trade agreement between the two countries, signed in Washington in May 1946, included provisions for quotas on films screened in French cinemas. As the climate of Cold War began to bite, the provisions were attacked (probably unjustly) as a sell-out to American imperialism, and were subsequently renegotiated. Catholics and Communists also co-operated in a move to limit the importation of American comics, resulting in the introduction of a law placing tight restrictions on publications aimed at young people. The legislation of 1949, still largely in force, is generally seen as protecting French-produced *bande dessinée*, in which Catholic and Communist publishers had the largest market share, with their respective flagship characters of Tintin the boy reporter, and Pif the dog.

The battle for the minds and hearts was not confined to Communists and Catholics, but they had the most developed networks of cultural activity, and the most publicly marked identities. Committed Catholic novelists like Mauriac or Cesbron, and Communist philosophers like Garaudy or Lefebvre were readily identified in the public mind, and generally wore their label of affiliation with pride. Their Protestant or Jewish equivalents were few in number and low in profile, and their Socialist or Gaullist counterparts, where they existed, tended to avoid a precise label of affiliation, cultivating an arms-length relationship with organised religion or politics in their professional activity. The same could be said of most of the cultural professions, including film-making, fine art, music, the theatre, and poetry, for example. In each case, amid the variety of political and spiritual orientations firmly or tentatively presented, a number of figures could be discerned who were identifiably champions of the Catholic or Communist cause.

These identifications began, however, to blur in the late 1950s. There were many reasons for this: the major political crisis of the Algerian War, which cut brutally across political and religious affiliations; the easing of the Cold War; leadership changes in the Kremlin and the Vatican; and the growing sophistication of techniques of persuasion (or marketing), which revealed the limited efficacy of direct political or religious propaganda. There were major reappraisals of policy among Catholics internationally, arising from the reforms of the Second Vatican Council (1964–6), spearheaded by French theologians, in a spirit of greater openness and dialogue with other belief communities. The French Communists undertook a far reaching review of the relations between politics and culture, signalled at a milestone meeting of the PCF's Central Committee, held in the Paris suburb of Argenteuil in 1966. The drive for reform was led by the poet and novelist Louis Aragon, who argued strongly for the need to encourage greater cultural and intellectual innovation without a tight political strait-jacket. Consequently, when the effervescent uprising of May '68 broke out, there were relatively few cultural barriers from these quarters to damp down the libertarian spirit of the students. Culture appeared, on the contrary, as a key to social emancipation, memorably encapsulated in the slogan 'l'imagination a pris le pouvoir' (imagination has taken power). Cultural diversity flourished, and it even became something of an orthodoxy that 'creation' should be unconstrained. In this climate, the role of political and religious organisations, and their associated networks (such as trade unions and charitable associations), became deeply problematic, since they could easily appear to be abusing culture by covertly promoting partisan objectives.

But the relative withdrawal of these intermediate bodies from cultural activity left in effect only two sources of funding support: the State and the commercial sector. Both had a clear interest in supporting culture, and both were at least ostensibly neutral in political and religious terms. The development of the cultural industries has resulted in a thriving economic sector, albeit one which is increasingly vulnerable to the internationalisation of the world economy. The State's role in providing resources and an infrastructure for culture has also continued to expand. It was explicitly recognised in the creation of the Ministry of Culture by de Gaulle in 1959. First headed by the writer André Malraux, its role grew through the economic downturn of the 1970s and underwent a massive expansion, with a greatly increased budget under Jack Lang during the first Mitterrand presidency, from 1981.

The renewed role of the State in culture has been well marked by its architectural presence in Paris, which was reasserted in the last quarter of the twentieth century. The austere General de Gaulle believed more in the symbolic power of words and personal appearances, and Malraux's mark on Paris was mainly confined to a major campaign of cleaning the façades of public buildings. Successive Presidents of the Fifth Republic strove to leave their mark in more enduring legacies. They began with Georges Pompidou's conception of a postmodern culture house in the Beaubourg area of the old market district, Les Halles, based around an art gallery and library. The Centre Pompidou was opened in 1977 by his successor, Valéry Giscard d'Estaing, whose own presidential *grands travaux*, including the Orsay Museum, were completed by François Mitterrand. The fourteen-year presidency of Mitterrand enabled him to complete a series of his own projects, including the extension to the Louvre, under a large glass Pyramid, a new opera house at the Bastille, and a large new national library. It is particularly noteworthy that these assertions of national pride were dominated by cultural monuments, especially libraries and art galleries. On the one hand, this reflects the belief in culture as a national heritage, for which the State must take responsibility on behalf of the nation. On the other hand, it reflects the key role which culture has been assigned in constructing and maintaining French national identity, both internally as a means of achieving national unity and underpinning the legitimacy of governments, and externally as a display to the rest of the world of French prestige, creativity and achievement.

Conclusion

At the end of the twentieth century and opening of the twenty-first, there are many events that in various ways combine the three issues that have been discussed here. In addition to the *grands travaux* of recent presidents, there have been major public events that would repay detailed analysis, including perhaps the celebrations of the bicentenary of the French Revolution in 1989 (with a spectacular parade on 14 July) or those marking the turn of the millennium in 1999–2000 (with fireworks on the Eiffel Tower and a millennial meal along the Paris meridian). In more conflictual mode, there are insights to be gained from the revocation of Bishop Gaillot from the diocese of Evreux in 1995, or the occupation of churches and public buildings in defence of illegal immigrants (*les sans-papiers*), for example, in the later 1990s. One of the most revealing recent events, which struck a powerful national chord, is the French national team's performance in the football World Cup of 1998. The final in Paris attracted a huge television audience, and was attended by the President, Jacques Chirac, a Gaullist, and his prime minister, the Socialist Lionel Jospin. Both of them strove to indicate not only their personal interest in the game but also their support for the team on behalf of the entire nation. The team's victory was an occasion for national rejoicing, symbolising the country's world status, and also expressing a new national unity. The players came from a variety of ethnic backgrounds, underlined by the fact that the hero of the match was Zinedine Zidane, the son of North African immigrants to Marseilles. Echoing the blue of the national sporting strip and the 'blue-white-red' of the national flag, 'les Bleus' were heralded as 'Black-Blanc-Beur', celebrating the visible ethnic mix of the national team, and the symbolic recognition of diversity within national unanimity.

In the context of the global village, sporting events are now cultural symbols at least as potent as churches and exhibitions. The images are seen by a wider audience, and may be endlessly repeated, accumulating meanings as they are recirculated. They increasingly involve the responsibility of the State, which commits enormous investment to infrastructure that supports these events, and reaps the social, economic and even political consequences of the outcomes. It may be too much to argue that sport (or any other cultural pursuit) has replaced religion or politics. But the ability to command loyalty, mobilise identities and encapsulate fundamental values is a social function which political, religious and cultural movements all share. And from the point of view of the State, cultural activities (such as football matches or libraries) are better able to support its consensual basis than the turbulent and conflictual fields of religion or politics. If this is so, then it is not too outrageous to contrast two gestures of national assertion: the young Third Republic's act of contrition on Montmartre Hill is answered by the mature Fifth Republic's sporting triumph at the *Stade de France*. Church-building is answered by team-building. In the postmodern condition of fragmented and diminished political and religious fields, a consensual state depends on the efficacy of cultural symbols to maintain a sense of national unity and maintain its place in the world.

FURTHER READING

Chadwick, Kay (ed.), *Catholicism, Politics and Society in Twentieth-Century France*, Liverpool: Liverpool University Press, 2000.

Cook, Malcolm, and Grace Davie (eds.), *Modern France: Society in Transition*, London and New York: Routledge, 1999.

Flood, Christopher, and Laurence Bell (eds.), *Political Ideologies in Contemporary France*, London: Pinter, 1997.

Flower, John (ed.), *France Today*, 7th edn, London: Hodder & Stoughton, 1993.

Forbes, Jill, Nick Hewlett and François Nectoux (eds.), *Contemporary France: Essays and Texts on Politics, Economics and Society*, 2nd edn, London: Longman, 2001.

Forbes, Jill, and Michael Kelly (eds.), *French Cultural Studies: an Introduction*, Oxford: Oxford University Press, 1995.

Hazareesingh, Sudhir, *Political Traditions in Modern France*, Oxford: Oxford University Press, 1994.

Hewlett, Nick, *Modern French Politics*, Cambridge: Polity, 1998.

Kelly, Michael (ed.), *French Culture and Society*, London: Arnold, 2001.

Larkin, Maurice, *France since the Popular Front: Government and People, 1936–1986*, Oxford: Oxford University Press, 1988.

McMillan, James F., *Twentieth-Century France, Politics and Society 1889–1991*, 2nd edn, London: Edward Arnold, 1992.

Mendras, Henri, and Alistair Cole, *Social Change in Modern France*, Cambridge and Paris: Cambridge University Press and Editions de la Maison des Sciences de l'Homme, 1991.

Todd, Emmanuel, *The Making of Modern France: Politics, Ideology and Culture*, Oxford: Blackwell, 1991.

9

The third term: literature between philosophy and critical theory

Introduction

In 1948, the philosopher and rising star of Parisian existentialism, Jean-Paul Sartre, recast a series of essays into book form as *Qu'est-ce que la littérature?* (What is Literature?) The question Sartre raised in the title introduced a set of concerns he deemed central to the programme of committed writing (*littérature engagée*) he and his colleagues sought to implement through the literary monthly, *Les Temps modernes*, they had launched in October 1945. Sartre's postwar ambitions for philosophy and literature were pragmatic and activist. Above all, he sought to mobilise the writer into an historical agent, a 'bad conscience' who spoke out in public – as often in speech as in writing – on the social and political issues of the moment. But while *Qu'est-ce que la littérature?* was a manifesto for *littérature engagée*, Sartre also saw the need to ground his programme in terms that addressed the nature of literature and of literary activity: what literature *was*, so to speak, as well as what he wanted it to *do*. It was, then, no small irony that much as Sartre sought to mobilise the writer of prose within a broad public sphere represented by mass media such as the daily press, theatre, film, the foundational questions he addressed in the opening chapters of *Qu'est-ce que la littérature?* – what is writing? why write? for whom does one write? – drew openly on a philosophical tradition whose origins in Greek antiquity included Aristotle's *Poetics* and Plato's *Republic*.

Qu'est-ce que la littérature? is my starting-point for this chapter because it posits necessary links between philosophy and literature understood from within, as a set of practices cast within constraints of discourses, sub-fields and categories; and from the outside, as variable social, political and symbolic functions attributed to these practices in a specific context. Beyond the specific conceptions of literature and the literary asserted by Sartre's 1948 manifesto, the interaction between internal and external approaches (alternatively expressed in terms as intrinsic and contingent) remains an ongoing feature of philosophy and critical thinking in twentieth-century France. The Sartre who wrote *Qu'est-ce que la littérature?* made literature a middle or third term between philosophy and critical theory, with the latter understood as the attempt to mobilise prose and the prose writer in the cause of social and/or political activism with a basis in human freedom.[1] Yet the questions that Sartre raised concerning literature also drew on a tradition of *poésie critique* (critical poetry) associated with literary figures such as Stéphane Mallarmé, Paul Valéry and André Breton, for all of whom the writing of poetry, in particular, and the creative process, in general, were inseparable from critical thinking. By extension, poetry designated the object of critical reflection that theorised literature and the literary in a Western philosophical tradition starting with Plato and Aristotle. Paul Verlaine made the point with concision and eloquence in his 1882 poem, 'Art Poétique', when he wrote that poetry was a touchstone, a verbal order of musicality apart, and all the rest was mere literature.

From another perspective, the intellectual links between *Qu'est-ce que la littérature?* and *poésie critique* illustrated the institutional distance separating Sartre's postwar programme from the erudite study of literature launched in the French educational system by the 1895 publication of Gustave Lanson's *Histoire de la littérature française*. The institutional impact of Lansonian methods overlaps significantly with what Vincent Descombes has described as the *university site* of modern French philosophy, whose formation was concentric and highly centralised: 'The *lycées* provide[d] the universities with the bulk of their audience in the form of future secondary-school teachers. The *lycées* teachers [were], in theory, recruited by the State by means of a competitive examination system. Given that the content of these examinations (*agrégation*, CAPES) [was] a function of the sixth-form (*classe de philosophie*) syllabus, the teaching of philosophy in France [was] more or less determined by the nature and function of that syllabus.'[2] In such terms, the university site of philosophy – and, by implication, that of literature, as well – was consonant with the educational reforms of the Third Republic and the transmission of a cultural legacy (*patrimoine*) by means of a universal curriculum. Sartre's postwar programme was all the more ambitious because he sought from the start to implement *littérature engagée* explicitly outside the university site.

From *poésie critique* to erudite study

The lyric verse of Paul Valéry (1871–1945) was inseparable from his critical conception of poetry as a mental act. Valéry's two major collections of poems, published at an interval of some thirty years, were far outweighed by essays and notebooks in which he pursued a lifelong enquiry into the creative act and the structures of consciousness it disclosed. This enquiry owed as much to the reasoned method Valéry found in the writings of René Descartes and Leonardo da Vinci as to the poetry of his immediate tutelary figure, Stéphane Mallarmé, who had remained at an eloquent impasse in the face of the duality between the sense content of poetry and the 'pure' idea to which it gave material form. Unlike Mallarmé, Valéry transformed this duality into an object of systematic interrogation he cast in terms of what I want to call a bisected poetics. In one sense, he followed traditional usage of the term, with reference to a systematic inventory or description of literary means available to the writer. Poetics was a practical guide to invention that set the strictly literary effects of language apart from other uses, such as everyday conversation. (In his 1886 essay, 'Crise de vers', Mallarmé had asserted a similar distinction between the crude or immediate state of language in non-literary usage and its essential state in poetry.) By implication, this primary sense of poetics disclosed conventions of literary discourse, understood as the sum total of the products resulting from such invention. Moreover, its orientation from the individual to the general showed the extent to which Valéry equated poetics with literary theory: 'A theory of literature, as we conceive it: the name Poetics seems to fit it'.[3] Yet poetics equated with a theory of literature failed to account adequately for the sustained reflection on 'creative action, considered in an abstract and non-individualized way' that led Valéry to focus on the process, making or fashioning of the literary work rather than its accomplishment or final product (Todorov, 66).

Valéry's concern with poetry as mental act countered the Romantic emphasis on inspiration and genius with a dynamic between an *état poétique* (poetic state) of heightened awareness or receptivity and its transposition into material form through processes of fabrication whose models were music and geometry. This also meant that the privilege accorded by tradition to the figure of poet and to the poem as aesthetic object yielded to the centrality of the poetic state. In 'Poetry and Abstract Thought' (1939), Valéry defined the poem as an artificial synthesis of the poetic state and its capacity to induce in the reader the heightened consciousness that led the poet to write. Because the poem elaborated the state of mind that gave rise to it, the activities of poet, reader and poem all centred on the poetic state: 'Whatever other functions it may perform (for it may also occur elsewhere), the poetic state becomes that criterion of difference through which poetry and non-poetry can be distinguished'.[4]

Some six years before he wrote the 1924 *Manifesto of Surrealism*, André Breton styled his first poems on those of Valéry. Much like Mallarmé and Valéry before him, Breton asserted the specificity of poetry by setting it against more mundane uses of language. But like Sartre some twenty years later, the Breton who wrote the *Manifesto* defined poetry as a means of liberating human experience from the fetters of a realist attitude he equated with utilitarian prose and reasoned thought. Much like Sartre two decades later, Breton was an activist for whom literature was an activity and means to an end. But where Sartre was to reject poetry in favour of a transparent prose that drove the writer through language and into the world, Breton posited the primacy of poetic language as a privileged means of disclosing aspects of human experience that prose and reasoned thought alone could not disclose. Accordingly, he wrote less about poetry than about the poetic image; less about what poetry was than what the poetic image might do. Breton was also at odds with Valéry because his sense of the poetic image as a construct on a par with the dream drew on what Sigmund Freud had analysed in *The Interpretation of Dreams* (1900) with a view towards the interaction of conscious and unconscious processes. The poetic image was thus one means of resolving the contradiction between day and night that Breton took as emblematic of waking and sleeping states. Yet this claim held only to the extent that creation linked to fashioning the poetic image took priority over prose literature in the form of the realist novel Breton took pains to reject.

Marcel Proust was a writer of prose – essays, fiction and letters – for whom criticism was a means of moving towards the personal and aesthetic understanding whose full expression took form in the 3,000 pages of his novel, *A la recherche du temps perdu* (Remembrance of Things Past). Proust was not a poet in a strict sense, but his critical sense of language, literature and fine arts such as music and painting touched significantly on aspects of *poésie critique* noted above in the writings of Mallarmé and Valéry. Like Mallarmé, Proust set the realm of aesthetics and creation apart from, yet fully within, everyday life. And like Valéry, he endlessly considered and reconsidered the similarities and differences among various arts. A more literal translation into English of the title of the *Recherche* as *In Search of Lost Time* in place of *Remembrance of Things Past* also helps to explain the associations throughout Proust's writings between literary criticism, aesthetics and the redemptive potential of artistic creation. Proust's literary career following his 1896–1901 work on the novel *Jean Santeuil* can be described as an enormous cycle that begins with the raising of aesthetic questions that only criticism and Proust's discovery of his artistic vocation could begin to solve.[5] The continuum Proust posited between critical and creative language also explains why his prose resembled nothing so much as the commentary of a poem yet to be written. The relevant point asserts the primacy of language and style as sources of understanding. It extends to the essay-within-the-novel form with which Proust first experimented in the texts republished posthumously in 1954 under the title *Contre Sainte-Beuve*.

The central role of memory throughout the *Recherche* has often prompted comparisons with philosophical considerations of reminiscence and knowledge from Plato to Henri Bergson. Much as the distinction between voluntary and involuntary memory was essential to genesis of creation as Proust portrayed it, Bergson's *Matter and Memory* (1896) set an acquired or habitual memory against a pure or spontaneous memory capable of withdrawing at the tiniest movement of the will. Of course, much depended on how the two kinds of memory are deployed as well as on the values attributed to them within the models of time of which they are part.[6] The term 'resurrection' used by Bergson and Proust evokes a sense that both grounded their respective notions of spontaneous and involuntary memory in transcendence or even spirituality. These parallels notwithstanding, the notion or model of time implied by Proust's equation of recurrence and repetition in the *Recherche* seems less akin to Bergson's attempts to account for temporality in terms of scientific laws and duration than to the mystical experience, as in Sören Kierkegaard's *Repetition*.[7]

The full trajectory of *poésie critique* towards aestheticism, the surreal and the mystical was the antithesis of an erudite practice whose methods dominated literary study in the French educational system during the first half of the twentieth century. Arguably, this trajectory extends forward in time as far as the infamous debate of the mid-1960s between the Sorbonne professor, Raymond Picard, and his New Criticism (*nouvelle critique*) adversary, Roland Barthes, surrounding their respective studies of Jean Racine's plays. Gustave Lanson's 1895 *Histoire de la littérature française* marked a singular triumph within the programme of educational reforms instituted by Jules Ferry and others. Lanson sought to replace the generalised categories of genre, technique and style linked to the teaching of rhetoric in the *lycées* and universities with the systematic study of individual texts. This shift from the general to the particular extended currents of positivist thought to the scholarly disciplines of literary study, philosophy and history. Lanson's *Histoire* combined the determinism that Hippolyte Taine had grounded in elements of race, environment (*milieu*) and moment with an emphasis on the evolution of literary genres set forth in the writings of Ferdinand Brunetière. In terms of method, Lanson achieved this shift from rhetoric to history by applying to literature's of all periods the techniques of philology that were more usually applied to ancient and medieval literature.

The undisputed key to Lanson's *Histoire* and single cause of its lasting influence on literary studies in France was the establishment and accumulation of facts on which systematic understanding would build. The pedagogical implications of this key quickly made the *Histoire* into a textbook that transformed literary studies in unique and lasting ways. In the classroom, Lanson's *Histoire* spawned the twin exercises of essay (*dissertation*) and textual analysis (*explication de texte*) meant to instil accurate and precise understanding. Outside the classroom in sites such as libraries, archives and publishing houses, erudite understanding promoted research activities that provided the materials and data needed to conduct systematic and reasoned understanding. These activities soon spawned a programme – referred to as Lansonian criticism or as Lansonism – that inaugurated the study of sources and influences. Elements of this programme included annotated critical editions, the publication of unpublished texts (*inédits*), biographies of writers and bibliographies of various kinds.

There were significant discrepancies between Lanson's conception of erudite study and the institutions of *lansonisme* that it inspired. For Lanson considered erudition less an end in itself than an instrument for determining the social conditions within/under which literary works were produced and, by extension, the qualities of uniqueness and genius that kept the best of them alive.[8] It is no small irony that Lanson's personal devotion to criticism as an aspect of judgement grounded in taste and genius came to be seen by many of his former disciples as dated and close to laughable. Along the same lines, the pedagogical goal of instilling inductive reasoning as an intellectual attribute of democratic and republican ideals at the core of instituted *lansonisme* was increasingly at a remove from the erudition Lanson had set out to accomplish in 1895. In the end, the Lansonian mania for sources and influences conformed to literary history under the sway of nineteenth-century positivism (Compagnon, 823). After the challenges to Lanson's ideas raised since 1950 by *la nouvelle critique*, structural analysis and deconstruction, the emergence of genetic criticism tracing the creative process through textual variants discloses the persistence of theories and practices of erudition inspired by Lanson's *Histoire* that many had long considered outmoded.[9]

From phenomenology and the three H's to existentialism

The theorising of literature and institution of literary studies linked respectively to *poésie critique* and Lanson were more or less home-grown, with distinctly French origins in late nineteenth- and turn-of-the-century poetry and positivism. The interface between literary theory and philosophy was assumed and tacit, with the latter understood in more general terms within a humanistic tradition of the history of ideas. The designation of national or linguistic origin becomes more relevant in light of the fact that a third model of literature and literary studies drew in method and ideas on social sciences and philosophy imported between the wars from German-language sources. Breton had based his conception of the poetic image in the 1924 *Manifesto* at least in part on readings – some might say misreadings – of Freud's *Interpretation of Dreams* and *Psychopathology of Everyday Life*. Substantial readings of texts by Georg Wilhelm Friedrich Hegel, Edmund Husserl and Martin Heidegger marked literary studies among two generations of writer-critics who came to maturity between 1925 and 1945. Initial interest in Hegel was spawned by a series of seminars conducted by Alexandre Kojève (born Aleksandr Vladimirovich Kozhevnikov) at the elite Ecole Pratique des Hautes Etudes between 1933 and 1939. The seminars focused on Hegel's 1807 *Phenomenology of Mind* and, in particular, on the element of negativity as the motor or force of a three-part dialectic charted in terms of thesis, antithesis and synthesis. The primal scene of this dialectic occurred in an early section of the *Phenomenology* devoted to self-consciousness and figures of domination and dependence whom Hegel identified respectively as Masterly and Slavish consciousnesses.

Kojève extended this sense of consciousness towards relations with others understood in terms of competing desires that resulted in violence to the point of death. He considered the idea of prospective freedom as a negative force that drove the Slavish consciousness to transcend the state or condition of dependency towards an ultimate coincidence of idea and reality. This transcendence became a model for a progression from a physical dependency linked to life and death towards a human and social existence founded on interactions with others. Kojève followed Hegel by casting the Master–Slave relation initially in the singular as interpersonal. Yet the full expression of what he meant by the notion of mind, also translatable into English as 'Spirit' from the German *Geist* and the French *esprit*, was an impersonal phenomenon set apart from individual agency. Beyond the specific passages devoted to the Master–Slave dialectic, what Hegel asserted in the *Phenomenology*'s final chapter as the end of history opened the dialectic to reconsideration from perspectives such as the Russian revolution of 1918 and the so-called 'American way of life'. Some philosophers have dismissed Kojève's reading of Hegel's *Phenomenology* as skewed and idiosyncratic. Yet its influence on those who attended his seminars either regularly or only on occasion – registration rolls included the names of Breton, Georges Bataille, Jacques Lacan, Maurice Merleau-Ponty and Roger Caillois – persisted well through postwar Parisian existentialism and absurdist theatre to essays of the 1960s by Michel Foucault and Jacques Derrida.

Translations of texts by Edmund Husserl and Martin Heidegger introduced phenomenology to many of the same generation that attended Kojève's seminars. Hegel had used the same term with reference to the evolving forms or phenomena of *Geist* he analysed as a series of stages or moments. Husserl's conception of phenomenology extended a model of subjectivity in a Cartesian tradition by rethinking human experience with a view to formal and logical thought as the necessary basis of any empirical understanding. In his *Ideas* (1918), Husserl asserted a notion of the phenomenology by which he sought to describe the objects of consciousness while abstaining from any judgement concerning their reality or unreality. One result of this method was a return to the material specificity of objects and thus, as much as possible, a return 'to the thing in itself' (*un retour aux choses mêmes*). The story goes that the young Sartre was so taken with what his friend, Raymond Aron, reported to him about this 'new German philosophy' that he decided to spend two years studying it in Berlin. The impact of Sartre's exposure to German phenomenology was visible in his essays of the late 1930s on the transcendence of the ego and on the imagination as well as in long passages of his 1938 novel, *La Nausée (Nausea)*, in which description bordered on the hallucinatory.

Elements of Husserlian phenomenology resurfaced between the late 1930s and the mid-1960s in essays by Marcel Raymond, Georges Poulet and Jean-Pierre Richard, and other critics of consciousness linked to the Geneva School. Poulet's essays on human time and Richard's analyses of vocabulary sought to re-create the imaginary world of the novelist, essayist and poet by simulating consciousness and sensibility reminiscent of early nineteenth-century Romantic literature in France and Germany. In this sense, readings that posited specific kinds of sensibility and consciousness extended the Lansonian bias towards authorship. At the same time, their textual focus resulted in less of an analysis or interpretation than a simulation of patterns that traced the act of reading. Additional variations on this phenomenological orientation occurred in studies that Gaston Bachelard organised around the four elements of fire, water, air and earth and in Maurice Blanchot's postwar essays on Mallarmé, Proust and Franz Kafka. Where Bachelard delineated archetypal patterns of imagery in poetry and prose, Blanchot explored the creative process as a movement towards the literary work (*oeuvre*) and what he described in a 1959 collection of essays as the book of the future (*le livre à venir*).

Martin Heidegger began as Husserl's disciple until the 1927 publication of his *Being and Time (Sein und Zeit)* allowed him to succeed his mentor in the Chair of Philosophy at the University of Freiburg-im-Bresgau. Translations into French promoted a cult following among philosophers and writers of Sartre's generation despite strong reservations on the part of many concerning Heidegger's activities in Nazi Germany between 1933 and 1945. Following World War II, his rethinking of fundamental questions of ontology set him into a dialogue of sorts with postwar French existentialism. Literary interest broadened after Heidegger met the poet René Char at a 1955 conference at Cerisy-la-Salle. Visits to France over the next fifteen years to Char's native region of Provence prompted Heidegger to consider the South of France a living version of the ancient Greece whose philosophy and poetry his writings sought to venerate. As with Hegel and Husserl, Heidegger came to represent a source of ideas and notions on which writers, critics and theorists drew in various ways. Strict attribution of textual sources mattered less than the simple fact that creative writers and critics drew on readings in philosophy to think and create in new ways.

The impact of the three H's in France evolved after World War II into a broad cultural and social phenomenon known as Parisian existentialism. Between 1944 and 1965, writings by Sartre, Albert Camus and Simone de Beauvoir popularised philosophical concepts such as 'being', 'nothingness', and 'the absurd' into a sensibility and fashion. Writings by these three recast traditional considerations of identity and freedom, spreading the vocabulary and models of ontology, metaphysics and ethics among writers, artists and scholars marked by the 1940–44 Nazi Occupation of France. Sartre, Camus and de Beauvoir wrote essays on topics such as ontology (Sartre's *Being and Nothingness*), the absurd (Camus's *The Myth of Sisyphus*) and intersubjectivity (de Beauvoir's *The Ethics of Ambiguity*). Significantly, they also wrote novels and plays that conveyed literary expressions of their respective philosophical visions to an international public sphere far beyond the Sorbonne and Parisian intelligentsia. All three filtered recurrent themes of freedom, resistance and commitment through the experience of the Nazi Occupation that fostered various kinds and degrees of commitment (*engagement*) in order to break with the recent past of the Occupation.

Human sciences and the structural paradigm

The heightened attention paid to German-language philosophy in interwar and early postwar France coincided with the growing institutional impact of social sciences such as sociology, psychology and anthropology within the university system and elite Grandes Ecoles. This impact extended as well to the revised methods of historical study promoted by the *Annales* group launched at the University of Strasbourg in 1929 under the leadership of Marc Bloch and Lucien Febvre. Social sciences of the period extended assumptions of positivist method and a scientism that clashed with the work of writers and scholars across disciplines. The postwar human sciences (*les sciences humaines*) differed from interwar practices of social sciences precisely in sustained attempts to rethink the method and ambitions of scientific enquiry apart from – and eventually in opposition to – the centrality of individual consciousness designated polemically with reference to a Cartesian subjectivity grounded in demonstrable knowledge. Earlier efforts in phenomenology and aesthetics had struggled with subjectivism. Husserl and Heidegger had sought each in his own way to rethink the centrality of the Cartesian subject in light of logic, theory of knowledge and metaphysics. Sartre and Jacques Derrida extended this critique of Cartesian subjectivity, the former as early as *Trascendence of the Ego* (1936) and the latter as early as *Speech and Phenomena* (1967).[10]

A more forceful break with the Cartesian tradition of subjectivity occurred following World War II in a pervasive emphasis on structure that emerged from methods of enquiry adapted from anthropology, linguistics and psychoanalysis. The structuralist project detached social science entirely from the centrality of consciousness and the Cartesian tradition, in favour of new models of critical thinking that dominated French thought during the twenty years following the 1949 publication of Claude Lévi-Strauss's *The Elementary Structures of Kinship* (*Les Structures élémentaires de la parenté*). Expressions and extensions of this model in guises from formalism to deconstruction continued to mark philosophy and critical theory in France during most of the second half of the twentieth century. Yet there is properly speaking no structuralist philosophy because structuralism is only the name of a scientific method whose *effect* upon philosophical discourse is nonetheless incontestable (Descombes, 77). The obvious but often overlooked point is that a critical concern with structure does not qualify on its own as philosophy. At the same time, the impact of this concern as it promoted a shift in critical thought between 1945 and 1966 made linguistics a pilot science guiding social science as a whole.[11]

In *The Elementary Structures*, Lévi-Strauss asserted that the laws of language were the key to understanding the dynamics of exchange he adapted from the 1925 *Essai sur le don, forme achaïque de l'échange* (The Gift, Forms and Functions of Exchange in Archaic Societies) by the sociologist and disciple of Emile Durkheim, Marcel Mauss. Like Mauss and Durkheim before him, Lévi-Strauss expanded from the phenomenon of exchange – which he linked to marriage, exogamy and incest prohibition – towards a generalised model of social cohesion on a par with what Dukheim had theorised as a total social fact. What set *Les Structures* apart from this Durkheim–Mauss lineage was the fact that Lévi-Strauss replaced the simple description of practices central to anthropology as an empirical science with analyses that sought to disclose the underlying structures that empirical observation alone left undetected. More importantly, Lévi-Strauss held that these underlying structures could be studied according to laws of language such as those set forth in the passages of Ferdinand de Saussure's 1916 *Cours de linguistique générale* (Course in General Linguistics) devoted to the study of signs in society that came to be known as semiology.[12] *The Elementary Structures* set emergent structural analysis at odds with phenomenology by asserting the primacy of language as a system over the conscious individual agent. This primacy was understood as functional. Because Lévi-Strauss held that the site of meaning originated outside or beyond the conscious individual, his analyses focused less on the meaning of specific rituals and customs than on the more basic (elementary) structures and processes that produced meaning.

Saussure's *Course* had posited linguistics as an element or subset of semiology. It provided three key notions on which postwar structural analyses of various kinds were to draw. The first of the three was a distinction between two levels of language, referred to in French as *langue* and *parole*, whose interaction constituted the language system in a specific time and place that was taken as the prime object of study. *Langue* (language) was the totality of extant rules, patterns and practices understood as a collective phenomenon or social construct within which instances of *parole* (speech or speech act) occurred. Saussure argued in the *Course* that meaning occurred on the basis of relations between elements understood both semantically and phonetically.

The second distinction involved the production of meaning on the basis of the interaction between a signifier or sound-image (*signifiant*) and the idea or notion (*signifié*) it designates. It was this interaction between signifier and signified rather than the elements in and of themselves that produced the sign (*signe*). The interaction between signifier and signified drew on interactions between semantic and phonetic specificity, with reference to what subsequent scholars have studied as the phenomenon of double articulation. What counted in both interactions referred to above were relevant relations whose intelligibility occurred in the form of differences. For example, the term 'mother' in English becomes meaningful both through its conceptual difference from related terms such as 'father', 'sister', 'uncle', and 'aunt' as well as through its difference in sound from similar terms such as 'other' and 'smother'.

The third and most significant notion in the *Course* asserted the arbitrary nature of the sign. By this Saussure meant that the link or relation between signifier and signified was neither natural nor intrinsic. Accordingly, the specificity of the sign was always open to change in terms of context. This assertion might at first seem reasonable, its implication being that language was something more or other than a nomenclature in which seemingly arbitrary names were assigned to pre-existing concepts and was open to question and debate. Yet the thesis was more radical: that *both* signifier *and* signified were arbitrary, *both* contingent functions of context-specific relations among speakers and/or writers. Saussure thus implied a degree of complex arbitrariness in both the *paroles* of speech acts and the *langue* of their cultural-linguistic systems. Because the arbitrariness of the sign ascribed a purely differential identity to the sign and sign-systems alike, these entities were negatively defined, so that 'their most precise characteristic is that they are what the others are not'.[13] Or as the *Course* reiterated the point even more concisely, 'in language there are only differences' (Saussure, 120).

The linking of the arbitrary nature of the sign with the assertion that everything in language is differential marked the polemical thrust of the *Course*. It is, then, all the more important to recall that the *Course* was explicit concerning the limits of arbitrariness and difference:

> The statement that everything in language is negative is true only if the signified and the signifier are considered separately; when we consider the sign in its totality, we have something that is positive in its own class. A linguistic system is a series of differences of sound combined with a series of differences of ideas . . . Although both the signified and the signifier are purely differential and negative when considered separately, their combination is a positive fact.
>
> (Saussure, 120)

The implications of arbitrariness set forth above were central both to the Saussurean model and to various ways it was appropriated on the part of those who tempered the Saussurean emphasis on *langue* as sign-system with a countervailing emphasis on the *parole*. Where *langue* assumed for Saussure a role akin to that of transcendental entity in the Cartesian tradition, a more extreme reading asserts the primacy of difference in determining the positionality of the speaking subject as neither pre-given nor transcendent.

The subject in question

The replacement of the Cartesian subject figured as a central source of vision emanating a conscious gaze outward towards the world with the speaking subject at risk within the vagaries of language and meaning spawned a variety of enquiries linked to a more generalised critique of the sign, for which the projected science of semiology set forth in the *Course* was a recurrent point of departure. Individual readings redirected the Saussurean models of sign and semiology towards a broad range of enquiries, almost all of which drew – most often in critical ways – on the history of Western philosophy that continued to be taught in France at the secondary and university levels. Roland Barthes first adapted aspects of the *Course* in the series of short articles on popular culture in postwar France that he republished in book form in 1957 as *Mythologies*. A decade later, he stated his aim in those articles both to disclose and to dismantle the production of social signs through close analyses of modern myths (literally, 'myths of the moment') as found in the daily press, mass-market journalism, advertising and film. Because Barthes read Saussure by way of Marx and Lévi-Strauss, his sense of semiology as a system of language entailed by necessity the critical breaking apart of the signs he termed 'semioclastics' and by which he asserted that signs were fashioned rather than natural.[14] By 1968, Barthes had also extended his critique of the sign with regard to literary conventions even more polemically towards what he characterised as the death of the author. In both cases, Barthes's appropriation of concepts from Saussure's *Course* extended the range of semiology by setting the study of signs into a critique of various social and literary conventions, understood as kinds of languages or language-systems.

A second form of the critique of the sign characterised the writings on ideology and representation in texts of the 1960s by Louis Althusser such as *For Marx* and *Lenin and Philosophy*. Althusser went significantly further than the Barthes of *Mythologies* by analysing the production of ideology as a process located in the concrete institutions built on notions of family, educational system and organised religions he linked under the general category of ideological state apparatuses. His analysis of these institutions in *Reading Capital* (1970) disclosed ideology's generalised structure and function as that of representing the imaginary relationship of individuals to their real conditions of existence. Even more pointed was Althusser's assertion that that ideology constituted concrete individuals by addressing them ('interpellating' is his preferred term) as subjects in what amounts to a specular relation founded by misrecognition. What Barthes had disclosed in the *Mythologies* as the mythic level of signification underlying the more visible interaction of signifier and signified became for Althusser a dynamic of subjection in which individuals were 'always already' subjects of ideology. In such terms, the autonomy of the individual subject was an illusion, formed from without by social and economic institutions in order to perpetuate an illusion of natural order within which individuals submitted to the processes of capitalist reproduction.

Where Althusser founded his notion of ideology on a return to Marx, Jacques Lacan's return to Freud drew on the writings of Saussure and Roman Jakobson in support of a general hypothesis asserting that the unconscious was structured like a language. For Lacan, this meant replacing received understanding of the unconscious as an autonomous force of repression and instinctual urges with a relation to the signifier and by extension, to language in general. Mastery of language and what Lacan called the 'symbolic order' was a developmental process staged in conjunction with concomitant orders of 'the imaginary' and 'the real' that continually precluded the unity and stability of the ego. The Lacanian subject was essentially a desiring subject that understood itself only in relation to an object of desire – a person or thing – it never succeeded in possessing. Self-understanding was founded on a recognition of lack with regard to this failed possession. A related recognition involved the absolute autonomy of the signifier whose expressions were best understood as a chain of signifiers by means of which meaning continually floated within dynamic poles of selection and combination that Lacan adapted from Jakobson's work on metaphor and metonymy.

Jacques Derrida's early work linked an initial enquiry into Husserl's later writings with a broader critique of the sign and the philosophical tradition on which it was founded. Derrida was trained as a philosopher, but his dense prose exuded a literary sensibility that attracted readers on both sides of the Atlantic. This attraction, in turn, created converts as well as dissenters to what came to be called deconstruction. The breadth of the questions Derrida's writing raised with reference to notions of writing, trace, supplement and difference – with the last term sometimes spelled in French as *différance* to illustrate that the phenomenon to which it referred could be written but not heard – was undeniable. So was the energy with which the notions attributed to deconstruction spawned disarming strategies of reading and interpretation among literary scholars receptive to the intellectual and stylistic rigors of Derrida's prose. In this sense,

Derrida's concerns have remained those of a philosopher for whom the semantic and graphic complexities of literary texts best disclose signifying processes he has explored in studies whose objects over the past forty years have ranged from Plato, Rousseau, Nietzsche and Freud to Blanchot, Antonin Artaud, Francis Ponge and Jean Genet.

Notoriety surrounding deconstruction has often obscured the fact its critique of hierarchical oppositions such as that between speech and writing or nature and culture extends a practice of critical thinking related to literature and critical theory as I have traced its evolution in France from Valéry and Sartre to the present. This critique is based in the history of Western philosophy from Plato to Husserl, via the central figure of Descartes. At the same time, it extends to the transmission of knowledge such as that raised by Vincent Descombes with regard to the university site of philosophy. Derrida's writings constitute a singularly comprehensive inventory of philosophical questions addressed to literature. As a set, they have recast critical thinking on various topics in literary studies as well as in visual media such as painting and film. And much like Sartre some three decades earlier, Derrida has understood the need for philosophy to enter a public sphere for which literature has served as a privileged site and third term between philosophy and critical theory.

NOTES

1. My invocation of the term 'critical theory' recalls its use as early as 1932 by Max Horkheimer. Along with Theodor Adorno and others at the Frankfurt School for Social Research, Horkheimer sought to ally all forms of knowledge with the emancipation of individuals and groups by setting critical reason against the dominating forces of instrumental reason. While the ambitions of *littérature engagée* overlap with those of the Frankfurt School, the only explicit mention of the latter I have found in Sartre's writings is a reference to Herbert Marcuse in a July 1968 interview in *Der Spiegel* reprinted a year later as part of *Les Communistes ont peur de la révolution* (Paris: John Didier, 1969).
2. Vincent Descombes, *Philosophy in France*, trans. L. Scott-Fox and J. M. Harding (New York: Cambridge University Press, 1980), p. 5. The *agrégation* and CAPES are competitive examinations administered annually in conjunction with the recruitment and career advancement of teachers in the secondary system.
3. Paul Valéry, *Variété V*, p. 291; cited in Tzvetan Todorov, 'Valéry's Poetics', *Yale French Studies*, 44 (1970), p. 66.
4. Ralph Freedman, 'Paul Valéry: Protean Critic', in John K. Simon (ed.), *Modern French Criticism: From Proust and Valéry to Structuralism* (Chicago: University of Chicago Press, 1972), p. 25.
5. Walter A. Strauss, *Proust and Literature* (Cambridge, Mass.: Harvard University Press, 1957), p. 214.

6. Roger Shattuck, *Marcel Proust* (New York: Viking, 1974), p. 143.

7. Robert Champigny, 'Proust, Bergson and Other Philosophers', in René Girard (ed.), *Proust: A Collection of Critical Essays* (Englewood Cliffs: Prentice-Hall, 1962), p. 130.

8. Antoine Compagnon, '1895: Gustave Lanson Publishes his *Histoire de la littérature française*', in D. Hollier (ed.), *A New History of French Literature* (Cambridge, Mass.: Harvard University Press, 1988), p. 822.

9. See, for example, Alice Kaplan and Philippe Roussin, 'A Changing Idea of Literature: the Bibliothèque de la Pléiade', *Yale French Studies*, 89 (1996), pp. 237–62. The entire issue, entitled 'Drafts' and edited by Michel Contat, Jacques Neefs and Denis Hollier, presents textual study in the evolved mode of genetic criticism. Some thirty to forty years earlier, Lucien Goldmann's studies of Racine's tragedies, André Malraux's novels, and Jean Genet's plays illustrated a genetic structuralism whose basis in sociology responded to Lanson's concerns for the literary life of France at odds with the textual orientation of recent genetic criticism. The writings of Goldmann (1913–70) also warrant reconsideration as antecedents of Pierre Macherey's writings on literary production, Pierre Bourdieu's notions of intellectual field, distinction, *habitus* and symbolic capital, and Roger Chartier's work on print cultures.

10. See also Derrida's long introduction to his translation of Husserl's 'The Origin of Geometry'.

11. François Dosse, 'Introduction', in *History of Structuralism, volume I, The Rising Sign, 1945–1966*, trans. D. Glassman (Minneapolis: University of Minnesota Press, 1997), pp. xix–xx.

12. Jonathan Culler notes the difficulty of distinguishing structuralism from semiotics as a general science of signs originating in the work of the American philosopher, Charles Saunders Peirce (Jonathan Culler, *Literary Theory: a Very Short Introduction* [New York: Oxford University Press, 1997], pp. 120–1).

13. Ferdinand de Saussure, *Course in General Linguistics*, trans. W. Baskin (New York: Philosophical Library, 1959), p. 117.

14. I have written on the linkage of semiology and semioclastics, in 'From Event to Memory Site: Thoughts on Rereading *Mythologies*', *Nottingham French Studies*, 36, 1 (Spring 1997), pp. 24–33.

FURTHER READING

Althusser, Louis, *Lenin and Philosophy and Other Essays*, New York: Monthly Review Press, 1971.

Derrida, Jacques, *Of Grammatology*, trans. G. C. Spivak, Chicago: University of Chicago Press, 1976; first published 1967.

  Writing and Difference, trans. A. Bass, Chicago: University of Chicago Press, 1978; first published 1972.

  Margins of Philosophy, trans. A. Bass, Chicago: University of Chicago Press, 1982; first published 1967.

Descombes, Vincent, *Modern French Philosophy*, trans. L. Scott-Fox and J. M. Harding, New York: Cambridge University Press, 1980; first published 1979.

Dosse, François, *History of Structuralism*, trans. D. Glassman, Minneapolis: University of Minnesota Press, 1997; first published 1993.

Ehrmann, Jacques (ed.), *Structuralism*, Garden City, NY: Anchor, 1970; first published 1966 as *Yale French Studies*, 36–7.

Lacan, Jacques, *Ecrits: a Selection*, trans. A. Sheridan, New York: Norton, 1977; first published 1966.

Lévi-Strauss, Claude, *The Elementary Structures of Kinship*, trans. J. H. Bell and J. R. von Sturmer, Boston: Beacon, 1969; first published 1949.

Montefiore, Alan (ed.), *Philosophy in France Today*, New York: Cambridge University Press, 1983.

Sartre, Jean-Paul. *'What is Literature?' and Other Essays*, Cambridge, Mass.: Harvard University Press, 1988; first published 1948.

Saussure Ferdinand, *Course in General Linguistics*, trans. W. Baskin, New York: Philosophical Library, 1959; first published 1916.

10

Narrative fiction in French

Introduction: towards a definition

The object of study that is both configured and analysed in this chapter is usually split into four categories: French literature (written in France), 'Francophone' or 'non-Hexagonal' productions (written in French outside of hexagon-shaped France) and within each field, a further separation occurs between canonical and popular literature. Because critical studies are often restricted to high culture, and have long treated France as the unquestioned centre of French studies, Francophone countries and popular literature are the vulnerable variables of the equation. In this chapter, we propose to redraw the disciplinary borders that have surrounded traditional fields ('popular culture', 'Francophone' and 'French' literatures) and focus on narrative fiction of French expression.

We do not pretend that France can arbitrarily be treated as just one Francophone area among others or that the distinction between high culture and low culture can be instantly abolished. The Hexagon has always had specific characteristics, notably a self-perception as the centre and point of origin. Even if we keep in mind regional cultures (Occitany, Brittany), France is a monolingual country whereas all other nations mentioned in this chapter will have French as one of their languages. In formerly colonised areas (North Africa, Sub-Saharan Africa, Vietnam, the Indian Ocean, the Caribbean) French has been associated with conquest and cultural domination. In yet other countries, French is a vulnerable cultural capital threatened by other expanding linguistic forces (English in Quebec for example).

We seek to loosen the tie between a language (French) and a nation (France), and to consider literary texts as well as popular culture, in order to resist the (positively or negatively encoded) marginalisation of both 'Francophone' and 'popular' texts: our goal is to suggest that one of the most remarkable features of twentieth-century narratives of French expression has been their ability to influence and revolutionise our conception of what constitutes the art of storytelling in French.

In this chapter, we thus address the question: 'who decides whose stories are legitimate?' by studying the relationship between narrative fiction and national or cultural institutions. We then move on to the issue of how narrative forms evolved throughout the century by concentrating on authors who either experimented with language and narrative genres or chose to adapt France's nineteenth-century realist legacy. Finally we focus on the relationship between narratives and modern identities by exploring the narrative representation of otherness (national or political identities in the case of historical texts, racial or ethnic identity in the case of colonial and post-colonial literature, gender or sexual identity in feminist and gay writings).

Narrative fiction and national or cultural institutions

The emergence, after the 1960s, of a vibrant corpus of non-Hexagonal Francophone narratives breaks with a long tradition of French centralisation which can be traced back to the creation of the Académie Française in 1635, and to Louis XIV's efforts at imposing his presence all over Europe: it is not a pun to say that French culture's 'rayonnement' (literally radiance) starts with the self-proclaimed Sun King (1638–1715). Today, the canonisation of narratives is both a cultural and a commercial enterprise as several institutions continue to intervene in the domain of narrative prose.

Literary prizes make authors famous in their own country and abroad. In France, every year, the novels chosen by the selection committees of the Goncourt, Fémina or Médicis prizes enjoy more than ten minutes of fame: they are celebrated by the media, by magazines such as *Le Magazine littéraire* (The Literary Review), *Lire* (Reading) or *La Quinzaine littéraire* (The Literary Fortnightly), and by popular TV shows such as Bernard Pivot's mythic (now extinct) *Apostrophes* (Apostrophes).

National education programmes play an even greater role in France: universities and Ecoles Normales Supérieures teach the same texts to students who take recruitment exams. Generations of teachers can thus be expected to have the same references and to share a relatively homogeneous canon, itself reflected in the programmes of the high school graduation diploma, the 'Baccalauréat'. Consequently, French students may not know the precise dates of publication of the seven volumes of Marcel Proust's *A la recherche du temps perdu* (Remembrance of Things Past, 1913–27), but they will all be familiar with the 'petite madeleine', the famous French biscuit that magically resurrects the narrator's past when he dips it into a cup of tea.

The obvious disadvantage of such a system is that it is very difficult for authors traditionally excluded from the list to be discovered at all except by individual readers. Women and non-Hexagonal writers have always been marginalised and it is theoretically and practically difficult to remedy the situation. The centralised nature of literary prizes has also historically penalised smaller, newer or not-so-Parisian publishers (out of the twenty Goncourt prizes awarded between 1980 and 2000, thirteen went to Gallimard, Grasset and Seuil, humorously renamed 'Galligrasseuil'). Marguerite Duras's career offers a typical example of the effect of prizes: while her first novels were admired by academics, she became enormously popular after being awarded the Goncourt Prize for *L'Amant* (The Lover) in 1984. Naturally, the principle of state intervention is not limited to France and the effects of all directives are not interchangeable: when African universities modified their programmes after the 1960s to include more African authors into their curriculum, when Quebec subsidises national literature, the strategy is interventionist but the ideological perspective is historically different. And canons are constantly challenged, drawing our attention to new frontiers (as when Aimé Césaire, the Martinican poet was put on the French 'Baccalauréat' programme).

There are, of course, different ways of questioning the principle of the canon from the inside: literary monuments can be, and are, reappropriated by popular culture and by the media. If a measure of an author's canonisation is the frequency with which his or her work reverberates through popular culture, Proust remains the emblem of the twentieth-century novel. He has inspired countless Francophone film directors (Chantal Akerman's *La Captive* [The Captive] and Raoul Ruiz's *Le temps retrouvé* [Time Regained] are adaptations of Proust's novels) but also rap musicians (MC Solaar includes references to the 'madeleine' in his lyrics).

Canonising institutions themselves are not always on the side of conservative forces even if their intervention is, by definition, ambiguous.

In 1921, the Goncourt prize was awarded to *Batouala: véritable roman nègre* (Batouala: a True Black Novel), a harsh satire of the colonial enterprise by a Guyanese author, René Maran. Ironically, he had to resign from his post in the colonial administration as a result of the scandal created by his book. Literary prizes have also celebrated many non-Hexagonal authors: between 1985 and 1995, the Goncourt prize singled out a Moroccan writer (Tahar Ben Jelloun for *La Nuit sacrée* [The Sacred Night]), a Martinican (Patrick Chamoiseau for *Texaco*), and an author of Lebanese origin (Amin Maalouf for *Le Rocher de Tanios* [The Rock of Tanios]). The prix Renaudot went to a Haitian writer in 1988 (René Depestre's *Hadriana dans tous mes rêves* [Hadriana in All My Dreams]), the Prix Fémina to the Quebecois Anne Hébert for *Les Fous de Bassan* (In the Shadow of the Wind) in 1982, and the Belgian writer Jacqueline Harpman was awarded the Prix Médicis in 1996 for her *Orlanda*.

As for publishers, they cannot simply be equated with the literary establishment: some have played a resolutely dissident role in times of crisis, risking their business and their lives for their ideas. During World War II, Minuit was founded as a clandestine publisher and published Vercors's *Le Silence de la mer* (The Silence of the Sea, 1942), a story that implicitly urges the French to resist German Occupation. During the war of Algeria, Minuit, Maspéro and Le Seuil spoke up against the use of torture. Other publishing companies were precisely founded to act as counter-canons, to correct absences that had become glaring to some intellectuals: Présence Africaine and Les Editions des femmes have become a home to African and women writers respectively.

Narrative forms: experiments and tradition, popular culture and the canon

What then, are the types of narrative fiction available to Francophone publics since 1900? Because the end of the nineteenth century is so clearly dominated by the realist and naturalist tradition, it is not surprising to find that twentieth-century prose writers have felt the need to position themselves vis-à-vis such literary monuments as Gustave Flaubert, Honoré de Balzac or Victor Hugo. Since no writer can altogether ignore that legacy, twentieth-century practitioners tend to fall into two categories: those who adopt nineteenth-century narrative techniques to express contemporary issues and those who perceive themselves as avant-gardists and seek to redefine the genre of the novel.

Realist fiction inspired by nineteenth-century Balzacian sagas survives in popular novels: the four volumes of Bernard Clavel's *Grande patience* (Great Patience) paint the harsh reality of bakers, Robert Sabatier's Parisian saga (including *Les Allumettes suédoises* [The Safety Matches]) has remained a best-seller. Depictions of bourgeois life and family drama abound in Henri Troyat's *Les Eygletière* (Eygletiere, 1965–7), in Hervé Bazin's *Vipère au poing* (Viper in the Fist, 1948). As for Françoise Sagan's *Bonjour tristesse*, her story of lost adolescence instantly became a formidable success in 1954.

Narratives whose authors privilege their rural, regionalist origin are often described as *romans de terroir* (regional literature). The ambiguous label implicitly endows non-urban centres with an aura of authenticity and tradition but it also relegates the genre to the periphery: rural life is idealised but seen as backward and old-fashioned. Louis Hémon's famous *Maria Chapdelaine* (1916) had a lasting influence on the way in which 'French Canada' was perceived and stereotyped. It also became the model against which other types of *romans de terroir* (such as Antoine Ringuet's 1938 *Trente Arpents* [Thirty Acres]) were written. In France, Marcel Pagnol's renditions of Provence popularised an exotic South in his plays, films and autobiographical narratives (*La Gloire de mon père* [My Father's Glory] or *Le Château de ma mère* [My Mother's Castle]). Recent adaptations of his novels include *Jean de Florette* and *Manon des Sources* (Manon of the Springs).

The genre of the detective novel deserves a special mention because of its remarkable ability to cross canonical frontiers. Television adaptations have immortalised the heroes of early detective fictions: Arsène Lupin, Belphégor, Rocambole, Fantômas or Léo Malet's Nestor Burma. As for Maigret, the famous inspector created by Georges Simenon (Belgium), he has become the Francophone equivalent of Hercule Poirot. From a stylistic and ideological point of view, we (often rightly) suspect such novels of being rather conservative: Gérard de Villiers's *S.A.S.* series, for example, is not exactly on the cutting edge of gender representations. Postwar authors, however, have very successfully subverted the political and literary conventions of the genre: in the 1950s, *nouveaux romanciers* such as Alain Robbe-Grillet or Marguerite Duras (*L'Amante anglaise*) wrote fake detective novels where the mystery is eventually exposed as irrelevant. Self-reflexivity also characterises the self-parodic San-Antonio or Hubert Aquin, the Quebecois author of *Prochain Episode* (Next Episode). More recent works have also added a distinctive left-wing and multicultural tonality to the detective novel. Didier Daeninckx explores the darkest hours of the war of Algeria in his 1984 *Meurtres pour mémoire* (Murder in Memoriam), an account of the 1961 deadly repression against Algerian demonstrators in Paris. Daniel Pennac's immensely popular *La Petite Marchande de prose* (Write to Kill, 1989) is as remarkable for its alert and humorous style as for its sympathetic depiction of Belleville, the working-class and ethnically diverse Parisian neighbourhood. The same interest in immigration and in new multi-racial French identities animates Jean-Paul Izzo's trilogy on Marseilles: *Total Kheops*, *Chourmo* and *Solea*. Women writers are no longer excluded from this traditionally male bastion and have learned how to adapt and reappropriate its conventions: if Sylvie Granotier, Estelle Monbrun or Fred Vargas are worth discovering, they have not yet gained the celebrity of Amélie Nothomb, the prolific, witty and acidic Belgian novelist, author of *Hygiène de l'assassin* (The Murderer's Hygiene) or of her compatriot, Harpman (*Le Bonheur dans le crime* [Happiness in Crime]).

The persistence of nineteenth-century models is obviously not limited to the popular novel nor can we assume that the tradition of realism is preserved only by backward-looking or nostalgic authors who will tend to favour literary and political conservative positions. At the very beginning of the century, Pierre Loti's novels do exemplify the type of exoticism that is now seen as the perfect example of (imperialistic) colonial prose. But when Jean-Paul Sartre, whose name is now synonymous with existentialism, asked himself what role literature should play in a modern society, his answer was two-fold: writers had to be 'engagés' (committed to social progress and equality) and should strive for maximum legibility: the ideal prose should be transparent like a pane of glass. Hence, his novels are a different type of philosophical language. And just as the hero of Sartre's *La Nausée* (Nausea) can be seen as the archetypal existentialist character, Albert Camus's novels, *La Peste* (The Plague) or *L'Etranger* (The Stranger), are often read as illustrations of humankind's 'absurd condition', a theory also illustrated in his more theoretical texts, *Le Mythe de Sisyphe* (The Myth of Sisyphus), or *L'Homme révolté* (The Rebel).

During and after the most active phase of existentialism and the great formal revolutions of the 1960s, Francophone readers have continued to enjoy beautifully crafted but not necessarily structurally revolutionary works by Marguerite Yourcenar (the first woman to be elected to the Académie Française in 1980), Jean-Marie Le Clézio (*Désert* [Desert], 1980), Harpman (*Moi qui n'ai pas connu les hommes* [I Who Have Never Known Men]) or Michel Tournier (*Le Roi des Aulnes* [The Ogre]).

A distinction should obviously be made between several types of mimetic prose: throughout the twentieth century, authors have hesitated between the baroque luxuriance of an Albert Cohen (*Belle du Seigneur*, 1968) or a Patrick Grainville (*Les Flamboyants*, Goncourt 1976 [The Flamboyants]), and the terse minimalism of Jean Echenoz (*Lac* [Lake], 1989) or Marie Redonnet (*Seaside*, 1992). But it may be worth noting that the early twentieth century enriched a tradition of narrative impertinence that can be said to go back to Rabelais. In 1959, Raymond Queneau invented a delightfully verbal phenomenon, the heroine of *Zazie dans le métro* (Zazie in the Metro) who accumulates witty remarks, colloquialisms, malapropisms, poetic neologisms. Another problematic literary monument can be mentioned in this category: Céline has the reputation of being both unavoidable from a literary point of view and unbearable from a political point of view. His *Voyage au bout de la nuit* (Journey to the End of the Night) obtained the Renaudot Prize in 1932 and earned him instant fame. Followed by *Mort à crédit* (Death On the Instalment Plan) in 1936, this first novel already displays a characteristic and unique style, an exuberant mixture of delirious humour and pessimism verging on the grotesque. Céline borrowed from all registers, merging epic passion and the truculence of oral parlance. But no one can forget that his prose is at the service of his virulent and paranoid anti-Semitism.

Such stylistic tours de force are however to be distinguished from another typically postwar literary intervention: a self-conscious and public determination to question the very foundations of nineteenth-century realism. The 1960s saw the rise of a series of highly visible literary movements whose primary goal was to emphasise the literariness of literature, i.e. the essentially formal nature of the production of texts and the ways in which the illusion of reality is created or exposed through storytelling. From radically different ideological perspectives, at least three Hexagonal collective enterprises sought to revolutionise the definition of narrative prose through their self-conscious and theoretical approach to the production of texts: a group of experimental writers known as 'Oulipo', a constellation of novelists who became known as the *nouveaux romanciers* and a team of radical and theoretical feminist authors whose books were so widely read that they came to represent 'French' feminism on the international scene.

Georges Perec and Raymond Queneau, two famous representatives of the *Ouvroir de littérature potentielle*, shared their companions' interest in logic and mathematical equations. With, respectively *La Disparition*

(A Void, 1969) a whole novel written without making use of the letter 'e', and the 1947 *Exercices de Style* (Exercises in Style), where the same insignificant episode of two men talking in a Parisian bus is narrated ninety-nine times in a different style, they brilliantly demonstrated that formal constraints are not the enemy of fantasy and that formal experiments are not incompatible with playful inspiration.

The writers associated with the *nouveau roman* were definitely less playful and their ambition to break with their literary predecessors resulted in difficult and often unpopular prose. André Gide and Marcel Proust are often presented as two obvious precursors of this movement, the former because of his interest in 'mise en abyme' (*Les Faux-monnayeurs* [Counterfeiters] is a novel about the writing of a novel) and the latter, for his fascination with self-reflexivity (*La Recherche* [Remembrance of Things Past] can be said to be the story of how the book was written). Both inspired an intense theoretical reflection on what it means to tell stories, on what it is to be a writer, to create novels. Thus, in Alain Robbe-Grillet's 1959 *Dans le labyrinthe* (In the Labyrinth), the labyrinth is a theme (a soldier is lost in a city), a metaphor for the story itself (the hero wants to give a box to the family of a friend but what is inside does not matter), and the model of our frustration as readers: the novel calls our attention to the fact that we are supposed to go through a disorientating experience during the reading. Similarly, Nathalie Sarraute and Marguerite Duras often deprive their readers of the comforting illusion that characters are just like real people. In *Disent les imbéciles* (Fools Say) and *Les Fruits d'or* (Golden Fruits), Sarraute's fragmented and elliptic prose betrays her lack of faith in the ability of traditional narrative prose to adequately express the tiny movements of human thought. Studied and encouraged by the most brilliant semiotician of their generation (Roland Barthes) and theoreticians themselves (Sarraute's 1956 *L'Ere du soupçon* [The Age of Suspicion], Robbe-Grillet's 1963 *Pour un nouveau roman* [For a New Novel] and Jean Ricardou's 1967 *Problèmes du nouveau roman* [Problems of the New Novel]), the *nouveaux romanciers* are often perceived as a group of elitist formalists. And yet, Duras's *Hiroshima mon amour* or Claude Simon's *Histoire* (*History*) or *La Bataille de Pharsale* (The Battle of Pharsalus) asked whether stories are capable of doing justice to the intricate workings of individual or collective human memory and history, anticipating issues that anticolonial or testimony literature would address during the next decades.

At the same time, the young Quebecois authors of the 1970s were turning their back on a relatively conservative generation, and experimenting with style. Relatively conventionally written *romans de terroir* were re-placed by texts made up of fragments and written in exuberant styles: *L'Avalée des avalés*, by Réjean Ducharme (1966), is the long interior mono-logue of a young rebel, Bérénice, who spews out insults and coinages, inventing her own language, the *bérénicien*. In Jacques Godbout's *Salut Garlarneau!* (Hail Galarneau!, 1967) the use of colloquial language and the fragmented structure of the text correspond to the protagonist's original and anarchic act of 'vécrire' (a coinage made of 'vivre' and 'écrire' [live and write]).

The genre of realist prose is not an infallible indicator of political sen-sitivity. A quick look at the works written by the feminists of the 1960s would convince readers that a fascination for the mechanics of writing is not incompatible with a militant and activist agenda. Although it would be a mistake to imagine that no French feminism existed before Simone de Beauvoir's 1949 *Le Deuxième Sexe* (The Second Sex), her monumental treatise did mark the beginning of a distinctive feminist generation in Europe and also in Quebec. *Ecriture féminine* perceives itself as a critique of universalist rationality whose binary thinking is identified as masculine. It seeks to invent a new polymorphous and polyphonic language to create a space of feminine freedom. It is characterised by its highly theoretical nature (Julia Kristeva's *Révolution du langage poétique* [Revolution in Poetic Language], Nicole Brossard's *L'Amèr ou le chapitre effrité* in 1977 [These Our Mothers; or, The Disintegrating Chapter]), its poetic opacity (*La Nef des sorcières* [The Writer in A Clash of Symbols], a 1976 Quebecois collective manifesto), its lack of distinction between prose and poetry (Monique Wittig's *Les Guérillères*), its interest in Lacanian psychoanalysis and struc-turalist theory (Luce Irigaray's *Ce Sexe qui n'en est pas un* [This Sex Which Is Not One]), and in lesbianism and bisexuality (Hélène Cixous and Cather-ine Clément's *La Jeune Née* [The Newly Born Woman]).

'Opacity' is also a literary and ideological tool in some of the most rev-olutionary postwar narratives. In his attempt to write a decolonised his-tory of his island, Martinican novelist Edouard Glissant questions the philosophical value of apparently objective categories such as chronol-ogy, geography and linearity. In his award-winning *La Lézarde* (Renaudot, 1958 [The Ripening]), the hero is a Martinican river. In the whole series of interconnected stories that Glissant subsequently published, he con-tinued to explore the fictional dynasties of Caribbean heroes, served by an unmistakable, dense, poetic, fragmented prose which he compares to the equations of chaos theory.

It is worth noting that narrative prose is not always the genre of predilection of revolutionary visionaries and that at least two fundamental movements influenced literature in general without being primarily concerned with the novel: Surrealism and *négritude*. The Surrealists' contempt for humanist values, their fascination with the intersection between desire and revolution, their interest in psychoanalysis and their remarkably early anti-colonial stance cannot be separated from their poetics: an international and interdisciplinary movement, they expressed themselves through manifestos, tracts, in reviews and exhibitions, in paintings and experimental poetry ('automatic writing') more systematically than in narrative prose. Similarly, the *négritude* movement was spearheaded by three poets, Césaire, Léopold Sédar Senghor and Léon Gontran Damas. And if only one work had to be mentioned in connection with them, it would be Césaire's *Cahier d'un retour au pays natal* (Notebook of a Return to My Native Land), a long lyrical poem as remarkable for its poetics as for its politics. Prefaced by André Breton, the 'pope of surrealism' who had met the Martinican poet on his island while fleeing occupied France, Césaire's cry of revolt is often credited with heralding the birth of 'Francophone literature'. And even if *négritude* is mostly represented by plays and poems, even if the Surrealists are often associated with a seething critique of the novel as genre, the radical agendas promoted by the Surrealists and by the *négritude* movement between the two world wars have had a lasting influence on the poetics and politics of future generations of storytellers. At one end of the spectrum, Julien Gracq is often associated with the Surrealists although he has always refused to belong to movements and structured groups or to abide by the laws of the market. The poetic prose of *Le Rivage des Syrtes* (The Opposing Shore), for which he won the Goncourt prize in 1951, is an example of radical storytelling. On the other hand, the ideas of the theoreticians and poets of the *négritude* pollinated the mimetic prose of early works by Tunisian Albert Memmi (*La Statue de Sel* [The Pillar of Salt], 1953) or Caribbean Michèle Lacrosil (*Cajou*, 1961). Maryse Condé's later vast historical African or transnational sagas, *Ségou* (Segu), *La Vie scélérate* (Tree of Life) and *Les Derniers Rois mages* (The Last of the African Kings) are noticeably different from Glissant's chaotic and 'rhizomic' prose (Glissant applies Gilles Deleuze and Félix Guattari's distinction to his own work: to the unique root, he prefers the rhizome, a diverse and multiple network of subterraneous stems).

Narratives and the representation of identities: nations, ethnicities, sexualities

If the twentieth century has spawned remarkable formal research and experiments, it has also generated a fascinating and ongoing debate about the relationship between narratives and identities: just as *écriture féminine* raised the controversial issue of a gender-specific prose, historical events forced writers to confront the always problematic interweaving of narratives and political opinion, sexual orientation and racial identities.

When history becomes cataclysmic (and the twentieth century has had more than its share of wars and atrocities), stories, like writers, must take sides and grapple with the disturbing intersection between history and fiction. World War II can be said to have inspired several distinct types of narratives: some stories were tales of resistance to the Nazi Occupation and the Vichy government, others are now referred to as literature of 'collaboration', a word connoting betrayal or even treason. Céline shared his sickening anti-Semitism with other 'collaborators' such as Drieu la Rochelle and Robert Brasillach who was condemned for treason and executed at the Liberation.

The other side of the political spectrum generated a more varied narrative production. Resistance literature sometimes fictionalised the fight against Nazism, sometimes bore witness to the horrors of life in concentration camps: among the most poignant accounts is Robert Antelme's *L'Espèce humaine* (The Human Race, 1947). Antelme's rescue from Dachau thanks to François Mitterrand is recounted from a more autobiographical perspective in one of Marguerite Duras's short stories, 'La Douleur' ('The War' in *The War: A Memoir*).

The incomparable nature of the Holocaust is reflected in a unique corpus: even if Jewish survivors describe experiences shared by other political prisoners (deportation and life in camps), their testimonies teach us that life at Auschwitz was different depending on whether they were deported as Jews, gypsies, political prisoners or homosexuals. In *La Nuit* (Night, 1959), Nobel Peace Prize winner Elie Wiesel remembers arriving at Auschwitz with his relatives. And in the 1970s, Charlotte Delbo published *Auschwitz et après* (Auschwitz and After).

For it was not immediately after the survivors' return from concentration camps that testimonies about the Holocaust were first heard by the French who were perhaps not ready to face their own responsibility

for the genocide. And it took almost half a century for a new generation of narratives to appear in print. Some Francophone authors wrote
about their own experience of deportation (Jorge Semprun's *Le Grand
Voyage* [The Long Voyage], 1963), others have stressed the fate of colonial
subjects fighting against the Germans, or the effect of Vichy on their
Caribbean island (Raphaël Confiant's *Le Nègre et l'amiral* [The Negro and
the Admiral]). Others still, like Patrick Modiano, write novels that revolve
around the issues of memory and identity (*Dora Bruder*). When narrative
fictions move away from testimony, despair is sometimes wonderfully expressed through comedy (in Gérard Oury's film *La Grande Vadrouille* [Don't
Look Now, We're Being Shot At], starring Louis de Funès and Bourvil) or
self-derision and tragic humour: Emile Ajar's *La Vie devant soi* (The Life
Before Us ['Madame Rosa'], lovingly portrays an old Jewish prostitute so
traumatised by World War II that, in the 1960s, she still carries ID papers
that prove that she has not been Jewish for generations).

Almost immediately after the Second World War, a new series of conflicts erupted between France and its colonial possessions. In the former
Indo-China and in Algeria, there were full-blown wars of independence.
Elsewhere a more gradual and sometimes incomplete process of decolonisation started, which led to an international political and cultural
upheaval. As can be expected, a vast array of narratives, including those
granted the legitimacy of 'history' by academic institutions, were written
in those troubled times where rhetorical as well as military battles were
fought with different weapons. If the body of texts written by colonised
or formerly colonised subjects has long suffered from marginalisation
and sometimes censorship (during the war of Algeria for example), it
has now become the primary object of study in the fields known as
Francophone and post-colonial studies. Literary histories are regularly
published and they have made us sensitive to the successive generations
of post-colonial narratives.

During the 1950s, several novels written in French insisted on the
dark and exploitative character of the 'civilising enterprise': from the
Caribbean (Joseph Zobel), from the Maghreb (Mouloud Mammeri,
Mohammed Dib), from Sub-Saharan Africa (Mongo Béti, Ferdinand
Oyono, Camara Laye), came out a first generation of anti-colonial prose
about which it is now said that it was mostly addressed to French audiences and to a small community of educated colonised subjects. Then,
in the 1960s and the 1970s, as anti-colonial feelings developed into more
radical nationalistic sentiments, narratives became forceful and lyrical

cries of revolt (Kateb Yacine's *Nedjma* has been read as the allegorical invention of the Algerian nation to come). In the 1970s and 1980s, critics paid attention to the fact that the number of women writers increased exponentially (Mariama Bâ, Ken Bugul). These authors added their voices to a new type of story where corrupt local governments and misogynistic traditions were often humorously but severely criticised as omnipresent forms of neo-colonialism (Sembène Ousmane, Ahmadou Kourouma). Even more recently a new trend has emerged: that of diasporic writings. Haitian writers publish in Quebec or in the United States for example. In France, a whole literary current is powered by the idea of 'second generation' or *métissage*. It forms an extremely varied community made up of recently arrived or long-established immigrants (Calixthe Beyala, Tahar Ben Jelloun), of children of immigrants originally from Africa (Azouz Begag, Nina Bouraoui) or Vietnam (Linda Lê), of Europeans who have adopted French as their language of publication (Augustin Gomez-Arcos, Andreï Makine, Milan Kundera) and also of long-established authors who now explore their own colonial past (Jacques Derrida, Cixous).

In this context, our commitment to comparative studies and our desire not to separate 'French' and 'Francophone' literatures creates one almost insuperable obstacle: if we adopt a chronological perspective, we must not only capitalise on the transnational similarities created by the global decolonising process but also remember not to lose track of the immense historical and cultural differences that exist between Francophone narratives. This is probably one of the reasons why very specific analyses of, say, the Moroccan novel, *Beur* literature (written by children of Arab immigrants or 'Beur' in slang) or Martinican folktales will continue to be necessary. But in this cross-national and comparative overview, what we would rather do now is consider the end of the twentieth century as an era where a type of story emerges and slowly becomes central: we suggest that they are examples of a global, cross-national (but not universal) 'post-colonial narrativity'.

Even in Francophone countries that were not directly involved in the creation of a colonial empire abroad (Canada), narratives now keep the trace of the process of decolonisation that has profoundly altered the balance of international relations. Although each country or geopolitical area will generate its own variation of what we call the global post-colonial narrative, it can now be argued that the post-colonial condition has modified readers' assumptions about what it means to tell a story. We suggest that post-colonial narrativity is characterised by a self-conscious demarcation from, and reappropriation of, literary codes that consumers of nineteenth- and early twentieth-century novels had gradually learned to take for granted because these codes had become familiar conventions. When addressed to post-colonial narratives both in and outside ex-metropolitan centres, three questions will typically obtain new answers. First, are some literary genres particularly well suited to express the post-colonial condition and why? Second, what is the status of the French language in a post-colonial narrative? And finally, who is the implicit public of such narratives?

In terms of genres, at least two reasons explain the abundance of post-colonial autobiographies. First novels, it is said, are often at least partly autobiographical and many early post-colonial writers were the first of their generation to have access to education and publication outlets. This phenomenon affects African and Caribbean texts from the 1950s and 1960s such as Camara Laye's *L'Enfant noir* (Guinea, 1953 [The Dark Child]), Mouloud Feraoun's *Le Fils du pauvre* (Algeria, 1950 [The Poor Man's Son]), but also children of immigrants in the Hexagon (Begag's 1989 *Béni ou le paradis privé* [Béni or the Private Paradise] and Nini Soraya's *Ils disent que je suis une beurette* [They Say I'm a Beurette, 1993] are two of many typical 'Beur' autobiographies). The other plausible explanation is that the process of rediscovery of one's identity is particularly well served by autobiographical genres. Like Joseph Zobel's *Rue Cases-Nègres* (Martinique, 1950 [Black Shack Alley]) or Bernard Dadié's *Climbié* (Ivory Coast, 1956) many texts denounce the cruel double bind imposed by colonial schools that taught children to despise their native languages and culture while making education the only way out of poverty.

Another particularly striking characteristic of post-colonial narrativity is the clever mixing of Western literary genres and autochthonous storytelling techniques. In an attempt to shatter the myth that no culture existed in Africa before the arrival of the coloniser, some authors have made a point of collecting folktales and legends (Birago Diop's *Contes d'Amadou Koumba* [Tales of Amadou Koumba], 1947), others wrote novels whose characters reveal the crucial cultural significance of oral performance in Sub-Saharan Africa, of the storyteller and of trickster figures in the Caribbean (Patrick Chamoiseau's *Solibo Magnifique* [Solibo Magnificent]), or in the Maghreb (Tahar Ben Jelloun's *L'Enfant de sable* [The Sand Child]). In *Le Jujubier du patriarche* (The Patriarch's Jujube Tree, 1993), Aminata Sow Fall questions the definition of the traditional 'griot' whose art consists of reciting long poems that function as the authorised genealogy of legitimate clans. Her 'griot' is not only a woman but a descendant of slaves and her narratives implicitly propose a counter-history. In another subversive move, Assia Djebar uses two modern Western genres (history and the novel) to write a poetic and revolutionary counter-narrative of the war of Algeria and the 1830 conquest: *L'Amour la fantasia* (Fantasia, An Algerian Cavalcade) is a polyphonic account where the words of dead soldiers and of nineteenth-century orientalist painters are presented side-by-side with old forgotten stories told by illiterate women, and with the personal vision of an Algerian woman whose relationship to the French language is always ambivalent.

In post-colonial narratives, French is never an obvious, self-evident linguistic tool. In his famous preface to Senghor's *Anthologie de la nouvelle poésie nègre et malgache* (An Anthology of the New Black and Madagascan Poetry, 1948), Jean-Paul Sartre brilliantly demonstrated that a language expresses hierarchies between races in its metaphors and in its vocabulary. Post-colonial narratives have used many different tactics to draw the reader's attention to the link between language and power. For example, authors who wrote in French can afford to let their silenced native language re-emerge through their text and the nature and the quality of this linguistic cohabitation is what makes their style unique: in each geographical area of multi-lingualism, a specific context of diglossia emerges. The first generation of post-colonial authors had to denounce a prevalent myth: the idea that French was superior, that it was the language of civilisation, and that the authors' native tongues were dialects, patois, not worthy of being taught or even spoken in class. And only after that (once revolutionary) point has been made, can we gradually realise and state that this question of dignity and linguistic respect is not qualitatively so different from other types of linguistic comparisons: in the 1920s, Charles-Ferdinand Ramuz was already advocating a form of 'Suisse' language that would be worth comparing to the Quebecois novels of the 1960s such as Godbout's *Le Couteau sur la table* (Knife on the Table, 1965) where the characters' identity is indistinguishable from their colloquial 'joual' (or Montreal slang).

But if it now goes without saying that French in general can no longer be synonymous with Parisian middle-class French, for colonised people whose native tongue was an African language, Arabic or Creole, this reconfiguration of linguistic skills had to be articulated during the long decade of the independences. In the Caribbean and in the Indian Ocean, where African slaves but also Chinese or Indian people were cut off from their original cultures, a new Creole language developed. After Césaire had initiated the mythical 'return to the native land', Confiant tried writing several novels in Creole, but the literary movement to which he belongs (the 'Créolistes') adopted a different strategy in their 1989 *Eloge de la créolité* (In Praise of Creoleness): Confiant, Patrick Chamoiseau and Jean Bernabé declared that neither the language of the coloniser nor the language of the colonised should be idolised. Typical of this attempt at 'creolising' is Chamoiseau's 1992 Goncourt prize *Texaco*, an international success. In the Maghreb, analyses of specific types of linguistic creolisation would have to take into account the often conflicting relationship between French, Arabic and Berber languages, as well as the power of state policies of 'arabisation' in Algeria for example.

That said, stories are constrained by, but not reducible to, a national context and each author will make specific decisions about how to deal with bilingualism or multi-lingualism. Some were at first content to introduce a few words from their native language into the text, and often, the words were explained in footnotes, which treated those items as a foreign element to be explained, justified. But glossaries can also be ironic and playful (as in Begag's 1986 *Gone du Chaâba* [The Kid from the Chaâba]). Other writers will let their native language colour the whole structure and syntax of their narratives. In *Les Soleils des indépendances* (The Suns of Independence), Kourouma writes in French but allows expressions and phrases from the Malinke to infiltrate all the elements of his novel. Other writers will multiply metaphors to explain what the French language represents for them. For Djebar, French is 'a threshold' but also the 'foster mother tongue' or 'Nessus's tunic'. For Yacine, it is a double-edged sword. Abdelkebir Khatibi writes that his French and Arabic mix to create phrases that are 'interwoven to death, indecipherable'. In *Amour bilingue* (Love in Two Languages), he equates French with a woman, a 'beautiful and malevolent foreigner' and he invents the concept of 'bilangue' which is not so much a form of bilingualism as the interstice between two languages, a way of listening to the world that Khatibi equates with a 'third ear'.

All these techniques have one major characteristic in common: they make it impossible to take it for granted that standard French is the only or even the most adequate tool of communication. Through their self-conscious use of 'French' as one of the possible languages, the mixing of narrative genres and the implicit questioning of a universal reader, post-colonial narratives force us to rethink the relationship between literature and oral performance, to ask ourselves how our stories are transmitted, and for whom. They remind us of the power of official histories to invent a world that we recognise as the only plausible real one. In other words, the 'us' itself, or the imagined community of readers is put into question by post-colonial narrativity: several techniques can be used to criticise the assumptions that the author and the reader belong to the same (national, cultural, linguistic) community, or the exoticising logic that tends to portray the stranger (never oneself) as fascinating but inferior. Blatant reversals of the anthropological gaze often result in comedy as in Bernard Dadié's *Un Nègre à Paris* (An African in Paris) and they also reveal that it has become foolhardy to impose Europe as a centre, or even the idea of the universal as self-evident. The twenty-first century may well be the century of what Bernabé, Chamoiseau and Confiant call 'diversality' in *In Praise of Creoleness*: 'the conscious harmonisation of preserved diversities'.

Meanwhile, twentieth-century narratives also grappled with the relationship between fiction and sexual or gender identities. Of course, gay themes and characters can be found in famous novels: Proust's *Sodome et Gomorrhe* (Sodom and Gomorrah) or Gide's *Corydon* (Corydon, Four Socratic Dialogues) come to mind. But the concept of 'gay novels' is a much more recent phenomenon, whose advent was prepared by the feminist and sexual revolution of the 1960s. Yves Navarre and Dominique Fernandez were both awarded the Goncourt prize respectively for *Le Jardin d'acclimatation* (Cronus' Children, 1980), a denunciation of the definition of homosexuality as a mental disease and *Dans la main de l'ange* (In the Angel's Hand, 1982), a fictional biography of Italian film-maker Pier Paolo Pasolini. A whole generation of AIDS writings emerged after 1982, as authors mourned the loss of their friends and lovers (René de Ceccatty's *L'Accompagnement* [The Accompaniment]), and of their own health (Pascal de Duve's *Cargo Vie* [Cargo Life]), but also wrote about their fear, anger and their sense of commitment. An aura of scandal has sometimes surrounded the most visible of these authors: it is especially the case for Hervé Guibert (1955–91), *enfant terrible* of AIDS literature since *A l'ami qui ne m'a pas sauvé la vie* (To the Friend: Who Did Not Save My Life, 1990), and for Cyril Collard who died in 1993, a few days before being awarded the César for best movie of the year for his film adaptation of his novel *Les Nuits fauves* (Savage Nights, 1989).

Narrative prose has also allowed women to explore the multiple facets of gender difference: just as we postulated the existence of a post-colonial narrativity, we would like to suggest that the twentieth century significantly contributed to include a gendered perspective in the definition of narrative fiction. Even if *écriture féminine* is still impossible to define, the legacy of the feminist 1960s is that it is much more difficult to argue today that language is neutral, and that gender is not a valid literary criterion. Thus, as we prepare a reading list for a class, if the relevant books that emerge as the result of our research happens to be made up of male authors only, it probably says something about the choice of our subject-matter. A list of exclusively or primarily female authors is quite easily compiled if one chooses the categories 'autobiographies' or 'sexuality'. Such topics would allow a critic to examine the link between storytelling and women identities in different national, cultural or racial contexts. Sexuality and lesbianism could be keywords if we read Colette's *Claudine à l'école* (Claudine at School), or Françoise Mallet-Joris's *Le Rempart des béguines* (The Illusionist; where the young heroine falls in love with her father's mistress). It would be interesting to compare Simone de Beauvoir's *La Femme rompue* (The Woman Destroyed) and Myriam Warner-Vieyra's *Juletane* for two different approaches to feminine madness and alienation. Class consciousness is notoriously crucial in Annie Ernaux's work, and more subtly explored in Redonnet's *Rose Mélie Rose* (Rose Mellie Rose), while colonial sexual politics are made obvious in Duras's *L'Amant* (The Lover). The intersection between sexism and racial discrimination as well as the articulation of non-Western feminisms is present in the work of all post-colonial women writers, from Djebar to Malika Mokeddem (Algeria), from Chantal Chawaf to Jeanne Hyvrard, from Condé to Cixous.

Conclusion

What then, can be said to be the most salient features of the twentieth century when we consider the narratives proposed to a public between 1900 and 2000? No simple synthesis will account for the multiplicity of genres and themes, of formal experiment and individual talents. We would like to suggest that, towards the middle of the century, a clear watershed separates those who believed that the future of narrative fiction laid in a revolutionary self-reflexivity, and those for whom narratives were subordinated to the quest of a political, sexual or national identity. After the beginning of the decolonisation process, the second type of vision prevails. Theoretically minded literary movements, that tend to insist on a radical separation between the realm of literature and the real now seem less attractive than narratives that directly grapple with the construction of identity, with the political, with the social. Clearly, a good story will always continue to exceed the representation of the real and the best narratives, at any given period, will be those that defy the formal constraints of traditional storytelling practices as defined by the dominant community. But at the same time, the revolutionary efforts of such visionaries change our expectations and readers' horizons. Since the 1960s, the efforts of previously marginalised storytellers who have insisted on sharing their gendered, ethnic or sexual perspectives have changed our expectations, and one of the lessons of post-colonial narrativity may be that we need to remain attentive to the criteria that we use to determine which stories are legitimate, true, good, well written before we uncritically pass them on to the next generation.

FURTHER READING

Bernabé, J., P. Chamoiseau and R. Confiant, *Eloge de la créolité/In Praise of Creoleness*, trans. M. B. Taleb-Khyar, Paris: Gallimard, 1993.

Davis, C., and E. Fallaize, *French Fiction in the Mitterrand Years: Memory, Narrative, Desire*, Oxford: Oxford University Press, 2000.

Hollier, D., and H. Bloch (eds.), *A New History of French Literature*, Cambridge, Mass.: Harvard University Press, 1989.

Hughes, A., and K. Reader (eds.), *Encyclopaedia of Contemporary French Culture*, London and New York: Routledge, 1998.

Lionnet, F., and R. Scharfman (eds.), *Post/Colonial Conditions: Exiles, Migrations, and Nomadisms*, vols. 1 and 2, *Yale French Studies*, 83, 2, 1993.

Unwin, T. (ed.), *The Cambridge Companion to the French Novel: from 1800 to the Present*, Cambridge: Cambridge University Press, 1997.

11

Poetry

Neo-Symbolism and renewal

Poetic modernity may be traced back to and even beyond Charles Baudelaire's searing paradoxes or Gustave Flaubert's clinical ironies, Stéphane
Mallarmé's retreat into textual interiorities or Arthur Rimbaud's aban-
donment of self-illumination, via his flight to Abyssinia and the recognition of the failure of his poetic enterprise. Twentieth-century poetic
modernity ushers itself in with a mixture of relatively silken-smooth
post-Symbolist manners and rather more jarring or vigorously rethought
modes that prefigure both Cubist and Surrealist preoccupations. The
principal figures on this early stage are nine in number: Valéry, Claudel,
Segalen, Péguy and Perse, Apollinaire, Cendrars and Reverdy, and one
often misunderstood woman, admired by Apollinaire and Cocteau and
the friend of Colette and Proust: Anna de Noailles.

Paul Claudel's work as a whole is marked by a spiritual questing
that conveys itself sometimes in surging lyrical, hymnal modes, sometimes in rather more emotionally taut tonalities to which the elastic and
free-flowing *verset claudélien* (Claudelian verset) or a poetically dramatised prose form bring suppleness and renewed rhythm. *Connaissance de
l'Est* (Knowledge of the East, 1900) offers a set of discreetly narrative/
descriptive and contemplative and emotionally charged prose poems
that caress the natural and human phenomena of a distant world, that
of the Far East. This world, however, refuses to provoke those very
twentieth-century feelings of alienation, doubt or revolt. The fourth
of Claudel's *Cinq grandes odes* (Five Great Odes, 1910), with its fluid verset, its 'stanzas' and 'anti-stanzas', its 'argument' and its 'epode', as
Claudel writes, sweeps majestically through its dialectic and dialogical

fervours, its 'desire . . . to be the gather[ing place] of God's earth'. *La Cantate à trois voix* (Cantata for Three Voices, 1912), like Claudel's considerable theatrical work and essay writing, seeks, both quasi-mystically and rather doctrinally, to experience 'paradise amidst the tenebrae! / . . . reality momentarily bursting forth for us beneath these fragile veils and a deep delight to our soul of all things God has created!'

This affective energy is not Paul Valéry's. His enthusiasms, though real, are more reined in. Philosopher, mathematician, a writer somewhat under the influence of Mallarmé, Valéry opted after a long silence (he was born three years after Claudel, in 1871), for a neo-Symbolist manner of relatively compact, late-classical forms involving only very occasionally the *impair*[1] or other prosodic modification (as in *Palme*, from *Charmes* [Charms, 1922]), never free verse, never the innovations of Rimbaud's *Illuminations* or Mallarmé's *Un coup de dés* (A Roll of the Dice, 1897). Cerebral, somewhat metaphysical, his poetry remains sensuously, even sensually rooted. His early work from 1890–1900 finally appeared in 1920, preceded by *La Jeune Parque* (The Young Parque, 1917) and followed by *Charmes* which contains his perhaps most famous poem, *Le Cimetière marin* (The Cemetery by the Sea). *Charmes* also contains characteristic aesthetically 'pure' miniatures such as the sonnet *Les Grenades* (The Pomegranates) with its modestly hermetic discourse on poetic creation and the structures of the mind.

If the fascinations of Valéry are, as his vast notebooks show, intellectually enormous and open-ended, as to their sense of being-in-the-world, those of Charles Péguy, like Claudel's, have an arguably narrower focus. A mystically inclined non-practising Catholic absorbed by the legend of Joan of Arc, an ardent lover of his native land with a strong sense of fidelity and social justice, a man closer to popular sentiment than most writers of his time, Péguy produced, before his death in action at the battle of the Marne, a rapid succession of inspired, surging poetic litanies. These are often of great charm and always of simple conviction, from *Le Mystère de la charité de Jeanne d'Arc* (Mystery of the Charity of Joan of Arc, 1910) to the various *Tapisseries* (Tapestries) and *Eve* (1913–14). The poetry of Saint-John Perse also reveals important patterns of repetition, both formal, prosodic and thematic, though Péguy's manner is more manifestly ritualistic, formulaic and recitative. Celebration remains, certainly, a dominant feature of Perse's poetry, as the early *Eloges* (Praises, 1911) makes clear, and persists despite a certain poetics of disenchantment and exile. As *Anabase* (Anabasis, 1924) soon shows, however – like the later volumes such as *Exil* (Exile, 1942), *Pluies* (Rains, 1943), *Amers* (Sea-Marks, 1957) or *Chronique* (Chronicle, 1960) – Perse is a poet alert less to the mystical than to the endlessly unfolding human and ecological epic of the planet. Teeming metaphor, technically brilliant description or evocation of the creativity and contradictions of humankind, the rhetorical intensification of observation and emotion, the general deployment of his atemporal, anhistorical landscapes by means of a muscular sinuous verset – these are some of the elements which give Perse that buoyancy of vision he expresses in his 1960 Nobel speech, *Poésie*.

Like Perse and Claudel, Victor Segalen travelled to the Far East, but the impact upon his work is more profound. *Stèles* (Stelae 1912), *Peinture* (Painting, 1916), *Odes* (1922), *Thibet* (Tibet, not published until 1963) and many prose writings attest to a sensibility at once still attuned to his very early *Synesthésies et l'école symboliste* (Synesthesias and the Symbolist School, 1902) but also very much plunged into an ascetic spirituality of 'essential exoticism' orientated towards some 'Attaining high and . . ./Being'. If, in rather lapidary, austerely lyrical forms, *Stèles* can speak of a 'Forbidden Violet City' where, beyond knowledge, 'the devastating torrent' may be experienced, *Odes* and *Thibet* venture further into the religious and the mystical, ever beyond a geography which Segalen loves.

If André Breton was soon to recognise in Valéry a thinker and poet of pertinence to his own nascent Surrealist consciousness, and in Perse a 'Surrealist at a distance', it is fair to say that the combined innovations of Reverdy, Apollinaire and Cendrars were much more visibly in tune with the more radical shifts of theory and practice that would soon proliferate, be they Surrealist, Cubist or others. Guillaume Apollinaire certainly began his career with lilting rhythms reminiscent of Verlaine, as in *Le Pont Mirabeau* (Mirabeau Bridge, in *Alcools*, 1913), and a Romantic and neo-Symbolist nostalgia lingers on in his work. But the *esprit nouveau*, or 'new spirit' he prescribes was rapidly given flesh and blood in the same volume via stunningly free-wheeling poems such as *Zone*. *Calligrammes* (1918) affirmed unambiguously a poetics of multiple perspective, flitting spatio-temporal consciousness, and apparent discontinuity that nevertheless provides a simultaneity of vision and (self-)analysis. The tight knots of Symbolist shimmer fly open, aesthetic nicety yields to the rawer beauty of experimentation, powerful spontaneity of impulse, even offhandedness, and convention yields to liberation. Exhilaration can dovetail with melancholy, and the energy of constantly self-renewing poetic option with existential anxiety. With Apollinaire's early demise, in 1918, due to the 'Spanish' flu, it was Pierre Reverdy who, by 1925, was deemed by the Surrealists (despite his distance from them) to be the greatest living poet in France. His *Poèmes en prose* (Prose Poems, 1915), followed by collections such as *La Lucarne ovale* (The Oval Skylight, 1916), *Les Ardoises du toit* (The Slates on the Roof, 1918), *Les Jockeys camouflés* (The Camouflaged Jockeys, 1918) and *La Guitare endormie* (The Sleeping Guitar, 1919), and his influential writings on art and poetry in the journal *Nord-Sud*, which he founded, all point to a poet radically renewing prevalent poetic manners and rhetoric. His conception of the image was to be snapped up by Breton's first Surrealist manifesto (though its notion of *justesse*, or 'appreciability', does not fit with Surrealist philosophy which privileges metaphoric 'distance'). Moreover, his disconnection of poetry from mimesis, narrative and raw emotion in order to create an 'antinatural' space of 'that emotion called poetry' both continues the logic of Mallarmé's meditation on book and poem and radically renews its textual practice. Closure is matched by a symbiotic link to the real world, whilst textual difference aims at a 'consubstantiation' of self, word and world. If, for Reverdy, the art of Braque is his true place of 'being', both the point of departure and the theatre of final accomplishment of any artist or poet remain the real, art thus emerging via a process of decanting and transmutation which Reverdy ceaselessly maps out in books like *Le Gant de crin* (Massage Glove, 1927) and *En Vrac* (In Bulk, 1956). Unlike Reverdy and Apollinaire, Blaise Cendrars was disinclined to theorise or critically historicise his own poetic production or that of poets and painters around him. His modernity lies, moreover, in a curious mixture of the lyrical, the autobiographical and the 'documentary' that recounts in long, free-verse poems his kaleidoscopic globe-trotting experiences. *Du monde entier* (The Whole World, 1919) opens with *Les Pâques à New York* (Easter in New York, 1912), *Prose du transsibérien et de la petite Jeanne de France* (Prose for the Transsiberian Railway and Little Joan of France, 1913) and *Le Panama ou les aventures de mes sept oncles* (Panama or the Adventures of my Seven Uncles, 1918). Spontaneous and incisive rhythms vie with a terse but open expression of sentiment, narrativity with a tendency to nominal style, 'elastic poems' with *enfantines* or 'childishnesses', constant search and movement with a sense of lack of self-coincidence. The tumbling lines of *Du monde entier* and *Au coeur du monde* (At the Heart of the World, 1919) may gather ephemeral, fragmented images of our early modernity, yet they speak too of its possible displacements and instabilities.

Anna de Noailles was not the only woman publishing poetry in these early years of the century. There were brief-lived pacifist poets, or poets such as Cécile Sauvage, Claudine Chonez, Andrée Sodenkamp, Gisèle Prassinos, Thérèse Plantier, Pierrette Sartin, mentioned in Jeanine Moulin's seminal anthology *Huit siècles de poésie feminine* (1963) and, perhaps especially, Renée Vivien with her powerful and moving, sometimes languorous sometimes pre-feminist lesbian ideals and tribulations, seen in work such as *Etudes et préludes* (Studies and Preludes, 1901), *Evolutions* (1903) or the posthumous *Haillons* (Rags, 1910). The classical prosodic conventions dominating the nineteenth century are largely respected by Anna de Noailles, as they are by Vivien, yet this friend of Colette achieves a freer manner via her anaphoric[2] flow, her varying manners and her use of poetic prose texts. Her work, from *La Domination* (Domination, 1905) to *Le Coeur innombrable* (The Countless Heart, 1918) and *L'Honneur de souffrir* (The Honour of Suffering, 1927), reveals a poetics of mortal consciousness and desiring reverie that, often motivated by the '[heroic] affirmers of life', constitutes a probing enquiry into our ephemeralness whilst demonstrating, in the face of pain, a joyous intuition of love's ever central discourse.

The avant-garde

In the 1920s even more pronounced changes in modern poetic practice become discernible, principally building consciously on the work of Reverdy and Apollinaire, yet also emerging with (neo-)Symbolist traces, and, above all, the marks of Dada's[3] demolitions and 'scandals' in the (dark) light of what was seen as the collapse of Western mythified 'progressive' ideals at the time of the 1914–18 war. If the poetic stage was soon to be occupied by Dadaists-turned-Surrealists such as Breton, Tzara, Eluard, Desnos, Aragon, Artaud and others, this is also a period allowing other new and differently significant voices to be heard. Pierre-Jean Jouve, for example, whose work goes back to 1909 (*Artificiel*), pursues a path that even today exercises its influence upon certain major poets, repudiating in 1924 all his early writings and, from the heart of a long spiritual crisis, giving us volumes such as *Les Mystérieuses noces* (The Mysterious Wedding, 1925), *Les Noces* (The Wedding, 1931), *Sueur de sang* (Sweating Blood, 1933), with his last volumes appearing in the 1960s. Lived tensions of guilt abound, caught in the polarities – for Jouve, often Baudelairian or Rimbaldian – of Eros and Thanatos, the mystical and the tragic. Jules Supervielle, too, like Lautréamont and Laforgue born in Montevideo, Uraguay, of French parents, found the fullness and independence of his poetic voice in these years, as in *Débarcadères* (Landing Stages, 1922), *Gravitations* (1925), *Le Forçat innocent* (The Innocent Convict, 1930). His poetry, recently crowned by a Pléiade edition (1996), is discreet and measured yet delicately intense and powerfully rhythmed with a wide range of emotion that includes the fanciful and the humorous and always conveys a sure cosmic sense of embrace. Marie Noël, finally, whilst drawing the admiring attention of Aragon and Montherlant, gives us, from the relative isolation of her native Auxerre, *Les Chansons et les heures* (Songs and Hours, 1920) and *Le Rosaire des joies* (The Rosary of Joys, 1930). The former provides lively, life-affirming yet self-enquiring 'songs' and popularly modelled 'fantasies' that, like the later volume, equally gentle and urgent in tone, still bear those marks of Catholic vision and concern which her two recorded spiritual crises of 1913 and 1920 document.

The Surrealist 'agenda', as developed by the movement's magus king, Breton, is ample and challenging in the extreme. It includes the pursuit of freedom; the exploration of the psyche beyond moral and aesthetic constraints; the penetration of the realms of the unconscious, dream, the irrational, impulse and intuition; the rendering 'available' of the self and an accompanying expectation; the opening up of the self to the 'marvellous' and to 'convulsive' beauty in their infinitely surprising forms; the realisation of the interlocking 'logics' of *amour fou* ('mad love'), communication, union, Communism, metaphor, all based on the conviction that 'there exists a certain point in the mind from which life and death, the real and the imaginary … cease to be perceived as contradictory'.[4] Automatic writing, free mental play, laughter and many similarly self-liberating tactics allow for a living – the literary is utterly secondary for Breton – of a primordial psychic energy that buoys up all his visions and texts – from *Les Champs magnétiques* (Magnetic Fields, with Soupault, 1920), *Clair de Terre* (Earth Light, 1923) and *Poisson soluble* (Soluble Fish, 1924) to his three manifestoes (1924, 1930, 1942), *Nadja* (1928), *Arcane 17* (1945) and beyond.

Tristan Tzara was invited by Breton to come from Zurich to Paris in 1920. He had already published Dadaist anti-texts such as *La Première Aventure céleste de Monsieur Antipyrine* (The First Celestial Adventure of M. Antipyrine, 1916) and *Vingt-cinq poèmes* (Twenty-Five Poems, 1918) before his arrival and would continue this vein of mild exuberance and eruptive, dancing, minimally coherent imagery before writing, in rather more Surrealist mode, his superb long poem, *L'Homme approximatif* (The Approximate Man, 1931), with its teeming, at once serene, poignant and obsessively trenchant outpourings, in which 'I think of the heat woven by language / around its kernel the dream we call ourselves'. Like Tzara, and indeed many Surrealists, Paul Eluard would flirt seriously with the Communist Party, whilst producing an oeuvre initially lightly and charmingly pre-Dadaist in colour (e.g. *Le Devoir* [Duty, 1916]), then vigorously Surrealist in tone, manner and preoccupation, as in volumes such as *Capitale de la douleur* (Capital of Pain, 1926), *Les Dessous de vie* (The Underside of Life, 1926) and *L'Amour la poésie* (Love, Poetry, 1929), as well as volumes in collaboration with René Char and Breton. Eluard's poetry reveals a great buoyancy of spirit, a trust both in life's natural 'fertility' and the 'anti-natural', 'Surreal' fertility and freedom of an imagination capable, precisely, of providing for humanity the freedom, joy and love it craves but, in the midst of its trials, barely believes in. His imagery of flickering yet casual transparency – 'I speak at random / Hintingly / Understanding myself', he wrote in the wonderful *Poésie ininterrompue* (Uninterrupted Poetry, 1946), adding 'I am my ray of sunshine / And I am my nocturnal happiness' – has made Eluard the most loved of the Surrealist lyric poets.

Two poets of great power and significance – Antonin Artaud, who was to turn his high-voltage energies towards a radical renewal of the theatre, and Robert Desnos, who gave himself increasingly to radio, film and journalism – found themselves 'excommunicated' from the Surrealist group. Artaud's dismissal came in 1926, after he had been head of the Centrale du Bureau de Recherches Surréalistes, heavily involved in the review *La Révolution surréaliste*, and after the publication of two splendid collections, *L'Ombilic des Limbes* (Limbo Umbilicus, 1925) and *Le Pèse-nerfs* (The Nervometer, 1925). 'Where others propose works, I claim nothing more than to show my mind', he writes characteristically in the first of these two volumes, 'Life is about burning questions. I do not conceive of any work as being detached from life.' His work constitutes total poetry, total theatre, always aiming to plumb 'the limbo of my consciousness', and to 'disturb'. Indeed, Artaud's own life was always disturbing, and disturbed, and he spent ten years in an asylum. Desnos, dying as a Resistance fighter in the Terezin concentration camp in 1945 just prior to its liberation, was not excluded from the Surrealist group until 1929, by which time his extraordinary mediumistic abilities had heightened Surrealist confidence in the belief that the unconscious can be tapped into and creatively mined, and his own collections had begun to multiply: *Deuil pour deuil* (Mourning for Mourning, 1924), *C'est les bottes de sept lieues cette phrase ≪Je me vois≫* (The Phrase 'I see myself' is like Seven-League Boots, 1926),

La Liberté ou l'amour (Freedom or Love, 1927). Witty, charming, tender, often magically supple linguistically, these and other poems, such as *Corps et biens* (Bodies and Possessions, 1930), with the 'marvellousness' of its *Rose Sélavy* or the dream-like beauty of *Les Ténèbres* (Darkness), make of Desnos a major voice belonging to what he was to call in the title of his posthumously published later work the true, free *Domaine public* (Public Domain) of Surrealism.

The extensive work of the Belgian-born Henri Michaux certainly exhibits elements of various Surrealist modes and fascinations, but his adventures of the self are more those of a loner. From his earliest work, *Qui je fus* (Who I was, 1927) and *Mes propriétés* (My Properties, 1929), Michaux's poetry, sometimes versified but often in prose, plots its course through the fantastical and aggressive (self-)exorcism towards lucid interrogation, the 'abyssal' self-knowledge of *Voyage en Grande Garabagne* (Journey to Great Garabrain, 1936), and those lived serenities of *Paix dans les brisements* (Peace in the Breakers, 1959), or *Vers la complétude* (Towards Completeness, 1967), at times drug-induced or at times glimpsed via music, painting, humour, children's creativity. His work is intensely poetic, yet defies classification. In revolt or tragically tinged, it always seeks 'absolutes' that slip away as he grasps their fleetingly lived reality. 'Suddenly, precipice', he writes later in *Connaissance par les gouffres* (Knowledge through Chasms, 1961) speaking of the movement of his own thoughts, 'Boiling away / torrential waters cascade to the canyon bottom / alive alive ultrahardy'.

The postwar period

To speak of Michaux is to remind ourselves that not all Francophone poetic genius originates in France and that even at this relatively early juncture in the twentieth century voices already made themselves heard, at times with very great innovative power, in the French-speaking world of Quebec, Africa, Belgium, the Antilles, Switzerland, in nearby 'corners' of Luxembourg, in the far-flung islands of the Pacific or the Indian Ocean. In Senegal, Léopold Senghor burst upon the world with *Chants d'ombre* (Songs from the Shadows, 1945), *Hosties noires* (Black Hosts, 1948) and *Ethiopiques* (Ethiopics, 1956) and became rapidly the foremost poet of Africa, at once elegiacal and celebratory, solemn and sensual, lyrical and sacramental, ritualistic and earthy. With the flexible *verset*, prose poetry, long dramatised and mystically orchestrated articulations, shorter, more abrupt texts, Senghor's range is considerable, even if his preference for more fully voiced modes dominates. Léon-Gontran Damas, born in French Guyana, is, like Senghor and Césaire, a poet of *négritude,* black identity. His work, from *Pigments* (1937), a powerful revelation of Black disinheritance, alienation and mocking resistance, to *Névralgies* (Neuralgias, 1966), for example, echoes oral and song traditions, yet is urbanely ironic. Similarly, whilst eminently able to convey sharp satire, it retains a resiliency, setting its sights on 'the infinite tenderness / that aims to survive'. Aimé Césaire, from Martinique and, like Senghor, destined to play a major political role in his still colonised land of Creole reality and African nostalgia, has given us unforgettable poetical works such as *Cahier d'un retour au pays natal* (Notebook for a Return to the Country of My Birth, 1939), *Les Armes miraculeuses* (Miraculous Weapons, 1946) and *Moi, laminaire* (I, Laminar, 1982), as well as theatre and essays. More manifestly surrealising in his imagery and elliptical in his syntax than Senghor, Césaire's poetry can fuse ampleness and concision; it can offer pounding free prosody or occasional most serene meditativeness; its lexicon can be brilliantly transparent or plunge us into dizzying kaleidoscopic reference and allusion. Far across the American continent, in Quebec, two great poets emerged, both of whom, like Senghor and Césaire in particular, were culturally and politically influential: Saint-Denys Garneau and Alain Grandbois. The former, with *Regards et jeux dans l'espace* (Visions and Games in Space, 1937) preceding his very early death only by six years, established himself as a poet of supple free verse rhythms, both intensely personal and ascetically inclined, ironic yet enthused, as in the celebrated *Le Jeu* (The Game). He was conscious too of a solitariness to which his 'joy of playing, [his] paradise of freedoms' destined him. Grandbois, widely travelled throughout Europe and the East, published his first *Poèmes* (1934) in China, followed by determining collections such as *Les Îles de la nuit* (Islands of the Night, 1944) and *Rivages de l'homme* (Shores of Man, 1948). Propelled by anaphoric and solemnly incantatory rhythms, his concentrated work is at once haunted by a thematics of death and birth, desire and guilt, cosmic (even apocalyptic, 'absolute') vision and yet attention to the earth's fleeting minutiae.

Back in Metropolitan France – at a time, let it be noted, of a high colonialism about to crumble under its own heaviness – various new poetic voices, freeing themselves up in significant measure from Cubist, Surrealist, even absurdist manners and philosophy, begin to exercise an influence that was to be felt well into the 1980s: Char, Frénaud, Prévert, Guillevic, Ponge, Follain, Queneau, Vilmorin. The work of the *maquisard*

Resistance captain, René Char, despite its poetics of 'fury', revolt and threatened destiny, manages to centre itself upon hope and a Rimbaldian 'future Vigour'. Its kingpins, both in the early *Arsenal* (1929), *Le Marteau sans maître* (Hammer without a Master, 1934), *Fureur et mystère* (Fury and Mystery, 1948) or the later collections, from *Chants de la Balandrane* (Songs from La Balandrane, 1977) to *Eloge d'une soupçonnée* (In Praise of One Suspected, 1988), are the earth's mystery and upliftment, human love and a continuing 'sovereign conversation' with great artists, poets, even oriental mystics such as Marpa and Milarepa. Char's achievements oscillate between a metaphorically dense and tightly aphoristic style and a supremely transparent manner, but they do not promote transcendence of the real, rather an embrace, at once exhilarating and difficult, of our passage, our traversal of being here and now. André Frénaud's attitude to life, poetry and creative endeavour at large swings about in unstable fashion between the pole of the tragic and the minimal and that of some maximum feasibility. Like many of the poets treated here, from Apollinaire and Reverdy, through Breton, Char, Prévert and Ponge, to Bonnefoy and Du Bouchet, Frénaud's relationships with contemporary artists and his writings devoted to them are of high pertinence. Irony, self-destruction and gaucheness vie with a self-assumption, a perseverance, a will to dignify existence, to perceive it even in heroic terms. His *Rois mages* (Magi Kings, 1943), as well as his *Poèmes de dessous le plancher* (Poems from under the Floor, 1949) or *Il n'y a pas de paradis* (There is no Paradise, 1962), demonstrate this compelling equivocalness that, as his interviews with Bernard Pingaud (*Notre inhabileté fatale* [Our Fatal Incapacity, 1979]) show, is not destined for resolution. Rough-edged and tender, tragic and driven on by an 'insane calling' to which he responds, now richly allegorical now fragmented and elliptic, Frénaud's oeuvre, with its superb *Sorcière de Rome* (The Witch of Rome, 1973) and its remarkable *Gloses* (Annotations, 1995), stands amongst the most authentic of the century.

Jacques Prévert's first collection, *Paroles* (Words, 1945), established him immediately in the eyes of a wide public as an original poet, witty, punning, satirically biting yet freedom-seeking and intrinsically 'festive'. He is today the most read poet of the century, and second only in popular readership to Hugo. He transcends genres, such as song, theatre, narrative, even music and image (as in his own collages for *Fatras* [Hodgepodge, 1966]), and all is grist to the poetic mill of a man who is also the greatest French scriptwriter of his generation (*Les Enfants du paradis* [The Children of the Gods, 1945], for example) and a poet whose poems were sung by performers such as Piaf, Gréco, and Montand, Nat King Cole and Sinatra. From *Histoires* (1946) and *Spectacle* (1951) to *La Pluie et le beau temps* (Rain and Shine, 1955), *Arbres* (Trees, 1968) and *Choses et autres* (Of This and That, 1972), Prévert's work, often thought simply anti-establishment (against church, army, nationalism), orientates itself implacably according to ideals of joy, innocence, liberty and love. Close in some respects to Prévert – they knew each other in their very early Surrealist days and one need only think of *Paroles'* famous opening poem, *Tentative de description d'un dîner de têtes à Paris-France* [Attempt at a description of a fashionable dinner-party in Paris-France] – is the ironic, at times burlesque pastiching and mathematically linguistic play of Raymond Queneau, subsequently editor of the *Encyclopédie de la Pléiade* and co-founder in 1960 of OULIPO, a group of authors dedicated to exploring the possible forms and structures of creative writing. Queneau's poetry, from *Chêne et chien* (Oak Tree and Dog, 1937) and *Les Ziaux* (Waterers, 1943) to *Petite cosmogonie portative* (Little Portable Cosmogony, 1950), *Cent mille milliards de poèmes* (A Hundred Thousand Billion Poems, 1961) and *Battre la campagne* (Scouring the Countryside, 1968), constitutes at once a self-satire, an implicit interrogation of literary purpose, and an investigation, both jubilatory and derisory, of improbable options remaining available in the face of existential self-doubt.

The three poets Ponge, Guillevic and Follain share, despite dramatically differing practices and conceptions, a deep fascination with everyday phenomena, 'things', from seashells, figs and 'landscapes', to stelae, stars and human presences as things amongst things. Eugène Guillevic's poetry – from *Terraqué* (Terraqueous, 1942) and *Exécutoire* (Writ of Execution, 1947) down to *Carnac* (1961), *Du domaine* (The Realm, 1977), *Requis* (Compelled, 1983) and *Possibles futurs* (Future Options, 1996) – commonly structures itself around notions of *choses* (things) and *conscience*, the interplay of matter and mind, the seemingly external givens of this world and a *dedans*, a human interiority that, ultimately, blurs the frontiers of our rationalised spaces and categories of self and other. Guillevic's writing is at once accessible and mildly gnomic, never truly dense or hermetic, and has a widely appreciated transparency that nevertheless offers subtle meditation on the fine, shareable detail of our being-in-the-world. There is no defeatism here, no real despondency, rather, a growing, earned, assumed ease, and a grateful caress of a world experience not scarred by a feeling of language's opaqueness. Similarly, Francis Ponge's instincts take him naturally towards the shimmering array of the earth's phenomena. Works such as *Le Parti pris des choses* (A Prejudice for Things, 1942), *Proêmes* (Proems, 1948), *La Rage de l'expression* (Expression's Fury, 1952), *Le Savon* (Soap, 1967) or *Comment une figue de paroles et pourquoi* (How a Fig of Words and Why, 1977) reveal a poet of great originality shifting his poetics from one of textual, expressive 'infallibility', closure and self-containedness, to one of incompletion, unfinishableness and the relativity of speech (*parole*). For Ponge world and word are non-coincident. To use Ponge's own terms, the *objet*, out there in the world of matter, can at best become textual *objeu* and, much better still, *objoie*. The poem, literature, all of language's discourse on being are thus held to be mere, but marvellous, 'obplay' and 'objoy' – joyous textual play that cannot, does not, hope to represent. The poem, with Ponge, thus leaps beyond realist illusion to its place of what he calls 'differential analogy' or homology in relation to the real. Jean Follain, however, does not concern himself with such thinking vaguely related to the theoretical journal *Tel Quel* or the New Novel. Nor does he, when all the dust has settled, seem to be any the worse for it. Admired by Frénaud, Guillevic and other contemporaries, and the recipient in 1970, just prior to his death, of the Grand Prix de Poésie de l'Académie Française, Follain plunges us right through the screen of language into the world of 'old wine-presses covered with soft lichens', 'frail dioscuri / go[ing] by the inn smelling of dark game stews', 'loves shining bright for a mere moment / in the stagless and flowerless forest'. This is a poetry of the lived, observed minutiae of our collective dailiness, essentially provincial, un-bourgeois, strangely primordial, though rooted in precise history and culture. Unrhetorical, even unlyrical, Follain's work nevertheless gives us, veiled and discreet, an intimate feeling of what two of his most important titles call *Usage du temps* (Use of Time, 1943) and *Exister* (To Exist, 1947).

Louise de Vilmorin came upon the French poetic scene in 1939, with the publication of her *Fiançailles pour rire* (Engagement for the Fun of It). A relatively rare woman's voice amidst the male din, it was nevertheless picked out by Malraux as distinctive, more truly oral, less concerned with the theory or practice of its textual inscription than many post-Mallarméan modernists. Prosodically more conventional than her contemporaries, whether in *Le Lit à colonnes* (The Four-Poster, 1941), *Le Sable du sablier* (Hourglass Sand, 1945) or *L'Alphabet des aveux* (ABC of Confession, 1955), Vilmorin's form can nevertheless veer to the unexpected, the rhythmically uneven, the smilingly 'coughing', as she unpretentiously puts it – albeit a 'cough' often set to music by Poulenc and Béart. Her 'marginality', as Malraux suggests – with respect to developing form, the image, and their theorisation – is deliberate. Her gift lies elsewhere, in what Malraux once again perceives, rightly, as 'an impulsive, impish fancifulness' that belies the delicately sober and enchantingly atemporal character of an oeuvre propelled by subtle intent. Such relative indifference to male avant-gardist preoccupation (in either aesthetic or philosophical terms) is visible in the poetic work of women such as Catherine Pozzi, Alice Rahon, Valentine Penrose and Claire Goll. The individual oeuvres of these four women may be slight in quantity, but their power can be very real and can never – as with a Follain or a Guillevic, of course – be attributed to a flagrant self-imposed aesthetic or philosophical ideology. Pozzi's virtues lie in expressive concentration that offers a subtle articulation of sentiment and metaphysical vision that Valéry would have been more than pleased to call his own. Valentine Penrose, admired by Eluard for the 'marvel of her language', opts for a Surrealist mode exploring difference, the shifting, even interchangeable realms of the oneiric and the real, a *merveilleux* that is 'true' and speaks of the radical 'otherness' of all that is. Penrose's companion in India, Rahon, operates, in *Sablier couché* (Recumbent Hourglass, 1938) and *Noir animal* (Black Beast, 1941), a bewitching fusion of body and dream, memory and imagination, and important intertextualities tie her work to Penrose's, as well as to her own painting. Goll, finally, generates in works from the 1928 *Une Allemande à Paris* (A German Woman in Paris) to her 1969 *L'Ignifère* (Igniferous), her own particular psychical surrealisation of the cosmic and the visceral, the mythical and the occult.

The new generation

In the mid- to late 1940s and early 1950s a new generation of poets ventured upon the scene, from all around the Francophone world, poets whose impact has frequently been very considerable. These include Bonnefoy, Du Bouchet, Des Forêts and Dupin, from France; Jaccottet, of Swiss origin; Mansour, born in England and brought up in Cairo; Schehadé, of Franco-Lebanese origins, born in Alexandria; Hébert, Miron and Giguère, from Quebec; Rabemananjara, from Madagascar; Glissant, from Martinique; Depestre, from Haiti; Tchicaya U Tam'si, from the Congo.

To speak of Yves Bonnefoy is to speak of a poet deemed by many to be France's greatest living poet today. His oeuvre is vast and multi-faceted: translations of Shakespeare and Yeats, art criticism from the Baroque to the hypercontemporary, intricate critical readings devoted particularly to Baudelaire, Mallarmé, Rimbaud and Verlaine; and, of course, a poetic corpus whose philosophical, psychological and spiritual urgency is always reflected in his other activities. From *Du mouvement et de l'immobilité de Douve* (Movement and Stillness of Douve, 1953) to his more recent *Début et fin de la neige* (Beginning and End of Snow, 1991) or *La Vie errante* (The Wandering Life, 1993), Bonnefoy's work seeks to offer itself as an act and a place of *présence* – of (self-)traversal, of openness, of both assent and (self-)contestation, of love and easeful 'open[ing up of] / the almond of absence in language'. 'Words like the sky', he writes at the close of *Dans le leurre du seuil* (In the Lure of the Threshold, 1975), 'Today, / something gathering, dispersing. // Words like the sky / Infinite / But entire and sudden in the brief pool'. The 'presence' of poetry thus functions against our temptation to make of it a place of Symbolist 'repose', 'image', a place of dream, closure, ideality – a structure as opposed to a mortal place of ephemeral experience. To 'conquer image *in* image' is Bonnefoy's hypermodern hope, to make poetry a non-place, exquisite, infinite, meaningful beyond conceptualisation, the rough equivalent of that described in *Ce qui fut sans lumière* (1987), 'amongst the brambles / That scratch our faces but are merely nothing scratching nothingness in the light'.

The relationships, human and philosophical, between Bonnefoy and his contemporaries du Bouchet, Jaccottet, Des Forêts and Dupin are significant, despite the many distinctive features that inform their separate oeuvres. André Du Bouchet, from early work such as *Air* (1951) and *Dans la chaleur vacante* (In the Gaping Heat, 1961) to *Qui n'est pas tourné vers nous* (That Faces Away From Us, 1972), *L'Incohérence* (Incoherence, 1979), *Axiales* (Axials, 1992) and beyond, articulates the (self-)doubtings and the intensity of the blind, compulsive questing that also continues, in a man and a poet for whom language, symbolic structuring of reality, never allows for that utopian access to being, and at best traces an imperfect trail in its direction. Incoherence, hiddenness, insubstantiality, fragmentation thus become 'themes', and acts of writing/being, that fall into tense and very terse relation with those of 'walking', forward movement, dour passage. For all such apparent signs of minimalism, Du Bouchet's work, as evidenced by his very many translations and critical meditations (for example, on Giacometti, Joyce, Shakespeare, Celan and Hölderlin), demonstrates a resilient buoyancy and a love of the rugged land of southern France which he long inhabited. Philippe Jaccottet, too, has both struggled, philosophically and psychologically, with language and the images that project the real, whilst never ceasing to immerse himself in their powerful universe, as poet, translator, critic and diarist. Speech may thus be 'imposture' or 'lie', as for Ponge or Michaux. Metaphor may, curiously and disfiguringly, move beyond, to the side and across, but there is upliftment, brief 'transport' available despite disillusion. Poetry may not allow for what Ponge calls a 'remaking of the world' and it is not really on Jaccottet's agenda, but it can allow for an occasional festive participation in being's natural beauties, a recognition and caressive 'combing' of the earth, distant, unreal but felt, as *Beauregard* (1981) suggests. From *L'Effraie* (Screechowl, 1953) to *A la lumière d'hiver* (In Winter's Light, 1977) and the wonderful prose and verse of *Cahier de verdure* (Green Book, 1990), Jaccottet thus shepherds his hesitant, at times fragile forms, seeking to provide via them a place of Heideggerian 'caring' rather more adequate to what he senses within those delicate 'groundsel, cow-parsnip, chicory' – phenomena of the world that, as he writes, boldly but still tentatively, in *Cahier de verdure*, manage to speak a language more eloquent than death and suffering themselves.

Louis-René des Forêts, co-founder with Bonnefoy, Picon and Du Bouchet of the review *L'Ephémère*, provides a sparse, bleak, paradoxical, even paroxystic oeuvre, initially novelistic (*Les Mendiants* [The Beggers, 1943], *Le Bavard* [Chatterer, 1946]), that has nevertheless caught the attention of poets and philosophers, notably Bataille and Blanchot. *Les Mégères de la mer* (Sea Shrews, 1967), *Poèmes de Samuel Wood* (Poems of Samuel Wood, 1988) and *Ostinato* (1997) show us a world of at once largely classical manner, yet devastatingly postmodern obsessiveness. It is a world, as Pascal Quignard has said, of 'writing and [its] disavowal', eked out over the years between 'reason and madness struggling in fine balance', as Des Forêts tells us in *Poèmes de Samuel Wood*. Jacques Dupin, too, knows well the traumas of psychic violence, that 'state of permanent insecurity' Des Forêts evokes. His poetic universe, from *Cendrier du voyage* (Journey's Ashtray, 1950), through *Gravier* (Gravel, 1963) and *L'Embrasure* (The Embrasure, 1969), to *Echancré* (Cut Low, 1991) and *Le Grésil* (Sleet, 1996), can be dense, abstruse, harsh, aggressive/defensive. Always deeply gouging into the real, it often portrays extreme dismay – 'in few words saying nothing/letting it all go' – or consequent derision, though it may suddenly veer away from being's, and language's, 'illegibility', to attribute meaning where none seemed feasible, a 'scintillation of signs in the profusion of ashes', 'the fragrance of named things / touched breathed infinitely / on your skin' (*Le Grésil*).

Joyce Mansour's Surreal world is at a distance from the 'group', though it was hailed by Breton, speaking of her 1958 *Les Gisants satisfaits* (Self-Satisfied Gisants), as 'the Garden of the century's deliriums'. This world is fiercely satirical, exhilaratingly but also nightmarishly erotic, offering a 'feminism' at once stunningly self-destructive and self-exorcising and radically liberating. Transgression is rife; literary ambition seems irrelevant. This is poetry – from *Cris* (Screams, 1953) to *Flammes immobiles* (Still Flames, 1985) – as 'pandemonium', 'scream', 'laceration', as certain titles suggest. As we cross the Atlantic, the signs of Surrealist influence fade in the work of a Quebec poet and novelist such as Anne Hébert, though the role of phantasm-driven metaphor and the 'exploration' of the so-called 'unconscious' remain manifest in most post-1940 work. This fading of flagrant Surrealism is largely true of modern Quebec poetry. The latter's resurgence more or less coincides with a renewed socio-cultural militantism that, more recently, has yielded to other at once private and more universal agendas. Tension, implicit or real threat, death and solitude motifs barely transmuted by images of continuing, crystalline voice: such are common fascinations in Hébert's early poetical work (*Les Songes en équilibre* [Balanced Dreams, 1942], *Le Tombeau des rois* [The Tomb of Kings, 1953]) which she herself argues is governed by a dialectics of 'night', 'struggle' and 'daylight'. Hébert's novelistic universe, in works such as *Kamouraska* (1970) or *Les Fous de Bassan* (The Loons, 1982), continues this search for equilibrium, as does her 1997 collection, *Poèmes de la main gauche* (Left-Handed Poems), caught between a desire for a few 'clear words' and a 'breathlessness', a near-exhaustedness deriving from a sense of 'unbearable and seemingly purposeless contingency'. Hébert's compatriots, the flamboyant and charming separatist Gaston Miron, founder of the Editions de l'Hexagone and contributor to *Liberté* and *Parti pris*, and Giguère, publishing in 1958 his *Adorable femme des neiges* (Adorable Snow-Woman), which, although revealing Surrealist influence, nevertheless espouses what Brochu calls 'temperate' modes and even themes, carve out a poetic territory significantly different in tone and vision from hers. Miron, perhaps the major poetic voice of his generation, gives us in *L'Homme rapaillé* (Gleaned Man) – texts gathered from the 1950s on, but only published in 1970 – a passionate 'anthropoetry', resistant, filled with desire and 'deferred love', visionary yet clear-eyed, a poetry moreover 'extremely written' and linguistically 'decolonising'. Roland Giguère, who refused Canada's Prix du Gouverneur, gathers together in *L'Age de la parole* (Age of Speech) his work of the 1949–60 period, and, in

La Main au feu (Hand in the Fire) his prose poems from 1949 on. Dense, muscular, curiously positioned between the lyrical and a symbolism that evacuates and purifies somewhat manifest, incarnate experience, Giguère's later work is at times less assured emotionally and philosophically. Wandering, brokenness of motion, disconnectedness may be given concise articulation, or else, as in *Illuminures* (Illuminates, 1997), he opts for frailer, haiku-like 'miniatures' that seem to contest their very status in their act of half-nostalgic affirmation.

What Georges Schehadé's poetic oeuvre, *Rodogune Sinne* (1947), *Les Poésies* (Poems, 1969), *Le Nageur d'un seul amour* (One Love Swimmer, 1985), may lose in its brevity, it gains in its discreetly intense drama of time and recovery, exile's forced reading of 'the great Bible of stones', its distanced trailing at best of 'the great paradises'. Metaphor here is always toned down, sober, solemn, far from Surrealist intoxication, and Schehadé's evocations are, curiously, at once visionary and reluctantly lyricising. The Malagasy poet of *négritude*, Jacques Rabemananjara, who was imprisoned for nearly ten years for his political views, opts instead for luscious, richly textured, incantatory free verse-forms. His poetry is one of recognition, resurgence and affirmation of the land and people he knows. Rather than orientate itself towards a past, it plants itself in presence and dreams of the future. Although one cannot say that the poetic oeuvre of Jean-Joseph Rabearivelo, also of Madagascar, accedes magisterially to a newness of form and manner, there is much to admire in his later writings such as the *Vieilles chansons des Pays d'Imérina* (Old Songs from the Land of Imerina, 1939). The compatriot of Césaire, Edouard Glissant, certainly joins Rabemananjara in his long cry for a self-assumption beyond plaintive historicism. Dense, superbly articulated epic combines with 'dialogues', 'dysodes', all the tactics of what Char called modernity's *art bref*, to form an oeuvre, from *Sangrivé* (Fixedblood, 1947–54), *La Terre inquiète* (Anxious Earth, 1954) and *Les Indes* (The Indies, 1955) to *Boises* (Wooden Deception, 1979) and *Les Grands Chaos* (Endless Chaos, 1993), not to mention important essays and novels, half-dreamed, half-real, chronicling myth and philosophical meditation. Beyond 'death, [knowing] the peppers mounting in gold / This high book of summits where the river sets up its stall, [and] o mystery / On the sand cockerels, unexpected sleepers',[5] Glissant's poetics roots itself in new relationship, a new totality of socio-ethical vision and discourse worthy of us all.

Born just across the Caribbean Sea from Glissant, René Depestre was soon to find himself in exile in France and, for some twenty years, Cuba.

His poetry – *Traduit du grand large* (Translated from the Open Sea, 1952), *Minerai noir* (Black Ore, 1956) down to *Journal d'un animal marin* (Journal of a Sea Creature, 1990) – is vigorous, animated, both felt and ironic. Culturally dynamic, in revolt and yet in possession of dreamed options, work such as *Poète à Cuba* (Poet in Cuba, 1976) can be simultaneously witty and touching, jubilant and cutting, tender and bitter, a veritable 'harbour of legends', nobly resilient, innocent. Across a vaster ocean, yet one linking Depestre to another lost homeland, Tchicaya U Tam'si has crafted a poetic, theatrical and novelistic opus of great range of tone, sentiment and formal mode. Pain and revolt, dignity and self-empowerment almost inevitably lie at the centre of such poetry, at once post-colonial and pre-postcolonial, pulled too between the poles of a cultural ancientness and a symbolism often Christian. It is sometimes memorialisation, sometimes 'passion-play', always a *cri du coeur* with its intimate ellipses, or else its litanical modes. Tchicaya's poetry, such as *Le Mauvais sang* (Bad Blood, 1955), *Epitomé* (Epitome, 1962), or *Le Pain ou la cendre* (Bread or Ash, 1978), often written in exile, constantly seeks to 'know how to make a balm of my voice'.[6]

After 1968

Yet another wave of powerful French and Francophone poetic voices broke upon the readerships of the 1960s and 1970s. In France itself, poets such as Edmond Jabès, Andrée Chedid and Salah Stétié, the first two born in Cairo, Stétié being from Lebanon, would bring to bear new languages and new sensibilities upon a poetic production already varyingly rethinking its manners via the work of Michel Deguy and Bernard Noël, Jacques Réda, Jacques Roubaud and Denis Roche. And elsewhere, although their echo was initially more dimmed in Paris, fresh works by, for example, Liliane Wouters (Belgium), Anne Perrier (Switzerland), Mohammed Dib (Algeria), Tahar Ben Jelloun (Morocco), Jean-Baptiste Tati-Loutard (Congo), Nicole Bossard, Gilles Vigneault and Gatien Lapointe (Quebec), impacted upon metropolitan French consciousness.

Deguy, for example, can initially give us a geopoetical oeuvre centred upon notions of the *phalène* or going-forth-into-the world, archaeology and self-world relationship – in *Fragments du cadastre* (Land-Survey Fragments, 1960) and *Poèmes de la presqu'île* (Peninsular Poems, 1961) – developing his practice to embrace large philosophical, ethical and cultural issues, whereas a poet such as Tati-Loutard can throw up a whole backcloth of intensely lived and half-politically, half-lyrically meditated post-colonial transformation, in works such as *Les Racines congolaises* (Congo Roots, 1968) or *La Tradition du songe* (Dream Tradition, 1985). If Bernard Noël, now fascinated and now repelled, can delve into the literal and allegorical experience of the body's fusion with the psyche in their ambivalent constitution of self, and if his preoccupations can lead him, in a prolific oeuvre from *Extrait du corps* (Body Extract, 1958) to *La Chute du temps* (Fall of Time, 1983) and beyond, to 'deconstruct' our 'language noises' and the 'sense/censuring' of the world we thus (mis)create, the Quebec poet and *chansonnier*, Vigneault, immensely loved for his re-energising of a both cultural and universal consciousness of appreciation, simple quotidian possibility and available upliftment, can demonstrate more freely those enthusiasms that Noël must often reserve for his brilliantly empathetic writings on art. Réda, on the other hand, tireless *promeneur solitaire*, can choose to write with freely chosen formal constraints that are nevertheless not essentially governed by Oulipian convictions in the production of works straightforward though often ludic, nostalgic yet dynamically present, engaged in the contemplative evocation of the city's – and, of late, even the countryside's – infinite ordinary visibilities and backwaters, or a poet such as Gatien Lapointe, more rooted arguably than Réda, yet more impulsively lyrical, more plainly political, too, in his attachment to a locality (*pays*), 'reddening sword in the eyes of our history', can, in the final, radically recast manner of his last poems, seem to echo Gaston Miron's argument that 'all poetry is a love story with language' – yet one whereby, as Lapointe writes, 'all of space grabs hold of you – brazier of meaning ultra-formulae a thousand tufts of swallows flap away crazily'.

None of this, of course, should be thought to represent an effort of systematisation of the poetic practices evoked. But it does quickly give some idea of the immense range of manners and focuses that proliferate in their inalienable specificities. If it is not unhelpful to proceed as has, for example, Pinson in his effort to orchestrate global aesthetic scenarios from a certain mass of recent poetic production (as in *Habiter en poète* [Poetic Dwelling, 1995]), textual and even conceptual particularity is what, surely, will govern our appreciation of any of the poets discussed in this brief study. Thus, if Jabès, with his *Livre des questions* (Book of Questions, 1973), his *Livre des limites* (Book of Limits, 1984–7) or his *Livre de l'hospitalité* (Book of Hospitality, 1991), can offer us a deep meditation on errancy and exile, 'subversion' and feasible place of being (after profoundly reorientating his style and perception from the early *Je bâtis ma demeure* [I Build my Dwelling, 1957]), and if this meditation and modal shift can be contrasted with what we find in the work of the Quebec feminist poet Nicole Brossard, this is not an occasion for odious comparison but rather an opportunity to celebrate the enormous and exhilarating difference separating, yet joining, their equally remarkable adventures. Certainly, the work of Brossard can be compared with that of Chedid or, the Swiss poet, Perrier, along purely formal lines, but is that (remembering Bonnefoy's caution against placing faith in 'the nothingness of any form') reason enough to launch into a structural and stylistic confrontation of their respective oeuvres, when it is clear that, for Brossard, 'to take place life-long / in one's native tongue' is far from a simple narcissistic pleasure? Similarly, for Chedid, language can reveal something 'over and above words' – a face 'behind the fur of the world' – while for Perrier, 'a courtyard sheltered by high lime-trees / honey blooming and dead bees', whilst pointed to via language and its 'forms', find their origin in 'a deep and concealed reality' that, ultimately, draws her attention beyond its poetic structurings. Brossard's fascinations, too, may be aligned with those of her two distant sisters. They, too, are humanist, implicitly if not overtly feminist, concerned with ethical and spiritual self-transformation, alert despite everything to the mysteries, beauties and potential 'simplicities' of the world. But this cannot come close to conveying the myriad sparkling distinctions of works such as Brossard's *Mordre en sa chair* (Biting into One's Flesh, 1966) or *Au présent des veines* (The Time of Veins, 1999), Chedid's *Seul, le visage* (The Face Alone) or *Territoires du souffle* (Territories of Breath, 1999), Perrier's *Pour un vitrail* (For a Stained-Glass Window, 1955) or *Le Livre d'Ophélie* (Book of Ophelia).

Wouters and Roubaud have both published important anthologies and have interested themselves in the evolution of poetic form and voice. Roubaud, however, a mathematician, novelist and Oulipian, has varyingly given himself to citational, 'recycling' poetic modes, discreet, restrained but felt lyricism, as well as humorous, more easeful, less abstract manners in an oeuvre extending from *E(psilon)* (1967) and *Trente et un au cube* (Thirty-One Cubed, 1973) to *La Forme d'une ville change plus vite hélas que le coeur des humains* (The Shape of a Village changes, alas, more quickly than the Human Heart, 1999). Wouters's poetic career goes as far back as *La Marche forcée* (Forced March, 1955) and *Le Bois sec* (Dry Wood, 1960), and includes theatre and essay writing. As with her more recent *Journal du scribe* (Scribe's Journal, 1990) or *Tous les chemins conduisent à la mer* (All Paths

Lead to the Sea), she can move between classical prosody and free verse in the same poem, which, more often than not, betrays anxiety and a sense of lack, whilst at the same time remaining tensely conscious of her felt residual strengths. If a poet such as Denis Roche – in work such as *Les Idées centésimales de Miss Elanize* (Miss Ellaneous' Centesimal Ideas, 1964), *Le Mécrit* (Miswriting, 1972), *Dépôts de savoir et de technique* (Deposits of Knowledge and Technique, 1980) and beyond – reveals a not entirely dissimilar, though wild, 'dancing', textually 'erotic' and frenzied, concentration on forms of occulted (self-)production or (self-)collaging that can be seen in some of Roubaud's work, his at times obscure but frequently exhilarating, desire-driven 'red' (mis)writing finds itself at some distance from that of, say, the Algerian poet Dib. The latter's poetical work (from *Ombre gardienne* [Guardian Shadow, 1966] to *L'Enfant-jazz* [Jazz-Child, 1999]), is a curious admixture of transparency and enigmaticalness, written in highly compact free but spontaneously disciplined verse of elliptical narrative character – modes stunningly different from Roche's but equally propelled by a desire for authentic relation. Ben Jelloun, a novelist like Dib, has written searing verse over some thirty years, gathered together in *Poésie complète 1966–1995* (1995), and has succeeded by the sheer energy of language in giving memorable poetic voice to obsessions less ethical and political than devastatingly and movingly human. It is an intensely lived work, yet a 'writing so as to no longer have a face [;] so as to speak difference'. Stétié, who has also known the trials of North Africa and the Middle East, and who has sought – no one better – to interlace the equally immense cultures and wisdoms of the Arab world and the West, chooses a poetic path (from *L'Eau froide gardée* [Cold Water Guarded, 1973] to *Fièvre et guérison de l'icône* [Fever and Recovery from the Icon, 1998]) of a more allegorical and ontologically symbolic character. In a preface to the 1998 collection, Bonnefoy has termed this most unusual oeuvre, 'a moving tapestry of representations coming undone in a great continuous stirring of verbal matter'.

Conclusion

Despite concerns and cautions that various poets, principally in France, have expressed about the current poetic 'state of affairs', the 1980s, 1990s and the first year or so of the new millennium have seen a dynamic and mushrooming production of work of great originality and power throughout the Francophone world. In metropolitan France itself, impressive oeuvres thus begin to build: the witty, erotically charged and lexically bewitching *povrésie* ('pooretry') of the latinist Jude Stéfan; the spiritually questing, yet terrestrially rooted work of poet and novelist Marie-Claire Bancquart; the free-flowing meditative spontaneities of James Sacré containing 'almost everything and anything at all put together properly'; the tumbling rhythmic cascades or the relentless *proses* of the feminist philosopher-poet Jeanne Hyvrard; the self-reflexive 'autobiographical' and allegorical manners of Jean-Claude Pinson; the restrained but committed lyricism of the ex-Telquellian poet Jacqueline Risset; the charmingly formal intrication and upbeat reflection on the quotidian of Yves Leclair; the telescoped poetic nuggets, (self-)probing, opaquely narrative/descriptive, of Esther Tellermann; the ironies and derisions of a poet chiselling out some adequate buoyancy of self in the work of Richard Rognet; the tug-of-war in the poetry of Michelle Grangaud between ethically, existentially anchored *geste* and formal play and recycling; the lucid, buzzing and nevertheless melancholy vigour of Jean-Michel Maulpoix's new lyricism; the surrealising energy of Vénus Khoury-Ghata's poetic *récits*. To these can be added: Pascal Commère, Anne-Marie Albiach, Emmanuel Hocquard, Denise Le Dantec, André Velter, Jeannine Baude, Marcelin Pleynet, Silvia Baron Supervielle, Jean-Claude Schneider and Heather Dohollau.

If in the rest of the Francophone world, the central issues of very recent contemporary poetry are often not intrinsically different from those dominating Hexagonal production – the ethics and ontology of self–world relations, questions of immanence and transcendence, closure and unfinishableness, language's both 'literal' and 'lyrical' relativities in the face of experience and dream – it remains true that the poetry of writers from Quebec, Acadia, the French Antilles and many parts of 'Francophone' Africa, whilst at once universalising and intimate and often interwoven with transcultural reference, may be coloured, or even heavily marked, by socio-political preoccupations, sometimes still essentially 'colonial', sometimes overtly post-colonial. The power and passion, as well as the private subtleties, of the following poets can make the reading of their work compelling: Emile Ologoudou (Bénin), Abdellatif Laâbi (Morocco), Frédéric Pacéré Titinga (Burkina-Faso), Hédi Kaddour (Tunisia), Fernando d'Almeida (Cameroon), Mohammed Khaïr-Eddine (Morocco), Quentin Ben Mongaryas (Gabon), Ahmed Tidjani Cissé (Guinea), Tshiakatumba Matala Mukadi (Zaire). Elsewhere, in Quebec, for example, strong poetic work is equally to be found, and in abundance: Madeleine Gagnon, Michel Beaulieu, France Théoret, Pierre Nepveu, Yolande Villemaire, Pierre Morency and many others; poets of Belgian origin are frequently well known: William Cliff, Jean-Pierre Verheggen, Christian Hubin, Eugène Savitzkaya; Swiss poets such as Pierre Chappuis, Alexandre Voisard, Pierre-Alain Tâche amply repay the effort of tracking down their collections, all too often (as with much non-metropolitan Francophone writing) not readily available in bookshops and even university libraries; the Luxembourg poet, Anise Koltz, the Antillean Monchoachi and Acadian poets such as Gérald Leblanc, Rose Després, Léonard Forest, France Daigle, all continue to write with a conviction and a delicacy that can, at times, belie their apparent marginality and self-doubt. A long, ever broadening panoply of written gazes upon self and world, their difficulties and their teeming exhilarations or, at very least, calls to continue, twentieth-century poetry, with, as the Mauritian Malcolm de Chazal wrote in 1948, its vast collective 'human gaze[,] is [indeed] a travelling lighthouse', a home from home, illuminated by, illuminating of, our difference and our strange sameness.

NOTES

1. Verse of uneven syllabic count.
2. Anaphora entails the repetition of a word or words at the beginning of successive lines, for rhetorical effect.
3. Dada was a revolutionary literary and artistic movement developing in 1916–17 and giving way to Surrealist philosophy and activity.
4. André Breton, *Second Manifeste du surréalisme*, Paris: Kra, 1930.
5. Edouard Glissant, *Poèmes complets*, Paris: Gallimard, 1994.
6. Tchicaya U Tam'si, *Arc musical*, Honfleur: P. J. Oswald, 1970.

FURTHER READING

Bishop, Michael, *The Contemporary Poetry of France: Eight Studies*, Amsterdam: Rodopi, 1985.
    Contemporary French Women Poets, 2 vols. Amsterdam and Atlanta: Rodopi, CHIASMA, 1995.
Bishop, Michael, and Christopher Elson (eds.), *Contemporary French Poetics*, Amsterdam and Atlanta: Rodopi, 2001.
Cardinal, Roger (ed.), *Sensibility and Creation: Studies in 20th-Century French Poetry*, London: Croom Helm, 1977.
Caws, Mary Ann (ed.), *About French Poetry from Dada to 'Tel Quel'*, Wayne State University Press, 1974.
Damas, Léon-Gontran, *Poètes d'expression française*, Paris: Seuil, 1947.
Greene, Robert W., *Six French Poets of our Time*, Princeton: Princeton University Press, 1979.
Igley, F., and G. de Reynold (eds.), *Poètes de Suisse romande*, Lausanne: Rencontre, 1964.

King, Russell, and Bernard McGuirk (eds.), *Reconceptions: Reading Modern French Poetry*, Nottingham: University of Nottingham Press, 1996.

Mateso, Locha, *Anthologie de la poésie d'Afrique noire d'expression française*, Paris: Hatier, 1987.

Maugey, Alex, *La Poésie moderne québécoise*, Montréal: Humanitas, 1989.

Memmi, Albert, *Ecrivains francophones du Maghreb*, Paris: Seghers, 1985.

Romanos, Maryse, *La Poésie antillaise d'expression créole de 1960 à nos jours*, Paris: L'Harmattan, 1998.

Stamelman, Richard, *Lost Beyond Telling*, Ithaca, NY: Cornell University Press, 1990.

Thomas, Jean-Jacques, and Steven Winspur, *Poeticized Language*, University Park, Penn.: Pennsylvania State University Press, 1999.

Wouters, Liliane, *Panorama de la poésie française de Belgique*, Brussels: Antoine, 1976.

12

Theatre

Introduction

Cultural history has little regard for landmarks suggested by the calendar, and, though the twentieth century was an active and highly distinctive epoch in French theatre, it did not begin neatly in 1900. Traditionally, French theatre performances were heralded by 'les trois coups' (three strokes of a broomstick against the boards behind the curtain). Likewise, twentieth-century theatre was heralded by three late nineteenth-century events: the opening of the experimental 'Théâtre libre' by André Antoine in the Passage de l'Elysée-Montmartre in 1887; the first public projection of moving pictures from a strip of celluloid in the Grand Café, Boulevard des Capucines, in 1895; and the opening – possibly just the opening line, 'Merdre!' – of Alfred Jarry's *Ubu Roi* (King Ubu) in Lugné-Poë's Nouveau Théâtre in the rue Blanche in 1896.

Several features of these events are worthy of note. First, they took place in, or just across the road from a single Paris *arrondissement* (the 10th) within an 800-metre radius of the corner of the Rue Montmartre and the Boulevard Poissonnière, a circle that also encompassed, at the time, a large proportion of Parisian theatres and private schools of art. The following century was to experience constant tensions between the roles of Paris as would-be creator, and the rest of France as consumer of theatre. Secondly, Antoine's company opened with a play by Tolstoy, and went on to be the introducer of Ibsen's plays, and their style of social morality, already internationally acclaimed and dubbed 'Ibsenism' by George Bernard Shaw, into France, while Jarry's first night was attended by a curious cross-section of French and European avant-garde writers and artists present in Paris at the time, including the Symbolist poet Mallarmé, the painter Toulouse-Lautrec and the Irish poet Yeats. For the first time since the 1820s, French theatre opened itself to the international scene, and this was to recur, especially during the 1930s, the 1960s and the 1980s. Thirdly, a feature of the century has been the double challenge of moving pictures, then of moving and talking pictures, for control of the performing arts in the group entertainment market – an extremely successful one, since by 1930 scores of small playhouses in Paris and the large provincial cities had closed or been converted into cinemas – followed, from 1950, by a second challenge to both cinema and theatre by television and its avatars. This has pushed theatre 'up-market': a fact welcomed by the artistic and intellectual avant-gardes, while at the same time causing successive crises of conscience amongst some of its proponents, and repeated attempts to de-commercialise the scenario, either by bringing theatre back to its popular cultural roots or by giving it a new civic basis.

During this period, dramatic forms and assumptions about the nature of performance have evolved considerably as a result of these factors, and also under the influence of technical improvements, though these have not been prominent in France because of very slow renewal of the fabric of playhouses until the 1960s: the first theatre to be designed for electric lighting and machinery was the Théâtre Pigalle, opened only briefly in 1928; the first electronically adjustable stage was installed in the refurbished Théâtre de la Ville as late as 1971. Drama has also developed in connection with wider literary and philosophical movements, and there have been considerable fluctuations in the status of the playtext, the concept of the author, the role of the producer. The respective semiotic roles of text, bodily expression and movement, material setting and plastic images, as well as concepts such as 'character' and 'plot', have been questioned, sometimes, as it seemed, destructively, though the phoenix has always risen again. The resultant picture is complex to draw, and does not lend itself to a purely chronological account, so the following sections overlap somewhat in time and reference.

Metropolitan entertainment

Throughout the century, French theatre has been underpinned by a genre which experimental dramatists and academic critics have often scorned, but which nevertheless has ensured that theatre-going never died out, even in the leanest years. This is known as *théâtre de boulevard*, which refers to the semi-circle of glittering metropolitan thoroughfares, opened up when the seventeenth-century walls of Paris were pulled down, which stretch from the Place de la République to the Madeleine on the Right Bank of the Seine, and reappear briefly on the Left Bank between Montparnasse and Port-Royal. To this day, they are lined with establishments offering Parisians and visitors pleasures of all kinds, from the sensuous to the artistic. Because, until the Revolution, unlicensed theatre had been tolerated outside the city walls, this area became, from the nineteenth century, an interface between seekers and providers of pleasure, and for the first sixty years of the century a significant proportion (as much as half) of French playhouses was situated there.

Boulevard theatre has gradually shrunk (some sixty playhouses in 1900, forty-five in 1945, and fifteen in 2000), but has shown a remarkable continuity since Paris's *Belle Epoque* (the forty years prior to the First World War), which contains its main cultural roots. It derives from the vaudevilles (playful social satires, with musical interludes) of the mid-nineteenth century and from the light social comedies of such writers as Labiche (wrote 1839–77) and Feydeau (wrote 1822–1916), which, being produced in almost industrial quantities and using well-tried formulas, were often referred to as 'well-made plays'. In its essence, it presents Parisian upper-middle-class audiences (and the provincial and foreign visitors in town to catch a glimpse of its sophisticated life-style), with a polished and idealised image of that style.

Theatre sets are always denotational (typically, Parisian apartments or houses) with many signs of luxury: it is common for the audience to applaud the set as the curtain first goes up. Characters tend to be unidimensional, defined by a specific habit, ambition or attitude. They interact in well-planned patterns, within a general design defined by an initial obstacle to surmount, a dramatic partial resolution at the end of each act posing more problems for the start of the next one, and a final untying of knots. The main parts are usually written to suit the known talents or established *personae* of specific actors (who also tend to be applauded when they first appear), which muffles variety and flexibility in characterisation. The English phrase 'drawing-room comedy' would describe this style, except that in the Parisian version the bedroom is invariably en-suite. Sexual transgression of a mild kind (extra-marital flirtation, infidelity with an established lover, bridging of modest age-gaps), tends to be its active agent, while the play may also pinpoint marginal inefficiencies of the prevalent social code: conflicts between generations, conventions on the distribution and transmission of wealth and respectability in the family, and minor misunderstandings involving outsiders – lower classes, provincial folk and foreigners. The main characters typically display a worldly satirical wit through punning and innuendo (replacing the comic couplets of the vaudeville), drawing on current society gossip or preoccupations. Plots are not socially disruptive: characters tend to be well-off and without professional worries, they are rarely encumbered with children or parents, and marital and legal codes are only temporarily questioned. Domestic servants remain a feature well into the 1960s, not as a reflection of reality but because the dramatic opportunities afforded by eavesdropping, gossiping, social blunders, master–servant exchange are part of the well-made play. The playhouses on which this genre centres are typically built in the Italianate horse-shoe shape, affording most of the audience a view of itself as well as of the play, upholstered in red velvet and provided with usherettes and cloakroom attendants who maintain the illusion of social stability and safety within conventions of conspicuous consumption.

Plays written for this type of theatre aimed at a potential audience estimated throughout the century to number about 400,000 (out of a Parisian population rising from 3 to 8 million during the period), whose social position allows them to stay out late: the conventional curtain-raising time was only brought back to 8.30 p.m. in the 1960s. An upper crust of three-or four-dozen actors (often with film careers) are available to star in them, and understudies are in plentiful supply to take the play on tour to the French provinces and even, until the 1960s, to some of the outposts of the French colonial empire. From the 1950s to the 1980s *boulevard* was practically the only form of theatre to be broadcast by the French television network, and it is significant that the series *Au théâtre ce soir* made a point of taking the camera into the theatre, with shots of the curtain and the sophisticated and appreciative Parisian audience, rather than adapting the plays to the television studio. From the *Belle Epoque* through to the 1980s, *boulevard* plays were also available in print through specific journals such as *L'Illustration*, *Commœdia*, *Paris-Théâtre*, *L'Avant-Scène*: reading them (and one sees how the staging conventions had therefore to be constant) was the next best thing to seeing them. The image of the metropolis plays an important part in national and imperial cohesion. And the more successful authors (Marcel Achard, Marcel Pagnol, Félicien Marceau) tended to be elected members of the Académie Française, that metropolitan body.

Among the significant playwrights in this genre were Henry Bernstein (wrote 1900–1949; see *Le Marché* [The Deal], 1900, *Le Secret*, 1913), Sacha Guitry (perhaps the most refined wordsmith of all, wrote 1905–48; see *La Jalousie* [Jealousy], 1915, *Faisons un rêve* [Just Suppose], 1918), André Roussin (wrote 1941–63; see *La Petite Hutte* [The Little Hut], 1947, *Lorsque l'enfant paraît* [The Adoration of the Child], 1951), Françoise Dorin (wrote 1967–83, see *La Facture* [The Invoice], 1968, *Le Tout pour le tout* [Going for Broke], 1978). Marc Camoletti is one of the most successful of the second half of the century, and his *Boeing Boeing* (1961) which rings the changes on the 'air-hostess in each port' theme and on the limitless possibilities afforded by multiple doors on stage, has often been revived. This type of theatre also (from the 1940s) adapts pieces from, and exports others to, London's West End and New York's Broadway, whose social backing is similar in nature. It is also (and this is a sign of its ultimate fragility) the only type of theatre which has been successfully adapted to the silver screen. Thus *La Cage aux folles* (A Cageful of Queers), a mild frolic on homosexuality, went around the Western world, on stage and film in the 1980s.

On the fringes of entertainment

For much of the first half of the century, most audiences had little choice beyond the *boulevard* offering, and the French classics presented institutionally by the Comédie Française (the only fully subsidised theatre company) and occasionally by directors working in the private theatres normally devoted to *boulevard*. More ambitious writing tended to address this known market, so that one finds, on its fringes, related and more ambitious forms, defining themselves against *boulevard*. Typically, the authors involved have been published in book form as well as in theatre journals: they achieve national and international respectability as intellectuals rather than just entertainers. Consequently, they reach bookshelves in France and abroad, interest academic observers, and the playwrights mentioned in this section are liable to be more familiar to non-French readers.

The first significant variant is genuine social satire. At the turn of the century, following on in the ambitious vein of Ibsen, Eugène Brieux (wrote 1890–1906) was introducing real controversy: for instance, the question of venereal disease amongst the bourgeoisie in *Les Avariés* (Damaged Goods), censured after the dress rehearsal in 1901. Henry Bataille (wrote 1894–1922) focused, not merely for comic purposes, on the double standards of morality applied to respectable women (*La Lépreuse* [The Leper-Woman], 1897, *La Marche nuptiale* [The Wedding March], 1905). In the 1930s, Marcel Pagnol made his name with *Topaze* (1928), which seriously challenged the value of honesty in the modern world, and went on to a highly successful trilogy (*Marius*, 1929, *Fanny*, 1931, *César*, 1936, made nationally famous by the film versions) which focused on provincial life and mores as more than laughable, and posed, albeit sentimentally, harsher questions about fidelity and family integrity. Later, the successful novelist Françoise Sagan (wrote 1954–70) briefly brought adolescent sexual liberation (causing scandal amongst parents) on to the stage (*Château en Suède* [Castle in Sweden], 1960, *Un piano dans l'herbe* [A Piano on the Grass], 1970).

In another variant, the denotational ties are relaxed, and the setting and language become more stylised. Whimsy replaces wit in order to question, for the duration of the evening, standard social assumptions and attitudes. This is the case with Marcel Achard (wrote 1922–57), whose main characters often speak with disarming sincerity of an old-fashioned belief in love and human kindness, to replace the prevailing cynicism of the age: *Voulez-vous jouer avec môa?* (Will You Play With Me? 1923), *Jean de la lune* (John of the Moon, 1929), *Patate* (Vegetable, 1957) stood out as quality literary comedy. Extravagance or chance disturbance in the midst of familiar surroundings was also the most successful vein explored by Marcel Aymé (wrote 1932–66), in *Clérambard* (1950) and *Les Oiseaux de lune* (Moonbirds, 1956). It is one of the main features of the plays of Jean Giraudoux (wrote for the theatre 1928–43), who amuses his ultra-sophisticated audience with quirkish and witty challenges to conventional life, and clever adaptations of traditional stories, while, however, conveying a far more powerful thematic, even political, message: reflections on religion and spiritual beliefs (*Amphitryon 38*, 1929, *Ondine*, 1938), and on social conflict and war (*La Guerre de Troie n'aura pas lieu* [Tiger at the Gates], 1935; *La Folle de Chaillot* [The Mad Woman of Chaillot], produced 1945).

Although its main official aim has always been to produce a repertoire of classics, with a special stress on Molière, from whose troupe it descends, the Comédie Française was also, until the 1970s, a supporter of *boulevard* style. It regularly revived Feydeau, that bastion of the *Belle Epoque*, but it also attempted to sponsor polished, mannered plays, based on the formula described above but with greater literary pretensions, expressed in a more stylised 'poetic' (certainly talkative) vein, though lacking any really coherent social or philosophical stance. These are closely related to Achard and Aymé, and have been at various times considered, wrongly, as in the forefront of writing for the theatre, mainly because critical attention does focus on the national theatre company. One example is Roland Dubillard (wrote 1948–78) with *Naïves Hirondelles* (Innocent Swallows, 1961), *La Maison d'os* (The Bone House, 1962). In the same category (though he was first produced outside the Comédie Française) one could place Jacques Audiberti (wrote 1946–60), with *Quoat-Quoat* (1946), *Le Mal court* (Evil Spreads, 1947), *L'Effet Glapion* (The Glapion Effect, 1959). Typically, these plays comprise all the elements of the 'well-made' variety, but partly dismembered and imperfectly reconstituted, like a Cubist painting.

In the French Classic and Romantic tradition, ambitious theatre was usually costume drama: in the political circumstances of the time, it was safer to displace contemporary political preoccupations on to other times or other places. Faced with the rather barren choices of the first half of the century (*boulevard*, enhanced *boulevard* or the classics), several writers of note tried to renew with this pseudo-historical convention. One way was to revisit the Greek and Latin classics, as the French theatre had done in the seventeenth century: in the interwar years, the novelist André Gide (*Œdipe*, 1932) and the poet Jean Cocteau (*Antigone*, 1922, *Orphée*, 1926, *La Machine infernale* [The Infernal Machine], 1934) dabbled with applying ironic anachronism to classical theatrical myths, and inspired Jean Giraudoux (above), Jean Anouilh (*Antigone*, 1943, *Médée*, 1953) and Jean-Paul Sartre (*Les Mouches* [The Flies], 1943, *Les Troyennes*, 1968). An interesting feature of these adaptations is often the foregrounding of what had been secondary characters or observers in the original versions, in line with modern political assumptions and with a consequently different perspective.

Another path, more central to the French Classical and Romantic tradition, led to plays based on historical events with mythical dimensions relating to the present, or even to create these for the sake of circumstances. Two playwrights of the mid-century stand out: Henry de Montherlant (wrote for the theatre 1929–60), with very literary pieces on personal and political responsibility, *La Reine morte* (The Dead Queen, 1942), *Le Maître de Santiago* (The Master of Santiago, 1948), *Port-Royal* (1954), and Jean Anouilh, with *L'Alouette* (The Lark, on Joan of Arc, 1953) and *Becket, ou l'honneur de Dieu* (Becket, or the Honour of God, on Thomas à Becket, 1956).

The most intellectually respectable offshoot of *boulevard* was existentialist theatre, which thrived for a decade after the Second World War, as some of the more ambitious playhouses (the Théâtre des Mathurins, the Théâtre Hébertot) became showcases for the very fashionable philosophical movement led by Jean-Paul Sartre (wrote for the theatre 1943–59). Sartre's own involvement in theatre criticism (texts collected in *Un théâtre de situations*, 1973) was considerable, and, as a Parisian, he found the stage a convenient place on which to project concrete illustrations of the concepts of individual responsibility and freedom which are the focus of his practical philosophy. In the main, he was not a dramatic innovator: he used the structure of the 'well-made play', even overtly referring to its conventions, in order to highlight the plight of heroes managing, or failing, to escape from the confines of their self-perpetrating image of identity and their apparently impervious social situation. His first two pieces (*Les Mouches*, 1943, and *Huis clos* [In Camera], 1944) were a costume drama and a parable both referring clearly to the situation of France under the German Occupation, during which they were nevertheless performed. In *Les Mouches* (an adaptation of the Electra story), Orestes, for once, braves the furies of hell and takes responsibility for the murder of his mother which has delivered his city of the pestilence caused by her earlier crimes. In *Huis clos*, three characters confined to a hotel room in hell for the crimes they committed in their lives, battle unsuccessfully against their existential bad faith. Later, Sartre was free to portray more overtly political figures – a Communist terrorist cell in *Les Mains sales* (Crime Passionnel, 1948), a left-over Nazi officer in *Les Séquestrés d'Altona* (Condemned of Altona, 1959) – though, in theatre as elsewhere, the overt often stands up less well than the covert to the test of time. His one venture into the realm of the avant-garde, *Le Diable et le bon dieu* (Lucifer and the Lord, 1951), an epic parable on the choice of good and evil, is his most ambitious one, though, again, he is making use of a dramatic structure (this time borrowed from Brecht) to express a philosophic dialectic.

Albert Camus, who pitted his version of existentialism against that of Sartre, also used the available production structures of Parisian theatre as vehicles for his ideas, though his personal experience of theatre as a practitioner made him more inventive than Sartre in choosing or adapting appropriate dramatic conventions: *Caligula* (written 1939, produced 1945) is a colourful and powerful examination of the human condition, and *Les Justes* (The Just, 1949) a much-translated portrayal of violent political commitment.

Avant-garde

This phrase, borrowed from the now questionable Romantic notion that art 'advances', was used by several groups during the first half of the century. They shared several ambitions. First, to reduce the exaggerated respect paid in the French theatre tradition to the spoken or declaimed word (whether the verse of the neo-classical and Romantic traditions, or the witticisms or oratory of *boulevard* and its offshoots), and to lay more stress on scenography, texture, costume, bodily expression and movement. Secondly, and in consequence, to open up communication with other plastic and performing arts (painting and ballet) and even music. Thirdly, because these trends were paralleled elsewhere, to look for inspiration to other European centres (notably Copenhagen, Moscow, Berlin) and to the cosmopolitan artistic community already in Paris.

The campaign against the word was, in the end, waged in vain. The whole of French culture is built on respect for the text, and the stranglehold of the declamatory Comédie Française and its attendant training school, the Conservatoire, was too great. To this day French actors believe they are being more physical by jumping on to a table and continuing to declaim. The one dramatist who could be seen as providing native pieces to the measure of these ambitions (Paul Claudel) was essentially a poet. The emphasis on other semiotic devices was more successful, although because of the small and antiquated playhouses available until the third quarter of the century, it was limited for a long time to associated arts easily available in Paris (costume design and painting). The large-scale European scenic innovators (the Russian Meyerhold, the Germans Piscator and Reinhardt) passed it by until 'decentralised' theatre was equipped with more modern machinery, and, even then, operating costs usually proved prohibitive. On the whole, although one can point to significant innovatory events, often involving foreign authors or companies, the overall effect has been muffled.

'Avant-garde' was first used to identify experiments made by Antoine in the 1880s, when 'modernism', understood to mean a reaction against academicism, was spreading out from the visual arts ('impressionism' and 'post-impressionism'), music ('Wagnerism') and poetry ('Symbolism'). The director Aurélien Lugné Poë (active 1893–1940) made a significant contribution at the start of his career, bringing the blurrings and suggestiveness of Symbolism on to the stage in a much-admired production of the Belgian poet Maeterlinck's *Pelléas et Mélisande* (1893), and following this up with Jarry's *Ubu-Roi* (1896), where actors were replaced by larger-than-life puppets, rhetoric by vulgarity, humanism by cynicism, and which prompted Yeats's dictum 'After us, the Savage God'. Lugné Poë introduced other Symbolists (Verhaeren) and European contemporaries (D'Annunzio, Gorki, Marinetti, Wilde) to Parisians, and found a French author to his measure in Paul Claudel, whose work he produced in 1912 and 1914.

In the first thirty years of the century, there was certainly some cross-fertilisation between different art forms. Parisians were vastly impressed in 1909 by the 'total experience' presented on tour by Serge Diaghilev's Russian ballet company, which returned several times and settled in France after the Russian Revolution, from 1917 to 1930. New types of dance were set off by contributions by painters and composers to a spectacle on a scale made possible by the largest auditoria then available (Châtelet, Champs Elysées, Opéra, all seating more than 1,500). In the more modest realm of theatre (where the largest had 1,200 places and most between 400 and 800) avant-garde poets (Apollinaire, Cocteau) occasionally wrote texts stretching dramatic conventions; painters (Picasso, Rouault, Chagall, Léger) made contributions to removing set and costume design from the realm of realism (though typically, Picasso worked more for ballet), and composers (Honegger, Milhaud) wrote scores playing an essential rather than a framing or allusive function. But these were specific, unusual occasions. Set design is perhaps the area which was most permanently modified. French theatre (again, for reasons of scale) did not take part in the vogue for 'expressionism', which the large German playhouses were demonstrating to the rest of Europe, but did conceive, between the 1920s and the 1960s, a related version for 'poor' theatre, which was particularly French. It was based on whimsically painted flats and toy props (one finds in many works of reference pictures of the one-sided static stage car with moving scenery in Jouvet's production of Jules Romain's *Knock*, the hobby-horses for horses in Anouilh's *Becket*, the minimalist painted flats used in practically all Ionesco's plays). In this tradition, the material stage, while remaining secondary to the text, asserts itself by its non-denotational style.

The term 'avant-garde' was in fact appropriated in France by five actor-directors who, from 1913 to 1950, dominated innovation in Paris: Jacques Copeau (worked 1913–40), who introduced new conceptions of scenography but soon retired to practise people's theatre in the country; Charles Dullin (worked 1907–43); Louis Jouvet (worked 1913–51); Gaston

Baty (worked 1919–46) and Georges Pitoëff, a Russian who had transited to Paris via Geneva (worked 1921–39). In 1926, the latter four, who were at that time all in charge of Parisian theatres (respectively the Théâtre de l'Atelier, the Comédie des Champs-Elysées, the Studio des Champs Elysées and the Théâtre des Mathurins) set up an informal association called *le cartel des théâtres d'avant-garde*. While continuing to address traditional audiences, they asserted their intention of enlarging their frame of reference.

The *cartel* was significant in bringing French theatre audiences in contact with Shakespeare and contemporary European playwrights, amongst whom Pirandello played a major role, and in renewing views of the French classics, Molière in particular. Partly through these fertilising influences, they were instrumental in bringing new French writing, in particular Claudel, Anouilh and Giraudoux, on to the stage. They also set a stamp on French theatre which was to endure until the end of the century: its dominance by actor-directors. While stopping short of expressionism, they nevertheless defended 'theatricality' defiantly (in opposition to film, which was choosing the path of realism), by giving a greater role to the actor than to the designer, and to the designer than to the scenographer. In doing so, they appealed strongly to the intellectual fringes of their audiences. This role was taken up from the late 1940s to the 1970s by a theatre company founded by two actors, Jean-Louis Barrault and Madeleine Renaud, originally a splinter group from the Comédie Française. They too introduced French audiences to contemporary European playwrights, played a part in encouraging young playwrights such as Beckett, and lent stage reality, through the visionary talent of Barrault, to a conception of theatre verging on the mystical, which had been formulated in the 1930s by Antonin Artaud in texts published after the Second World War as *Le Théâtre et son double*.

Paul Claudel now appears central to the ideals of the 'avant-garde', though he did not fully intend to be. A career diplomat, somewhat removed from the Parisian scene, he wrote texts in dramatic form, as one might write poems, without much hope of having them produced. His spiritual roots in the Catholic faith, his attachment to traditional rural rather than urban values, his experience of North and South America, China and Japan, combined with his early interest in poetic Symbolism to remove him completely from some of the strictures of established theatre in his time. Some of his plays (*L'Echange*, written 1894, performed 1914; *Partage de midi* [Noontide Deal], written circa 1905, performed 1947) are little more than *boulevard* in heightened prose. But *Tête d'Or* (Gold Head, written 1888, performed 1962), *L'Annonce faite à Marie* (The Annunciation, performed 1912), and *Le Soulier de satin* (The Satin Shoe, written *c*. 1922, performed 1943) are stories told in epic mode, set in a cosmic non-referential dimension, which need large-scale, non-denotational stage space, a sophisticated use of the actor's bodily presence, of sound and of light. After the initial revelation of Claudel by Lugné-Poë in 1912, it needed another director of strong and divergent talents, Jean-Louis Barrault, and exceptional circumstances (the thirst for spiritual renewal amongst Parisian elites after the defeat of 1940) to consecrate him, in the first, war-time, production of *Le Soulier de satin*, experienced as a ray of hope in the midst of the German Occupation. It is significant that, even after this, the play only really found complete expression in a double-evening revival by Barrault in 1985 and an eleven-hour outdoor version by Antoine Vitez at the Avignon Festival in 1987.

One can consider Jean Genet (wrote for the theatre 1947–61) as another reluctant member of the avant-garde, for social rather than ideological reasons. Taken into care as a child and into prison as a young man, Genet was discovered by the intellectual establishment (notably Cocteau and Sartre) to be one of the most original and powerful writers of the century. He created paragons of theatricality, built on complex interplays between characters and their imagined or imposed roles, and shot with heretic ritual, in which language reaches a sumptuous dimension. At their centre is crime and violence, as well as relevance to contemporary political issues such as racism, revolution and the end of colonialism, but these facts are an almost hidden symbolic core, radiating evil and salvation. Like Claudel, Genet has been imperfectly served by the French theatrical establishment. *Les Bonnes* (The Maids, 1947), though produced by a member of the *cartel*, Jouvet, was first mistaken for a thriller with social overtones. *Le Balcon* (1956), *Les Nègres* (1960) and *Les Paravents* (The Screens, 1961) were taken in hand with greater understanding by the very talented producer Roger Blin. But the far-reaching symbolic dimensions of the texts have only occasionally found the expression they deserve, in countries equipped with more opulent theatrical means.

Though he too would strongly resist this (together with any other form of classification), Armand Gatti (wrote from 1959) is the third really powerful French playwright of the century whose work could have fulfilled the ambitions of the avant-garde, though it has been produced in a piece-meal way by directors of varying talent (often in the *décentralisation* – see below), and he has himself removed it from established playhouses into different cultural contexts, such as factories and community centres. Like Genet, he is at the opposite end of the social spectrum from Claudel (being descended from anarchist Italian emigrants to Chicago), and his career, also notably undiplomatic, has been less secluded than that of Genet, putting him in closer touch with the live ethical nerves of the times – the Resistance movement, imprisonment in and escape from a German labour camp, the battle of Arnhem, journalism, tireless campaigns for non-denominational social and political awareness. But he is similar in the quality of his writing, the cosmic dimension to which his plays reach out, from everyday political reality through dream and myth, and his sense of the wider potential theatrical spaces: no one else has written a play for kites. His plays cover a wide range of issues specific to the second half of the century: concentration camps (*La Deuxième Existence du camp de Tatenberg* [The Second Life of Tatenberg Camp], 1962), trade unionism (*La Vie imaginaire de l'éboueur Auguste Geai* [The Imaginary Life of Augustus G, Dustman], 1964; *Chant public devant deux chaises électriques* [Oratorio in Front of Two Electric Chairs], 1966), the Chinese civil war (*Un homme seul* [A Man Alone], 1966), the Spanish civil war (*La Passion du général Franco*, banned by de Gaulle's government in 1968), social disruption through urban redevelopment (*Les Treize Soleils de la rue Blaise* [The Thirteen Suns of Blaise Street], 1968), Hiroshima (*La Cigogne* [The Stork], 1971), the Vietnam War (*V comme Vietnam* [V for Vietnam], 1967), immigrant worker communities (*Le Lion, la cage et ses ailes* [The Lion, the Cage and its Wings], 1975).

Provocative experiments

The most dramatic renewal French theatre has known since the early nineteenth century took place in the 1950s and 1960s, and it consisted in a radical questioning of the conventions on which the existing dramatic system was based. Because several of its proponents were also trying to give theatrical expression to the existentialist concept of the 'absurd' (briefly, the world is without meaning unless the human mind can contrive to project one on to it), that label was affixed to them. They can, however, be considered to be related to a more general movement, which had appeared almost a century earlier in painting and poetry, in which established conventions were radically questioned.

In what was still the dominant dramatic system (*boulevard* theatre and its avatars), a play contained a series of events in a chronological sequence given coherence by a title and a beginning and end. It involved characters with personal histories and family and social relationships, reacting to events according to personality traits which they were, individually or collectively, capable of understanding and describing. They were represented in a material setting, the denotational stage with its props and costumes, which confirmed their historical and social background as well as defining and explaining their behaviour. They expressed themselves in discourse which, whether it used everyday or heightened forms, demonstrated communication between them and conveyed meaning to the spectator.

All four conventions were memorably called into question in Eugène Ionesco's *La Cantatrice chauve* (1950). The title has no meaning (there is no bald prima donna present), the events are only occasionally sequential and they turn back on themselves like a Moebius strip (the paradoxical three-dimensional shape obtained by twisting a strip of paper and gluing its ends together upside-down). The characters are only distinguishable by their names, do not have personal histories, and swap places in the final scene. They appear to be in a drawing room in the suburbs of London, but it has no time dimension (a clock strikes random hours) and its Englishness is a joke. What they say to each other consists of recognisable speech acts, but is devoid of referential meaning or coherence, and at one point language breaks down into babble. There are similar features in Samuel Beckett's *En attendant Godot* (Waiting for Godot; first performed in Paris in the author's French version in 1953). The play's two acts are broadly variations on the same events, the characters have contradictory histories, nothing significant happens, the only props to which attention is drawn (a tree and a pair of boots) fail to relate to a time dimension, and the discourse consists of bantering cross-talk except at one point where a character who can only talk when wearing his bowler hat (an old circus turn) emits a parody of philosophical writing.

These two events put into sharper focus experiments which had appeared fitfully at the turn of the nineteenth and twentieth centuries and in the 1920s in the context of avant-garde, whether associated with 'Symbolism' or 'Surrealism', though theatre had, at those earlier times, only been an occasional vehicle for experimental writing, whose power base lay more in poetry, and was frequently side-tracked into opera or ballet.

Some were of a more formal kind. These include the much-noticed *Les Mamelles de Tirésias* (The Mammaries of Tiresias, 1917) where the poet Guillaume Apollinaire cocked a snook at the realistic stage convention (and, incidentally, invented the word 'surréaliste'), and Cocteau's less famous *Les Mariés de la Tour Eiffel* (The Eiffel Tower Wedding Party, 1921) which consists of a dialogue between two gramophones with no reference to marriage or to the Eiffel Tower, and where the music is more significant than the speech. Others were attempts to sharpen and widen the relevance of theatre to larger issues, outside the confines of the cosy *boulevard* conventions. It was in this vein that Alfred Jarry (wrote 1894–1907) produced his *Ubu-roi* (1896), a schoolboy's adaptation of *Macbeth* to an ahistorical sphere, replacing actors by larger-than-life puppets, ridding the stage of all denotational props and replacing them by circus gadgets (Ubu's symbol of majesty is not a sceptre but a toilet brush). Ubu, who reappears in a sequence of plays (*Ubu cocu, Ubu enchaîné, Ubu sur la butte* [Ubu Cuckolded, Ubu Bound, Ubu in Montmartre]) becomes a grotesque metaphor for all forms of evil associated with power-seeking and human vanity, and can serve either as an abstract or, in eventful times (such as the *coup d'état* of 1958), a direct political comment. Similarly, Roger Vitrac (wrote 1927–51) used Surrealist language games and the progressive subversion of character and story in his *Victor: ou les enfants au pouvoir* (Victor: Or Child Power, 1928), where trivial *boulevard*-type marital and social irregularities deepen into a near-cosmic indictment of French society in the new (twentieth) century as a purveyor of death.

In a less provocative vein, other dramatists of the 1930s and 1940s had begun to react against the conventions of referential theatre (if only in order to emphasise the connotational superiority of drama over film) while remaining within the theatrical establishment. The early plays of Jean Anouilh (wrote 1932–65) broaden the time references beyond the chronological convention and question, though often in a bantering way, the concept of character. In *Le Voyageur sans bagages* (The Traveller with No Luggage, 1937) a shell-shocked survivor of the First World War is presented with several possible personalities; *Le Rendez-Vous de Senlis* (The Appointment at Senlis, 1941) develops the mismatches between personality and social expectations, while a prolific series of variations on the Pirandellian model such as *Le Bal des voleurs* (The Thieves' Picnic, 1940), *Ardèle*, 1948, *La Répétition* (The Rehearsal, 1950), *La Valse des toréadors* (The Waltz of the Toreadors, 1952), *L'Hurluberlu* (The Crank, 1959), explore the revelatory powers of make-believe. For a time, Armand Salacrou (wrote 1925–61) was also seen as an innovator intent on bending the conventions in order to make theatre a better vehicle for moral philosophy and modern psychology: he is best remembered for his *Les Nuits de la colère* (Nights of Anger, 1946), a moving evocation of covert society in occupied France, and for *L'Inconnue d'Arras* (The Unknown Woman of Arras, 1935), a postmortem time-search for a key missing episode in a character's life.

Unlike Anouilh and Salacrou, who provided unconventional entertainment for conventional audiences, the main mid-century experimenters worked for a theatrical elite, which, from 1945 to 1965, centred, not on the 10th arrondissement, but on the Left Bank. They worked, not so much in a moral as in a philosophical dimension, which was inspired by existentialism (though, as we have seen, the 'official' existentialists such as Sartre and Camus wrote more conventional plays) and by dark reflections on the failure of moral progress inspired by the two world wars, the holocaust and the prospects of atomic Armageddon. It is not surprising that their work, with its universal appeal, should have been translated and produced all around the world, nor that three of the four main ones emerged, not from Parisian high society, but from the cosmopolitan Paris of artistic and political exiles.

The Russian exile Arthur Adamov (wrote 1948–63) first set the pattern. His inspiration, derived from Tchekhov and Kafka, is in the mainstream of the modern European mind. Whether he is concerned with emblematic expressions of failure such as *La Grande et la petite manœuvre* (Manoeuvres Big and Small, 1950), *Le Sens de la marche* (The Meaning of Walking/Facing the Engine, 1952, *Le Professeur Taranne* (1952) or with historical failure, like *Le Ping-Pong* (1955), on capitalism, or *Paolo Paoli* (1957) and *Printemps 71* (Spring of '71, 1963) on the Commune. The Rumanian exile Eugène Ionesco (wrote 1950–75) also brought the darker side of the human condition on to the modern stage. After a series of plays largely concerned, like *La Cantatrice chauve* (The Bald Prima Donna), with undermining the conventions, as in *La Leçon* (The Lesson, 1951) where a private lesson leading to murder becomes a metaphor for intellectual violation, *Les Chaises* (The Chairs, 1952) which attacks the idea that a performance can convey a message), he turned to more general reflections. A series of plays revolving around a recurrent Everyman character called Béranger illustrate the prevalence of evil in advanced societies: *Tueur sans gages* (Crime without Pay, 1959), the danger of political ideologies: *Rhinocéros* (Rhinoceros, 1959), and the disaster of individual death: *Le Roi se meurt* (The King lies Dying, 1962).

Samuel Beckett (wrote for the theatre 1948–85) was concerned from the start with metaphysical despair and how to express it on stage. This led him to a series of experiments in reduction of stage means, which began by seeming provocative and were later clearly systematic. In *En attendant Godot* (Waiting for Godot, 1953), as we have seen, character, plot and setting are rubbed out; in *Fin de partie* (Endgame, 1956), two characters are imprisoned in a room, and two others in jars; in *La Dernière Bande* (Krapp's Last Tape, 1958) and *Oh les beaux jours!* (Happy Days! 1961) there is only a solitary person, in a closed room or buried up to her neck in sand; in *Pas moi* (Not I, 1975) the character is reduced to a mouth. The essentials of the human quest for meaning and communication are thus brought into sharp focus.

The audiences who were delighted, or shocked, by the provocative methods of Ionesco and Beckett, were soon to witness, in the 1960s and 1970s, even more radical questioning of underlying theatre conventions. These include the separation between performance space and audience space (in *1789*, produced by the Théâtre du Soleil in 1971, part of the audience found itself enacting the crowds in the streets of Revolutionary Paris); the safety of the audience (in Fernando Arrabal's *Ils passèrent des menottes aux fleurs* [They Handcuffed the Flowers, 1969], spectators were given direct experience of Franco-type Fascism by being separated from their companions and being frog-marched to a seat in pitch dark by a jailer/usher); the sequence of performance (plays consisting of scenes which were enacted each evening in a random order), its predictability (in the late 1960s companies took to the streets, in festival towns and even elsewhere and organised *happenings*); its length (performances lasting from five to fifteen hours instead of the conventional two to three – thus Robert Wilson's *Le Regard du sourd* (The Deaf Man's Gaze, 1974), Vitez's complete performance of Claudel's *Le Soulier de satin* (The Satin Slipper, 1987), Olivier Pÿ's *Oedipe*, 1996; its association with a recognisable playhouse (André Engel's productions of Brecht's *Baal* in a stud farm, 1976; of Kafka texts for spectators billeted in single hotel rooms in *Hôtel Moderne*, 1979; of extracts from Dante's *Inferno* accessed by mystery train in a disused railway marshalling area on the side of a canal, 1982).

One of the most significant, and, for a time, successful challenges to conventions consisted in ousting the playwright and getting the actors and director to compose the play themselves, starting with historical or documentary texts and improvisations. The fashion was famously started by the Théâtre du Soleil, under the guidance of Ariane

Mnouchkine, with its scenes from the French Revolution (*1789*, 1970; *1793*; 1973) and later experiments in adapting *commedia dell'arte* styles to modern social satire. It helped to identify the new theatrical communities, which had been impressed by visits by American experimental companies such as the Living Theatre, as a focus for an alternative life-style which echoed for many young people the hopes they had entertained during the revolutionary events of 1968. Though remnants of this attitude survived until the end of the century (for instance in the mime-based satirical shows performed by Jérôme Deschamps's companies in theatres and on television), it gradually foundered, as had some of the hopes of the avant-garde before it, on the respect for the written word.

Widening the appeal of theatre

Market forces, we saw, have tended to narrow the popular base of theatre in the twentieth century. This is not only because of competition from recorded moving pictures. Theatre, a labour-intensive and plant-wasteful activity (where, typically, thirty people need to be employed to make a large building on a prime city site productive for three hours a day), has also been particularly exposed to the increased costs on all service industries since the 1930s (better protection of workers through minimum wage, pensions schemes and social charges on employers) and the enormous increases in the productive value of city property. The market-led rationale results sooner or later in casts of three actors playing to audiences able to afford five times the price of a cinema ticket for a seat.

Working against that trend, and since the more or less permanent establishment of the republican regime (1870), there have been repeated calls for a publicly owned and sponsored theatrical system. Theatre directors and government have responded in various ways, and the situation has evolved rapidly since the 1960s, so that by the end of the twentieth century France had in place a network of state or community theatres stretching to most areas of the country, side-by-side with a dwindling private system practically limited to Paris.

The early republicans considered that theatre, as a shared ritual, could be an ideal way of reinforcing a single national ideology. The first French Revolution (1789–1800) had experimented with pageantry and festivity to promote itself. On a more modest scale, the Second Republic (1848–50) had brought in free theatrical performances for the poor, just as it opened the museums free for them on Sundays. Early Third Republic politicians such as Jules Bonnassies (1872), Jean Jaurès (1900) and theatre directors and writers such as Maurice Pottecher (*Le Théâtre du peuple*, Theatre for/of the People, 1899) and Romain Rolland (*Le Théâtre du peuple*, 1903) advocated various forms of institutionalised people's theatre. Subsequently, the idea moved forward mainly during periods when cultural interventionism was politically in favour: under left-wing or centre-left governments (Combes, 1902–05; the Popular Front, 1936–40; the first Mitterrand presidency, 1981–8) but also under paternalistic right-wing regimes (Vichy, 1940–44; the Fifth Republic under de Gaulle, and, especially André Malraux, his Minister for Culture from 1958 to 1965). Many variants have found favour, but it is significant that France has set up three separate institutions called *Théâtre National Populaire* (1920–24 and 1951–72 in Paris; 1972–present in Villeurbanne, near Lyons), while state involvement in theatre policy and funding is symbolised by the existence of the 'direction du théâtre' at the Ministère de la culture.

In its most simple form, popularisation has consisted in establishing theatre in communities who have no access to it (following the example set by Maurice Pottecher in the village of Bussang at the turn of the century, half-a-dozen small-town community theatres were set up by government in 1902; in the late 1920s the successful Parisian director Jacques Copeau famously abandoned Paris and spent ten years based in the Burgundy countryside, taking productions on tour to villages). It can also travel to these communities from a metropolis: thus the 'Théâtre Ambulant' set up by Firmin Gémier in 1911 was a scheme for moving the whole apparatus of a Parisian theatre around France by rail; while the present 'Théâtre National Populaire' based in Villeurbanne is supposed to spend most of its time on tour. At other times, directors have advocated retaining a fixed playhouse but widening audiences by bussing them in from working-class or merely remote suburbs or nearby towns, cultivating links with works councils, schools and other community groups, distributing neighbourhood-friendly news-sheets widely in the town, and programming plays with popular appeal, which has often meant well-known classics, or plays with contemporary social and political relevance.

This latter philosophy was spread mainly under the influence of the actor-director-manager Jean Vilar (active 1943–62) who created the annual theatre festival at Avignon in 1947, and was director of the second version of the Théâtre National Populaire in the Palais de Chaillot in Paris from 1951. He defended his concept in various writings, collected under the significant title *Le Théâtre service public* (Theatre as a Public Service).

His success in making the TNP, for a dozen years, into a large enterprise addressing, not mainly workers, but a fair cross-section of Parisian society, has had, for two reasons, a widespread effect on the development of French theatre. First, there had appeared in several provincial towns in non-Occupied France, between 1940 and 1943, movements dedicated to the promotion of regional culture, both because they were now more distant from Paris (in the Occupied zone and no longer functioning properly as capital) and because the mood (not just among collaborators in the values promoted by Vichy) was for national regeneration from regional roots. Several of these movements focused on actors or theatre directors who had returned to their home province in 1940, and in the aftermath of the war several theatres with a regional brief were established by government in large provincial towns: notably Aix-en-Provence, Grenoble, Rennes, Saint-Etienne, Strasbourg, Toulouse. The affair moved into a new dimension with the appointment of André Malraux as Minister for Culture in 1959. A full programme of *décentralisation* was put into effect, which led, within fifteen years, to recognition and sponsorship of thirty-six theatrical ventures (of several types, depending on the proportions of national, regional and municipal financial support, on the degree of specialisation in theatre as opposed to other performing arts, plastic arts and music). As a result, there have, since the late 1960s, been major local focuses of dramatic production (in addition to those mentioned above) in Caen, Lille, Lyons, Marseilles, Montpellier, Nancy, Nice, Rennes, Villeurbanne, as well as in Parisian suburbs (Aubervilliers, Créteil, Gennevilliers, Nanterre). A real network of subsidised theatres has come into existence, of which each one typically produces two to four plays a year and takes them on tour to several of the others), and those responsible for establishing it all paid obeisance to Jean Vilar's principles and practices.

The most significant effect of *décentralisation* has been the construction of new playhouses or the major technical investments made into older fabrics. From the 1980s there were over fifty theatres in the Paris suburbs and the provinces, equipped with modern sound and lighting, and capable of adapting the audience–stage interface to practically any type of production. On the other hand, because running expenses were handed out more sparsely, these theatres have tended to take minimum risks, and rely on productions of classics, particularly those appealing to school audiences. As a result the system has only had a marginal effect on new writing for the theatre. Only a few significant contemporaries can be said to have been nurtured by *décentralisation*, though typically they have tended to emerge as actors or directors, not only as playwrights, a feature which has characterised some of the healthier periods of theatre history: thus Armand Gatti (see above), Bernard-Marie Koltès (see below), Serge Valletti (wrote from 1969), Annie Zadek (wrote from 1976). This is mainly because of the audiences it caters for. In spite of its ideological base, the new network has not brought factory workers and farmers, or even white-collar workers and tradespeople, to theatre in more than marginal numbers. It has appealed more to the professional classes in large suburban and provincial communities, and has been especially successful in attracting school groups. Neither of these sections of the audience are particularly attracted by little-known authors, overtly political pieces or plays using genuinely popular dramatic structures.

During the first twenty years, the men in charge of the movement made it their business to introduce French audiences to the plays of Bertold Brecht, whose 'Berliner Ensemble' made four epoch-making visits to Paris between 1954 and 1960. Brecht could be seen as a paragon because he combined a politically attractive stance (opposition to the Nazi regime in the 1930s, position as state theatre director in Communist East Germany in the 1950s – a time when the French Communist party, to which many French intellectuals subscribed, still looked to Eastern European models) with the power to create genuinely new dramatic structures for a politically responsible theatre: the use of historical parable, poetry and music, and ballad-type narrative to crack open audience passivity and shape new political myths. Brecht's subjects were, naturally, rooted in the preoccupations of pre- and postwar Germany, though they had a certain more universal appeal. They inspired a few French authors to form, for a time, a modest Brechtian school: Adamov (see above), with *Paolo Paoli* (1957) and *Le Printemps 71* (Spring 1971, 1971) and Roger Planchon (*La Remise* [The Out-House], 1961; *Le Cochon noir* [The Black Pig], 1972) are among the very few who broke through the media barrier described above.

Brecht's more lasting influence on the 'décentralisation' has been on styles of performance. Brecht demonstrated that scenography can be freed from realism, actors from total investment into one character study, and dramatic rhythm from strict chronology, and the resulting spectacle achieves a wide effect far removed from the conventions of film and television. These principles became, in the fourth quarter of the century, the hallmarks of French theatrical output. With the equipment and theatrical space now available within *décentralisation* and in open-air theatre festivals in southern climes (particularly Avignon, which has become an annual professional gathering) they have been applied widely and imaginatively, particularly to Molière and Shakespeare, who have constantly topped the charts: the first because he is a must for school parties, the second because he is a source of texts which, when freed from their native British tradition, can be freely adapted to all sorts of experimental uses.

Within this network, a playhouse is almost invariably placed under the authority of a theatre director on a limited contract involving three or four new productions a season, and funds do not usually stretch to establishing a company of actors, unless (as at Nanterre and Strasbourg, for instance) it is associated with an acting school under the authority of the same director. This, together with the stress on styles of production of classics, rather than on new plays, has given the director a greater role in the second half of the century than he ever had before. In the previous century, theatre was dominated by dramatists and actors. The 'avant-garde' directors of the 1930s were all primarily actors and are remembered as such. Now it is not uncommon to hear of 'Planchon's *L'Avare* (The Miser), Chéreau's *La Dispute* (The Dispute), Vitez's *Hamlet*' with Molière, Marivaux and Shakespeare relegated, as it were, to small type. In the modern scheme, directors have a style and a following – one could almost say a school; they have favourite authors and texts, they employ dramatic assistants to research their sources and to provide the public with glosses on their reading of classical works; and, even more importantly, they choose the plays and employ the actors.

Among the significant names in this new dispensation have been Marcel Maréchal (worked 1960 to 1998, associated with Lyons and Marseilles); Roger Planchon (worked from 1953, associated with the Théâtre de la Cité in Villeurbanne, later become TNP); Jérôme Savary (worked from 1965, first in a company of his own called Grand Magic Circus then in various state theatres); Antoine Vitez (worked 1966 to 1990, associated with the theatre in the Parisian suburb of Ivry, then with the Théâtre de Chaillot and the Comédie Française).

Revisiting realism

Ambitious French theatre since the 1890s had directed a great deal of its efforts towards escaping from realism, until the example of Brecht suggested that politically committed theatre needed to reanchor itself in some way to reality. As a result some of the prominent playwrights of the late twentieth century have returned to writing rooted in social reality, whether of a documentary or historical kind, though they have learned, at the same time, to emphasise the essentials of theatricality: an awareness of styles and levels of representation, modulation of the powers of the spoken word, and the newly identified opportunity to draw on the many forms of theatre that the century has invented or rediscovered.

Jean-Claude Grumberg (wrote from 1967) exhibits this kind of versatility in his plays on France's recent Jewish history, such as *Dreyfus* (1974), *L'Atelier* (The Workshop, 1979), *Zone libre* (The Unoccupied Zone, 1990), and on the foundering of humanistic ideals in the twentieth century, as in *Amorphe d'Ottenburg* (Amorphe of Ottenburg, 1971), *En rev'nant de l'Expo* (The Expo and After, 1975). Tilly (wrote from 1980) roots his pieces in 'documentary' reality, where stage time equates with real time, but contrives to make them relevant to society in general: see *Charcuterie fine* (Quality Pork Butcher, 1980); *Les Trompettes de la mort* (Deadly Fungi, 1985); *Minuit chrétien* (Christian Midnight, 1999). Jean-Marie Koltès (wrote 1970–88) also begins with striking images of social exclusion or violence while lending them a more profound texture through his versatility with words: *Combat de nègre et de chiens* (Nigger Fights Dogs, 1982; *Quai ouest*, 1986; *Roberto Zucco*, 1990).

Conclusion

The image and place of theatre in French culture evolved considerably during the twentieth century. In 1900 it was a widespread form of urban entertainment dispensed by actors commanding admiration in, but not admitted to, polite society. It was based almost entirely on French contemporary writing reflecting the preoccupations of a newly urbanised class-based society (social stasis or mobility, distribution and use of wealth, sexual mores, metropolitan anonymity and broken lineage), though experiments were taking place with new forms. It was an entirely Parisian artefact, of which the more entertaining products were consumed on loan by the provinces.

In the new millennium, theatre has split into three strands: a tiny and entirely Parisian remnant of the 1900 model; an educational exploration of the classical heritage aimed mainly at schools and spread fairly evenly among most medium and large towns; and a small set of experimental forms, mainly presented in Paris and the Avignon theatre festival, and of greater interest to theatre professionals than to the wider public. It now relates regularly to an historical and international repertoire of texts and dramatic forms and adapts them, by the licence afforded to its proponents and their alternative life-style, to the preoccupations of a post-industrial society where issues of class are less prominent than tensions arising from race, age, sex and consumer relations, and worries about the source and nature of political power and group and national identity. As cinema is increasingly attracted by the siren calls of techno images and cartoon-style psychology, French theatre still manages to survive, against the odds, as a small-scale humane interface between living actors and living audiences.

FURTHER READING

Bradby, D., *French Theatre since 1940: Modern French Drama 1940–1990*, Cambridge: Cambridge University Press, 1991.

Campos, C. (ed.), *People's Theatre in France, Theatre Quarterly*, 23 (1976).

Corvin, M. (ed.) *Dictionnaire encyclopédique du théâtre*, Paris: Larousse-Bordas, 1998.

Guicharnaud, Jacques, *Modern French Theatre: from Giraudoux to Genet*, New Haven: Yale University Press, 1967.

Knowles, Dorothy, *French Theatre in the Inter-War Years 1918–1931*, London: Harrap, 1967.

13
―――――

Music

When Charles Baudelaire, at the dawn of the French modernist period, wrote that music sometimes overwhelmed him like an ocean, he was heralding what would happen in France throughout the twentieth century. A musical map of France at the beginning of the period would have shown all sorts of geographical divisions and class hierarchies, with high art music the purview of a happy and wealthy urban few, regional musics retracting into provincial backwaters, and 'popular' forms of musical expression subject to the vagaries of the growing commercialisation of the music-halls. By the century's end, democratisation and technological advances had led to the breaking of all barriers. With the advent of radio, recording, cinema, television and the Internet, music of all kinds is simultaneously everywhere, giving individuals exponentially increasing choice in what they want to hear and when. For music-makers, too, the parameters have been infinitely extended: conventions of composition and harmony have dissolved; the potentials of sound production have been multiplied by the possibilities of electronic synthesis as well as by the recovery of ancient instruments; the spaces in which music can occur have become unlimited. France has not, of course, been alone in experiencing this revolution, and what it means in the French context is one measure – a significantly sensitive one – of the great changes that have swept the world in the modernist era.

Any definition of what constitutes 'Frenchness' in music is bound to be fraught. In his classic study of modern French music, Rollo Myers explored notions of national and nationalist characteristics, concluding that French music, as distinct in particular from the German experience, showed little evidence of such nationalist aspirations. But Myers also believed that although France had produced some great musicians, the

French were basically not a musical people, lacking spontaneity, and according excessive attention to technique, balance, clarity and detail – in short, to style. He describes this aesthetic consciousness as an instinctive intellectual attitude whose roots reach deep into the whole tradition of French civilisation. While it is generally true that French music is stylistically recognisable, the usefulness of Myers's concept of 'national' is not so clear, because it derives from an analytical paradigm predicated upon the nation-state, whose application is necessarily limited. A broader, more embracing notion of Frenchness in music may be found through the idea of a particular 'cultural community' and its organisation of the production, transmission and reception of its musical life. It is this model that will guide the analysis of this chapter, which will cover the high culture tradition, different aspects of folk and popular music, recent musical fusions, together with some of the most important interfaces between musical creativity and institutional organisation of music. Rather than being derived from any pre-emptive overarching definition, it is from the work itself that the defining characteristics of French music will emerge. It is hoped that in this way, the analysis of music in the French cultural space will contribute to greater general understanding of modern French culture.

The high culture tradition

Historical French state commitment to the high visibility and prestige of the nation's cultural activities received sharper focus during the presidency of François Mitterrand, whose policies drew together a number of new and pre-existing plans for major architectural projects in Paris. Two of these projects were concerned with music: the *Cité de la Musique* (Music City) on the northern edge of Paris, which houses the new buildings of the Paris Conservatorium, a music museum and a medium-sized concert hall; and the *Opéra de la Bastille*, which, since 1990, has housed, under the auspices of the Paris Opera Company, the city's operatic programmes, with the former Opera house (the Opéra Garnier) now reserved for dance. The decision to move the opera, which had already been mooted in the 1960s, carried with it a symbolic affirmation that opera, as an art form of the people, should be situated geographically in a part of Paris associated with France's popular revolutionary traditions. While one must be sceptical about such an aim, given the elite nature of today's opera audiences, both the Opéra and the Cité de la Musique stand as forceful statements about France's continuing role as an influential world centre of music. As prominent performance spaces, they evoke the impressive lineage of instrumentalists and singers that France has produced across time, and continues to produce. They are also, even more strikingly, reminders that the creation of music, like that of literature, cinema and the other arts, lies at the heart of the nation's cultural enterprise. The precise role of music in French culture evolved considerably, however, over the course of the century.

During the Belle Epoque, the major establishment composers, Saint-Saëns, Massenet, Fauré and d'Indy were reaching the end of their productive careers, and a new generation was appearing which included Roussel, Koechlin and Dukas. It was a time of dramatic socio-cultural contrasts, with industrial change simultaneously breeding unparalleled wealth and enormous demographic upheavals. In the arts, rebellious and radical experimentation coexisted with self-satisfied middle-class frivolity and conventionality. The figure who embodies most completely this period of transformation is undoubtedly Claude Debussy (1862–1918), whose music was pivotal in the creation of the framework of a musical modernism in France. Debussy's apprenticeship included an encounter with the colossal influence of Wagner as well as the discovery of the scales and timbre of Javanese music. Closely associated with many of the leading writers of his day, he used the poetry of Baudelaire (*Cinq Poésies de Charles Baudelaire*, 1887–9) to mark out a musical territory free of Wagnerian hegemony in which he would develop a language of sound that combined equivalents of what the Symbolists had achieved in poetry and the Impressionists in painting. His first masterwork, *La Prélude de l'après-midi d'un faune* (1892–94), was based on Mallarmé's celebrated text: it had an explosive impact on the musical world and can be considered as the foundation of the composer's future work. Debussy composed across a wide spectrum – song, ballet, opera, symphonic work, chamber music and a substantial body of music for piano. Among the most durably popular of his works are the opera *Pelléas et Mélisande* (1902), *Le Coin des Enfants* (1906–8), which includes music inspired by ragtime,[1] the two books of twelve *Préludes* (1909–12) and the *Etudes* (1915). Eschewing diatonic conventions for modes[2] and Eastern scales, he created a tonal fluidity and a richness of harmonic colour that are at the base of his uniquely mobile musical language. A highly conscious artist, Debussy was also an insightful and incisive musical critic whose reflections on his art illuminate the birth and development of the modernist era.

Less experimental than Debussy, but also a composer of great import, Maurice Ravel (1875–1937) reached his musical maturity early. Although some commentators have found his music to be artificial and aloof, based more on formal concerns than on feeling, it can be argued that the virtuosity and control that characterise Ravel's composition are in fact ways of distilling emotion into greater potency. His restraint is balanced by a taste for exoticism, which showed him to be a keen listener to his Russian contemporaries as well as to folk music from Spain and his native Basque country. His two piano concertos (1929–31), both masterpieces, also exploit the rhythmic possibilities of jazz. Like Debussy, Ravel's musical production is diverse, and his style is equally demonstrated in works for piano, chamber groups and larger orchestras. Within a predominantly modal framework, the hauntingly delicate melodic lines, the varieties of rhythm, and the subtle shifts of harmony are evident in all his compositions. His quest for perfect balance between intellect and feeling is most successful in *Pavane pour une infante défunte* (1899), the suite *Ma mère l'oye* (1908), the ballet *Daphnis et Chloë* (1912), *Le tombeau de Couperin* (1919) and the lyric fantasy, *L'enfant et les sortilèges* (1925), based on a text of Colette. It is perhaps unfortunate for Ravel that his best known work, *Boléro* (1928), written as a self-imposed challenge, has often obscured wider knowledge of his production. Based on a repeated gypsy dance motif, and on the principle of a relentless crescendo, while *Boléro* is one of the stalwarts of the orchestral repertoire, and continues to excite audiences, it does not do justice to the fine ambiguities of Ravel's homage to classical forms and his explorations of the stimulating and troubling dissonances of modernity.

Born between Debussy and Ravel, Erik Satie (1866–1925) is one of the most enigmatic and eccentric figures of French music. Founder of the *Eglise Métropolitaine d'Art de Jésus-Conducteur* (Metropolitan Art Church of Jesus the Conductor), Satie was from the beginning a bizarre thinker whose ideas anticipate the development of Surrealism, a movement in which he was to participate occasionally through his full engagement with the musical avant-garde. In his early period, his three *Gymnopédies* (1888), much loved by Debussy who orchestrated them, combine delicate linear melodies with quite hypnotically unresolved harmonies, giving the lie to Satie's proclaimed interest in Wagner. Later, he experimented in various ways. He suppressed time and key signatures and bar-lines – important conventional guidelines in the written score to mark the pitch and the development of the music. And he added quirky verbal commentaries to the music, inviting the performers, for instance to 'open their heads' or to 'postulate within themselves'. Titles such as 'Flabby Preludes', 'Desiccated Embryos', 'Pear-shaped Music', 'Second to Last Thoughts' caused Cocteau to suggest that Satie, to protect the modest seriousness of his work, had opted to hide behind a mask of ironic absurdity. His greatest works are commonly held to be *Parade* (1917) and *Socrate* (1918). *Parade* was a landmark event in French performance art, in which Satie collaborated with Cocteau, Picasso and Diaghilev's Russian Ballet, and it contains music that echoes the sounds of the contemporary world, with its mechanised rhythms and its underlying discordant violence. It also contains a ragtime that heralds France's entry into the jazz age. *Socrate* is more meditative, being a setting for voice and small orchestra of Plato's dialogues. Satie continued to experiment until his death, and his composition and personal appearance in René Clair's *Entr'acte* (1925) are a moving testament to this man whose life and work so poignantly illustrates the transitional nature of his times.

One of the symbolic markers of the vitality of the period following the First World War was the group of composers dubbed 'The Six'. The group consisted of Georges Auric (1899–1983), Louis Durey (1888–1979), Arthur Honegger (1892–1955), Darius Milhaud (1892–1974), Francis Poulenc (1899–1963) and Germaine Tailleferre (1892–1983). Although their subsequent careers demonstrate as many differences as similarities among these composers, they shared an aesthetic of rebelliousness (including an anti-Wagnerism common to many French composers) mixed with a tendency to cultivate traditional melodies, polytonal[3] discords, and crude or emphatic rhythms, often borrowed from ragtime. In the immediate postwar years, they moved in the avant-garde circles of Cocteau and Satie. After a 1918 concert in Paris, which provoked enough of a scandal to launch their reputation, they collaborated on only two collective works: Cocteau's ballet *Les Mariés de la Tour Eiffel* (1921), and *L'Album des Six* for piano (1920). Of the group, Milhaud has probably left the most significant heritage, with a large number of compositions covering many genres. His 1923 *La Création du monde* is emblematic of a musical inspiration that draws on all cultures and all epochs. Milhaud took refuge in the United States during the Second World War, and afterwards, his status as a national composer was somewhat diluted, as he shared his time between Mills College in California, as a resident composer, and the Paris Conservatorium. Poulenc crafted many exquisite pieces for piano, but also a significant number of works for voice, some of them like his *Dialogue des Carmélites*, emanating from his religious beliefs, and others like *Les*

Mamelles de Tirésias (1944) of more secular nature. The populist aspect of Auric's resolute modernism is best exemplified by his significant contributions to film music, while his years spent as Director of the Paris Opera (1962–8) remind us of The Six's conception of music as an art that bridges both high culture and popular traditions.

Writing against the neo-classicism of his contemporaries, Edgar Varèse (1883–1965) was from the beginning of his musical studies inclined towards considering music in terms of a quasi-architectural organisation of sound that, in turn, he thought of as raw material rather than as anything inherently musical. Varèse's life as a composer alternated between Europe and the United States and the international qualities of his personal biography are reflected in his work. Characterised by Henry Miller as the 'stratospheric Colossus of Sound', Varèse appears as a committed, wilful innovator. Abandoning traditional notions of melody, harmony and tonality for compositional forms based on the layering of sound and the creation of processes of flow, he works with equal originality in very large orchestral pieces such as *Amériques* (1918–23), chamber works like *Intégrales* (1925) or, one of his most often played compositions, *Ecuatorial* (1934), for solo flute. His *Ionisation* (1929–31) was the first Western musical score for percussion not based on folklore, and it demonstrates the way in which the composer transforms rhythmic figures into almost melodic ones, and the different depths of percussive sound into a kind of harmonic structure. Throughout all his work Varèse uses percussion as a distinctive and integral voice of musical development, rather than as a form of accompaniment or emphasis. The performance in 1954 at the Théâtre des Champs-Elysées of *Déserts* (1950–54), where the sounds of the orchestra were interspersed with tape-recordings made in factories, triggered a scandal, the likes of which had not been seen since Stravinsky's *Sacre du printemps* in 1913. Both in France and internationally, Varèse's status grew as the century advanced. Viewed from today's perspective, he appears more in the lineage of Schoenberg, Saguer, Xenakis and Boulez than as a representative of the period that produced Debussy, Ravel, Satie and The Six.

Olivier Messiaen (1908–92) entered the Paris Conservatorium at the age of eleven, and studied composition with Dukas and organ with Marcel Dupré, as well as many other musical forms, from Hindu rhythms to Gregorian chant. Winner of numerous first prizes, he rapidly established a strong reputation as a composer and a performer. His first major work, *Le Banquet Céleste* for organ, led to his nomination in 1930 as organist at the church of La Trinité, one of Paris's most sought-after residencies, where his improvisations provoked passionate interest over many decades. Messiaen was a deeply convinced and practising Catholic and, although he denied being in any way a mystic, his beliefs underlie almost all his work. For him, there was no paradox in his embracing and extending of the principles of contemporary music: on the contrary, driven by a desire to regenerate the aesthetic and spiritual power of French music, he saw the universalism of his religious beliefs as providing the unifying context for a compositional practice that ranged across quite distinct tonal and modal traditions. He is credited with putting an end to the limits of Schoenberg's serialism and with inaugurating a new era in French music.

During the Second World War, as a prisoner of war, Messiaen composed one of his most searingly demanding works, the *Quatuor pour la fin du temps*, that both expresses and seeks to transcend the pain and horror of the tragic catastrophe that had befallen humankind. After the war, as Professor of Harmony at the Paris Conservatorium, he added to his impact as a composer his influence as a teacher. In this dual capacity, he shaped the development of French music right down to the present and contributed significantly to musical development internationally: among his students were Boulez, Stockhausen, Xenakis, Tremblay, Mâche, Grisey, and many others. One of his more eccentric originalities was his love of bird songs which he collected and transcribed from sites all over the world, and which he integrated into a number of his compositions, such as *Catalogue d'oiseaux* (1959), a piano work that takes more than an hour to perform, or the orchestral *Chronochromie* (1960) which contains a passage reproducing sounds of eighteen species of birds singing together. Although some of his liturgical compositions provoked a degree of controversy, Messiaen attracted to his classes composers from all around the world. His opera *Saint François d'Assise* (1983) typified the conflictual reactions that his work produced for most of his career. Perhaps his most monumental composition was the ten movement *Turangalîla* symphony, which, with its immense orchestra, including piano, the Ondes Martenot,[4] and a vast array of percussion instruments, was intended to explore the complex and difficult tensions between Eros and Agapê, physical and divine love. This work provides impressive examples of the richness of Messiaen's musical language with its blend of intellectuality and violence.

In the high culture tradition, the towering musical figure of the end of the twentieth century was Pierre Boulez (*b.* 1925), a significant experimental composer, celebrated conductor, eminent theoretician, and the most influential power-broker for musical developments within France's cultural institutions. After studying with Messiaen (against whom he later rebelled quite acrimoniously) and Leibowitz (a pupil of Schoenberg's), Boulez worked for a time as music director in the Barrault-Renaud theatre company, making his debut as a composer in 1946 with a sonata for piano. A number of his early works were written in homage to Schoenberg and demonstrated a dominant modernist spirit: thus the song-cycle *Le Visage nuptial* (1946–50) and *Le Marteau sans maître* (1952–4) involved settings of poems by the contemporary poet, René Char. For some time, Boulez was interested in the 'concrete music' experiments of Pierre Schaeffer (1910–95). Schaeffer was seeking new ways of conceptualising musical experience, by recording and manipulating sounds from a diversity of sources, and his *Groupe de Recherches Musicales* (Musical Research Group, 1958) was to remain an important centre of activity. Boulez, however, quarrelled with Schaeffer, and indeed with much of the French musical establishment, which he accused of 'imbecility'. This led to almost two decades of self-imposed exile in Germany, during which his reputation as a world-class conductor was established. He was to head both the BBC Symphony Orchestra (1971–5) and the New York Philharmonic (1971–7). After extensive negotiations, Boulez returned to France in 1977 as the Director of the *Institut de Recherche et de Coordination Acoustique / Musique* (IRCAM – Institute for Accoustics/Music Coordination and Research) and as the Head of the *Ensemble InterContemporain* (the InterContemporary Ensemble), giving him a solid platform for both creation and performance of contemporary music at the interface of emerging technologies. He was also a key figure in the planning and creation of the Cité de la Musique.

Although its intellectual importance is uncontested, the work of Boulez, along with that of his disciples and other contemporary composers, points to a serious gap between the practitioners and their potential public. While Boulez himself attracts reasonable audiences among the cultural and intellectual elite, such audiences represent only a tiny proportion of the public at large, and both the IRCAM and the Ensemble InterContemporain depend heavily on subsidies from the French State (in the order of 80 per cent).[5] This problem of small audiences for contemporary 'serious' music is not of course unique to France, but it does help explain why in France, where culture is very much a matter of government preoccupation, considerable attention has been given, and increasingly so in recent years, to the support of more obviously popular forms of music.

Popular music traditions

Popular music in France has developed through a number of different vectors, which correspond to the complex and progressive emergence and evolution of the French cultural community. Three of the more important areas will be focused on here: French regional music; the *chanson* (song); and other musical fusions of various kinds that have occurred in the course of the twentieth century through the encounter between French and other cultures.

The defence of regional cultures in France has a history as long as the nation's thrust to build a centralised, dominant culture. After several centuries of centralism, government acknowledgment of the need to give greater linguistic and cultural autonomy to regions began under de Gaulle in the 1960s and was brought to fruition under Mitterrand in the early 1980s. The revitalisation of traditional musics, with their use of local languages and folk music forms has greatly benefited from this changed environment. From the 1960s and 1970s, strong movements have grown up across France, motivated in part by a nostalgic desire to reclaim the simpler truths of the past, but also by a determination to demonstrate that contemporary creation is possible within the traditional frameworks. Music is seen both as an example of cultural renewal, and as a means of achieving it. Such movements often combine the use of ancient traditional instruments with the possibilities of electronic technology, and their audiences extend well beyond the regions and, thanks to the global popularity of world music, even beyond France. What often began as a practice of amateur performances was by the end of the century significantly professionalised, with trained musicians, dedicated recording companies and well-organised performance circuits.

Brittany has led the way in the regional music revival and it has attained a high level of institutionalisation in its initiatives to maintain and foster Breton culture (e.g. the 'Dastum' Association of Rennes, created in 1972 to collect, research and showcase the region's cultural patrimony[6]). One of the more enduring participants in the resurgence of Breton music is Alan Stivell (*b.* 1944). Stivell began his career as a specialist of the Celtic harp and other folk instruments, with which he managed to create a very considerable new audience following the success of a concert at the Olympia in Paris in 1972: the concert album sold nearly 1.5 million copies. Later, he experimented with electronic music as well as with instruments and sounds from other traditions and through the 1980s and 1990s, he toured throughout the world, performing before large live audiences and maintaining a strong output of albums. One of the musicians from the Stivell band, Dan Ar Braz (*b.* 1949), created his own group as well as building a career as a solo performer, promoting the values of the Celtic heritage through tours in France and abroad and through very prolific recording. Other regions of France have also been active in nurturing their local music and in drawing attention to it. The Corsican group *I Muvrini*, for instance, has since 1979 sought to use music and song as a way of educating the public about Corsican culture. Similarly, groups using the Provençal language such as the *Massilia Sound System*, formed in 1984, and the *Fabulous Trobadors* (1986) draw on a variety of musical traditions to transmit the strongest possible message promoting the values and rights of local cultural communities.

The French *chanson* also has a very long history, and it covers a great diversity of subjects and styles. The twentieth century, with its development of new modes of transmission, witnessed a marked upsurge of song production, and the recognition of the *chanson* as a legitimate art-form in its own right. *Chanson* is a melding of music and poetry capable of expressing the most complex aspects of individual perception, sensibility and ideas which, at the same time, remains accessible to popular audiences. At the beginning of the century, singers performed in cabarets, in cafés, and, after the First World War, in music-halls such as the Alhambra, the Ambassadeurs, the Apollo, and Bobino. (Bobino is still in operation, together with the Olympia and the Zénith, as an important performance base for *chanson*.) Mistinguett (Jeanne Bourgeois, 1875–1956) developed a career of almost half a century and was without doubt the major female star of the interwar years, while Maurice Chevalier (1888–1972), also enormously successful in France, came to incarnate the stereotypical French entertainer for audiences abroad, particularly in the United States. The success of the 1957 film *Gigi*, in which he starred with Leslie Caron, ensured Chevalier's ongoing celebrity. During the 1930s, Charles Trénet (1913–2000), nicknamed 'Le fou chantant' (the singing madman) established his reputation as a brilliant performer and a composer whose songs captured the edgy dynamism of the times. Trénet also enjoyed a long career, which continued almost until the time of his death.

It was just before the Second World War that Edith Piaf (Edith Gassion, 1915–63) broke into the stardom that would make her the world-wide emblem of French song that she became in the decades following the war. Her diminutive size (which earned her the name 'Piaf' – slang for 'sparrow'), the expressivity of her heart-rending voice, the themes of her songs with their emphasis on unhappy and damaged lives and on social outcasts, the tragedy of her own life: all these factors contributed to making of her a legendary figure. Her song, 'La vie en rose' (1945), became something of a signature tune: the music and lyrics capture the mixture of pain and hope that underlie her work, and performed by her, it has a wrenching, timeless intensity. Piaf composed almost eighty songs, and despite interruptions caused by periods of depression and problems with drugs and alcohol, she continued to perform until 1960. Her grave in the Père Lachaise cemetery is a national monument, constantly visited by new generations of fans. As a singer, Piaf has become a classic: her work is regularly performed by major stars internationally and in many languages. It is symbolic of her philosophy of confronting and overcoming even the most despairing of situations that her final performance at the Olympia was of 'Non je ne regrette rien'.

While the Occupation period was notoriously rich in musical life – Chevalier and Piaf continued to sing at this time – the Liberation was marked by a burst of renewal of the *chanson*. In the Saint-Germain-des-Près area in Paris, where Sartrean existentialism had become a cultish fashion, Juliette Gréco (b. 1927) was the husky voice of the new youth culture. Her image was that of the rebellious, restless young people who sought emancipation from the oppressive atmosphere of the Occupation and the constraints of bourgeois morality and values. Her bohemian, intellectual appearance – long black hair, all black clothing – contrasted with the traditional expressivity of performers, and it inspired numerous writers and musicians to create songs for her: Prévert, Sartre, Queneau, Brassens, Ferré, Gainsbourg, Aznavour. The other major figure of Saint-Germain was Boris Vian (1920–59). His songs represented only one aspect of his eclectic creativity – which embraced novel writing, acting and jazz – but they cover a very broad territory, both musically and poetically. Vian's recorded performances of his work have a deceptive lightness of voice: the apparent deadpan delivery is, in fact, a vehicle for a cutting wit and underlying fury. Songs that at first hearing appear quirky or trivial reveal complex melodic and harmonic craftsmanship and messages of profound import. Thus, the theme of social satire in 'Je suis snob' (1954) hides an ontological dimension, and the sarcastic humour of 'La Java des bombes atomiques' (1955) carries the deep unease of the Cold War era. Vian's most famous song, 'Le Déserteur' (1954), which takes the form of an open letter to the President of the French Republic, was an anti-war protest and was taken by the authorities as inciting young men conscripted into the Algerian War to desert. It was accordingly banned, a fact which served to consecrate Vian's reputation as an iconoclast.

The postwar period saw the emergence of many singers whose work has become integral to France's musical patrimony. Georges Brassens (1921–81) is undoubtedly the most celebrated of them. He came to performance relatively late, beginning only at the age of thirty, but his subsequent success was both critical and popular. The words of his songs have been accorded the full status of poetry, so much so that he was awarded the Poetry Prize by the Académie Française in 1967. Famous for his reticent personality and the complete lack of showmanship in performances in which he appeared either simply with his guitar or with a double bass accompaniment, he came to embody the notion of musical integrity. Brassens's voice is gravelly, and his accent bears traces of his southern France upbringing. His music, developed around his texts, is generally uncomplicated, in the folk tradition. His thematic material, on the other hand, can be quite involved, even though it deals with familiar topics – love ('Je me suis fait tout petit'), friendship ('La canne de Jeanne'), nature ('Auprès de mon arbre'), death ('Pauvre Martin) – in everyday situations of modern life. From early on, he earned a reputation for anti-conformism and even anarchism, with songs whose language highlighted slang and crude swearwords which, in the 1950s, still had the power to shock. His attacks on authority figures, like police, priests and judges, and on what he saw as the irrevocable stupidity of the guardians of public morality ('Les trompettes de la renommée', 'Le temps ne fait rien à l'affaire') ensured both a rejection by cultural conservatives and an enthusiastic reception by the young. One of his songs, 'Le Gorille', which recounts the adventures of a sex-starved gorilla having to make a choice between a decrepit old woman and an uptight young magistrate – and choosing the latter – was found to be so offensive that it was banned for some years from the radio.

If the work of Brassens is above all an expression of warmth and humanity, with a healthy dose of scepticism, that of the Belgian Jacques Brel (1929–78) whose career and rise to fame were very much contemporary, resonates with the pain and passion of a man for whom performance and life are synonymous. Many of Brel's songs reflect the conflicts inherent in his upbringing as a French speaker in Flanders, and the Belgian landscape is a constant point of reference ('Les Flamandes', 1959; 'Le Plat pays', 1962; 'Bruxelles', 1962). Brel was a driven man, and his performances were legendary for the fierce energy that he deployed during unusually long concerts. His voice was rich, deep and adaptable to great emotional range. The dark and oppressive atmosphere evoked in a song like 'Amsterdam' (1964), the spasms of despair in 'Ne me quitte pas' (1972) and even the nostalgic sentimentality of 'Quand on n'a que l'amour' (1960) are delivered with extraordinary force of conviction. Brel sang as he lived – with unrelieved urgency, and it was perhaps this sense of turbulent acceleration that made his audiences see him as such a great witness of the spirit of his time.

Other notable singers of this period include Yves Montand (1921–91) who, like Charles Aznavour, divided his career between singing and cinema acting, in both of which he gained considerable international reputation. Léo Ferré (1916–93), for his part, built a strong and faithful audience within France for his musical settings of Rimbaud, Apollinaire and Aragon as well as of his own rather anarchistic and pessimistic poems. In the early 1960s, the influence of the new American popular music (early rock'n'roll, the twist etc.) led to another dramatic transformation of the French *chanson*. The rapid expansion of television, radio and sophisticated record-playing equipment, together with the appearance of the transistor, and the fashion for mini-skirts and motor scooters spawned what became known as the *yé-yé* generation (from the American 'yeah'). The main singers of this blandly commercial movement of superficial sentiments and simplistic melodies were Johnny Hallyday (*b*. 1943), Françoise Hardy (*b*. 1944), and Sylvie Vartan (*b*. 1944) all of whom survived it and went on to more varied musical careers.

One genre of *chanson* particularly appreciated by French audiences, but virtually unknown outside of the Francophone world because of the linguistic difficulties it can present, is the humorous or comic song, which has had some very distinguished representatives. Boby Lapointe (1922–72), who was most active during the 1960s and 1970s, built his songs out of highly sophisticated plays on language, absurd onomatopoeia, clever puns and percussive rhythms. His performance of these works was often a *tour de force* in its own right, of galloping, tongue-twisting difficulty. Pierre Perret (*b*. 1934) shares something of Lapointe's playfulness, but is more overt in his deployment of slang and popular speech. His wit is particularly mordant when he attacks questions of sexual inhibition, such as his 1974 song 'Le Zizi' (slang for the male organ), which, with more than 5 million copies sold, has remained one of the great hits in the whole history of French song. Not all of Perret's work is humorous. There are songs of social comment, and more intimate pieces about friendship; there are also heartily erotic songs and works that sing the pleasures of the table and the eye. Marie-Paule Belle (*b.* 1946) also developed a successful and extended career based essentially on humour. Her work employs parody and pastiche, and a series of rapid, glancing allusions to the preoccupations of contemporary urban French life, with its frenetic pace, its psychological uncertainty and turmoil and its tangled values. 'La Parisienne' (1976) is a good example of this work in its breathless portrayal of a young provincial woman getting the hang of what it means to be a Parisian.

Any anthology of recent French *chanson* production is bound to reflect above all the tastes of its creator, but certain figures do seem to impose themselves as likely to be of durable presence. Serge Gainsbourg (1928–91), despite a complete absence of a conventional singing voice, was inspired by Boris Vian to take up composition in the late 1950s, and for three decades he worked at evolving a radically personal musical style. Drawing on jazz, reggae, rock, funk and other musical forms, he sought out controversy through his continual confrontation of social and musical habits. There is a deliberate coarseness about Gainsbourg's music, just as there was in his hard-drinking, provocative life. The vulgar eroticism of a song written for and performed with his wife, Jane Birkin, 'Je t'aime moi non plus' (1968) led to its banning in several countries. His reggae version of the 'Marseillaise', 'Aux armes etcoetera' (1979), produced much patriotic outrage – and much joyful assent. Paradoxically, his writing also reflects a deep appreciation of literature. He wrote songs for Bardot, Françoise Hardy, Vanessa Paradis and others. His biggest selling album, 'Love on the beat', appeared in the mid-1980s.

Among other stars of the 1980s and 1990s were Claude Nougaro (closely identified with the city of Toulouse), Anne Sylvestre, Georges Moustaki, Jacques Dutronc, Michel Jonasz, Renaud, France Gall, Francis Cabrel, Jean-Jacques Goldman and Vanessa Paradis. Patricia Kaas (*b.* 1966) stands out because of the extent of her success, which is world-wide, with record sales in the many millions. Regularly compared to Piaf, Kaas has a similarly big voice which with its slight raspiness, exudes warmth. Her first album, 'Mademoiselle chante le blues' (1988) 'went gold' within a month and her second, 'Scène de vie' (1988) was even more successful. In 1991, she received the World Music award for 'Best French Artist of the Year', and has subsequently released new albums every three or four years.

The steady flow of new talent into the *chanson* genre promises a healthy artistic future. *Chanson* has been established as a major industry, watched over and fostered by the Société des Auteurs, Compositeurs et Editeurs de Musique (SACEM – The Society of Authors, Composers and Publishers of Music). Politically, too, it has its role to play in the French government's cultural promotion of French language abroad. *Chanson* often poses problems of access for non-French-speaking audiences who, unable to understanding the interplay between lyrics that are often in themselves poetic and linguistically challenging, and music that, in its allusions and borrowings, can seem naïve and even silly to ears attuned to American music. With its high degree of social and political commitment, however, the *chanson* remains an important indicator of many of the issues facing contemporary French society, and is hence an invaluable source for understanding the pressures at work in French culture.

Over much of the modernist period, French culture has continued to encounter other forms of musical expression and to interact with them. Just before the First World War, the tango became a popular dance form whose role as a vector for Latin American influence would be continuous. Even more importantly, the impact of jazz, from 1918 on, was to affect all kinds of music in France, in both the high culture and popular traditions. An indigenous French jazz culture also grew strongly, producing groups and musicians who reached undisputed international status in the jazz world. Guitarist Django Reinhardt (1910–53) was the first of these in the 1930s with *The Quintet of the Hot Club of France*, especially the work that included the violinist, Stéphane Grappelli (1914–97). After World War II, Martial Solal (*b.* 1927) demonstrated brilliance of invention as a performer (piano, saxophone) and as a composer and arranger. The saxophonist Michel Portal (*b.* 1935) came into jazz through the Basque folk tradition as well as formal training at the Paris Conservatorium and was one of the pioneers of the Free Jazz Movement in France. The virtuoso pianist, Michel Petrucciani (1962–99), in his short career won the admiration of the most difficult of jazz audiences, that of the leading American jazz musicians. It is worth noting, too, that many American modern jazz musicians, including Miles Davis, Bill Evans and their followers, have drawn liberally on the harmonic vocabulary and modal techniques of such composers as Debussy and Ravel. Jazz has provided opportunities for significant cultural exchange, and while its influence in France is undeniable, it is also true that French music has contributed to the establishment of jazz as a universal musical language.

Since the 1960s, France has been fully engaged with the musical pluralism that has swept through the world, blurring generic boundaries as well as opening listening possibilities to the musical productions of a multiplicity of times and places. Like individuals anywhere in the Western world, French people at the beginning of the twenty-first century have virtually unrestricted access to any and every form of musical expression, and it is difficult to distinguish between French reception of musical trends and fashions and those that occur elsewhere. Contemporary audio-visual technology – the Walkman, the video clip, the dedicated radio and television programmes, the Internet – has transformed the presentation of music in ways that are universal. French participation in world-wide youth musical culture is not, however, insignificant, with various explicitly French groups such as Daft Punk and Air occupying high positions on the world pop and techno charts. MC Solaar (*b.* 1969) has shown how rap culture imported from America can be adapted to the French situation, just as *Noir Désir* (1981) has explored the possibilities of rock. France's post-colonial connections in Africa and North Africa have also been a fertile source of musical cross-pollination; groups like *Les Négresses Vertes* (1987) and the performers of *raï* (originally an Algerian fusion, but later the basis of manifold musical interweavings), such as Khaled (*b.* 1960), have attained high levels of multi-cultural and international popularity.

Another area of popular culture where musical creation has been of great importance is the cinema, which has been the principal vehicle of expression for a number of composers. Joseph Kosma (1905–69) attained immortality with his setting of the Prévert poem 'Les feuilles mortes' – one of the rare French tunes to become, as 'Autumn leaves', a worldwide jazz standard; but in addition, his contributions to many of the films of Jean Renoir are also notable as is his work for Carné's *Les Enfants du paradis* (1945) and *Juliette ou la clef des songes* (1951). Georges Delerue (1925–92) composed music for more than 130 films including those of the major New Wave directors, Resnais, Truffaut, Godard and Melville. Michel Legrand (*b.* 1932) is responsible for the score of one of France's few cinematographic musicals, Jacques Demy's *Les parapluies de Cherbourg* (1964) and many other film scores.

Conclusion

In 1982, following a directive from the then Minister of Culture, Jack Lang, France instituted a day of national celebration of its music and musicians, the 'Fête de la Musique'. Held on 21 June at the summer solstice, this day has been ritualised ever since as a symbol of the complete integration of musical activity in French daily life. All through the nation, in rural villages, provincial towns and major metropolitan centres, in churches and concert halls, in railway stations, barns and in the streets, many thousands of musical performances take place, amateur as well as professional, solo performers as well as full orchestras and choirs. Today a Baudelairean *flâneur* strolling through the France of the Fête de la Musique would witness the comfortable coexistence of an almost unlimited array of musical styles, just as individual citizens in today's France would experience no sense of paradox in personal music collections containing Satie, Ravel, Alan Stivell, Messiaen, Patricia Kaas and Les Négresses Vertes. Hundreds of musical networks, from amateur clubs and professional associations to the regional and national conservatoriums, are involved in the organisation of this festival. Every possible form of music is represented, from every time and tradition. In the mid-1980s, the French initiative was taken up at the level of the European Union and in 1997, an international charter was signed by many other countries. Today more than 100 countries join the annual celebration of music-making.

Like the iconic Cîté de la Musique, the 21 June event is both an emanation of the lively musical activity of France as a cultural community, and a way of drawing the attention of the rest of the world to the esteem in which the nation continues to hold the art of music. It is perhaps at the level of state policy that one can most readily see how the French music sector is a most useful indicator of wider cultural shifts, and particularly, the dramatic transformation of a centralist cultural model into one that explicitly supports not just variety, but an ethos of geographical and generic pluralism that would have been impossible in the pre-modernist period.

NOTES

Colin Nettelbeck's work on this project was greatly facilitated by the research assistance provided by Kirsten Newitt.
1. Ragtime is a syncopated music that emerged from African American culture in the late nineteenth century, and that rapidly became popular in Europe. Its best-known composer was undoubtedly Scott Joplin (1868–1917).

2. Diatonic scales (major and minor) are made up of tones and semitones and correspond to a given key. Originally part of the medieval modal system, which offered a wider range of scales, the diatonic scale was dominant in European musical composition from the seventeenth to the nineteenth centuries.

3. Polytonal: the use of two or more keys simultaneously.

4. An electronic instrument invented in 1928 by *Maurice Martenot* (1898–1980). Its effects are based on reverberation and unlimited pitch variation.

5. Pierre-Michel Menger, 'L'élitisme musical républicain: la création contemporaine et ses publics', *Esprit* (March 1985), pp. 5–19.

6. 'Dastum' derives from the Breton word for 'gathering together'.

FURTHER READING

Bernard, François, *Histoire brève de la chanson française*, Paris: RFI, 1999.

Blake, Jody, *Le Tumulte noir: Modernist Art and Populist Entertainment in Jazz Age Paris 1900–1930*, University Park, Penn.: Pennsylvania State University Press, 1999.

Goddard, Chris, *Jazz away from Home*, New York and London: Paddington Press, 1979.

Les Inrockuptibles (weekly magazine).

Myers, Rollo, *Modern French Music: its Evolution and Cultural Background from 1900 to the Present Day*, Oxford: Basil Blackwell, 1971.

Jean-Michel Nectoux *et al.*, *The New Grove Twentieth-century French Masters: Fauré, Debussy, Satie, Ravel, Poulenc, Messiaen, Boulez*, London: Macmillan, 1986.

Stovall, Tyler, *Paris Noir: African Americans in the City of Light*, Boston and New York: Houghton Mifflin, 1996.

Tournès, Ludovic, *New Orleans sur Seine: Histoire du Jazz en France*, Paris: Librairie Arthème Fayard, 1999.

Vernillat, France, and Jacques, Charpentreau *La Chanson française*, Paris: Presses Universitaires de France, call. '*Que sais-je?*', 1971.

Von der Weid, Jean-Noël, *La Musique du XXe siècle*, Paris: Hachette, 1997.

France's official Ministry of Culture website http://www.france.diplomatie.fr/culture/france/ind_musiq.html

The richest source of information about traditional French music groups and activities is to be found on their Internet homepages.

14
_____

The visual arts

Introduction

France's contribution to the visual arts is arguably her outstanding achievement in the twentieth century. Paris became the world centre of modernism: the greatest non-French artists such as Pablo Picasso from Spain and Piet Mondrian from Holland would make Paris their home before the Second World War. The far-reaching impact of Cubism on architecture, from Le Corbusier onwards, changed the face of cities across the world. The Ecole de Paris saw artists from Russia, subsequently the Soviet Union, such as Chaim Soutine or Jacques Lipchitz come to live or stay for long periods in Paris, together with artists from Poland and Eastern Europe such as Jules Pascin, from Italy (Amadeo Modigliani), from Switzerland (Meret Oppenheim, Alberto Giacometti, Jean Tinguely), from Denmark (Asger Jorn) and of course from America, from the Synchronist painters before the First World War to photographers such as Man Ray and Lee Miller in the 1920s or William Klein in the 1960s.

Paris, meanwhile, reciprocated, not only as a place of freedom, bohemian lifestyles, purpose-built artists' accommodation, and the café conversation that was so essential a complement to long hours in the studio, but with a structure of annual and varied Salons, a growing, professional and internationally orientated dealer system and, in terms of both spectacle and artistic information, the great exhibitions that marked the first half of the century: the Exposition Universelle of 1900, the Exposition des Arts Décoratifs in 1925, the Exposition Coloniale in 1931, and the Exposition Internationale des Arts et des Techniques de la Vie Moderne in 1937.

This immense concentration of creativity demonstrated the economic viability of fine and decorative arts production, which was intimately linked to Paris's status as a centre for fashion and luxury goods, gastronomy and sexual pleasures. France's very late industrialisation, compared to competitors England, America and Germany, contributed to this development. After the First World War, massive manpower losses encouraged a policy that welcomed the setting up of immigrant workers' communities in various Parisian arrondissements. These provided the multi-cultural infrastructure that invisibly subtends the familiar narratives of the lives of well-known artists and writers. For every name that posterity has retained there were hundreds of stylistically secondary disciples, together with jobbing artists who made a living with portraits, landscapes and still-lives, a host of bohemian dabblers and Sunday painters. Paris was hit, however, at the end of the 1920s by the world economic recession: the art market slumped. Economic factors were only part of the story. The persecution of intellectuals and artists under totalitarian regimes accounted for the renewed presence in Paris of Wassily Kandinsky, Marc Chagall (both of whom had initially accepted positions in the new Soviet State), the Cologne Dadaist Max Ernst, whose early photomontages pilloried German belligerency, and later the anti-Nazi sculptor and Surrealist photographer, Hans Bellmer, among many others. The intense poverty of some artists in Paris after 1945, such as Bram van Velde or Asger Jorn in the 1950s, continued the story of struggle and success or failure, while Paris continued as a magnet: for the painter Zao Wou Ki from China for example in the late 1930s, or Ousmane Sow from Dakar, who became a sculptor while studying in the metropolis in the 1960s.

The visual arts before the First World War

Fauvism may be seen to initiate the establishment of art as an 'autonomous' language, in its deployment of colour without naturalistic reference to the depicted object: red and blue tree trunks, green facial shadows, lime and crimson contours. It had an evident heritage in late nineteenth-century decorative arts and *japonisme*. The Salon d'Automne of 1905 heralded the baptism of the *cage aux fauves* (wild beasts' cage) by the critic Louis Vauxcelles. In this exhibition space, Matisse's *Woman with a Hat*, 1905, painted in violent colours, took its place with works by André Derain, Maurice de Vlaminck, Charles Camoin, Albert Manguin and Louis Marquet. Complementary strokes of colour, red versus green, blue versus orange, were based 'scientifically' on the chromatic contrasts of Chevreul's colour wheel – in the wake of the Impressionists' conception of coloured shadows, post-impressionist theories of optical mixtures reconstituted in the eye of the beholder (Georges Seurat) and the neo-impressionists' development of broader *taches* – broad dabs of colour – to depict open-air, quasi-mythological scenes of naked bathers (Paul Signac, Henri Cross). Thanks to the expansion of the French railways, the opening up of the south of France to artistic tourism was demonstrated by fauvist views of nascent seaside resorts such as Estaque and Collioure, while in the north of France, Raoul Dufy painted beach scenes at Honfleur and Trouville. His *Posters at Trouville*, 1906, in particular, abandoned the shoreline views made classic by the Impressionists, for the vulgar world of advertisement hoardings – with products easily recognisable through colours and formats alone – bringing popular culture into the fauve arena, while anticipating the reintroduction of bright colours into Cubism in the work of Robert Delaunay.

Georges Braque, who had spent a holiday in Estaque painting fauvist seascapes with Dufy, returned there in 1908, after the impact of seeing the Cézanne retrospective at the Salon d'Automne of 1907. His vision of the hinterland – Cézanne's own territory – was painted in what the critic Vauxcelles now derided as *petits cubes* (small cubes). A new movement was born, Cubism: and an argument about priority would develop, Braque's Cézannisme being pitched against Picasso, whose *Demoiselles d'Avignon*, 1907, had been conceived in isolation in his so-called 'Bateau-Lavoir' studio in Montmartre. The *Demoiselles*, named after a Spanish brothel rather than the French city, was the violent and disturbing end-product of literally hundreds of sketches. The large, square-format canvas was inspired, it has been argued, by Picasso's encounter with El Greco's large *Temptation of Saint Antony*, a sexual theme he would also have discovered in early Cézanne. Picasso's contorted figures are based in part on El Greco (particularly the play of light on blue and white draperies) and in part on Michelangelo's sculpture, *The Dying Slave*, in the Louvre, with its twisting body position (*controposto*) and raised arms. Ingres's famous painting, *Le Bain turc*, a mass of female figures pressed against the canvas (exhibited in a retrospective at the Salon d'Automne of 1905) was also important. Most notorious, however, was the transformation of the faces of the female figures with violent striations, evoking Picasso's encounter with African sculpture at the Trocadéro museum. Thus the *Demoiselles d'Avignon*, uncompromisingly modern, with its shocking subject-matter, was rooted in Picasso's study of the past. Picasso also realised that the designation of forms and features in African art was the result of a *conceptual*, not a representational logic. His constructed sculpture, imitating the protruding eye-sockets of African masks, would represent the sounding hole of a guitar with a cylindrical protuberance – literally a reversal of negative into positive space. As Cubist experiments progressed in painting, a new conception of space came into being, dictated by the flattening properties of an overall conceptual grid, which nonetheless permitted a play with conceptions of four-dimensional space and multiple viewpoints: a glass seen both in profile and with a circular rather than ovoid top, for example. Cubist subject-matter, especially still-life, was very definitely linked to the shallow spaces of the café table, evocations of the Suze *apéritif* bottle, or the Anis loved by the Spaniard Juan Gris. Yet the still-life could evoke the more intellectual theme of the *vanitas*, particularly when collage and *papier collé* (pasted paper) was involved. Picasso emphasised both his artifice and the 'reality' of the world in his celebrated *Still Life with Chair Caning*, 1912: with a piece of industrially printed imitation chair-caning cloth stuck on to the canvas. Braque, whose father was a house-painter, 'combed' his paint to achieve *faux-bois* (fake wood panel) effects, or pasted *faux-bois* printed dado papers on to the canvas, with fragmentary evocations of bottles or clarinets in the background. The use of newspaper introduced poetic and semantic dimensions into Cubism, with parts of words stuck or painted on to the pictorial surface, notably *Jou*... suggesting *journal, jour, joujou, jouir* (newspaper, day, toy, to enjoy) or whole phrases involving in-jokes, such as Picasso's collage of 1912 with its newspaper slogan 'La bataille s'est engagée...' (the battle has begun). Subsequent definitions attempted to structure the development of Cubism into three historical phases: 'analytical Cubism' in which objects were broken down into their planar and facetted components, 'hermetic Cubism', in which an almost monochromatic portrait or still-life recedes into a grid, leaving the odd conceptual clue (a piece of cord, a violin silhouette) and 'synthetic Cubism' which built up towards objects starting from shapes and forms. Cubism thus reasserted the flat, autonomous surface of the picture plane and painting's status as an 'object in the world' rather than a 'window on to a represented world'.

The poet Guillaume Apollinaire, author of *Les Peintres cubistes, Méditations esthétiques* (The Cubist Painters, Aesthetic Meditations) 1913, characterised the work of the couple Robert and Sonia Delaunay as Orphism. Delaunay reintroduced the spectral colours of the prism into the cubist grid of his *Windows* series, finally approaching pure abstraction, and abandoning Paris's rooftops for motifs of the sun, moon and Blériot's biplane, introducing a sense of deep space. Sonia Delaunay would extend Orphist principles into fashion design. The unifying concept was *simultanéité* – the simultaneous registering of disparate events – whether referring to the scientific contrast of colours or the movement of patterns in a dress. The American Synchronists, such as Stanton Macdonald Wright and Morgan Russell adapted Orphist colour and space, while, via the *Blaue Reiter Almanach* collaboration with German artists in 1911, the Delaunays influenced German expressionism (Franz Marc, Paul Klee).

Filippo Tommaso Marinetti published the founding manifesto of Futurism on the front page of the Parisian newspaper *Le Figaro* on 20 February 1909, in which he exalted 'great crowds, excited by work, by pleasure and by riot'. What Marinetti saw as the 'beauty of speed' was related to the attempt to convey in two or three dimensions the imaginary lines of force around an image or sculpture in motion, while what he called the 'telegraphic imagination' affected poetic syntax. Often *parole in liberta* (words in liberty) were painted – released from all syntax – directly on to the canvas as well as printed page, a development indebted to Apollinaire's poems known as *calligrammes*, where typographic arrangements created objects made of words. The first Paris exhibition of the group, including Umberto Boccioni and Gino Severini, was held in 1912. However, its anti-feminist stance and 1909 manifesto sentiments such as 'We will glorify war, the world's only hygiene' and 'We will destroy the museums, academies of every kind', intimated the dangers of a creed that led some of its members towards Fascism under Benito Mussolini. The model of charismatic leader, manifesto, printed tracts and journals (derived from politics) became the blueprint for future avant-garde art movements.

From the First World War to 1939

The First World War saw many young French artists and intellectuals called up to fight for their country. Apollinaire, though not a French national, also volunteered; he subsequently died of influenza in 1918. With the extinction of its most brilliant spokesman and critic, an intellectual as well as an historical era seemed to have come to an end. While from 1911 cubist imitators of Picasso and Braque known as 'Salon Cubists', such as Albert Gleizes and Jean Metzinger, continued to flourish with

Figure 6. Marcel Duchamp, *Nude Descending the Staircase*, 1912. Philadelphia Museum of Art, the Louise and Walter Arensberg Collection, 1950.

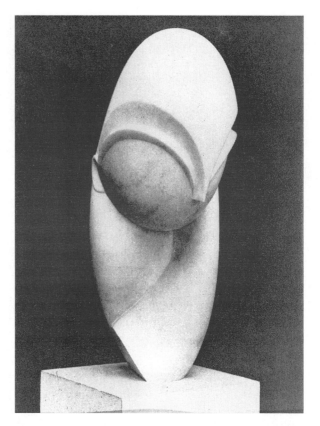

Figure 7. Constantin Brancusi, *Mademoiselle Pogany*, 1928–9. Philadelphia
Museum of Art, the Louise and Walter Arensberg Collection, 1950.

innumerable converts, Dada now erupted in Paris. Marcel Duchamp's
Nude Descending a Staircase (1912) mocked the seriousness of his peers, and
provocatively fused Cubism with a debt to Etienne Marey's chronopho-
tography (the photography of sequential moments of time). Duchamp
also fixed a bicycle wheel on top of a stool in 1913, and in 1914 purchased a
Bottlerack from an ironmongers, which he treated as sculptures. In 1917
in New York, the most celebrated of his so-called 'ready-mades' *Foun-
tain*, was exhibited: it was an industrially produced urinal, inverted and
signed 'R. Mutt', moreover it was subsequently removed from the Independents' Salon – as an 'invisible' object, it became even more notorious.
The apparently random selection of an object, the bestowing of a title
and an 'artist's signature', together with the contextualising frame of the
exhibition space, had created the work of art.

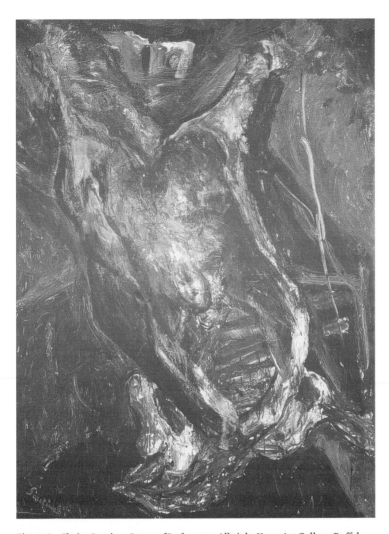

Figure 8. Chaim Soutine, *Carcass of Beef*, c. 1925. Albright Knox Art Gallery, Buffalo, New York. Room of Contemporary Art Fund, 1939.

The absurdist thrust of Dada had its origins in the Cabaret Voltaire, a café-cabaret founded in neutral Zurich during the war. Against a back-drop of cubist and German expressionist art, avant-garde performances were staged, delivering a searing indictment of the times. In Cologne, the Alsatian artist Hans Arp introduced aleatory principles into collage composition by placing fragments of cut or torn paper as they fell 'ac-cording to the laws of chance' – he used this phrase as the title for some pieces. Arp, Max Ernst and the Romanian Tristan Tzara, whose Dada manifestos proposed the creation of poetry from cuttings pulled out of a hat, came to Paris: Dada's 'anti-art' revolution embraced poetry, typography and performance, and works such as Picabia's 'mechanomorphic' painting or his *Portrait of Cézanne* (1921) adorned with a stuffed toy monkey. Scandalous Dada soirées at the Salle Gaveau and Théâtre de l'Oeuvre consolidated Dada's success. Performances such as Tzara's *Le Coeur à Gaz*, 1923, and the Ballet Suedois's *Relâche* with the interval film *Entr'acte* (both involving Picabia) define Parisian Dada as an ultimately elitist – if joyously anarchic – phenomenon, compared with its early counterpart in Zurich, or, indeed, with Berlin Dada, where photomontage techniques were immediately co-opted to aggressively political ends.

Surrealism, founded by André Breton, attempted to go beyond Dada in a Hegelian spirit of the 'negation of the negation'. It attempted to explore the psyche and the unconscious at a time when the works of Sigmund Freud were gradually appearing in French. Breton's first manifesto of 1924 defined Surrealism as 'Pure psychic automatism, by which an attempt is made to express, either verbally, in writing or in any other manner, the true functioning of thought, in the absence of all control of reason, excluding any aesthetic or moral preoccupation.' While experiments with 'automatic' writing took place, 'automatic' drawings made with closed eyes had to be carefully enlarged on to the canvas (Joan Miró, André Masson). Masson's use of poured sand in paintings such as the *Battle of the Fish* (1927) exemplified automatism at work. The symbolism of the painting was inspired by the metamorphic and animalised prose fantasies of the *Songs of Maldoror* (1868–9), written by the Montevidean-born writer Isidore Ducasse, Comte de Lautréamont, who had been rediscovered by the Surrealists.

In 1929, Breton's second manifesto excluded several former members of the group. Surrealism's revolutionary ethos was now repositioned, not in the individual psyche, but within Communist politics: the group's review, *La Révolution Surréaliste*, became *Le Surréalisme au Service de la Révolution*. In 1931, the Surrealists protested against France's Exposition Coloniale, a vast array of exotic pavilions in the landscaped Bois de Vincennes, dominated by a scaled-down stucco reconstruction of the magnificent Cambodian temple of Angkhor-Wat. This spectacle gave no hint of the injustices of a French colonialist system sustained by repression and violence. The Surrealists' emphasis on the 'marvellous' and their eager embrace of African and Oceanic art sit rather uneasily with their protest in this context; moreover Marxist commitment from a group of artists and writers who disdained 'work' was problematic to sustain. The next visual development in Surrealism is best likened to a 'hand-painted dream photograph' – minutely realised depictions in oil mingling the real with the fantastic – promoted by the Belgian René Magritte and the Spaniard Salvador Dalí. A key feature was the improbable visual juxtaposition or metamorphosis on the lines of Lautréamont's celebrated and enigmatic phrase from a canto in *Maldoror*: 'as beautiful as the juxtaposition of a sewing machine and an umbrella on a dissecting table'. Here, the unconscious 'appears' in quasi-Freudian dream tropes of displacement and condensation, but painting technique, far from being 'automatic', is painstakingly academic. In the later 1930s, Dalí would taunt Breton's promotion of the 'absence of all control … or moral preoccupation', with paintings referring to Hitler which acknowledged the libidinal energies harnessed by national Socialism.

Surrealism of the late 1920s, embracing painting, the *explosion-fixe* (fixed explosion) of Man Ray's solarised photography, or films (Dalí and Luis Buñuel's *Le Chien Andalou*, 1929, for example), was provocative and avant-garde at a time when Art Déco was transforming late Cubism into an ultimately decorative style. The Exposition des Arts Décoratifs of 1925 had embraced this jazzy, syncopated mode in all its variations. It was here that the architect Le Corbusier constructed his *Pavillon de l'Esprit Nouveau*, an uncompromisingly modernist pavilion of white, geometrical forms based on Cubist principles. The title came from his review, *L'Esprit nouveau* (the 'New Spirit') and Purism, the movement in painting (devolved from Cubism), which involved Le Corbusier and Amadée Ozenfant. The pavilion included works by the Purists, together with Juan Gris and Fernand Léger. Léger's film *Le Ballet mécanique*, of 1924, had included not only production-line imagery – Purism promoted the merits of standardisation and mass production – but the lips of the notorious model Kiki de Montparnasse and silent movie star Charlie Chaplin. Film as well as popular culture was penetrating modernist art.

In a reaction to modernism partly conditioned by the First World War, the so-called *rappel à l'ordre* (the *Call to Order*, title of a book by Jean Cocteau) heralded a return to realism. In Picasso's case, this realism recalled the nineteenth-century artist Ingres. Picasso's new mode appeared as a major public statement in his stage curtain for the ballet *Parade*, first

Figure 9. Nadia Khodassievitch-Léger, *Self-Portrait*, 1936. Private collection.

staged to some scandal in 1917. As the 1920s progressed, many artists turned away from modernist abstractions, and the nude, portrait and still-life became staple productions. A signature style was crucial, however, from a market point of view: witness the elongation of Modigliani's female bodies with their blank, almond-shaped eyes, the fine 'Japanese' lines and pearly, flat skin of Tsuguhara Foujita's nudes, or the expressionist handling and exaggerated pathos of Chaim Soutine's low-life subjects such as hotel bell-boys. The Louvre museum was still the major point of

reference (together with the live model) for students in the various painting academies and the Ecole des Beaux-Arts. Thus, Louvre masterpieces
such as Chardin's *La Raie* (The Skate) and Rembrandt's *Flayed Ox* may be
seen directly to inspire Soutine's still-lives and Jean Fautrier's disturbing
black boars. These paintings with their deep sense of tradition coexisted,
paradoxically, with the proliferation of modern'isms' which were sum-
marised in 1925 by Arp and the pioneering Soviet artist and designer El
Lissitzky with a three-language publication, *Der Kunstismen, Les Ismes de
l'Art, The Isms of Art*, published in Zurich.

At the same time as the Purist ethos affected avant-garde art and
architecture in Paris, a completely non-referential form of abstraction
was evolving around the Dutchman Piet Mondrian, whose theosophical
beginnings, repressed during a period of cubist influence, re-emerged as
a hermetic key to his pure white canvases striped with black vertical or
horizontal lines and the occasional square or oblong of primary colour –
red, blue or yellow (Neo-plasticism). This 'non-objective' art (which had a
utopian Socialist agenda in his native Holland) rapidly inspired acolytes,
ranging from the Frenchmen Jean Hélion and Jean Gorin to the Paris-
based Englishwoman Marlow Moss. This 'school of Mondrian' in all but
name became part of the wider grouping, Cercle et Carré (Circle and
Square), formed by the Belgian critic Michel Seuphor. Its first exhibition
and review was published in 1930. By 1931, along with the rival Art concret
group, this became absorbed by the Abstraction-Création exhibiting Salon and review. Its precepts were entirely antithetical to the contempora-
neous Surrealist movement, with which, however, it may be interestingly
contrasted, for it was comparable both in terms of the number of its converts and its international scope. The Surrealists held international exhibitions in Santa Cruz, Tenerife in 1935, London 1936 and Paris in 1938.
The antagonistic trends, abstraction and surrealism, were consecutively
contrasted by the curator of New York's Museum of Modern Art, Alfred
Barr, in two historic exhibitions of 1936. With their now celebrated
catalogues, *Cubism and Abstract Art* and *Fantastic Art, Dada and Surrealism*,
these shows laid the foundation for modernism to pass to New York after
1945.

The Paris World Fair of 1937, known as the 'Exposition International
des Arts et Techniques de la Vie moderne' celebrated art and technology in modern life; important artistic commissions were given to French
nationals such as Raoul Dufy. His vast mural for the Pavilion of Light,
The Electricity Fairy (still visible in the Musée d'Art Moderne de la Ville

Figure 10. Henri Matisse, *Woman in Blue*, 1937. Philadelphia Museum of Art, Gift of Mrs John Wintersteen.

de Paris), traces electricity in a frieze-like procession of figures from Lucretius and the ancient Greek philosophers to modern radio broadcasts of symphonic music. Artist Robert Delaunay masterminded abstract geometric murals for the Aeronautic pavilion, while Marcel Gromaire created more realist decorations for the Sèvres porcelain pavilion. 'Maitres de l'Art indépendant' at the Petit Palais showed an impressive display of generally French artists. The largely émigré international Ecole de Paris was excluded from this nationalistic celebration. In riposte, the exhibition 'Origines et développement de l'art international indépendent' was organised for the Jeu de Paume museum by Christian Zervos, the Greek director of the luxury review *Cahiers d'Art*. It deliberately focused on artists such as the Russian expressionist Kandinsky, who had spent his formative years in Munich – at a time when reports of Hitler's 1937 campaign against 'degenerate' art, targeting Dadaists and German Expressionists in particular, was reported in the French press.

The World Fair was also notable for the modernist pavilion by José Maria Sert, which housed Picasso's superb, post-Cubist protest painting *Guernica* – a jagged, monochromatic response to the first ever bombing of a civilian population by German aircraft during the Spanish Civil War. Even more ominous was the confrontational display of totalitarian art and architecture in the pavilions designed by the German Albert Speer and the Soviet architect Boris Iofan. In the latter, modernist forms of photomontage propaganda were countered by chilling examples of Stalinist Socialist realist painting. By this time Joseph Stalin's anti-modernist, international Communist ('Comintern') propaganda was impacting internationally; from the USSR, avant-gardism was pronounced both obsolete and decadent, with great impact on Communist intellectuals world-wide, including France. The former Surrealist poet, Louis Aragon, changed his allegiance and in 1935 published a series of lectures promoting Soviet Socialist realism as a model for French painters. The Communist-backed Maison de la Culture absorbed the French branch of the Association of Revolutionary Writers and Artists; its photographic wing welcomed documentary photographers such as Willy Ronis. Documentary photography, published in reviews such as *Regards* and *Vu* which were based, in part, on Soviet and German models, focused on workers' lives, protests and strikes, and provided an important complement to the push for a Socialist realism.

The later 1930s were a tense period in the arts. The Forces Nouvelles group co-opted a 'French tradition' dating back to artists such as Jean Fouquet, Georges de la Tour and the Les Nains brothers, in paintings which responded to the Spanish Civil War, but whose realism and academic handling, ratifying conservative and reactionary tendencies, sat uneasily with notionally left-wing agendas. A discourse of anti-Semitism in the arts, which had begun as early as the late 1920s, intensified. The destruction of Jacques Lipchitz's 1937 exhibition commission, an allegorical, anti-Nazi work, *Prometheus and the Vulture*, thanks to right-wing pressure, heralded tragic developments. Over 125 artists of the Ecole de Paris were among the thousands of Jews from France who died during the war – sixty-four identified artists met their ends in the gas chambers.

In Occupied Paris, exhibitions such as 'Le juif et la France' (The Jew and France, 1941), were well attended, while the pillage of Jewish art collections, now comprehensively documented, was co-ordinated and centralised.

From the Second World War to the 1970s

The immediate postwar period saw the increasing influence of the so-called 'Young Painters of the French Tradition' who had relaunched a patriotic and Catholic French art during the Occupation. Artists such as Charles Lapicque and Jean Bazaine employed a generally red and blue palette, an armature indebted to the cubist grid and a warmth of colour and facture that showed a renewed influence of the veteran painters Pierre Bonnard and Jacques Villon. Rapidly artists and intellectuals returned from America, including André Breton who reasserted the vitality of Surrealism with an internationally based exhibition at the Galerie Maeght in 1947. Seasonal exhibiting salons continued to govern the art calendar, while new groupings emerged: the Salon des Realités Nouvelles became the focus of a relaunched, internationalist Geometric abstraction. Similar in its tastes and antagonisms to its 1930s roots (the 'Abstraction-Création' movement) it now included many new converts. The Hungarian Victor Vasarely was an influential abstract geometric painter; his gallerist, Denise René, became a major force promoting this tendency internationally.

Fernand Léger returned from America in 1945 and in Picasso's wake joined the Communist party at the height of its post-Resistance prestige and the Communists' participation in the first postwar tripartite government. Picasso's Occupation portraits of skull-like women with distorted features had been physically attacked at the autumn Salon of 1944 (the 'Salon de la Libération'); his modernism now competed with realist depictions of postwar austerity by Francis Gruber or the fashionable Bernard Buffet. In 1947, Stalin's new 'Cominform' (Communist information) organisation was launched as Cold War antagonisms intensified: Europe was split into East and West. In France the Communists left the government. Cultural policy from Moscow was promoted via Communist parties in Western Europe, particularly Italy and France. How should modernist artists such as Picasso and Léger be accommodated with the new Communist push for a Socialist realism? The answer was a two-tier policy with a strongly nationalist flavour: the Maison de la

Pensée Française mounted exhibitions of Picasso, Léger, Matisse or Jean Lurçat's tapestries near the presidential Elysée palace, while realist works such as Boris Taslitzky's *Small Camp at Buchenwald* (an eye-witness testimony transformed into a realist history painting), or André Fougeron's *Mining Country* sequence (showing miners killed or deformed in accidents), could be put to propaganda use. Fougeron used sources from the Louvre, in particular Jacques-Louis David to reinforce a patriotic 'nouveau réalisme' (new realism – Socialist realism by another name), but could descend to an extraordinary level of bathos, especially when depicting popular fêtes, political demonstrations and the 'cult of personality' of party leaders.

A completely new art, known as the Informel (literally 'formless' art) emerged in 1945 with exhibitions by Jean Fautrier, Jean Dubuffet and the German artist Wols (a pseudonym). In Fautrier's *Hostage* series, his waxy encaustic surfaces from the late 1930s gave way to the use of special pastes, *hautes pâtes*, raised and worked with a palette-knife on face- or body-sized canvases, then painted, one by one, with the lines of a profile or scarred torso. The discovery of the caves of Lascaux in September 1940, with their prehistoric animal paintings on rough, raised and rugged surfaces ratified Fautrier's debt in terms of colour and texture to this primeval art. Dubuffet took up the *haute pâte* but added gravel, anthracite and other matter to the surface on which representations were incised like graffiti; his was a dark anarchist humour with Nietzschean overtones (a naked male figure was titled *Volonté de Puissance* – 'will to power' – after the philosopher). Wols moved from watercolour to oils in 1947; his picture surface lost all residual figuration and became a mess of trickles and scratches in which forms were dissolved. This new art, the Informel may be interpreted in the light of Fautrier's friendship with Georges Bataille in the 1940s: the dissident Surrealist writer had investigated the collapse of form via a philosophical discourse on the 'low' or the 'base'. Alternatively, in a period of ruin and reconstruction, the notion of the *informel* artist's gesture as a choice or act of will, in an absurd universe, seemed close to Jean-Paul Sartre's existential philosophy. In the case of artists such as Georges Mathieu or Hans Hartung, where gesture became more important than surface (often painted with one colour as a flat monochrome), the terminology shifted: these works were categorised as Abstraction lyrique (lyrical abstraction). A patchier, splashier application of paint, in the works of Henri Michaux, for example, was known as Tachisme. The almost scholastic debates and the necessity for artist to have a distinct signature style cannot be detailed here – but the division

Figure 11. Jean Fautrier, *The Pretty Girl*, 1944. Private collection, Geneva.

existed largely between so-called Abstraction chaud ('hot' i.e. gestural abstraction) and Abstraction froid ('cold' i.e. geometric – precisely drawn and coloured – abstraction). Within a situation of universally recognised Cold War tensions, these tendencies became politicised: only Communist Socialist realism claimed an art form legible by the proletariat; abstract art was denounced as bourgeois – yet politically non-affiliated realist or abstract artists coexisted with their antagonistic counterparts. In general, however, the choice of an artistic style was always seen as an ideological statement.

Figure 12. Alberto Giacometti, *City Square*, 1950, installation photograph. Mrs Edward Hutton Collection, Witt Library, Courtauld Institute of Art, London.

Artists of the CoBra (Copenhagen, Brussels and Amsterdam) group, while based in Paris, became impatient with the critical debates of the time – and with Parisian self-satisfaction. Their expressionist art which was produced from 1948 to 1951 was informed by sources explored in the periodical, *Cobra*: child art, graffiti, European folk art. Concurrently, an 'art without origins' by institutionalised schizophrenics but also naive artists, was collected, studied, exhibited and promoted in Paris by the painter Jean Dubuffet, who coined the successful label Art Brut for this broad category of works.

By the end of the 1950s, the existential, 'martyred' aspect of the rough-surfaced, spindly bronzes of the human form by Alberto Giacometti or Germaine Richier no longer corresponded to a changed climate of materialist consumer confidence, and – after Stalin's death in 1953 and its repercussions – the beginnings of de-Stalinisation. In the context of the forward-looking 1958 Brussels World Fair, artists such as Yves Klein wished to harness the positive aspirations of a new nuclear age. Klein was influenced not only by Kasimir Malevich – the pre-First World War Russian painter of one-colour squares, white or black, whose 'Suprematist' monochromes were displayed in Amsterdam in 1958 – but the veteran Matisse's blue cut-out paper nudes of the 1950s. Other inspirations

Figure 13. Nicolas de Staël, *Standing Nude*, 1953. Nathan Gallery, Zurich.

included his trip to Japan and his own physical and mental experiences as a black-belt judoka. Klein's own unframed monochromes were coated with 'International Klein Blue', a paint medium he patented whose fixative evaporated leaving a velvety reflective surface. Klein applied 'IKB' to his naked models, creating what he called *femmes-pinceaux* (female paintbrushes) who pressed their bodies on to canvas: the imprints he called *Anthropometries*. This event took place, in a gallery space in 1960, to the one-note orchestrated accompaniment of Klein's *Monochrome Symphony*.

During the 1960s geometric abstract art acquired a new vibrancy, introducing optical effects and movement, heralding Op and Kinetic art, sometimes with a neo-dada irony (Jean Tinguely's animated *Métamalevich* series). The gallerist Denise René promoted her artists such as Vasarely, the Russian, Nicolas Schöffer and the Israeli artist, Agam, internationally, notably in the 'Responsive Eye' exhibition which toured America in 1965, and in the 'Art et Mouvement' exhibition held in Montreal, the same year as the international Expo '67.

Nouveau Réalisme, the name of the group, including Yves Klein, whose manifesto was drafted by critic Pierre Restany on 27 October 1960, aimed at a post-dadaistic 'sociological grasp of the real'. Arman's 1960 exhibition 'Le Plein' (literally 'full up') filled Iris Clert's gallery with trash – a riposte to Klein's 1958 show 'Le vide' (the void): a room of empty, 'sensitised' space. Arman filled and sealed glass boxes with individuals' discarded rubbish: he called these *portraits robots* ('identikit' portraits). Analogous to reliquaries of bones and personal effects, the *portrais robots* personalised themes of consumerism and waste. The sculptor César's cars, crushed at the car dump into rectangular blocks (from 1961), were also reliquary-like, combining the immediacy of the present with a sense of archaic presence. The Affichistes (torn poster artists), Raymond Hains and Jacques de la Villeglé, exhibited parts of street hoardings or accumulated layers of posters in the art gallery, in particular those ripped or defaced with graffiti by anonymous passers-by: the cohabitation of adverts for festivals and cinemas with political posters and slogans, here, demonstrated the dilemmas of a newly commercialised France at the time of Algerian war atrocities. The French-American artist Niki de Saint-Phalle shot with a rifle at cans and bladders of paint concealed behind the picture surface or within moulded chicken-wire and plaster 'body-effigies' (*Tirs*). The paint seemed to 'bleed' over her shot-at altarpieces – indictments of the inactivity and hypocrisy of the Catholic Church on issues ranging from Algeria to birth control – or works such as the

Siamese-twin effigy, *Kennedy-Khrushchev* (1963), a carnivalesque yet bitter comment on Cold War power politics. These works, which may be seen to challenge the premises of patriarchal society as a whole, correspond to the artist's explicitly feminist viewpoint, rare for France at the time.

The American painter Robert Rauschenberg's prize at the Venice Biennale exhibition of 1964 is seen as the symbolic moment when art world dominance passed from Paris to New York. It produced an assertive riposte in the 'Mythologies quotidiennes' exhibition in Paris that year (the title a homage to Roland Barthes's 1957 analysis of contemporary society, *Mythologies*). The advent of Pop art in Paris, coming from London as well as New York in the early 1960s, encouraged a figurative painting that engaged with popular culture, especially the *bande dessiné* or comic strip (see works by Bernard Rancillac) and the *film noir* (see works by Jacques Monory with their frozen, 'B'-movie narratives). Long before American hyperrealism arrived in France in the early 1970s, these French artists copied images or outlines projected with slides or an epidiascope on to canvas, often achieving photographically 'realist' effects. Some members of this movement, known as Figuration narrative or Figuration critique, were active Communists, such as Henri Cueco, who organised a Vietnam protest exhibition in 1968–9. The export of the contents of the Salon de mai spring exhibition, together with many of its artists, to Cuba in 1967, saw art from France deployed as anti-American propaganda. Against the increasing stridency of this generally figurative political work, Daniel Buren's abstract stripe paintings (some paraded on the street) advocated a modernist abstraction itself as a strategy of camouflage, concealing, not 'reflecting', the political cacophony.

May '68 saw the apotheosis of 'art on the street' as the Ecole des Beaux-Arts was occupied and turned over to militant poster production. Old Surrealist slogans were juxtaposed with new exhortations daubed on to the walls of the Universities of Nanterre and the Sorbonne, notably 'Imagination au pouvoir' (All power to the imagination). The politico-artistic group called the Situationnists, who had provoked the first student unrest in Strasbourg in 1966, were active in this context. Their initial ideas in the fine arts were linked to the Lettrist movement, founded by the Romanian Isidore Isou in the 1940s, who called for a 'poetry of the letter'. Lettrist paintings depicted signs and rebuses on canvas. Isou also drew and painted directly on to rolls of film, producing more challenging experimental work. The writer Guy Debord's 'Lettrist International' took over Isou's ideas and expelled him from the new grouping; subsequently the *Internationale Situationniste* journal (1958–69) expounded Debord's key principles: *détournement* (literally a 'turning away or awry'), the critical appropriation and perversion of meaning, and the *dérive*, or 'swerving away' from an accepted path, either metaphorically, or as literally 'drifting' through the city. *Psychogéographie* (psychogeography) was a new concept here in which the 'mapping' of Paris's new urban landscape was subject to the desires of the individual psyche. Debord's prophetic publication of 1967, *La Société du Spectacle*, anticipated the world-wide transmission of televised violence. Jean-Jacques Lebel brought the American-style 'happening' to Paris in 1964: artists and public alike mingled in events where spontaneous behaviour (often sexually liberated) challenged not only the traditional artist and art-object but the controlling perimeters of a gallery space. Lebel was a key figure on the barricades in May '68. In the deflated aftermath of May and increasing anxiety about the Vietnam War, much figurative art appeared increasingly melancholy: Jean-François Lyotard, whose influential book *The Postmodern Condition* was first published in French in 1979, interestingly anticipated the irrevocable change in late twentieth-century consciousness with his critical writing on Jacques Monory's blue paintings at this time.

In sharp contrast, the Supports-Surfaces movement was linked via the critic Marcelin Pleynet to the literary periodical *Tel Quel* which had structuralist affiliations. While working through the heritage of Matissean flatness and colour (Claude Viallat, Louis Cane) and Duchampian principles (Daniel Dezeuze), Supports-Surfaces purported to investigate the physical and semantic components of a painting according to structuralist principles. Simultaneously the abstract paintings produced by this group acknowledged the impact of the Americans, Mark Rothko, Barnett Newman and American Minimalism – all shown in Paris during the 1960s. Yet the Supports-Surfaces artists simultaneously attempted to provide a Maoist theoretical base for their art. For example, 'sculptures' consisting of long, narrow reed mats unrolled and spread across the gallery floor evoked the Eastern traditions of the scroll and a certain philosophical asceticism; the art work, moreover, became the 'materialist' complement to aggressively political writing of group members such as Marc Devade. Aware of New York art critic Clement Greenberg's formalist, modernist position and his immense power over artists and the American art world, the *Tel Quel* writer Pleynet moved from a similar formalism in his art criticism towards a more psychoanalytic mode during this period. The intractable formal and political differences between the abstract Supports-Surfaces artists and the Figuration Narrative painters continued the epic of France's twentieth-century stylistic battles: moreover national identity and revolutionary credentials were at stake. The Figuration Narrative artists heralded David and the figurative painting of the French Revolution as they contested American hyperrealism in Paris. The abstract Supports-Surfaces group acknowledged Malevich's monochromes – contextualised by the October Revolution of 1917 – as the origin of avant-gardism; their *tabula rasa* aesthetic of the 'blank slate' promised new beginnings. Parallels were all too evident at the time between these artistic confrontations and neo-Marxist debates in contemporary philosophy and politics.

From the Centre Georges Pompidou to the millennium

Several exhibitions happened under the auspices of the Centre Georges Pompidou before the official opening, in 1977, of the extraordinary building designed by the young architects Richard Rogers and Renzo Piano. Rehousing the formerly conservative Musée National d'Art Moderne, the opening show was a retrospective of the works of Marcel Duchamp. Following important Duchamp shows in America and Britain in the 1960s this was a very *late* reclamation of France's arguably most important twentieth-century artist. While demonstrating the unease of the artistic community with the doyen of 'anti-art', the exhibition reinforced the brief of a cultural centre whose populist ethos aimed to demonstrate the possibility of an 'anti-museum'. This was not a mausoleum of the past but an experience for the present, with an emphasis on interdisciplinarity: a meeting of fine art, film, literature – a free city library – and debate, all linked by the social spaces of the building and its transparent-glass inner and outer walls. The major exhibitions of the 1970s, 'Paris–New York', 'Paris–Berlin' and 'Paris–Moscou' reasserted Paris's magnetism and impact on the European and transatlantic art scene. 'Paris–Paris' coincided with the access to power of the Socialist government of François Mitterand in May 1981. Even its title was an untranslatable pun – on Paris's 'bets' (*paris*) during the years 1937–57. In a later article curator Germain Viatte spoke of a 'soi-disant Paris perdu' (a so-called lost Paris) implicitly positing the 'paradise lost' of Parisian arts hegemony, which various upbeat exhibitions, culminating with his 'Made in France 1947–1997', could not dispel. This show, a provocative mélange of artists and generations, daringly juxtaposed late Picasso with

Figure 14. Gérard Fromanger, *The Artist's Life*, from the series 'Desire is Everywhere', 1975.

the comic, painted caricatures of Robert Combas, a painter who emerged in the 1980s along with the Figuration libre (Free figuration) generation; its streetwise, graffiti-based take on contemporary France was typically unable to attract international attention.

Ironically, the Socialist government did not completely regenerate French art, despite the formidable investment, restructuring and decentralisation programmes. The 'Fonds régionaux d'art contemporain' (FRAC) and the 'Délégation aux arts plastiques' (DAP) initiated by Mitterrand's Minister of Culture Jack Lang, were supremely important; massive purchases were made: yet often works of art were displayed infrequently or stockpiled. Enduring successes, however, include the FRAC Centre, in Orléans, a circulating archive of architects' drawings and models, and the birth of several international centres for contemporary dance.

Particularly during – and after – the initial period of Communist cohabitation with the Mitterand government in the early 1980s, the whole anti-establishment thrust of an ageing left-wing Communist and neo-Marxist avant-garde found itself without an adversary: ironically the symbolic heritage of this moment is the collection of 'revolutionary' works by Narrative Figuration artists such as Gérard Fromanger within the Assemblée Nationale – the parliament building – itself. While, in the 1980s, an artist such as Gérard Garouste replied with painterly and mythical works to strong expressionist and figurative developments in painting in Italy (for example, Sandro Chia), Germany (the 'Neue Wilden' movement) and America (Julian Schnabel, David Salle), he was happy to decorate François Mitterrand's presidential private apartments and bedroom ceilings. He allied himself, here, to a tradition which stretched back to Pompidou's 'Op art' reception rooms at the Elysée Palace, Georges Mathieu's quasi-Royalist work for the Sèvres porcelain and Aubusson tapestry manufactures under Giscard d'Estain in the 1970s, and, ultimately, a history of court commissions. Many left-wing artists of the 1960s accepted commissions for the Church or for former church or abbey buildings – continuing the 'art sacré' (sacred art) movement of the 1950s – thanks to the link made by government between contemporary art and cultural heritage organisations concerned with the *patrimoine* (France's 'patrimony'). Notably involved were artists from the Supports-Surfaces movement, even the Protestant Daniel Dezeuze or the erstwhile Maoist, Pierre Buraglio, who in 1992 created a spiritually ascetic décor and ecclesiastical furnishings for a chapel within the church of Saint-Germain-des-Prés in Paris – in explicit homage to Matisse's 1951 Chapelle du Rosaire in Vence.

Quite distinct from this grouping, Christian Boltanksi has emerged as the most significant artist from France to engage with issues of memory and the Holocaust. His altar-like sculptures made of ordinary objects, such as tin boxes, often incorporate transferred, photographic images of 'lost children', images whose meaning is constituted through anonymity and the presence of 'absent' identities. Boltanski has associated his work with the writer Georges Perec, whose fictions with their language games and missing letters likewise may be seen to treat the event of the Holocaust obliquely – as an imperceptible absence.

A profound relationship to Catholicism and the sacred was also a distinguishing feature of France's most striking performance artists of the 1970s (both deceased), the homosexual Michel Journiac, who trained initially as a priest, and the Italo-French artist Gina Pane, whose work involving ritual practices and self-mutilation deliberately evoked saintly martyrdom. Only the Paris-based artist Orlan was able to sustain her performance work through the 1990s, with the series of shocking operations on her body carried out under a local anaesthetic which allowed her to read and 'perform' under the knife, while the most radical cosmetic surgery gave her facial implants. Her discourse on beauty, blasphemy and

Figure 15.   Daniel Buren, Photosouvenir: *Les Deux Plateaux*, Sculpture *in situ*, 1985–6. Cour d'honneur, Palais Royal, Paris (detail).

monstrosity claimed feminist credentials, yet she was omitted from the major Centre Pompidou exhibition 'fémininmasculin, le sexe de l'art' (femininemasculine, the sex of art) in 1996. France's own feminist history of the 1970s and 1980s, still denied by the French establishment, was symbolically omitted in this show: France's tardy attempt to engage with Anglo-American gender discourses.

Jean Baudrillard, whose theories of the 'simulacra' of reality within the postmodern world have been internationally influential in the arts, together with Paul Virilio, whose daring architectural propositions of the 1960s have been eclipsed by his writings on speed and warfare – were both involved in polemics in the late 1990s in which they – and respected museum curators such as Jean Clair – virulently attacked contemporary art in France. Their generation, formed in the 1970s, continues to hold power in an art world whose controlling structures are still elitist and highly centralised; a top-heavy administrative apparatus discourages individual initiatives: France has few 'artist-run spaces'. Despite magnificent individual achievements assisted by the Association Française d'Action Artistique which organises shows abroad, this curatorial bureaucracy has not thus far provided a memorable narrative of post-1945 developments in the visual arts for consumption outside the Hexagon.

Conclusion: French art today

New vocabularies coming from anthropology, literature, video and television offer a means for artists in France – and elsewhere – to escape
the co-ordinates of Picasso, Matisse, gesturalism or the proliferation of
the post-Duchampian ready-made. Sophie Calle's *Venetian Suite* (1983), for
which she became a chambermaid at a hotel in Venice, documenting the
lives of the hotel inhabitants, displayed as an intriguing 'photo piece'
what would once have found form in the novel; Calle, indeed, collaborated in various ways with the American novelist Paul Auster in 1996.
Sylvie Blocher's *Living Pictures/Tell Me* (1997) uses video images and narrative as a confessional device; Pierrick Sorin's comi-tragic 'sit-coms' create three-dimensional installations involving televisual spaces. Video in
combination with sculptural installations is ubiquitous, witness Fab-
rice Hybert's prize-winning installation of TV sets in the French Pavilion at the 1999 Venice Biennale, punningly called *Eau d'or, Eau dort, Odor*
(golden water, water sleeps, odour). The success of France's decentralisation policies are evident in superb and scholarly museum exhibitions
held from Lille to Antibes and in Paris's Ecole des Beaux-Arts itself, where
teaching is now enlightened and internationalist. One may argue, however, that contemporary art in France – despite or perhaps because of its
substantial state support – seems to have neither the political urgency
of art from Russia or a now-reunited Germany, the daring of the best
American art (from Jeff Koon's topiary puppy sculptures to Bill Viola's
spiritual video installations) nor the satirical and self-deprecating wit
of 'Young British Art'. Moreover, despite France's promotion of *la francophonie*, the French language still creates barriers for artists in a world
increasingly united by the English language and the Internet. Would
a young artist from China in the year 2000 choose Paris, rather than
London, Los Angeles or Sydney to live and work – or choose to stay in
a developing Beijing? The larger questions raised here concern France's
role within a global cultural, economic and political community. The visual language of twentieth-century modernism was forged in Paris; its
imprint on the cities of the twenty-first century – Shanghai, for example –
is uncontested. The hierarchy of the arts, uncontested at the Exposition
Universelle in the Paris of 1900, gave a pre-eminent place to painting and
sculpture, categories which were challenged by the broadening field of
visual culture throughout the twentieth century. As this heritage is re-
assessed within an increasingly globalised and digitalised culture, the

place of 'high art' itself as a form of cultural production becomes relativised. France's artistic achievements and current dilemmas are symptomatic of those of any nation state concerned with its national and cultural identity at the millennium.

FURTHER READING

Books

Ardenne, Paul, *Art. L'Age contemporain. Une histoire des arts plastiques à la fin du XXe siècle*, Paris: Editions du Regard, 1997.

Berk Jimenez, Jill (ed.), *Dictionary of Artists' Models*, London: Fitzroy Dearborn, 2001.

Bertrand-Dorléac, Laurence, *L'Art de la défaite, 1940–1944*, Paris: Seuil, 1993.

Blake, Jody, 1999, *Le Tumulte noir: Modernist Art and Popular Entertainment in Jazz-Age Paris, 1900–1930*, Philadelphia: University of Pennsylvania Press, 1999.

Bois, Yve-Alain, and Rosalind Krauss, *Formless: A User's Guide*, New York, 1997 (French version: *L'Informe, mode d'emploi*, Paris: Musée National de l'Art Moderne, Centre Georges Pompidou, 1996).

Bouqueret, Christian, *Des années folles aux années noires. La Nouvelle photographie en France 1920–1940*, Paris: Marval, 1997.

Clair, Jean, *Art en France, une nouvelle génération*, Paris: Chêne, 1972.

Cone, Michèle C., *Artists under Vichy: a Case of Prejudice and Persecution*, Princeton: Princeton University Press, 1992.

French Modernisms: Perspectives on Art before, during and after Vichy, Cambridge: Cambridge University Press, 2001.

Francblin, Catharine, *Les Nouveaux Réalistes*, Paris: Editions du Regard, 1997.

Gee, Malcolm, *Dealers, Critics and Collectors of Modern Painting: Aspects of the Parisian Art Market between 1910 and 1930*, London and New York: Garland Publishers, 1981.

Gervereau, Laurent, with David Mellor (eds.), *The Sixties. Britain and France, 1962–1973. The Utopian Years*, London: P. Wilson, 1997 (French version: *Les Sixties, années utopies*, Musée d'Histoire contemporaine, Paris, 1996).

Golan, Romy, *Modernity and Nostalgia: Art and Politics in France between the Wars*, New Haven and London: Yale University Press, 1995.

Green, Christopher, *Art in France, 1900–1940*, New Haven and London: Yale University Press, 2000.

Cubism and its Enemies: Modern Movements and Reactions in French Art, 1916–1928, New Haven and London: Yale University Press, 1987.

Guilbaut, Serge, *How New York Stole the Idea of Modern Art*, Chicago and London: University of Chicago Press, 1983.

Michaud, Yves, *La Crise de l'art contemporain, utopie, démocratie et comédie*, Paris: Presses Universitaires de France, 1997.

Millet, Catherine, *L'Art contemporain en France*, Paris: Flammarion, 1987.

Minière, Claude, *L'Art en France, 1960–1994*, Paris: Nouvelles Editions Françaises, 1994.

Moulin, Raymonde, *The French Art Market: a Sociological Perspective*, London and New Brunswick: Rutgers University Press, 1987.

Ory, Pascal, *La Belle Illusion, culture et politique sous le signe du Front Populaire, 1935–1938*, Paris: Plon, 1994.

Perry, Gill, *Women Artists and the Parisian Avant-Garde: Modernism and 'Feminine' Art, 1900 to the Late 1920s*.

Perry, Gill, and Sarah Wilson, 'Training and Professionalism: France. Twentieth Century', in Delia Gaze (ed.), *Dictionary of Women Artists*, 2 vols., Manchester and London: Manchester University Press, 1997, pp. 92–8 (and relevant entries).

Pleynet, Marcelin, *Les Etats-Unis de la Peinture*, Paris: Seuil, 1986.

Pradel, Jean-Louis, *La figuration narrative*, La Seyne-sur-mer and Paris: Hazan, 2000.

Stallabrass, Julian, *Paris Pictured, 1900–1968*, London: Royal Academy of Arts, 2002.

Exhibition catalogues

1972 *Douze ans d'art contemporain, 1960–1972*, Paris: Grand Palais.

1977–1981 *Paris–New York, 1905–1965*; *Paris–Berlin, 1900–1933*; *Paris–Moscou, 1900–1930*; *Les Réalismes, 1919–1939, Paris–Paris, 1937–1957*, Paris: Musée Nationale de l'Art Moderne, Centre Georges Pompidou.

1982 *Aftermath, France, 1945–1954, New Images of Man*, ed. Sarah Wilson, London: Barbican Art Gallery.

1986 *L'Amour fou: Photography and Surrealism*, ed. Rosalind Krauss, London: Hayward Gallery.

1993 *Paris Post War: Art and Existentialism, 1945–1955*, ed. Frances Morris, London: Tate Gallery.

1998 *Les Années Supports-Surfaces dans les collections du Centre Georges Pompidou*, Paris: Galerie National du Jeu de Paume.

2000 *L'Ecole de Paris, 1904–1929, la part de l'autre*, Paris: Musée d'Art Moderne de la Ville de Paris.

2001 *Denise René, une galerie dans l'aventure de l'art abstrait, 1945–1978*, Paris: Musée National de l'Art Moderne, Centre Georges Pompidou.

2002 *Paris, Capital of the Arts, 1900–1968*, ed. Sarah Wilson, London: Royal Academy of Arts.

2003 *Art Deco, 1910–1939*, ed. Charlotte Benton, Tim Benton, and Ghislaine Wood, London: Victoria and Albert Museum.

15

Cinema

Introduction

A century of French film-making has provided us with a unique perspective on a range of aspects of French culture: from the earliest recordings of the Belle Epoque period, to the twenty-first century appetite for fairytales like *Le Fabuleux destin d'Amélie Poulin* (*Amelie*, Jeunet, 2001), the cinema has revealed, like no other medium, the myriad moments of a national life lived in modern times. People, places, events, ideas: as all have passed in front of the lens, so they have left behind them not only a wealth of creative products that speak to us of the country, its citizens and their artistic energies, but equally a record of patterns of cultural practice and production that reflect the wider apparatus and structures of national life. This would be true in any culture, but as the birthplace of cinema, the midwife of much global debate and theory about film practice, and the school yard of many of the world's most significant players, France provides a rare insight into how cinema functions as the locus of art, industry and intellectual interest, and thus as a significant indicator of questions of national identity.

The early years

When a series of short films by the Lumière brothers was first shown in *Le Grand Café de Paris* in December 1895, cinema constituted little more than an elitist curiosity, 'an invention without a future' as Lumière *père* quickly decreed. And yet the medium experienced such massive growth in popularity that by the time of the Exposition Universelle of 1900 it had become a permanent feature of the fast-developing leisure culture in all its various incarnations: projections in established bourgeois theatres like L'Olympia and L'Eldorado were frequent, but equally, screenings were a feature of much popular entertainment, from sideshow attractions at itinerant *fêtes foraines*, to music-hall repertoire. By the time of the Exposition Universelle, the international showcase of French modernity, cinema's appeal as a spectacle for a mass public could no longer be doubted: among many other attractions, the Lumière brothers' giant screen in the Pavillon des Machines attracted more than one million visitors in only six months.

This trajectory constitutes what cinema scholars would call a *mise-en-abyme*[1] of debates about high and low culture that have been articulated in relation to many arts and media – particularly those related to performance and the visual arts – and which have dominated commentary about the cinema since its inception. Should French culture rejoice in this democratising force, welcoming an art form that could be distributed in ways that cut across social and class divides? Or should it despise this inferior offspring of painting, photography and drama, relegating it to the margins of 'popular culture', topographically as well as artistically? Could cinema ever be an 'acceptable' diversion for those schooled in classical artistic and philosophical traditions? Or was it no more than a cheap and cheerful distraction for those of poor literacy and limited financial means? These questions were to be asked over and over again, and, some would say, have not yet been fully resolved. But these are important questions, the consequences of which translate into the realities of funding, visibility, and national prestige. Given the very close relationship between State and culture in republican France, the 'ownership' of cinema has been perhaps more a site of conflict in France than anywhere else in the world.

What is unique about the cinema is that, unlike most other creative expressions, it was arguably an industry before it was an art. The early years saw huge capital investment in French technology and materials, resulting in a very short time in a complex network of production companies, studios, and distributors. The medium was initially supported not by the artistic community, which was much more interested in avant-garde developments in painting, poetry and prose, but by financiers and industrialists such as Charles Pathé and Léon Gaumont. These were commercial entrepreneurs who saw the development of the film industry as a fantastic financial opportunity, and their investment paid off in record time: by the early years of the century, the globe – including the United

States – was peppered with Pathé and Gaumont filials. These two companies dominated the world market and were instrumental in determining the shape that the industry took in its formative years.

The first fixed cinema halls with dedicated projection facilities began to appear in Paris around 1906, and the appeal was such that by the end of 1907, Paris had over one hundred such venues. The expansion of venues was more than amply matched by increased film production: Pathé alone produced more than 500 films in 1903, an average of around ten per week. By the late 1920s, the landscape of French culture had been changed dramatically, with around 4,500 functioning halls across the French mainland, and a developing infrastructure in the colonies.

Thus, the popularity of the cinema surpassed all expectations, including those of its early sponsors, who would soon be overtaken by the developments that were taking place in the global market and on the world political stage. Many advances in technology were embraced by the industry, but sound technology was regarded with some suspicion; the view that prevailed in France – one that was encouraged by musicians and cinema owners – was that it was a novelty that would not last. But last it did, and the investment in sites dedicated to modes of provision that were soon to become obsolete was to prove its own stumbling block to forward momentum. Indeed, as the sound revolution took off at the end of the 1920s, only 254 halls in all of France were suitably equipped to accommodate what were inevitably mainly US films. Provincial audiences were prevented from keeping up with new trends and stars, while metropolitan spectators were quickly seduced by both the novelty of sound, and the magic of the US star system. The industry hung on for a time, thanks largely to income generated by the high taxation of cinema premises and admissions, but its failure to anticipate the impact of a globalised industry dealt a fatal blow. If the French thought that films in a foreign language posed no threat to their position, they were soon proved very wrong. For audiences unused to synchronised sound, dubbing was an acceptable feature of films. Charlie Chaplin and Buster Keaton were as immediately identifiable to a French audience as the fabled Max Linder; but the modernity of sound meant that France's stars of the silent era were cruelly eclipsed, destined to remain very much for domestic consumption.

Even before sound, though, the industry was in trouble, and the impact of the First World War on the industry cannot be underestimated. Mass mobilisation meant an almost overnight dispersion of technical, artistic and commercial personnel, while the studios and all their facilities were requisitioned by the military; as they closed, so cinema production in France ceased almost overnight. As would happen again at the outbreak of the Second World War, major figures such as Charles Pathé left France for the USA, where they spent the war. Those films that were authorised for production were often clumsily patriotic in content, and subject to heavy censorship. The industry thus lived through a period of massive undercapitalisation in equipment, technology and infrastructure, leaving it depleted and directionless when the war ended in 1918. It is from this point that we can date the definitive loss of the European cinema market to the USA.

The canon of early cinema in France was varied and imaginative, and many of the aesthetic currents we now identify as 'genres' can be traced to this period. The *féerie*, or fantasy film, as directed by Georges Méliès is a distinctive example of the output of the period, but so too are documentaries, literary and historical adaptations, serial films, and 'actualités reconstituées', what we might today call 'docudramas'. Méliès's reconstructions of the Dreyfus Affair, and the coronation of Edward VII are rich examples of the innovations of early practitioners.[2] The *Film d'art* company led the way in creating prestigious theatrical productions, featuring stage stars such as Sarah Bernhardt (*La Dame aux Camélias* [*Camille*], 1910) and Gabrielle Réjane (*Madame Sans-Gêne*, 1911), whose popularity with the public was already legendary. Louis Feuillade was a pioneer of the serial format with *Fantômas* (1913–14), a series of five feature films, and later *Les Vampires* (1915–16) and *Judex* (1916): his work was the first to feature stars in roles that were reprised from film to film – in this case the legendary iconic screen actress Musidora in the role of Irma Vep – and popularised the 'sequel format' that is such a standard feature of modern popular cinema. Elsewhere, ethnographic and journalistic film-making developed to such an extent that by the 1930s, newsreels were a staple feature of all cinema programmes.

The overall shape of the pre-sound period in French cinema was greatly influenced by the emergence of an experimental avant-garde with its sights on film. Artists such as Louis Delluc, Marcel L'Herbier, Jean Epstein, Germaine Dulac, Abel Gance, Man Ray, Salvador Dali and Luis Buñuel were part of a broad intellectual current which extended beyond film alone, and into theory, criticism, dedicated film journalism, and education through film groups, an early pre-cursor of the *Ciné-club* movement,[3] as well as into other art forms. Thus, although the Lumières and Méliès are generally taken to be representative of the two main impulses that launched and sustained cinema – the documentary and the magical 'trick photography' of the fantasy film – as the above examples show, this is too reductive a perspective on the period. Indeed, contemporary scholars have reviewed the contribution of a range of directors, designers, technicians and cinematographers very favourably, rejecting long-standing claims that theirs was a 'primitive' type of cinema, highlighting instead a clear notion of filmic language at work in their very different narrative forms. It is right to term the cinema of the early years in France a 'cinema of attractions', as the attraction and attractions of the cinema were distinctive and defining elements of the broad culture of the period.

The 1930s

Once sound had been established as a permanent feature of cinema, the French industry regathered itself, and entered into a dynamic period of immense creativity: the 1930s were to be 'the golden age of French cinema', aesthetically, creatively and technically. But this was nevertheless a period of considerable economic depression and great political instability in Europe, which suffered the fallout from the Wall Street stockmarket crash of 1929, as well as the rise of aggressive Fascist regimes in Germany and Italy, and these anxieties are often reflected in films which interrogate questions of social status and the mood of despair of 'ordinary' French people.

A range of forms mark the first half of the decade. Initially, spectators were drawn towards the 'filmed theatre' of playwrights-turned-directors such as Marcel Pagnol and Sacha Guitry, whose work was already familiar to large sections of the population. This contrasted with a more experimental vein of film-making, promoted by artists such as René Clair, which explored the lyrical and visual possibilities of cinema, and which enjoyed considerable popular success: *Sous les toits de Paris* (*Under the Roofs of Paris*, 1930), *A nous la liberté* (*Freedom for Us*, 1931), and *Quatorze juillet* (*Bastille Day*, 1933) are all now regarded as precursors to the '*cinéma d'auteur*' of the Nouvelle Vague directors. A third vein was that of musicals, on the one hand sophisticated extravaganzas featuring exotic stars such as the black actress Josephine Baker or the romantic Maurice Chevalier; and on the other, that of the *comique troupier*, or military comedy, which was held in enormous public affection.

As the 1930s went on, the extent of French creativity became more obvious, as a series of directors working in a predominantly naturalist vein, and exploring new concepts of *mise-en-scène* came to prominence. The most important director of the era is undeniably Jean Renoir, whose prewar work has become synonymous with classic European cinema. The artisanal impulse in his work – highly crafted films, made by 'teams' of artists, accessible to a popular audience – announced new forms of cinematic expression, which brought together the political, the aesthetic and the technical. The later era was marked by the stylistic trend known as 'poetic realism', of which the major exponents were Renoir, but equally Marcel Carné, Jean Vigo, Jean Grémillon, Jacques Feyder and Julien Duvivier. Their work, although very different from director to director, was characterised by a shared stylisation in black and white of contemporary urban settings, and more precisely of working-class milieux, whose streets housed flawed heroes and criminals, all caught up inexorably in a closed world of pessimism and doomed romance. Studio-based filming was the key to the creation of this style, relying as it did on very elaborate studio sets designed by East-European émigré artists such as Alexander Trauner and Lazare Meerson. Carné's *Hôtel du Nord* (1938), set on the Canal St Martin in Paris, was filmed entirely in the studio, and is a typical example of how poetic realism expresses a tension between the artificial and the real. This film, like others, often has the quality of a beautiful moving painting, oneric in its poeticism, yet authentic in its visual appearance. The films of the era are characteristically set at night or in shadows – *Le Quai des Brumes* (*Port of Shadows*, 1938) is a good example – a technique which adds to the pessimistic overtones of the themes, and they rely for their effect on a sophisticated studio-based technical apparatus: sound, photography, music, lighting. It is the case that many of the technical personnel of the era such as the composer Joseph Kosma, are as well known and revered as the directors whose names announce the films.

These trends led to the emergence of a new domestic star system: Jean Gabin, Pierre Brasseur, Arletty, Michèle Morgan are some of the stars whose distinctive voices – speaking the words of a new generation of 'dialoguistes'[4] such as Jacques Prévert and Henri Jeanson – and equally distinctive looks came to mark the films of the era. Revered actors like Louis Jouvet moved into the cinema from the stage, as did a whole generation of new stars whose background was in music hall and cabaret: Fernandel and Raimu were among the most successful of those whose comic tone and physicality found favour with the public. Others such as Bernard Blier, Michel Simon and Jules Berry played 'types' rooted in French habits and customs, and were easily identifiable as a 'family' of character actors. French cinema could soon lay claim to its very own matinee idols in the form of Gérard Philipe, Martine Carol and Jean Marais.

Politics were rarely far away from the films of the 1930s. The Front Populaire government (1936–8) actively sought to democratise 'culture', and many of the leading cinema personnel such as Renoir, Prévert and Duvivier were prominent activists. Films like *Le Crime de Monsieur Lange* (*The Crime of Monsieur Lange*, Renoir, 1935) and Duvivier's *La Belle equipe* (*They were Five*, 1936), provided cinematic illustrations of political debates about collective enterprise, while celebrating the solidarity and creativity of the workers and their affinity with a popular cultural apparatus. These were popular, and often upbeat films that thematised the dominant political impulses of the time, while remaining hugely popular at the box office.

However, two more 'reflective' films prefigured the débâcle of 1940. Jean Renoir's *La Règle du jeu* (*The Rules of the Game*, 1939), with its cast of rich landowners engaged in frivolous and trivial pursuits whilst Hitler invaded Czechoslovakia, and Marcel Carné's *Le Jour se lève* (*Daybreak*, 1939), in which a man commits a murder and then takes his own life after twenty-four hours locked in a room at the top of a building, having resisted all police efforts to make him come out, were both held by the wartime censors to be so potentially demoralising that they were banned; both films have, subsequently, been interpreted as exemplifying the culmination of the atmosphere of moral decadence and defeatism often said to have permeated France in the late 1930s.

1940s and 1950s: Occupation cinema and the reorganisation of the industry

If this was so, such an atmosphere was rapidly dispelled from the film industry, which, in a strange paradox, experienced a second 'golden age' between 1940 and 1944 – a paradox because wartime shortages of raw materials and the priority accorded to the German-owned film production company Continental Films turned making films into a procurement nightmare. A paradox too, because since the double censorship imposed by the Occupants and the Vichy regime was draconian, since Jewish-owned production companies had been expropriated and Jews were forbidden to work in the industry, and since many of the best directors and actors had fled abroad, among them Clair, Renoir, Duvivier, Jouvet, Gabin and Morgan, the likelihood of French film production flourishing under such circumstances might have appeared extremely slim.

Yet flourish it did. Goebbels's stated aim to cut the film industry down to size was undoubtedly what galvanised the Vichy regime into taking a close interest in the cinema so that it could promote the image of French culture. Indeed, the close relationship between the State and the film industry and the strong belief in cinema as a crucial mechanism for forging a national identity and promoting it abroad can be traced back to the Vichy period, with the establishment of the COIC (Comité d'Organisation de l'Industrie Cinématographique – it became the CNC in 1946), uniform contracts, guarantees for investors, advances and the creation of the IDHEC (Institut des Hautes Etudes Cinématographiques, known since 1986 as the FEMIS – Institut de Formation et d'Enseignement pour les Métiers de l'Image et du Son). As the Ministry of Information stated, propaganda was 'the defence of morality and respect for natural traditions' ('Unification du marché', February 1941).

The period of the Occupation saw the release of approximately 220 French feature films, all subject to pre-production censorship. Unlike the output of the American, British and German film industries, these were remarkable for their tendency to avoid explicit or implicit propaganda and, instead, their aesthetic concentration on narratives of escapism and depictions of closed communities: *Les Visiteurs du soir* (*The Devil's Envoys*, Carné, 1942), *Les Inconnus dans la Maison* (*Strangers in the House*, Decoin, 1942), *Goupi mains rouges* (*It happened at the Inn*, Becker, 1943) and *Le Corbeau* (*The Raven*, Clouzot, 1943) are all classic illustrations of this trend. All display an aesthetic propensity towards stasis, in content and form, which is only partly explained by the material constraints of the time. The transitional film of the Occupation/Liberation is Marcel Carné's *Les Enfants du paradis* (*Children of Paradise*, 1945), a tour de force of this type of film, displacing the action of the film to a distant place and time, but one whose relevance to an enduring sense of French national identity is powerfully apparent. Its popularity in the postwar period and beyond is testament to its impact on the national psyche.

The Liberation of France brought a determination on the part of the government and the trade unions to develop and support a national cinema. Symbolic of this effort was the blacklisting of Henri-Georges Clouzot, whose film *Le Corbeau* was held to have embodied a spirit of defeatism inimical to the robust nationalism now required, exemplified in stirring semi-documentaries such as René Clément's *La Bataille du rail* (*The Battle of the Rails*, 1946), which recounts the heroic efforts of Resistance saboteurs working in the French railways.

The future of the postwar French film industry was to depend, in part, on the Americans, who were determined to open up European markets to Hollywood products. In Italy and Germany, defeated powers, they were completely successful, in Britain, moderately successful, while in France negotiations took a highly political turn, exacerbated by the beginnings of the Cold War. Films were among the commodities included in the so-called Blum-Byrnes agreement, negotiations on a range of cultural issues, concluded in May 1946, which provided the framework for American aid to French reconstruction and included the provision for a 'screen quota' obliging French exhibitors to reserve four (five from 1948) weeks per quarter for screening French films, while during the remaining weeks they could screen what they liked. Initially welcomed by the French industry, the Agreement was later denounced as a sell-out to the Americans and a fierce media campaign was whipped up especially by the Communist press after the start of the Cold war. However, the quota more or less corresponded to the capacity of the French industry at the time, enfeebled as it was by the impact of the war. In the latter part of the 1940s, therefore, large numbers of Hollywood films were screened in France, including many made in the period 1940–44 which had been banned during the war: *Gone With the Wind* (Fleming, 1939), *Citizen Kane* (Welles, 1941) and *Casablanca* (Curtiz, 1942) were just some of the classics that the French were eager to see on their screens. The impact of this backlog on the subsequent history of French cinema cannot be understated. In addition to leading to the definition of an entirely new genre, 'film noir', which was widely imitated by French directors in the 1950s, the exegesis of Hollywood film led to the development of the 'politique des auteurs' – a seminal statement valorising 'authorship' in film-making – by the critics of the journal *Les Cahiers du cinéma* (including François Truffaut, Jean-Luc Godard and Jacques Rivette), founded in 1951. Their appetite for the work of directors like Alfred Hitchcock, Howard Hawks, Billy Wilder, Ernst Lubitsch and John Ford was insatiable.

Other important government measures to support cinema were enacted in the late 1940s and throughout the 1950s which, taken together, helped to maintain a flourishing film industry in France, while the film industries in other European countries languished under the combined competition of Hollywood and television. Various forms of government aid and subsidy were on offer for films of 'artistic merit', initially for short films and, from 1959, for features: *Loi d'Aide* (1948); *Fonds de développement* (1953) and, in 1959, *Fonds de soutien (avances sur recettes)*. The latter – a loan against future profits, available to unestablished young directors – was particularly significant and continues to benefit the industry to this day. Whilst supporting low-budget art films in this way, bigger budget films were encouraged by the Franco-Italian co-production agreement initiated in 1949 in an attempt to bring together sufficient capital to compete with Hollywood. By the end of the 1940s, French cinema was firmly back on track. It was a more secure industry than it had been for at least thirty years, and was well placed to become a vibrant and competitive postwar industry. The formal establishment in September 1946 of the Cannes Film Festival as a showcase for a revitalised industry (held over from 1939) spoke of an optimism on the part of both the authorities and practitioners that was to prove well founded.

The 1950s: the 'cinéma de papa'

The postwar period saw the foundations laid of what later came to be called film culture. Particularly active was the influential critic André Bazin who, through the government supported organisation *Travail et Culture*, visited schools, factories, union meetings in order to screen films, deliver lectures and organise debates. Such activities were considered valuable agents of education and democratisation, especially in rural areas. Bazin also worked in the French-occupied zone of Germany. The *Cinémathèque française* organised its superbly eclectic screenings, while journals such as *L'écran français* (1943), *Image et son* (1946), *Les Cahiers du cinéma* (1951) and *Positif* (1952) educated a wide public to understand and appreciate film.

Against this background the films of the 1950s may sometimes appear rather less disappointing, perhaps, than critical wisdom held until recently. The apprentice-based structure of the industry made it difficult for directors to make a hit feature film until they reached the age of about forty. For this reason, the period is primarily characterised by the directorial activities of a generation that began working in film-making in the 1930s: Becker, Clouzot, Christian-Jaque and Decoin were reliable names who could produce high-quality films, and attract large audiences. Their staple material tended to be either the literary adaptation (Christian-Jaque) or crime films (Decoin), that privileged plot, character and costume over cinematic innovation. The categorisation of their cinema as a 'quality cinema' was in fact a condemnation of its forms and priorities: 'la tradition de qualité' has become synonymous not only with the films produced under the Fourth Republic, but also with the notion of an unambitious and 'static' profession and industry.

Despite the telling example of Italian neo-realism, French films remained, for the most part, studio-bound. This did give rise to masterpieces such as Ophuls's *La Ronde* (*Roundabout*, 1950), but Carné, the darling of the industry when *Les Enfants du paradis* was released in 1945, saw his reputation plummet with *Les Portes de la nuit* (*Gates of the Night*, 1946): his designer Trauner re-created in the studio a perfect replica of the Métro station Barbès-Rochechouart, but the film's cynical pessimism was out of touch with the times.

In the main, however, a combination of studio production and generic conservatism meant that the films of the period were characterised by an avoidance of reflection on recent history and politics. Costume dramas such as Claude Autant-Lara's *Le rouge et le noir* (*The Red and the Black*, 1954), Christian-Jaque's *La Chartreuse de Parme* (*The Charterhouse of Parma*, 1948); *Fanfan la Tulipe* (*Fan-fan the Tulip*, 1952) *Lucrèce Borgia* (*Lucretia Borgia*, 1952), *Madame du Barry* (1954), *Nana* (1955), and Max Ophuls's *Le Plaisir* (*House of Pleasure*, 1952) and *Lola Montès* (*The Sins of Lola Montez*, 1955) were immensely popular. The colourful personal life of stars like Martine Carol, Simone Signoret and Yves Montand only added to the attraction.

On the other hand, straws in the wind indicated change. Independents such as Jean-Pierre Melville or Jacques Tati pursued the *auteur* tradition undertaken by Renoir and reclaimed by Truffaut in his celebrated 1954 diatribe against the power of the screenwriters, published in *Les Cahiers du cinéma*; with the publication of 'Une certaine tendance du cinéma français', the *cinéma de papa* was not quite dead, but it was certainly wounded. Another wound was initiated by Roger Vadim, whose 1956 *Et Dieu créa la femme* (*And God created Woman*) revealed a pouting, nubile Brigitte Bardot to an astounded world. The explorations of female sexuality that this unleashed – Jeanne Moreau and Anna Karina were other exciting new stars of the French screen – became, and until recently remained, an element distinguishing it not just from Hollywood but from most other national European cinemas. This tradition has remained characteristic of French cinema, with recent films such as *La Belle noiseuse* (*The Beautiful Troublemaker*, Rivette, 1991) or *Romance* (Breillat, 1998).

The 1960s and 1970s: new wave and post-new wave

The most long-lasting and internationally significant change in French cinema occurred at the end of the 1950s with the birth of the *Nouvelle Vague* (New Wave), symbolised by the award of the Director's Prize for *Les 400 coups* (*The Four Hundred Blows*) at the 1959 Cannes Festival. At more or less the same time, Jean-Luc Godard, Claude Chabrol, Jacques Rivette, Agnès Varda and Eric Rohmer all made their first feature films, leading the epithet 'new wave', originally applied by Françoise Giroud to the generation of young people reaching maturity in the late 1950s, to be applied almost exclusively to cinema. The *ciné-club* movement had gone from strength to strength, with ten official federations established in the 1960s, and hundreds of thousands of members all over France. Henri Langlois energetically promoted the Cinémathèque as a forum for debate about film, and was instrumental in the development of a 'cinémas d'art et d'essai' network. Young people began to claim the cinema as their own, forcefully rejecting the 'cinéma de papa' as aesthetically outmoded and socially irrelevant.

It is traditional to consider Truffaut's polemical 1954 article claiming that a film director should be considered an 'auteur' in much the same way as the author of a book, to be the first statement of the *nouvelle vague* creed – ironically, since at the same time, literary criticism was moving away from the 'auteurist' approach towards Structuralism. And it is indisputable that the *nouvelle vague* brought about a revolution in film-making whose effect still reverberates today. Nevertheless, with hindsight, it is possible to understand the *nouvelle vague* as a product of technological and social change as much as of the genius of a few talented individuals.

The first revolution, perhaps, was one of subject-matter. Most new wave films are intimist in a way that most 1950s French cinema is not; with plots, such as they are, based on the often trivial concerns of young people. Thus Truffaut's anti-hero Antoine Doinel is a teenager who gets into a series of scrapes because he is at odds with his parents, whilst Michel, the male protagonist of *A Bout de souffle* (*Breathless*, 1960), spends much of the film trying to persuade his American girlfriend to go to bed with him. These 'small topics', as Chabrol called them, reflected the interests and life-styles of the principal film audience remaining in the late 1950s, and, as Edgar Morin suggested, the key to the films' success was the almost perfect coincidence between the preoccupations of audience and characters.

As important was the technological revolution on which the *nouvelle vague* was predicated. In terms of the film industry, the *nouvelle vague* directors were all extremely young at the time of making their first features, and they did so without any of the large crews and cumbersome equipment until then considered *de rigueur*. Thanks to lighter cameras, faster film and better sound recording, the cost of film-making could be reduced to the point where a semi-amateur was able to raise the cash for a production budget. Several *nouvelle vague* directors were scions of wealthy families (Chabrol, Godard) or married into the film industry (Truffaut) and were able to combine funds offered from these sources with smaller sums from the newly created *avances sur recettes*, and so to scrape together enough money for a low-budget film. The use of actors who were then unknown (Jean-Paul Belmondo, Jean-Pierre Léaud) and of locations rather than studio sets further reduced the cost of filming. The result was that early *nouvelle vague* films closely resemble documentaries in style and tone, so much so that part of their continuing charm is the image they provide of France, particularly Paris, in a period now long past. This is especially true of a film such as Varda's *Cléo de 5 à 7* (*Cleo from 5 to 7*, 1962) which is in part intended as a portrait of the city, but it is also true of *Les 400 coups* (1959), *A Bout de souffle*, and, of course, Rivette's *Paris nous appartient* (*Paris is Ours*, 1960).

However, perhaps the most influential and long-lasting change brought about by the *nouvelle vague* was in pace and narrative style. The *nouvelle vague* broke with the 'grammar' of Hollywood film with its clarity of exposition and neatly turned stories. Instead, *nouvelle vague* films are characterised by fast-paced, often elliptical open-ended narratives, classic instances of which might be the freeze-frame on Doinel's face at the end of *Les 400 coups* or Patricia's enigmatic repetition of Michel's words and gestures at the end of *A Bout de souffle*.

Throughout many *nouvelle vague* films, but especially those of Godard and Truffaut, there is also a consistent interrogation of the State of France, seen especially in Godard's use of the tricolour palette – blue, white, red – in colour films such as *Une Femme est une femme* (*A Woman is a Woman*, 1961) and *Pierrot le fou* (*Pierrot goes Wild*, 1965), chronicling the rapid modernisation of the country which took place in the 1950s and 1960s. These film-makers were led to posit a relationship between French and American cinema which is worked through in the many references and pastiches in the films. Thus the colonial relationship they perceived between Hollywood and the French film industry not only did much to determine public policy towards the cinema in the subsequent decades, but also turned cinema into a prime vehicle for the discussion of social transformation.

Internationally, the influence of the *nouvelle vague* cannot be overstated. The concept of 'auteurism', and its associations with innovative narrative style and low-budget independent art cinema, had repercussions for all significant developments in film theory and practice in the years that followed. That we talk about film the way we do today is largely a result of what was said and done in film-making in France in a few short, but explosive, years.

The 1970s

The auteurist approach has remained a constant feature of French cinema since the 1960s, and certainly of those films designed for export. Popular cinema in France, meanwhile, declined dramatically in significance in the face of rising competition from television. By 1970, 90 per cent of households had acquired TV sets (a decade later than in Britain or Germany) and television rapidly became the principal means by which feature films were distributed. By the end of the 1970s, TV had also become a major source of finance for French feature films, putting an end to competition for audience between the two media, and this has remained a distinctive feature of the French film industry as well as, arguably, a source of its continuing strength.

May '68 proved a watershed in film-making, as with so much else in French cultural life, and the changes can be seen both in the themes and content of films as well as in their narrative. Throughout the early 1970s cinema became strongly politicised. Many film-makers had, in February '68, criticised attempted government interference in the management of the *Cinémathèque française* and this initial politicisation led to the summoning of the Estates General of the Cinema, held during the month of May '68. Proposals which emerged from these meetings concerned the structure of the film industry, the distribution of films, and the issue of representation in cinema. Such debates continued until the middle of the 1970s, especially in the journal *Cahiers du cinéma* which became strongly Maoist at the time. During the events of May themselves, many film-makers produced short films recording or commenting on events in the street from a point of view that often contradicted the 'official' filmed versions of events put out by state television. Such activity had a profoundly radicalising effect on conceptions of the role of the film-maker and the control of cinema.

The career of Jean-Luc Godard at this time may be taken as exemplary. In company with Jean-Pierre Gorin, he first created the Dziga-Vertov group dedicated to the production of political films – *Le Vent d'est* (*East Wind*, 1969), *Pravda* (1970), *Luttes en Italie* (*Lotte in Italia*, 1970), *Vladimir et Rosa* (1970) – outside the traditional commercial structures. Godard, nevertheless, returned to commercial film-making with the ironically titled *Tout va bien* (*All's Well*, 1972), starring Jane Fonda and Yves Montand, a film which narrated the representation of a strike in a sausage factory. *Tout va bien* is also noteworthy for its foregrounding of sexual politics, a theme which was to preoccupy Godard for much of the 1970s. After 1972, Godard left Paris for a number of years and, with his new collaborator Anne-Marie Miéville, attempted to discover how the 'new medium' of video could be used for the production of a radical cinema.

Another important strand of film-making to emerge from May '68 was women's cinema, reflecting in its themes the rise of the women's movement and its demands, such as the legalisation of abortion, but also the desire for women to become significant actors in the film industry in a manner that had been infrequent up to then. The idea that women should have a 'voice' in film-making was part and parcel of the more general 'prise de parole' subsequent to May '68 which claimed the right for all subordinate groups to be able to speak and be heard. In this respect, the career of Yannick Bellon is exemplary: she was unable to make her first feature film *Quelque part quelqu' un* (*Somewhere, Someone*) until 1972 (when she was forty-eight), despite a long career in the industry, but she went on to make a series of films in the 1970s and early 1980s – *La Femme de Jean* (*John's Wife*, 1973), *L'Amour violé* (*Rape of Love*, 1976), *L'Amour nu* (*Naked love*, 1981) – which focus squarely on 'women's issues' such as divorce, rape and breast cancer.

However, the three film-makers who came to prominence as both women and feminists in the 1970s were Agnès Varda, Marguerite Duras and Chantal Ackerman. With *L'Une chante l'autre pas* (*One Sings, the Other Doesn't*, 1977), Varda nailed her feminist colours to the mast. After a period in the 1960s when she had been accused of saccharine flacidity (*Le Bonheur* [*Happiness*], 1965; *Les Créatures* [*The Creatures*], 1966, with *Sans toit ni loi* [*Vagabond*], 1985), she went on to make the film which remains emblematic of debates about the representation of women in the media. Duras, likewise, with *Nathalie Granger* (1972) and *Le Camion* (*The Truck*, 1977), added to an already considerable reputation as a novelist a talent for radical feminist film-making, while, with the compelling *India Song* (1975) and *Son nom de Venise dans Calcutta désert* (1976), she combined, as she had in her novels, minimalism and melodrama in equal portions. Chantal Akerman's *Jeanne Dielman 23 Quai du Commerce 1080 Bruxelles* (1975) casts, almost in real time, Delphine Seyrig as an oppressed housewife who takes to prostitution and kills one of her clients, while *News from Home* (1977) and *Les Rendez-vous d'Anna* (*The Meetings of Anna*, 1978) investigate diasporic culture from the point of view of a Jewish, Belgian lesbian.

The 1970s was, in retrospect, an exceptional period for women's cinema. Whilst it certainly opened up new career paths for women in the film industry, the feminist vein which characterised the decade gradually petered out, so that although there are now many women directors of talent working in France, few, if any, would claim to be feminists. Indeed, many, such as Catherine Breillat or Claire Denis appear deliberately to take on overtly 'masculine' subjects almost as though they wish to prove a degree of gender-blindness.

Cinema in the 1980s and 1990s

The 1980s began on a wave of political optimism, and the new left-wing regime brought with it new prospects for French culture. The Socialist administration saw it as part of their mission to make a serious investment in cultural policy, not only politically, but also financially. The budget was immediately doubled in 1981 (from 3 billion francs to 6 billion francs) and, in spite of the constraints of the politics of austerity espoused by France during the recession of the 1980s, continued to be increased until 1993 when it finally reached the symbolic figure of 1 per cent of total national spending. For film-makers this meant a greater general fund to draw on (the *avances sur recettes* alone was more than doubled in 1982). Furthermore, the options for investment were quickly extended beyond the purely public sector: new modes of investment were actively encouraged by the Minister for Culture, Jack Lang, whose many initiatives included the creation of SOFICAs in 1985 (Sociétés de Financement des Industries Cinématographiques et Audiovisuelles), deregulation of the broadcasting industry, and the successful defence of French audio-visual interests during the GATT talks in 1993, which resulted in cultural products being recognised as exceptions to the Maastricht Treaty on free trade.

In part, this unprecedented investment in the cinema industry constituted an attempt to reverse a pattern underway since the end of the 1950s: that of falling audiences. From around 400 million per annum in the immediate postwar period, attendance figures had fallen to an alarming

179 million by 1980. Increased television ownership and domestic VCR usage were identified as culprits, but it was acknowledged by the government that other factors were also to blame: those who did still go to cinemas were increasingly found to be watching American films in preference to home-grown products. As audience figures continued to fall throughout the 1980s (reaching a low of 121 million in 1989), so the French/US imbalance intensified in America's favour: in 1982 French films were seen by 53.4 per cent of cinema-goers compared with only 30.1 per cent for US films, but by 1995, the figures were practically reversed: 35.4 per cent for French films, against 54.2 per cent for US films.[5]

Attempts to reverse this trend were apparent on all kinds of levels, but none has so far proved to be the saviour of the industry: the annual *fête du cinéma* was introduced to encourage participation and pride in French films; the international community was embraced through the conferring of French awards like the Chevalier des Arts et des Lettres on figures like Sylvester Stallone and Warren Beatty; most significantly of all, the didactic function of cinema as a beacon of national identity was actively promoted through the support given to the 'heritage film' industry. What this meant was that, once again, 'prestige products' had their place in French cinema culture: the vogue for literary adaptations of canonical texts by literary giants like Pagnol (*Jean de Florette*, *Manon des Sources*, *La Gloire de mon père*), Zola (*Germinal*), Flaubert (*Madame Bovary*) and Balzac (*Le Colonel Chabert*) was encouraged, and financially sustained by state investment. Such projects were prioritised for funding in the hope that they would give good cultural and financial returns to France through foreign distribution. And to a large extent, this was the case.

Other aesthetic currents define the last twenty years of twentieth-century French film-making, most particularly the 'cinéma du look', and the popular domestic comedy. The *cinéma du look* is a stylish, image-driven form of film-making, that celebrates its hybrid cultural heritage in advertising, music videos and popular literary culture. Fusing genres as diverse as the crime thriller, science fiction, the cartoon strip and documentary, films from *Diva* (Beineix, 1981), through *Subway* (Besson, 1985), *37.2 le matin* (*Betty Blue*, Beineix, 1986), *Nikita* (*La Femme Nikita*, Besson, 1990) and *Les Amants du Pont-neuf* (*The Lovers on the Bridge*, Carax, 1991) have become cult favourites on the global art-house circuit. The style has been much derided by cinema critics in France, who have deemed it to be 'all style, no substance'; but the neo-Baroque extravagance of the films has proved to be popular with the public, and has given French cinema a new family of stars such as Anne Parillaud, Béatrice Dalle and Juliette Binoche.

Home-produced comedies have always enjoyed great affection in France, and the 1980s and 1990s have been no exception. From café-théâtre adaptations such as *Les Bronzés* (*French Fried Vacation*, Leconte, 1978) and *Le Père Noël est une ordure* (Poiré, 1982), to mega-hits like *Les Visiteurs* (*The Visitors*, Poiré, 1993) and *Le Dîner de cons* (*The Dinner Game*, Veber, 1998), French comedy has thrived in the modern market. The brand of comedy that the French enjoy is firmly based in classical theatrical traditions of farce, mime and vaudeville, and as such, has never exported particularly well; the satire and targets are almost entirely French, and are enjoyed almost exclusively by the mainland French population.

Advances have been made in more overtly political areas of film-making, such as *beur* film-making (*Le Thé au harem d'Archimède* [*Tea in the Harem*], Charef, 1985; *Hexagone*, Chibane, 1993; *Douce France* Chibane, 1995), and in socio-realist modes (*Les Nuits fauves* [*Savage Nights*], Collard, 1991; *La Haine* [*Hate*], Kassovitz, 1995; *La Vie rêvée des anges* [*The Dream Life of Angels*], Zonca, 1998): these are films which have given a voice to tra-ditionally marginalised elements of society such as homosexuals, immi-grants, the homeless. French cinema has also gained a new 'international' flavour through the English language work of directors like Besson (*Léon* [*The Cleaner*], 1994; *The Fifth Element*, 1997) and Jeunet (*Alien Resurrection*, 2000) who have taken on US cinema at its own game and on its home ground. French stars such as Gérard Depardieu and Sophie Marceau have made films in English, while the many remakes of French films by US stu-dios (*Three Men and a Baby*, Nimoy, 1987; *Point of No Return*, Badham, 1993) have taken French ideas and creativity, if not the films themselves, be-yond France's borders.

Nevertheless, the French remain cautious about the future of their industry. The continuing attraction of the French public for American blockbusters such as *Jurassic Park* (Spielberg, 1993) and *Titanic* (Cameron, 1998) (the latter alone took 12 per cent of the 1998 box office) understand-ably undermines national confidence. Whether or not new trends are un-derway on the back of the phenomenally successful *Amélie* remains to be seen.

NOTES

1. The term *mise-en-abyme* is used by cinema and literary scholars to designate a scene, sequence or chapter of a work that encapsulates the wider narrative and thematic base of the work in question.

2. These films and new genres are discussed at length by Elizabeth Ezra in *Georges Méliès* (Manchester: Manchester University Press, 2000).

3. The *Ciné-club* movement was an influential amateur 'film appreciation society' whose members included many later prominent film-makers and critics (for example, André Bazin, Henri Langlois and François Truffaut).

4. Dialoguistes were scriptwriters whose forte was dialogue, and whose words, phrases and witty exchanges quickly became filmic references in their own right.

5. René Prédal, *Le Cinéma français depuis 1945*, Paris: Nathan, 1991, 833.

FURTHER READING

Abel, Richard, *The Ciné Goes to Town: French Cinema 1896–1914*, Berkeley and London: University of California Press, 1998.

Andrew, Dudley, *Mists of Regret: Culture and Sensibility in Classic French Film*, Princeton: Princeton University Press, 1995.

Austin, Guy, *Contemporary French Cinema*, Manchester: Manchester University Press, 1996.

Crisp, Colin, *The Classic French Cinema 1930–1960*, Bloomington, Ind.: Indiana University Press, 1997.

Ezra, Elizabeth, and Sue Harris, (eds.), *France in Focus: Film and National Identity*, Oxford and Washington, DC: Berg, 2000.

Forbes, Jill, *The Cinema in France: after the New Wave*, Basingstoke: Macmillan, 1992.

Forbes, Jill, and Sarah Street, *European Cinema: an Introduction*, Basingstoke: Palgrave, 2000.

Grantham, Bill, '*Some Big Bourgeois Brothel': Contexts for France's Culture Wars with Hollywood*, Luton: University of Luton Press, 2000.

Hayward, Susan, *French National Cinema*, London and New York: Routledge, 1993.

Jeancolas, Jean-Pierre, *Le Cinéma des Français: la Vème République (1958–78)*, Paris: Stock, 1979.

Quinze ans d'années trente: le Cinéma des Français 1929–1944, Paris: Stock, 1983.

Loosley, David, *The Politics of Fun: Cultural Policy and Debate in Contemporary France*, Oxford and Washington, DC: Berg, 1995.

Monaco, James, *The New Wave*, Oxford: Oxford University Press, 1976.

Nowell-Smith, Geoffrey, and Steven Ricci (eds.), *Hollywood and Europe: Economics, Culture and National Identity*, London: BFI, 1998.

Powrie, Phil, *French Cinema in the 1980s*, Oxford: Oxford University Press, 1997.

French Cinema in the 1990s, Oxford: Oxford University Press, 1999.

Prédal, René, *Le Cinéma français depuis 1945*, Paris: Nathan, 1991.

Williams, Alan, *Republic of Images: a History of French Filmmaking*, Cambridge, Mass.: Harvard University Press, 1992.

Index